CHOOSING TO CARE

CHOOSING TO CARE

A Century of Childcare and Social
Reform in San Diego, 1850–1950

KYLE E. CIANI

UNIVERSITY OF NEBRASKA PRESS · LINCOLN

© 2019 by the Board of Regents of the University of Nebraska

Elements of the following chapters were previously published: Chapter 1 as "A 'Growing Evil' or 'Inventive Genius': Anglo Perceptions of Indian Life in San Diego, 1850 to 1900," *Southern California Quarterly* 89, no. 3 (Fall 2007): 249–84. Chapter 2 as "The Power of Maternal Love: Negotiating a Child's Care in Progressive-Era San Diego," *Journal of the West* 41, no. 4 (Fall 2002): 71–79. Copyright ABC-CLIO, LLC © 2002. And chapter 5 as "Revelations of a Reformer: Helen D. Marston Beardsley and Progressive Social Activism," *Journal of San Diego History* 50, no. 3–4 (Summer–Fall 2004): 102–23.

Library of Congress Cataloging-in-Publication Data
Names: Ciani, Kyle, author.
Title: Choosing to care: a century of childcare and social reform in San Diego, 1850–1950 / Kyle E. Ciani.
Description: Lincoln: University of Nebraska Press, [2019] | Includes bibliographical references and index.
Identifiers: LCCN 2018052336
ISBN 9781496214591 (cloth: alk. paper)
ISBN 9781496216762 (epub)
ISBN 9781496216779 (mobi)
ISBN 9781496216786 (pdf)
Subjects: LCSH: Child care—California—San Diego—History. | Child care services—California—San Diego—History. | Child welfare—California—San Diego—History.
Classification: LCC HQ778.67.S25 C53 2019 | DDC 362.709794/985—dc23 LC record available at https://lccn.loc.gov/2018052336

Set in Sabon Next LT Pro by Mikala R. Kolander.

For Douglas Anthony Cutter and our daughter,
Margaret Ciani Cutter

CONTENTS

List of Illustrations. ix

Acknowledgments xi

Introduction xvii

List of Abbreviations. xxix

1. Indentured Care:
   Anglo Solutions to "Civilizing" American Indian Children . . . 1

2. Maternal Care:
   Childcare for Working-Class Families 21

3. Court-Appointed Care:
   Interventions for Troubled Families. 53

4. Professional Care:
   Expert Protocols for Childcare Programs. 89

5. Neighborhood Care:
   Localizing the Settlement House Movement. 127

6. Emergency Care:
   Collaboration during Economic Recovery. 163

7. Wartime Care:
   Navigating the San Diego Home Front. 193

Conclusion. 223

Notes 233

Bibliography 273

Index 293

ILLUSTRATIONS

1. American Indian boys, 1890 17
2. Angelita Luzo with a child and a dog, 1904 18
3. Children's Home and Day Nursery at the edge of the
   city park, 1889 23
4. The Boys Dormitory at the Children's Home, c. 1924 24
5. Women laundering at the foot of D Street at the
   waterfront, 1912 38
6. The Electric Laundry Company, 1915 39
7. Vocational education in City Heights, c. 1913 71
8. Newsboys for the *San Diego Sun*, 1925 74
9. Girls and women packing cherries, c. 1905–7 75
10. Mexican refugee women and children, 1916 101
11. Boys working in the yard of the Helping Hand
    Home, c. 1920 107
12. A boy who resided in the Children's Home, 1921 114
13. Girls who resided in the Children's Home, 1921 115
14. Women at a San Diego County Welfare
    Commission meeting, 1921 121
15. Women preparing sardines at the Normandy
    Company, 1924 135
16. Women packing olives for the Old Mission
    Olive Factory, 1928 136
17. Visiting nurse taking a baby's foot impression, c. 1928 . . . 169

18. Children at Mesa Grande government school, 1931 174
19. Workmen run to receive their paychecks, 1934 187
20. Women sorting peppers for packing, c. 1935 189
21. The Pacific Parachute Company employees, c. 1943 198
22. During the war years at the Sisters of Mercy Hospital, 1942 . 209

ACKNOWLEDGMENTS

This book is the product of long-standing and strong relationships with colleagues, friends, and family, and I am thrilled to be
able to publicly thank them. Since 2001 my professional home
has been in the History Department at Illinois State University
(ISU), and it could not be a better fit for my family and me. The
department, the College of Arts and Sciences, and the university
have provided generous financial support through a sabbatical
leave, travel and publication funds, a Summer Faculty Fellowship,
a Pre-Tenure Faculty Initiative Grant, and a New Faculty Initiative
Grant. My sincere thanks to chairs John B. Freed, Paul Holsinger,
Roger Biles, Diane Zosky, Anthony Crubaugh, and Ross Kennedy,
who all devoted their time to understanding and supporting my
research, especially as it slowed when I took on administrative roles.
Thank you for your trust in my scholarship. In the best situations,
colleagues become friends, and I am fortunate to live that reality at ISU. Special thanks to Katie Jasper, Monica Noraian, Patrice
Olsen, Touré Reed, Georgia Tsouvala, and Christine Varga-Harris
for cheering me along; Faith Ten Haken and Kera B. Storrs, who
saved me with their bibliography skills; Linda Spencer and Sharon Foiles, who always find ways to make systems run smoothly;
librarian Vanette Schwartz for performing her magic in tracking
sources; Linda Clemmons for being a first-rate walking partner,
reading the book at various stages, and giving me excellent advice
on how to revise it; and Katrin Paehler, who defines how a neigh-

bor, at both office and home, can provide comfort and laughter to flip the script in the roughest of storms. I appreciate you all.

The Women's and Gender Studies Program is my other home at ISU, and it comes with a wonderful group of scholars whose scholarship I value and friendships I cherish, especially Alison Bailey, Cynthia Edmonds-Cady, Kass Fleisher, Ann Haugo, and Melissa Johnson. Beyond ISU, women's history colleagues Stacy Cordery, Sandra Harmon, Deborah Kuhn McGregor, Stacey Robertson, and April Schultz offered me a supportive space in their reading group and provided important critiques of my research in this book.

My hunger for women's history was first fed as a graduate student at Michigan State University (MSU) through studying with Lisa M. Fine. She taught me how to create a woman-centered research agenda and curriculum, and through her example I learned how to find a balance between academia and mothering; I am deeply grateful for her mentorship. While adjusting to the Midwest, I found the friendship of Vibha Bhalla, Tammy Stone Gordon, Maria Quinlan Leiby, Mary Mapes, Cathy Oglesby, Patti Rogers, and Susan Stein Roggenbuck, who along with MSU faculty David Bailey, Julia Grant, Peter Levine, and Gordon Stewart helped me navigate academic life. I so wish that Bailey had been able to read this research in book form before his untimely death. The MSU History Department and the College of Arts and Letters awarded me Graduate Merit Completion, Research, and Incentive Fellowships, which allowed me to spend initial time at the San Diego History Center and the Social Welfare History Archives (SWHA) at the University of Minnesota. At SWHA, I worked with archivist David Klaassen and, much later, archivist Linnea Anderson, and I appreciate their combined expertise.

Staff at the University of Nebraska Press have been a joy to work with from proposal to final production. Special thanks to senior acquisitions editor Matthew Bokovoy, who has been a champion of this research. His suggestions for clarity and emphasis have only improved the final product, and I so appreciate his confidence in my scholarship. Heather Stauffer and Joeth Zucco make an author feel as though you are the only person in their inbox, and the editing skills of Lisa Williams thoroughly clarified my points; I appreciate their keen attention to every one of my questions. My thanks also to Merry Ovnick, editor of the *Southern California Quarterly*, and coeditors of the *Journal of San Diego History*, Iris H. W. Engstrand and Molly McClain, for bringing elements of this research to life in earlier publications. I benefited from the anonymous reviews of this manuscript at much earlier stages, as well as that by David Wallace Adams. I deeply admire his work and am humbled by his thoughtful reading of my scholarship. I paid attention to the advice offered by all of these scholars and am fully responsible for the outcome.

The bulk of my research occurred in San Diego, and I hope this book shows scholars a bit of its rich archives. Iris H. W. Engstrand introduced me to archival research when I was an undergraduate at the University of San Diego (USD), nurtured me through a master's degree, and encouraged me to pursue a doctoral degree. She remains incredibly supportive, and I can't thank her enough for the time she has devoted to my family and me. The USD College of Arts and Sciences awarded me a Visiting Assistant Professorship, which allowed me the opportunity to hone my teaching craft and continue my research. In addition to Iris, thanks to Maureen Byrnes, James Gump, Molly McClain, Michael Gonzalez, Yi Sun, and Louis Warren for welcoming me and Doug Cutter into the History Department.

I am grateful to the many archivists who helped me maneuver their collections: Lynn Olsson and Bill Payne at San Diego State University's Special Collections and University Archives at Malcolm A. Love Library, and later, Robert Ray and Amanda Lanthorne, who helped with permissions; Debra Day at the Scripps Institute of Oceanography Archives; Larry Johnson and Ryan Morris from the United Way of San Diego; and Rick Crawford at the San Diego Central Library. Special thanks to the staff at the San Diego History Center, which became a second home for me. There, former archivist John Panter, photo archivist Carol Myers, and digital imaging specialist Natalie Fiocre turned around my many requests with unwavering efficiency; and archivist Renato

Rodriguez went above and beyond, including securing SDHC volunteer Katy Phillips to validate my citations. I am eternally grateful for this collective help. As with David Bailey, I wish that Gregg Hennessey, Ethel Mintzer Lichtman, and Edwina B. Sample had lived to see this book in print. I benefited from conversations with them about San Diego life, appreciate their published scholarship, and hope my analysis honors their own work.

Access to childcare is personal for me. When our childcare fell through the day before classes started, Nicole DeMore saved us by coming to our home once a week for our daughter's first two years, and we are forever grateful to her. Then teachers at Kensington Preschool and the USD Manchester Family Child Development Center provided a nurturing environment that embraced the children's multicultural and bilingual lives. When we moved to central Illinois, we benefited from teachers at parent cooperative the Mulberry School and at the ISU Laboratory Schools. Because I knew these people cared about my daughter, I could focus on my work at ISU, including interacting with the many and diverse students who come with teaching at a large public institution.

This book has taken a very long time to bring to publication, but I have never felt alone. Our San Diego circle has shifted as some of us have moved to other parts of the country, but we continue to support one another's goals and dreams, and make sure we get to the beach. Thanks for your friendship, Sharon Belknap, Cheri and Reid Cooper, Page Harrington, Margot Howard, Barb Neault Kelber and Rob Kelber, Cindi and Michael Malinick, Rosalie and Dave Meyer, and Jane Walstrom. Carmen Cutter and Guillaume Escarguel, thank you for being both friends and family, and always opening your home.

My beloved parents, Ametilio "Tom" and Alice Ciani, and my father-in-law, Donald C. Cutter, did not live to see this book in print, but I know they would be so proud. My mother-in-law, Charlotte Lazear Cutter, shared her memories of being in childcare when her mother worked in a cannery, and I cherish those conversations. I marvel at how over several decades they all immersed themselves in the labor of child rearing, loving unconditionally, and teaching their children to enjoy our lives to the fullest. I married into a large and loving family of nine siblings, their spouses, children and grandchildren, and along with my siblings, their spouses, children and grandchild—Mike and Michele, Kim and Mark, and John Ubidio—I am reminded of how lucky I am to be a part of the Ciani and Cutter families. Margaret, you've lived with this book your entire life; thanks for never complaining and always being up for an adventure. You learned those things from your dad, who is a parent extraordinaire, and you both bring me joy on a daily basis. Doug, moving from Normal Heights to Normal Avenue created big changes in our lives—thank goodness for your enchiladas and home renovation skills—but our love for one another made it work. Thanks for always being on my side and by my side.

When the Creator designed this beautiful world, it would seem
as though he had chosen San Diego as the spot in which to
concentrate all earthly blessing.

—David Gochenaur, MD, First Annual Report of the Board of
Health, 1888

Squeals of laughter rang out from the grounds of the Children's
Home and Day Nursery (CHDN) and comforted Marie O'Malley
(a pseudonym) when she registered her three young daughters.[1]
Located on the edge of San Diego's city park, CHDN had opened
in 1888 to provide a safe space for children to stay for a day, a week,
or even months while their parents worked for wages or conva-
lesced from sickness. Boarding her daughters at CHDN would allow
the sisters to stay together in a safe and clean space while Marie
headed south into Mexico to search for her missing husband. Three
months earlier he had left them to find fortune in the Mexican
mines, but Marie had not heard from him since, and she feared
he could be sick, injured, or dead. The existence of CHDN helped
Marie decide to follow her husband's path and find work to support her family. By 1890, when she needed the institution's help,
work had dried up in San Diego, but plenty existed in the soap
and textile factories of Ensenada.[2] Securing a job seemed likely;
finding her foolhardy husband less so. After six months of paying
CHDN a monthly fee of five dollars, Marie collected her daugh-

ters and reported she had found a housekeeping job in town, so no longer needed their services. Whether her husband ever reappeared in their lives remains a mystery.[3]

Another mother, Anna Lee Gunn Marston, experienced the Children's Home and Day Nursery in very different ways. As one of its founders, Anna Lee volunteered countless hours to ensure children like the O'Malley daughters received care and comfort. Anna Lee married George Marston in May 1878, and together they raised five children in San Diego.[4] The couple had profited financially from land speculation in the 1880s, and they used their wealth to open San Diego's first department store, support local politics, and fund several budding charities, including the Woman's Home Association, whose members established CHDN.[5] George regularly took out-of-town buying trips, knowing full well that during these lengthy absences his wife would handle the household functions, including parenting their children. Like most women of her social position, Anna Lee embraced the nineteenth century's true womanhood ideals: efficiently run the family home, nurture her children's growth, support her husband's public endeavors (which included two unsuccessful runs for mayor in 1913 and 1917), and involve herself in charitable works.[6] Anna Lee fully immersed herself in the spheres of parenting her own and others' children, and her involvements positively influenced some of San Diego's most enduring social programs.

The familial situations of the O'Malleys and Marstons demonstrate how childcare concerns connected women from vastly different social circles in a common cause. They understood that their families' livelihoods depended on the success of their husbands, but these women knew *their* work was the labor that stabilized their children's lives. Indeed, for Marie, her waged work proved pivotal in reconnecting her family in spite of her husband's failings. Ultimately, their husbands' actions set the parameters for how they could parent: the absence of Marie's husband and the family's poverty limited the ways she could mother her daughters, whereas Anna Lee could shower her children with attention because of her husband's absences and financial success. But childcare brought these women together.

   Interactions among parents and reformers from diverse backgrounds proved critical in the development of social reform programs in San Diego. *Choosing to Care: A Century of Childcare and
Social Reform in San Diego, 1850–1950* examines how a variety of
people—from destitute parents and tired guardians to benevolent
advocates and professional social workers—connected over childcare concerns. Childcare took many forms during San Diego's first
one hundred years of American governance, and as with programs
established across the country in this era, racial, ethnic, gender,
and class identities defined the options available to families. Yet
the programs initiated in San Diego differed from those established in larger, more industrial cities, due to its close proximity
to the United States–Mexico border, and the dramatic population
changes, especially those resulting from the city's military connections. Social boundaries influenced how parents could advocate for their children; cultural boundaries prescribed how San
Diegans accepted certain families into the web of assistance; and
geographic boundaries ordered the delivery of childcare.
   Childcare tends to be defined as the custodial care of children
due to the inability of a parent to do so because of work. A broader
definition can include efforts taken to maintain and nurture the
mental, social, and physical health and development of minors no
matter the reason for the absence of the primary caregiver. In San
Diego this included adults searching for strategies to help rear children considered delinquent, deviant, or disruptive. As such, San
Diegans often struggled with the moral, legal, and economic obligations connected to implementing childcare programs. A critical group of reformers (most of whom were white, middle-class
women) chose to care about the custodial and educational needs
of children from impoverished and working-class families. In the
late nineteenth century, they established social service programs
to try to remedy the growing poverty in the region, and typically
those programs included a childcare component. By the twentieth century, legal mandates professionalized these options and
expanded the possibilities available to families, including a vocational skills curriculum in the public schools, a settlement house

in a predominantly Mexican neighborhood, and accepting qualified children from all cultures at nurseries developed on an emergency basis. However, many civic leaders (most of whom were
white, middle-class men) did not see the need to budget time and
money toward childcare in their own businesses. Essentially, they
understood childcare as social welfare and not as a benefit spon-
sored by employers. That ideological stance influenced how the
city's general population understood childcare, mainly by defining it as a resource needed by unstable families.

An investigation of childcare initiatives in San Diego highlights
the importance of the United States–Mexico transborder relationship to the work of crafting effective childcare programs. In San
Diego the needs of a multilingual and multicultural community
dictated the implementation of childcare programs and differed
from other urban areas in California because of its geopolitical
position as a transborder urban system.[7] By the twentieth century, international involvements in the Mexican Revolution, concerns over repatriation practices, Prohibition, and labor protests
halted the fluidity between borders that had long characterized
the area. These transnational issues moved authorities to secure
the national borders and consequently defined who could access
childcare resources in San Diego.[8]

Examining when and why San Diegans asked for childcare
resources uncovers how people with little political or social power
struggled to improve their lives in San Diego, and the responses
by civic leaders to those needs. Tourists, health seekers, and military personnel sparked much of the city's urban growth, yet few
studies have focused on the lives of the working poor during these
transformative eras.[9] Over the course of the years 1850 to 1950, thousands left their familial networks behind when they moved to the
San Diego area, and those moves forced many of them to turn to
strangers to help them raise their children. Sources show us how
neighbors, teachers, social workers, nurses, and settlement house
workers reached out to families in need. Reformers established
shelters, day nurseries, and juvenile centers, and then learned to
coordinate agency responses so that families could make the most

out of troubling situations. Local advocates, not national activists, touched children's lives in these intimate ways. The size of the city and familiarity of people holding civic power allowed for such personalized attention; however, this changed after 1910, when the sheer size of the city and the infusion of professional standards into childcare prevented such interactions.

Journeys taken by families like the O'Malleys and the Marstons have been the backbone of American West tales: fathers engaged in farming, mining, or land speculation; mothers holding together the family; and children making the most of parental decisions. New West historians have complicated these stories by embracing the messiness of historical experience and challenging narratives that assumed the legitimacy of territorial expansion, patriarchal dominance, and racial hierarchy; moreover, they have debated the complex forms of control within class groups, the heightened agency among marginalized groups, and the fluidity of racial and sexual borders.[10] California history figures prominently in New West analysis, with Los Angeles dominating the scholarship.[11] An analysis of childcare concerns is one way to bring San Diego more squarely into the histories of the American West and California, and demonstrates how a family's racial, ethnic, and class position always influenced how reformers directed a family toward care options.[12]

Historians have also highlighted the complex ways in which benevolent and professional reformers in the United States interacted with parents, and the effects of those interactions.[13] By the mid-nineteenth century, women's access to and need for childcare programs grew alongside opportunities for female wage earning, but a woman's ability to protect and care for her children remained dependent upon how her legal identity positioned her in society. Because the need for childcare has often been understood as an impermanent stage in a woman's life, employers and much of the larger society avoided seeing it as a benefit of employment and instead cast it in terms of social welfare. The general belief in women's innate ability to care for children, tend to the sick, and provide for their elderly relatives defined expectations for who provided familial care.[14] The political and economic transformation that arrived with the nineteenth century gave Euro-American men access to new civil and political freedoms, which tied the concept of independence to waged labor. It also created conflict for those excluded from sustainable waged labor, such as the wives and children of these free men.[15] Instead of seeing women as contributors to the family income, society viewed women and children as "dependents," devalued their labor, and overlooked the influence of their participation in a community.[16] Yet women increasingly moved into the public sphere as both wage earners and reformers.

Maternalist activism tempered the sting of underfinanced and overutilized public programs as middle-class women inserted themselves into decision-making processes through local school boards, club movements, and city beautiful agendas. Similar to women operating in the country's major cities, San Diego's female reformers redefined the use of public spaces.[17] The core of this group migrated into the area in the 1870s and 1880s, emerged as civic leaders during the tumultuous 1890s, and deepened their commitments into the early twentieth century. As white, middle-class women, they operated within a socially privileged arena that kept them isolated from the pains of poverty and discrimination, although their class status also encouraged their involvement in social reform, namely, concerns over sick, abandoned, orphaned, and destitute children. A second generation of female reformers came of age in the 1910s and expanded childcare resources to better accommodate the needs of San Diegans. Their community activism caught the attention of national childcare advocates and led to this group's securing federal grants to improve public healthcare and support for nursery school education in the 1930s, and daycare centers during World War II. However, international borders and the influx of military installations defined their advocacy differently from that of their sisters situated in other centers of progressive energy.

Evidence of childcare in San Diego shows the strength of the "female moral reform authority" in a small but growing community.[18] Like female reformers in larger American cities, San Diego's advocates believed civic fathers paid little attention to solving the social problems spreading through the community. They adopted "maternalist" language and strategies—actions that "transformed motherhood from women's primary *private* responsibility into *public* policy."[19] In the American West, maternalism often operated against the cultures of American Indian, Asian, and Mexican-descent people, but some maternalists learned to confront their "gendered politics of race and citizenship" and accept alternate ways of living and parenting.[20] We see both this civilizing agenda and consequent confrontation in San Diego.

Benevolent-minded women, social workers, philanthropists, and employers made it their business to record their ideas and promote their agendas, leaving behind a cache of source material for scholars to document the evolution of childcare. Organizational papers from local agencies—such as CHDN, Associated Charities, the Public Health Department, Visiting Nurses Association, Travelers Aid Society, and Neighborhood House—underscore the critical roles played by women in the design, maintenance, overhaul, and success of childcare programs in San Diego. These sources also reveal that some projects harmed rather than helped children, and they highlight the inherent boundaries connected to child-centered reform agendas. The local sources along with governmental reports and testimony, oral histories and memoirs, and assessments from national associations emphasize how cross-cultural interactions helped keep some families together but tore others apart. They give voice to mothers and fathers who desperately needed to find solutions to their childcare problems but instead landed in a sphere of regulation.[21] They also provide evidence of children rebelling against the new child protection system that removed them from their households.

But perhaps most importantly, the combination of these sources reveals how difficult it is to establish programs for underrepresented groups. In San Diego, we see a case study of how best to integrate local, regional, and national energies, expertise, and funding, and it offers a lesson in how to listen to the recipients of these social programs. It is terribly difficult to provide a basic resource like childcare to families with widely diverse needs—language and cultural expectations being only two examples of characteristics that create difference—but parents and guardians asserted their right to decide how to care for their children, and reformers often succeeded with the smallest of budgets to offer options to those families.

Yet some pieces of the story remain missing. Since the Children's Home and Day Nursery served as the primary childcare program in San Diego for decades, researchers had studied its organizational papers to understand the city's white, middle-class benevolence but not to learn about the families who used it.[22] Others had studied the collection in search of birth mothers or for clues about an adopted child, and by the time I began my research, the first visitor's log had gone missing. It could have helped me assess the involvement of a parent or community official by tracing visits to a child, but the facility's case records gave me a solid foundation to assess how San Diegans dealt with the complicated processes of providing care to a variety of children over a significant period of time.

Prior to the establishment of CHDN, the community viewed childcare as a private concern. This attitude changed a bit as the town developed and a slightly diverse population moved into the area, especially during the "boom" period of the 1880s. The 1892 depression forced thousands to rethink their decisions about relocating to San Diego, and by 1900 only 17,700 people claimed the city as home. Industrial energy would rekindle migration patterns, and by 1910 San Diego's population grew to 39,978 and then doubled to 74,683 by 1920.[23] Businessmen and politicians pinned their economic hopes on tourism and contracts with the military, and these ventures were highly successful by the 1910s. Sailors, airmen, and soldiers brought their wives and young children with them to the coastal community, as did laborers who hoped to find work in the construction and manufacturing sectors. Civic leaders touted the benefits of living in San Diego by launching two international expositions, one in 1915 and the other in 1935, and by supporting manufacturing interests associated with food production and military expansion. Combined, these efforts helped transform the relatively isolated town into a growing international metropolis, but with a large community of people who were vulnerable to the ever-present economic fluctuations.[24]

Social welfare programs helped stave off the worst effects of the depressions in the 1890s and 1930s, but the problems associated with San Diego's growth continued throughout the boom years of World War II. The population of 147,995 in 1930 swelled to 203,341 in 1940, and to nearly 500,000 by 1944, leaving the city hard-pressed to suitably accommodate its newcomers.[25] The 1930s and 1940s proved incredibly challenging for reformers to stabilize the city's child, health, and social care needs, and they turned to state and federal governments for assistance. Business leaders and politicians, however, clung to the belief that childcare was a temporary problem caused by unique national emergencies, rather than a permanent obstacle faced by a significant sector of the workforce.

The city's first public health official, David Gochenaur, MD, noted in 1888, "When the Creator designed this beautiful world, it would seem as though he had chosen San Diego as the spot in which to concentrate all earthly blessing," but he challenged that statement by documenting the many health concerns in the area.[26] San Diegans survived smallpox and influenza epidemics in the 1860s and 1910s; droughts, floods, and crop-destroying pests; regular bouts of tuberculosis; spurts of white supremacist violence; and racial segregation and ethnic prejudice. *Choosing to Care* analyzes the effects of these events from the perspectives of those who needed childcare or provided that care, starting with when California joined the Union in 1850. Chapter 1 charts the perceptions and actions of Anglos who began migrating into San Diego in the 1850s. State leaders adopted the use of indentured servitude and boarding schools as childcare strategies for some American Indian children, especially for orphaned, captive, or indigent Indian children. In 1880 only 2,637 non-Indians lived in the San Diego area, but Anglo residents controlled the legal, political, and economic power. While the solidification in the 1890s of the reservation system in California ended the practice of indentured servitude, it also kept American Indian children and their families isolated in the remote, rural areas of the state. That isolation provided a rationale for the expansion of federal boarding schools, thus assuring that these children would remain segregated from the majority population.

Chapter 2 reviews the important influences of maternal reformist energy in the late nineteenth century and its effects on San Diego. Organizations at the local, state, and national levels began establishing resources for families to stabilize their lives, such as the CHDN, the Girls Rescue Home, and the Helping Hand Home. These organizations provided a collaborative foundation that would support the city through difficult economic times. Reformers recognized a connection between the spread of vice in San Diego's downtown and the need for childcare, and female reformers tackled the problem head-on by demanding leaders close the district and think differently about the girls and women embedded in the prostitution trade. The San Diego evidence shows that fathers also approached agencies in search of day care because their wives were sick, had died, or abandoned them and their children.

Chapters 3 and 4 detail how professional actions changed childcare practice. Reformers trained in family medicine, social work, and early childhood education began arriving in the area starting in the 1880s, and some of their initial actions came in response to San Diego's concerns over juvenile delinquency. The effectiveness of juvenile justice programs in large cities such as Los Angeles and Chicago has received the greatest attention from historians, yet evidence from agencies in San Diego shows that smaller communities also found success in using these sorts of progressive measures. San Diegans participated in the new juvenile justice movement by establishing juvenile-specific programs that included an order of commitment system; vocational education opportunities; building a local center to house children in need of foster care; and collaborating with existing resources to keep children connected to their local communities. The mandated policies emerging from that movement required San Diegans to implement professional standards in its programs. That allowed for collaborations between local agencies as well as the integration of governmental funding to support the new practices.

Chapter 5 outlines the influences of the settlement house movement, which arrived in San Diego with the opening of Neighborhood House in 1914 by members of the College Woman's Club (cwc). Tensions over increased poverty and homelessness had been exacerbated by the presence of refugees from the Mexican Revolution and transients dislocated by the closing of the city's world exposition in 1917. First Mexican-descent and then African American families benefited from the settlement's programs, which included a clean milk station, immunizations, hygienic public baths, and pre- and postnatal parenting classes. cwc members included several reformers with local and international connections, and these women established a strong commitment to providing medical, childcare, and educational resources to families in this neighborhood.

Chapters 6 and 7 assess the importance of federal programs established during the Great Depression and expanded upon during the 1940s. The Works Progress Administration Emergency Nursery Schools utilized existing spaces in the city, such as in Neighborhood House and public elementary schools, to provide cannery and munitions workers with day care. These sites employed teachers, artists, and craftspeople as childcare workers in an effort to provide steady work to adults affected by the economic crisis of the 1930s. Early childhood educators also received support for their curriculum from the state and federal governments, and when local organizers of the California-Pacific International Exposition in 1935–36 agreed to feature the demonstration nursery school on its grounds. San Diegans survived the Great Depression only to face the population explosion resulting from military preparedness that rocked the city from 1939 through 1945. The federal Lanham Act and California's Child Care Center program allowed the city to open more childcare centers, but those did not solve the problem of infant care and offered parents too little too late. Instead, parents resorted to lifestyle changes such as embracing swing shifts, taking in roommates, and boarding out their children to accommodate their childcare needs. Parents who had recently moved into the area did not benefit from extended kin networks to piece together solutions, and, unfortunately, their choices were not always the ones they hoped would exist for their children.

Providing childcare for families in San Diego proved to be a complicated process. Programs offered safe spaces for some children but controlled and acculturated others. Although never perfect, at least some types of childcare existed in the city and continued to be altered from their inception in the 1850s through the boom years of the 1940s. In the process, childcare played a key role in establishing social reform agendas and contributing to the urbanizing energy of what would develop by the twenty-first century into the nation's eighth-largest city. The history of childcare shines a light on the people in San Diego who chose to care about the health and well-being of strangers, and the parents who chose to trust that care.

ABBREVIATIONS

AC	Associated Charities
BCC	Board of Charities and Corrections
BCIM	Bureau of Catholic Indian Missions
BGAS	Boys and Girls Aid Society
CAC	Consolidated Aircraft Corporation
CCCC	California Child Care Centers
CH	Children's Home
CHDN	Children's Home and Day Nursery
CGC	College Graduate Club
CWC	College Woman's Club
CWLA	Child Welfare League of America
DH	Detention Home
ENS	Emergency Nursery School
FERA	Federal Emergency Relief Administration
FIS	Free Industrial School
FSASD	Family Services Association of San Diego
FWSAA	Family Welfare Services Association of America
HHH	Helping Hand Home
JLSD	Junior League of San Diego
NCLC	National Child Labor Committee
NH	Neighborhood House
SDBA	San Diego Benevolent Association
SDCWC	San Diego County Welfare Commission

SERA	State Emergency Relief Administration
SFIS	San Francisco Industrial School
TASSD	Travelers Aid Society of San Diego
VNB	Visiting Nurses Bureau
WCC	Women's Civic Center
WCTU	Women's Christian Temperance Union
WHA	Woman's Home Association
WPA	Works Progress Administration
YMCA	Young Men's Christian Association
YWCA	Young Women's Christian Association

CHOOSING TO CARE

CHAPTER ONE

Indentured Care

Anglo Solutions to "Civilizing" American Indian Children

We want the Indian girl until she is of age.

—Andrew Jackson Chase to Ephraim Weed Morse, 1862

When eight-year-old Frederico arrived at the San Diego courthouse with his guardians, he knew they planned to indenture him to an Anglo rancher. That winter a small-pox epidemic and flooding had caused great hardship for his family, and he could help them survive by working as an indentured laborer.[1] As the trio entered the courthouse, the boy noticed a tall Anglo looking his way, and Frederico realized this man would soon dictate when and where he worked, ate, and slept. Another Anglo carrying some papers appeared, sat behind a large desk at the front of the room, and began reading the material. Frederico's guardians whispered to him that this man, the justice of the peace, would determine his fate. The hearing took only a few minutes, ending when the official declared, "I do hereby certify that the said Joseph Smith is authorized to have the care, custody, control and earnings of said Frederico minor until he obtain the age of fifteen years." Signatures from the adults in the room secured the justice's proclamation that on December 16, 1861, Joseph Smith owned the boy's labor for the next seven years.[2]

From 1850 into the 1880s, Anglo-Californians, including those living in San Diego County, accepted indenture as a rational prac-tice and legal strategy to care for American Indian children.[3] At a time when social reformers in American cities began to establish nurseries for destitute children, Anglo-Californians put American Indian children to work as a childcare solution. Like off-reservation boarding schools, indenture separated American Indian children from their clan networks and isolated them from childhood experiences.[4] Americans in the colonial era used indentured servitude as a control mechanism for economically vulnerable people until they replaced it with chattel slavery.[5] Californians entered the Union in 1850 as a free state, yet they fully accepted indentured servitude as a method to control American Indian people. The effects of that practice are the focus of this chapter.

In California, Spanish colonists established a chain of missions and used American Indians in what Stephen Hackel describes as a "semicaptive" labor force that Spaniards controlled by providing them "food and community life" at the missions.[6] Indians resisted the captivity, and their resistance to these conditions is a major theme in Spanish–Indian relations.[7] When the secularization of the missions in 1821 "freed" Indians from their colonial Franciscan obligations, secular Mexicans continued to use Indian labor, including children. In studying the Los Angeles case, Michael Gonzalez found that traders operating between Los Angeles and Santa Fe raided Paiute villages for children, convincing destitute parents "who needed guns, horses, or, as some witnesses remembered, a 'plug of tobacco,'" to sell their children into service.[8] Anglos also embraced these practices.

The 1850 Act for the Government and Protection of Indians (California State Statute, chapter 133) legitimated indenturing American Indian children and became a de facto form of state-sanctioned childcare.[9] The act essentially erased the 1832 United States Supreme Court decision *Worchester vs. State of Georgia* by investing the State of California with final authority to manage Native peoples located within the state boundaries. That introduced a system of indenture whereby Indians paid off vagrancy fines and court costs through their labor and/or the labor of their children. Justices of the peace gained jurisdictional authority in all cases of complaints by and against Indians, including decisions regarding contract lengths, provisions expected of employers, and third-party consent to indenture. Moreover, through this act some Anglos assumed custody of Indian children, which essentially erased the parental rights of numerous Indian parents.[10]

The act was amended in 1860 to strengthen the parameters of what lawmakers referred to as "apprenticeship," so as to develop responsible behaviors among Indians.[11] Tragically, these changes encouraged the murder of Indian parents by nefarious traders who sold the orphaned children into this labor. Historian James Rawls notes, "Set in the context of the national controversy over slavery, the situation in California was certainly ironic," considering the territory petitioned for entry into the Union as a free state but essentially sanctioned the enslavement of Indian nations. Potential employers no longer needed to obtain parental consent for child laborers but instead could rely on third-party consent. In addition, the act made any Indian—child or adult—who had "no settled habitation or means of livelihood" eligible for indenture. Under the 1860 law, adults could be impressed into service and terms increased considerably from one or two years to as much as fifteen years for a child. Those terms led to an increased demand for Indian "apprentices" and served as legal mechanisms to fully control a new generation of American Indian people.[12]

While the practice drew some criticism from the general public in California, this transformation occurred through the legal, economic, and political machinations of Anglo-Americans who adopted statehood in the midst of national controversy over captive labor. The state's constitutional convention in 1850 cemented racial stratification by granting state voting rights only to white male citizens of the United States and Mexico. Political privilege gave "white" men the ability to construct racial boundaries and left "nonwhite" individuals little currency with which to argue their citizenship rights. Through this state convention, "white" men affirmed a legal and political system that defined all people who were not "white," male, and mature (twenty-one years) to be legal and political dependents.[13] Thus, in addition to enduring economic instability, "nonwhite" men, women, and their children found themselves vulnerable to further abuses because of the legal system.[14]

Anglo settlement escalated the incidence of domestic violence, environmental scarring, spread of disease, and cultural disruption in the region. Historians agree that nations who lived near the centers of "gold fever" in northern California experienced the greatest harm to their families, but people in all areas of California suffered from the changes.[15] Indians over the age of twenty-five at the time of their capture could be held for up to ten years, and kidnapping children so as to "apprentice" them to employers became a serious issue. Sherbourne Cook estimated that from 1852 to 1867, between three thousand and four thousand children fell victim to apprentice kidnapping in California, with many children being as young as six and seven years old.[16] Boys indentured under the age of fourteen could be held till their twenty-fifth birthday, and girls until they turned twenty-one. Boys contracted between the ages of fourteen and twenty years could be indentured until they were thirty, whereas girls served until the age of twenty-five. Typically, girls worked as domestics, and boys labored on wharves, on ranches, and in mines. Indentured labor integrated children into white spaces, but only as exploited workers who were disconnected from their Native families and dependent on employers for their basic needs.

San Diegans participated in these practices. In 1850 San Diego's population included American Indian nations, *Californios* (descendants of Spanish colonizers), Mexican nationals, Anglos, and a small group of African Americans.[17] As newcomers from east of the Mississippi entered the area, they brought their imagined visions of "savages" made popular by the penny press. But instead of encountering hatchet-wielding warriors, Anglos met people who belonged to clan networks of the Kuupangaxwichem (known by the Spanish as Cupeño), Takhtam (Serrano), Cahuilla, and Kumeyaays (Diegeño). Unprepared to recognize ethnic distinctions, Anglos collectively referred to these groups as "Mission Indians," thereby erasing whole systems of vibrant culture and further establishing their power.[18] Both Anglo men and women participated in sculpting a segregated landscape: whereas white men defined the boundaries of property ownership and political participation, white women used their privilege in private spaces, which included mandating how nonwhite children should be parented.[19]

Like sympathizers of chattel slavery, some proponents of indenture used the language of "assistance" to argue they were saving the "savages" from a life of poverty, thus characterizing indenture as a benevolent rather than an exploitive practice. Even some abolitionists believed that Indians who interacted with whites had a better chance to learn skills that would make them more productive members of society. Abolitionist Jessie Benton Frémont, the wife of explorer and national politician John C. Frémont, shows this attitude in her travel narrative from the 1850s. Frémont commented that the "Mission Indian" servants in her household had been transformed from illiterate vagabonds to civilized domestics.[20] She treated these servants well; however, the assumption that their poverty defined their character underscores the cultural thinking of a mid-nineteenth-century politician's wife. Whereas only white men held the legal authority to contract an indenture, white women served as key instruments in the implementation of "civilizing" projects through domestic spaces, which in California included the care of children.[21]

Some Anglos permitted Native people to remain on their ancestral land in exchange for their labor. Such was the case with J. T. Warner. Originally from New England, Jonathan Trumball Warner (aka Don Juan José Warner) entered California in 1830 as part of a trading expedition captained by Jedediah Smith. Within a couple of years, Warner became a Mexican citizen, changed his name to embrace his new citizenship ties, and began a chain of events that secured his title to forty-seven thousand fertile acres in northeastern San Diego County, the ancestral home of the Kuupangaxwichem. One link in that chain was his marriage to Anita Gale, whose father had left her in San Diego to be raised by an important *Californio* family, the Picos.[22] Born "American," both Jonathan and Anita became Mexican and adopted the *Californio* tradition of patronage connected to labor, which embraced a practice of gift giving to and support of loyal workers.[23] For Warner, that included allowing Kuupangaxwichem families to stay on the land in exchange for their labor on his *rancho*.[24]

When white businessmen arrived in the 1850s, they altered the barter and gift exchange practices used by *Californios*, "Mission Indians," and bilingual Anglos like the Warners. The system had secured loyalty and protection between workers and employers across several generations, but recent transplants challenged the centuries-old practice and invoked beliefs clearly informed by the social purity movement's call for alcohol temperance. Consequently, they judged *Californios* and Anglos who used alcohol in this manner as irresponsible employers.[25] Instead, some white newcomers supported Indian removal policies and indenture practices.

Anglo newcomers rationalized that indenture offered multiple solutions to controlling the problems generated by chronic vagrancy among American Indians, and especially among women. To the point, in his 1877 travel narrative *Letters from California*, D. L. Phillips described the Indian women he encountered as "very much like the men, almost wholly given to a vagabond life, swarming about the towns ... utterly oblivious to the obligations of the marriage relation. The Indians ... are simply doomed, by their laziness and vices, to early extinction."[26] Rumors of Native women offering themselves in prostitution or being sold by a male relative had long circulated in the region, dating to narratives by Spanish soldiers and Franciscan priests written during the conquest and mission periods.[27] In truth, these narratives documented the rapes and assaults of Indian women by colonizers. One example dates to 1775, when six hundred men (defined by some scholars as "Diegueño warriors") descended on the San Diego Mission as a revolt against colonial abuses and burned it to the ground. Over time the history of the revolt lost its connection to the protection of Indian women and became one more misreported account of Native savagery.[28] Yet the laws and ordinances passed in the 1850s show the Anglo disconnect with colonial realities and instead held non-Anglos responsible for the expansion of the vice trade and the evil elements that accompanied it. Indenture became one solution forwarded by Anglo authorities to remedy the issue.

The combination of legislative state law and federal treaty policy paved the way for increased Anglo migration into the San Diego region despite its lackluster commercial endeavors.[29] Newcomers arrived at the way station with a mixture of excitement and trepidation, as most had never ventured west of the Mississippi. Travelers accustomed to oaks, maples, and spruce trees, and an adequate water supply, found scrub brush, yucca, the occasional piñon tree, and little potable water. They also discovered a racially mixed population. In a letter to his brother dated October 18, 1855, Thomas Rylan Darnall mentioned the environment—its excellent bay, the preponderance of fish, and the temperate climate—and emphasized the "heterogeneous combination and amalgamation of all nations and kinds ..."[30] Darnall was struck by people whose physical appearance resembled that of enslaved people in his home region, and he was surprised by their freedom of movement—not "required to show their passes"—and perhaps nervous as to why San Diegans did not control these people. Travelers like Darnall had grown up with tales of wild Indians and uncultured Mexicans, making it easy to believe Indian fathers prostituted their daughters, drunken husbands disturbed the peace at all hours of the day, and whole families stole foodstuffs and livestock from *ranchos*.

San Diego's non-Indian population increased from 650 residents in 1850 to only 731 residents by 1860, but these people used a legal system legitimated through state politics to control the area.[31] In defending the indenture system, Anglo rancher Cave Johnson Couts insisted that under his authority the Payómkawichum (known as the Luiseño by the Spanish) were "well regulated" rather than vagrant drunks.[32] One of the most controversial and vicious employers in the San Diego area, Couts accumulated the thirty-plus laborers needed to work his 23,000-acre Rancho Guajome by exploiting the law. The son of Tennessee slave owners, Couts believed his racial superiority gave him the right to own and control his workers and use brutal punishment if they stepped out of line. Some of that workforce labored in his fields under his supervision, while others worked domestically for his wife, Doña Ysidora Bandini de Couts. Their indentured servants included vagrants, an orphaned six-year-old girl, boys whose mothers agreed to the contract in exchange for their child's clothing, food, and shelter, and "Francisco, an Indian boy," who was ordered by the court in 1858 to serve Couts.[33] Michael Magliari found that Couts used a combination of convict leasing, debt peonage, and formal indenture to effectively control his un-free labor force. Between 1855 and 1870, his reputation as a cruel disciplinarian prompted the San Diego County Grand Jury to issue "no fewer than four indictments" against him for homicide or violent assault. But, as Magliari explains, "well-heeled, well-connected, and well-represented in the local courts, Couts always succeeded in escaping conviction."[34]

Statehood allowed Anglo San Diegans, like Couts, to take control of the area. In 1851–1852, Indian agents negotiated eighteen treaties that affected groups from Klamath near the Oregon border to Temecula at the northernmost reach of San Diego County. The treaties called for 7,488,000 acres to be set aside for reservation land, meaning the twenty thousand or so Anglo squatters living on these acres would be required to relocate. A special legislative committee investigated the treaties and consequently overturned them, ruling to remove to Indian Territory all Indians except for those converted by the missions.[35] In response, some residents, like J. J. Warner, rejected the action and campaigned against Indian removal. Warner asserted that Anglos and Indians needed one another's labor, and he penned the "Minority Report" to disagree with the legislature's relocation plan.[36] Basically ignored, his document had little effect, as Anglos succeeded in pushing most of the Indian families away from the coasts and into the remote interior areas of San Diego County, leaving plenty of farmable land for Anglo settlement.

Some Indians managed to remain in the growing town and to find work as day laborers. Women and girls found domestic labor among *rancheros*, town merchants, and soldiers at the presidio, while men and boys herded livestock, cleared brush, planted and harvested vegetables, and worked in construction. During San Diego's whaling and shipping boom from 1855 to 1875, men and boys also earned wages as sailors, longshoremen, and blubber renderers.[37] But within a generation, Indians lost access to day labor when land-owning Anglos and *Californios* broke with tradition and began hiring poor non-Indians for unskilled jobs. The 1861 indenture of Frederico whose story opened this chapter shows that shift away from hiring Indians for day labor.

The boy's contract certainly gave his family a needed respite, but it also left the eight-year-old vulnerable to abuse by severing him from his clan network and culture. Indeed, because the indenture contract refers to him only as "Indian," the familial strength of his tribal affiliation is lost to history. Frederico spoke Spanish, which gave him some space in which to maneuver outside his culture, and gives us one clue about his heritage: he was probably not from the southern Kumeyaay clans. In San Diego County, indigenous groups first adjusted to life under Spanish colonial rule in the eighteenth century.[38] The Poyomkawish, Kuupangaxwichem, Cahuilla, and northern Kumeyaay learned Spanish and interacted with Europeans through representatives of their clan or village. Those relationships continued when Mexico took control in 1821. Landowners hired clan members conversant in Spanish as shepherds, shearers, field hands, and domestics. In contrast, the southern Kumeyaay resisted European influence and domination by retaining their language and refusing to learn Spanish. For the southern Kumeyaay, resistance to adopting European culture resulted in their greater dislocation and discrimination, especially because they did not speak Spanish. Those results lasted throughout the nineteenth century and into the twentieth century.[39] Language skills probably saved Frederico from starvation as he maneuvered in a culture "curdled" by contact with Anglos, and the boy probably learned to become invisible to his employer as a protection against harsh discipline.[40] He was not alone.

Correspondence between merchants in the 1850s and 1860s reveals evidence of the trade in Indian children. Andrew Jackson Chase, a wholesale grocery dealer in San Francisco, and his friend Ephraim Weed Morse, a San Diego retailer, exchanged several letters regarding Chase's hope to purchase an Indian servant.[41] In 1857 Chase wrote (emphases in the original), "Friend Morse, I should like an Indian Girl and had about concluded to send for one, but Mrs. C found by inquiry of ladies who had had experience in this kind of *property*, that they weren't to be trusted, especially if their masters are fond of *vanity*. Wife thinks *we* had better not run the risk, and I think if anything should *turn up* it would be awful." The Chases seemed to accept stereotypes that depicted Indian women as dishonest, and the Chases were not willing to risk any loss of property or reputation.[42]

Several years later, in 1862, Chase revisited the request and called on Morse to find him an "Indian girl." In outlining his wishes, Chase explained, "We want the Indian girl until she is of age. We wish to treat her well and give her a good English education. We should not consent to any dictation from her Father, as to the mode of her education either domestic or religious." Chase concluded, "When you have an opportunity to make that contract with the Father of the Indian girl please do so."[43] Since Christian Anglos believed "whiteness" sat at the top rung of the social ladder, they also understood their attempts to convert and civilize the so-called heathens as benevolent acts.[44] The Chases saw their intentions to educate a servant as charitable, and the resulting control of the girl's life seemed inconsequential to them. They dismissed any paternal protection coming from this girl's father, which highlights how Indian parents lost their abilities to care for their children, especially through labor practices such as indenture.

Emma, the girl found by Morse for the Chases, was from a Kumeyaay band in southern San Diego County and proved a satisfactory domestic for the Chase family—so much so that others in their social circle began inquiring as to how they might "procure one." These wealthy Anglos used a language of possession: they understood these children as possessions, using phrases such as "like much to have one" and "get one like her," which highlight their embrace of Indian children as commodity. For them, the girl Emma held value as property and not as a child in need of care. Although Andrew Chase and Ephraim Morse hailed from the antislavery strongholds of Newbury and Amesbury, Massachusetts, they obviously believed that the control of some people's labor fell within the parameters of their male citizenship rights. Indeed, they seem to understand their trade in Kumeyaay children as benevolent. After all, Mrs. Chase emphasized, they agreed to treat Emma "well and give her a good English education."[45] Interestingly, Emma was from a clan that had historically *resisted* acculturation, as the southern Kumeyaay worked to preserve its clan networks and culture by not learning Spanish and not working for Spaniards. However, we also learned from the indenture contract of Frederico that the early 1860s were difficult years for people living in the San Diego region, so Emma's family probably resorted to her indenture in San Francisco out of desperation.

Other documents show some indentured children remained in San Diego but lived in the homes of their employers. José Rosario, "an Indian," consented to bind his eight-year-old daughter, Dolores Rosario, to Hannah Schiller for a "term of twelve years," where she would live in the Schiller household. The contract of February 11, 1867, stipulated the girl would "serve her mistress faithfully, honestly, and industriously [in] all lawful commands." In exchange for her service, Mrs. Schiller would provide "suitable and sufficient clothing and food."[46] The wife and daughter of Old Town merchants, Mrs. Schiller likely needed Dolores's labor to help her keep the store clean and stocked, as well as to help with childcare and other domestic chores.[47]

Day labor existed in San Diego County, so why would a child be indentured rather than be a day worker? The need for food and housing may be the key. Families suffered terribly from the floods, drought, and smallpox epidemics in the mid-1860s. Rosario probably indentured his daughter to give her a chance at surviving the poverty and disease that enveloped the community. When Frederico became indentured to Joseph Smith, his guardians and not his parents accompanied him to the courthouse. The records do not indicate a clan relationship between the boy and his guardians, but by the early 1860s, Frederico could have been separated from his parents by kidnap or orphaned through any number of tragedies, complications of poor diet, smallpox, or influenza. Even though most murderous traders operated in northern California, we cannot discount the possibility that Frederico and his parents could also have been victims of such evil. The records simply do not detail these important factors in Frederico's life.

Twenty years later the "apprenticeship" document for seven-year-old Ramón Culfa shows a continuation of this survival strategy. On July 12, 1884, the clerk of San Diego County's Board of Supervisors recorded the boy's apprenticeship to farmer Andres Scott. Despite his age and legal status as a dependent minor, Ramón made his mark—an X—on the document that bound him to Scott until he turned twenty-one years old. Contract conditions were typical for the era in that they required Ramón to "serve his master faithfully, keep his secrets, obey his lawful commands," and conduct himself in a respectable manner. He could not "play at cards, dice, or any other unlawful game, whereby his master may be injured," nor could he "haunt saloons, taverns, or play houses." Ramón relinquished personal liberties such as his right to marry; to buy or sell goods; and to "absent himself day or night from his master's service." In exchange, Andres Scott agreed to teach Ramón to farm, to provide him with "sufficient drink, food, clothing, lodging and washing fitting for an apprentice"; and to offer an environment in which Ramón could be taught to read, write, and know the "ground rules of arithmetic," presumably in the English language. The contract required Scott to provide Ramón at the end of his service with "two full new suits of clothes (worth at least sixty dollars) and the sum of fifty dollars gold."[48]

The contract spells out the conditions agreed upon for children like Ramón Culfa, but important mysteries remain. Why did the boy enter into the arrangement? Were his parents deceased, or did he belong to a family who pieced together a living with odd jobs for Anglo ranchers? Had his family joined the migration of Kumeyaay dislocated by negated treaties and now forced south into Mexico?[49] Was Ramón apprenticed to preserve ties in the United States? We also do not know the outcome of Ramón's life as Andres Scott's apprentice. Did Scott provide food, lodging, and an education for Ramón as contracted; likewise, did Ramón keep the secrets of the Scott household? At the start of San Diego's boom period in 1884, the court approved Ramón's contract during a summer when Anglos passed curfews that forbade any Indian to be in town past sundown. Approving this contract may have been influenced by these actions.

By 1884 business leaders had been unsuccessful in securing a railroad connection linking San Diego to major cities, and without such links the community could not effectively compete with markets to the north, especially Los Angeles. Developers argued that health seekers and entrepreneurs would never move to the town if they saw Indians roaming through it, and several editorials in the *San Diego Union* emphasized the baser qualities of Indians. A November 14 editorial declared that "the squaws frequent the back streets after night for the purpose of indulging in immoral practices for gain" and claimed that "it is well known that the Indians of this section are without morals."[50] As remedy, San Diego leaders passed an ordinance outlawing all "Indians" from being seen within the town boundaries after sundown.[51]

Another solution to the so-called Indian problem was to racially segregate the school system. Beginning in the early 1870s, Anglos complained about their children attending school with "Natives" and began consciously segregating schools.[52] Mission Indian advocate Father Anthony Dominic Ubach recognized the discrimination and wrote to his superior Bishop Amat, "It affects my very heart to see their great wants, their rights so very often violated, by unscrupulous white settlers, taking every advantage over them on account of their social and financial condition, without giving them any chance for redress."[53] Ubach eventually opened St. Anthony's Industrial School for Indians in 1886 as a way to deal with these prejudices, but the school came too late for children like Ramón Culfa. Run by the Sisters of St. Joseph of Carondelet, the boarding school trained the children in Catholic dogma and vocational trades, with boys learning to plow and plant fields and girls learning how to harvest crops and labor as domestics. While St. Anthony's protected students from Anglo prejudices, it also took children away from their families and imposed strict discipline on the ninety to one hundred children who attended the institution each year. Established at the height of a land boom that attracted in two years over thirty thousand newcomers to San Diego, the school met with the approval of Catholic officials, likely as a way to placate Protestant anxieties over a decidedly Catholic and Indian presence in the community.

The nationally situated Bureau of Catholic Indian Missions (BCIM) funded the school that operated in San Diego's Old Town for five years before Ubach relocated it to a more remote location on Mission San Diego de Alcalá property. Initially Ubach's recruitment at San Pascual, Temecula, San Luis Rey, Pala, and Mesa Grande proved frustrating despite his offers to pay for the children's transport to the school, and Ubach believed that certain Anglos were at the heart of Indian families' keeping their children at home.[54] He feared that the prostitution trade figured prominently in their decisions. Ubach understood that the problem lay in "the malice and depravity" of "a good many white settlers," explaining that a "certain kind of commerce in human flesh" had occurred for many years. Whereas popular lore blamed Indian men for pimping their daughters and wives, Ubach emphasized that Anglo men were the real culprits. He wrote that the "wretches [white settlers] know fully well that if the Indian girls go to the Sisters School, they will be taught the merits and beauties of virtue and morality," and Ubach wanted to give those girls that opportunity.[55] Yet he also expressed frustration over how some parents pulled their children from the school because it took them away from their culture. Ubach and the sisters noted how Indian families rejected "white man's medicines and remedies," and they worried about the traditional use of herbs and roots for medical treatment. Ubach feared alcohol and narcotics abuses among Indian families and requested information from the BCIM on educating the community about their harm.[56]

The children attending St. Anthony's may have been sheltered from the taunts of Anglos in the town, but students who rejected the school's mission faced harsh punishments. The nuns indoctrinated their young charges in the benefits of Catholicism, speaking the English language, and living with tightly defined gender roles, and they used shame to keep the children in line. When the school's administrator, Sr. Octavia, caught two girls trying to run away, she cut their long hair as punishment. To their credit, the nuns at St. Anthony's cared for all children in need of shelter, and the school developed a reputation for also taking in poor Mexican children. But the children worked hard for the "privilege" of attending St. Anthony's; by 1893 they cultivated 120 acres of land, on which they raised vegetables, fruits, grain. and cattle to feed themselves and their teachers, and to sell to support school operations.[57]

As historian Margaret Jacobs makes clear, "In the American West, it was neither widespread sexual contact between Euro-American men and Indian women nor the resulting mixed-race children that alarmed authorities. Instead it was decades of costly Indian wars that drove government authorities to recommend assimilation and the removal of Indian children to boarding schools as the means to solve, once and for all, the so-called 'Indian problem.'"[58] Removal also protected non-Indian children from attending school with American Indian children. St. Anthony's closed in 1907 as a casualty of bureaucratic consolidation when the federal boarding school, Sherman Institute, opened in Riverside. Its complex history of saving children from Anglo abuse as well as contributing to that abuse exemplifies the problematic agenda of "saving" Indian children from their cultures.

Indenture in San Diego decreased in the 1880s because of St. Anthony's; however, into the 1920s some Indian families who lived in extreme poverty continued to lose their children to persons using disreputable practices. Delfina Cuero, a Kumeyaay mother, resorted to trading her twelve-year-old son, Aurelio, to a Mexican man and his wife in exchange for food to feed her younger children. The couple had told Cuero that "they wanted a son because they had no children . . . [but] they didn't treat him like a son." Cuero remembered that "they were mean and made him work like a man all the time and even beat him. The food they gave us to pay for him lasted a month." Aurelio stayed with the family for three or four years, then ran away to escape the abusive beatings.[59]

Indian children fell victim to indenture in San Diego because their parents could no longer freely earn wages in the town, and contracting a child to work provided some families with the ability to survive in desperate situations. No matter when each child entered service, Frederico, Dolores, Emma, Ramón, and Aurelio were expected to complete the work assigned to them and not complain about its rigor, and to be grateful to the Anglo they served. They all experienced traumatic separation from their kinship networks, heightened loneliness due to isolation from their families and cultures, and possible physical and sexual abuse. Unfortunately, the Indian families and guardians of Frederico, Dolores, and Emma had few options available to them. Delfina Cuero believed selling her son for food would save her younger children from starvation, and we know too little about Ramón's background to make an assessment of his options. Yet indenture practices required all these children to maneuver across cultural boundaries and enter an Anglo world. Once there, they had to learn how to communicate in English, abide by Christian customs, and, at least in the case of Aurelio, steel themselves against the pain of physical violence.

Interactions with Anglos like rancher Cave Johnson Couts or retailer Ephraim Morse certainly taught Indian children how to survive in a racially charged environment, and the increase of Anglo migrations influenced the tone of these relationships. Beekeeper Rufus Morgan migrated to rural San Diego County in 1879 from North Carolina, and in several letters to his wife, Mary, he wrote of his concern about finding good servants. Morgan observed that most whites handled tasks that in North Carolina would have been relegated to African Americans. Intending to ease his wife's nerves about joining him in the distant land, Morgan explained that many of his neighbors "live with squaws . . . though I have not seen any such" and emphasized that "what impresses me very much so far is that their moral status is higher here than with us." He later underscored he had "not seen a single drunken or noisy person since [he] landed." The one moral problem Morgan noticed was with "dirty Indians." But that did not stop him from hiring "a stout, intelligent Indian girl" who spoke Spanish to help him with

FIG. 1. American Indian boys (probably Kuupangaxwichem) near Warner Hot Springs in 1890. They likely worked the fields in the area. Photographed by Henry L. Davis, Edward H. Davis Collection. © San Diego History Center.

both domestic and field chores. This girl was not indentured, and she did not live with him. Morgan's letters suggest he intended to employ her long term and pay her eight dollars per month, indicating that by 1879 indenture was on the decline in San Diego. Or perhaps the fact that Rufus Morgan was new to the area influenced his decision to hire out rather than indenture an Indian girl.[60] A third possibility connects to this girl's ability to communicate in English, Spanish, and her own language. Given her language skills, she was probably not southern Kumeyaay.

By the 1880s most of the area's 2,500 Indians lived in San Diego's backcountry. Small pockets of Kumeyaay were present between Thirteenth and Seventeenth around K Street and on the bay at the foot of Fifth Street, and some bands lived in the river valley adjacent to Old Town. The growth of the Anglo population dislocated these groups and forced families like Delfina Cuero's into a nomadic state.[61] Some Anglo reformers, most notably Helen Hunt Jackson, called for federal intervention to save California

Fig. 2. Angelita Luzo working in a basketry hopper with a child and a dog next to her in 1904. By the twentieth century, American Indian families lived in the remote areas of San Diego. Edward H. Davis Collection. © San Diego History Center.

Indian nations.[62] But at the point that San Diego's economy took off in 1885, Anglos in the town had effectively contained all Indian groups to living on barren, dry lands outside the town limits. The Mission Indian Relief Act, passed in 1891, directed "Mission Indians" in San Diego County to live on fifteen separate reservations, which forced some Indian bands onto reserved lands in the county's backcountry. Tragically, the government deserted others who could not adequately prove their lineage, an act experienced by Delfina Cuero.[63] Federal officials also expanded the off-reservation boarding school system, which forced them to physically leave their communities and disconnect with their culture.

That complex social environment defined the conditions that allowed for children like Ramón Culfa to make their marks on Anglo documents. In this era Anglo concern over the care of Indian children would be complicated by the lack of medical resources for residents and the growth of San Diego's red-light district. Health concerns had been on civic leaders' minds since the 1870s, and in 1876 it became one of the first communities in California to establish a city health department. To enforce "state and local health and sanitary regulations and preventive measures," it opened a hospital, but only the very sick were admitted, making it a last resort for those dying from wounds, viruses, or infections.[64] Many families simply refused to go near the hospital and recognized it as a place of death. Civic leaders also feared that the expanding vice district would jeopardize the goal of attracting respectable families, but leaders should not have been concerned, as the community would soon experience a population boom.

Once "Mission Indians" no longer lived in the main town, Anglos switched their concerns to Chinese laborers, who had begun moving into the area in the 1870s. Work on the California Southern Railroad increased their numbers by 1885 to an estimated eight hundred men and about a dozen women in San Diego.[65] As they had with Indians, Anglo men became nervous about Chinese men mingling with their daughters and wives; they segregated the Chinese into the poorest-built housing, located in the seediest part of the town. Surrounded by saloons, houses of prostitution, and gambling joints, the Chinese could not escape stereotypes that characterized them as opium-smoking deviants. Even as more Chinese women entered the town as the wives of these men, the stain of rumored prostitution tainted their reputations and encouraged the continuation of segregation. A small group of Anglos developed some assistance for Chinese families, but these programs were focused on Americanizing and Christianizing rather than on providing basic survival services. As a result, Chinese people in San Diego lived in a tightly bound neighborhood where they raised their children in isolation from other cultures.[66]

Indian children living in the San Diego area experienced racism, prejudice, and segregation. By the 1890s leaders in San Diego accepted that the federal reservation system would solve the problems of destitute Indians and turned their attentions to problems posed by whites migrating into the town, such as children left alone during the hours their parents worked. Backed by the national growth of the club movement, benevolent women in San Diego embraced social purity movements such as temperance, closing vice districts, and banning child labor. When San Diego's boom economy failed, female benevolence organized to try and repair some of the damage. In that effort they left the care of American Indian children to the federal government.

CHAPTER TWO

Maternal Care

Childcare for Working-Class Families

They have the appearance of being in a happy home watched over by a devoted mother to whom they constantly turn with zealous affection and confidence.

—Woman's Home Association, 1890

Footsteps creaking across the front porch alerted the matron of the Children's Home and Day Nursery (CHDN) that something was amiss. She should have been sleeping, but the muggy air that July night had made several children restless and kept her from falling asleep. She peeked out the window and spotted some clothes on the porch. When the pile moved, she flew to the door and found an infant loosely swaddled in a silk shawl and lying within a worn quilt. She quickly carried the baby inside and conducted a basic examination. The infant appeared to be relatively healthy, about three months old, and a boy, but unfortunately the matron did not discover any note with identifying information on him. In the morning, she reported the situation to the county Board of Supervisors and chief of police, who agreed that the baby should stay at the CHDN, where he would receive good medical attention, clean clothes, nutritious food, and comfort from the matron and nursery assistant. Six weeks later a married couple attempted to adopt the boy, only to return him to the home within days, because he cried too much. CHDN staff then took full control of the baby's care. He lived at the CHDN with twenty or so other children, who ranged in age from one month to six years. In addition to meeting his custodial needs, staff took on more intimate tasks, such as naming him Willie and securing his christening. When Willie turned two, another couple adopted him, but that arrangement ended three years later when his adoptive mother abandoned the family. Willie's father tried to care for the boy, but a county supervisor, prompted by CHDN staff, removed the now five-year-old boy from the father, because "he was not treated right." Abandoned by two mothers and rejected by a third, Willie received stability and motherly attention from the CHDN through his formative years.[1]

By 1900, when the CHDN matron discovered Willie, a basic social welfare structure existed in San Diego, with the CHDN as its cornerstone. This chapter identifies the social welfare concerns residents in San Diego dealt with during the late nineteenth century and the people who worked to remedy those problems. One of the most pressing issues in the city involved the lack of childcare due to the many newcomers entering San Diego with few familial contacts and economic reserves. Civic leaders had set up basic programs to help indigents get on their feet, but the work of devising and delivering childcare so that parents could maintain employment came from benevolent women, signaling that childcare became understood and defined as a social welfare program rather than as a benefit of employment.

As witnesses to the dramatic changes in their community, women from San Diego's elite families believed they could help heal the traumatic effects of family dislocation. Like many benevolent-minded women of the nineteenth century, CHDN organizers moved into the public sphere through their childcare work. Across the country, benevolent women used their economic stability, social connections, and honored positions as respectable mothers to attend to the custodial needs of women and children. They organized day nurseries and boarding homes, established shelters for unwed mothers, created moral reform associations as a foil to prostitution, devised work exchanges, campaigned to raise the age of

Fig. 3. Children's Home and Day Nursery at the edge of the city park, 1889. ©
San Diego History Center. © San Diego History Center.

consent, and arranged for adoptions of orphaned or abandoned
children.[2] San Diego's maternalists embraced all this work.

A look at San Diego's urbanization in the 1880s helps explain
why these reforms were necessary. Railroad expansions, such as
the completion of the southern link in 1883, sparked explosive
population growth in much of Southern California, with San
Diego's population growing from three thousand residents in
1885 to thirty-five thousand in just three years.[3] Most of those people were white, like the Weddle couple who arrived in San Diego
in 1882 with their five children. They had left New York's Gene-
see Valley for Texas, then New Mexico, and finally landed in San
Diego, where they farmed grapes and olives on 460 acres in the
eastern part of the county. Nonwhite families were not so successful in their migrations. African American Noah Morgan, his
wife, Catherine Fauntroy Morgan, and their children left Kansas
in 1884 with hopes of finding opportunity in San Diego. Instead,
Noah could only find work as a cook for the railroad doing surveys on the international border, which took him away from his

Fig. 4. The Boys Dormitory at the Children's Home, c. 1924; it was added in 1909. Other additions included a hospital and a cottage for infants and children under five years. © San Diego History Center.

family for long periods of time. In the 1880s only about ten to fifteen African American families lived in San Diego County, and they worked in poorly paid service-sector jobs.[4] Gertrude Gildos, another African American, arrived in the city with her family in 1891. The eleven-year-old girl believed she would see "wild Indians," but instead she saw a scene all too familiar: black men serving whites. The sight was devastating for Gertrude, and she could not understand why her family had moved to yet another town where racism would rule her life.[5]

As with the Chinese immigrant community, Mexican-descent families congregated within an ethnic enclave named Barrio Logan (or Logan Heights to English-speakers), which developed southeast of San Diego's business district. Figures for Mexican immigrants in San Diego County and the City of San Diego are unclear prior to the 1910 census; however, demographers have estimated that these earlier figures were similar to the 1910 figures, which indicate numbers in the 3 percent range. In 1910 the county population totaled 61,665, with 2,224 enumerated as Mexican-born immigrants, and the city population was 39,578 in 1910, with 1,222 enumerated as Mexican-born immigrants.[6]

Town boosters appreciated the population growth, yet the existing infrastructure simply could not handle the influx of people. Electricity arrived in 1886, but officials did not secure water delivery until the San Diego Flume Company completed the Cuyamaca Dam in February 1889.[7] Even then the water situation remained precarious, due to the region's generally low water supply. Inadequate housing forced people to share a boardinghouse room with a stranger or to live in tents. The problem created a boon for the San Diego Tent and Awning Company, but headaches for sanitation officers and city planners trying to devise long-term solutions. Public officials did what they could to bring order to the chaotic development, but limited funding prevented them from adequately solving infrastructure problems, and private businesses simply could not keep pace with delivering services and products to everyone who needed them.[8] A small but dedicated group of white, economically privileged families established the San Diego Benevolent Association (SDBA) in 1872, yet the association went bankrupt by 1889. The demise of the SDBA resulted in additional responsibilities for the county Board of Supervisors, which by 1890 maintained the combination almshouse/hospital, financed the care of orphaned children, and reviewed all relief requests. Decreased funding meant the board approved far fewer requests, and those it did approve benefited white families who tended to use the assistance to leave the city.[9]

The severity of the economic situation convinced an estimated seventeen thousand people (nearly half of its population) to leave the area, resulting in a population decrease as dramatic as its increase: by 1900 San Diego's city population had dropped to 17,700. For those who stayed, distance from family networks proved a salient problem, as they had no resources to help them care for their children. Even the nationally situated organizations with a presence in the city could not offer effective assistance. By 1882 San Diego was home to local branches of the Young Men's Christian Association (YMCA), Catholic Charities, fraternal orders of the Masons, the Grand Army of the Republic, Knights of Pythias, and the Benevolent and Protective Order of Elks. Assistance such as food, burial funds, and money for medicine was provided to member families and relatives, and they made sure to keep aid secret so "that none should suffer from the fear and shame of asking."[10] George White Marston attempted to organize an Associated Charities in 1889, but the group met only three times before disbanding over issues of direction.[11]

Additionally, many of the newcomers who moved to San Diego as a remedy for their poor health learned that pleasant weather did not immediately heal their tuberculosis or pneumonia. Their medical needs soon overwhelmed both the County Hospital staff and the capabilities of the few physicians who had set up private practices. One attempt to improve medical care came from the Catholic order of the Sisters of Mercy, who established a dispensary at Sixth and Market in 1890 and, one year later, opened St. Joseph's Sanitarium.[12] In 1894 the private and locally organized Helping Hand Home (HHH) began housing destitute families, with attention paid to families who had been treated by the county physician. Sanitary conditions at the County Hospital had become so dire that the Board of Supervisors instructed the county physician to admit all sick or injured persons to the HHH rather than the hospital.[13] But these programs did not directly address the two concerns identified by local reformers as specifically affecting women and children: the absence of childcare and the expansion of vice.

Benevolent reformers from the city's Women's Christian Temperance Union (WCTU) formed its Woman's Home Association (WHA) and opened the CHDN in 1888. The establishment of the CHDN brought San Diego in line with other urban areas that had been offering that type of childcare for over a generation. The CHDN operated as both a boarding home and day nursery, offering the only organized day care in the city until 1910, when the HHH opened a day nursery; however, HHH was continually cited for its poor delivery of care and within five years stopped providing childcare. The community's first settlement house, Neighborhood House, would include a day nursery when it opened in 1914, but for twenty years the CHDN was the only facility in San Diego that provided day or long-term childcare. Employers hoped the facility would alleviate absenteeism *among their male* employees whose wives also earned wages outside their home. With few or no family members to help them care for their children, these parents depended on the CHDN.

The CHDN attracted the attentions of national agencies and resulted in their opening local offices, including the Salvation Army and the Children's Home Society of California (a national agency that found permanent homes for orphaned and abandoned children) in 1888. Five years later, in 1893, the Salvation Army also brought a rescue home for unwed mothers to the city, known in San Diego as the Girls Rescue Home. Bent on redemption, the Girls Rescue Home admitted girls and women under the age of thirty who were "desirous of moral reformation and . . . not otherwise objectionable." The organization helped an average of five women each month, but it did not allow admittance to African American, American Indian, or Asian women, highlighting another incidence of segregation in the city.[14]

Members of San Diego's WCTU organized the WHA as a way to address the growing childcare problem, but first they involved themselves in cleaning up San Diego's vice district. The presence of children living in the vice district gave credence to the rumors that unsuspecting youngsters were being lured into a criminal life, and members of the WCTU turned their full attention to eliminating the problem by acting to close the district. As with other WCTU chapters across the country, San Diego's membership dedicated their advocacy to understanding the multifaceted problem of vice, especially its harmful pull on women who had few options to enter into respectable work. A popular strategy adopted by many urban communities across the country was to control vice by containing it within a regulated district (known as red-light districts), which is how San Diego's civic leaders handled its problem.[15] However, the WCTU rejected that tactic and argued that the businesses operating in the area should be closed completely; ultimately, city authorities opted for regulation rather than closure.

San Diego's red-light district, known as "the Stingaree," consisted of several blocks of ramshackle buildings near and around the wharf. Beer and other spirits flowed freely, and one could easily find a gambling game, prostitutes, opium smoking, and cockfighting. The district's attractions drew in transients traveling to and from Mexico, fishermen relaxing after weeks on the sea, soldiers tired of the mundane post, confidence men anxious to make a quick buck, and day laborers looking to blow off a bit of steam. Named for the spiny fish found in San Diego's bay, the Stingaree became well known as an area filled with unsavory types, and a rumored 120 brothels by 1900. While such exaggerations cannot be validated, census information from 1870, 1880, and 1890 indicates a steady increase of single women living in locations where known prostitution occurred in the neighborhood.[16] The WCTU saw that increase as a call for it to connect with these vulnerable women, and they organized the WHA in 1884 in hopes of aiding sick, helpless, or unemployed women.[17] The WHA agenda fell in line with the national mission directed by WCTU national president Frances Willard to "combine the benefits of education with those of a social service to working mothers."[18]

While WHA members believed the Stingaree should be shut down completely, male civic leaders reacted differently to the district's problems. Men recognized the uptick in violent crime in the Stingaree and often blamed women living there for the increase. Yet evidence from coroners' inquests suggests that as with other vice districts in western communities, much of the criminal activity in the zone was directed at women rather than being initiated by them.[19] In the period 1881 through 1889, six women died by gunshot, starting with Maggie McCutcheon (otherwise known as Maggie Bangs), whose "lover," Charley Gordon, killed her on June 20, 1881. The term "lover" was nineteenth-century slang for a prostitute's pimp, and most of the women who died gunshot deaths had ties to prostitution. Some prostitutes survived the violence; one such was Hattie Ruth, who swore out a warrant against her "lover," James "Bull" Conrad, when he tried to kill her. Conrad retaliated by turning her in to the police for keeping a house of prostitution but decided not to follow through on charges when word seeped out he ran a gambling game on Fifth Avenue.[20] Authorities directed the 1884 curfew against American Indians, who they thought were engaged in prostitution and vagrant, and while newspaper editorials blamed American Indian women for these problems, court records show that whites were those prostitutes being arrested for deviant behavior and vagrancy. They believed this criminal behavior could be contained through zoning and controlled by legal action. The role of the WCTU in the passage of the curfew is unclear, but the fact that it organized in the same year as the curfew is certainly not coincidental. Authorities used these incidents to prove the city was experiencing an escalation of crimes committed by women and to emphasize the connection between prostitution and other forms of vice.

A precarious infrastructure and an unpredictable economy contributed to an unstable community, but the uncontrolled spread of vice raised some of the loudest protests among residents. Stories emerged describing the perils of young white girls who had too easily slipped into the life, sending the community into frenzies over the best ways to protect future victims against these kinds of incidents. They were not alone in their fear. Across the country social commentators and charity organizers wondered about the security of single women and girls traveling alone into cities to find jobs, even devising the moniker "women adrift" to describe the vulnerable group. They believed white females were vulnerable to falling into a "white slave" market in prostitution and worked to publicize the issue to the general public. Originating in 1885 with English journalist William T. Stead's article "The Maiden Tribute of Modern Babylon," the outrage over the sexual exploitation of young, working-class girls crossed the Atlantic and "had an immediate impact on the American moral reform community," especially with Frances Willard and the WCTU.[21] During the Progressive Era, and peaking between 1910 and 1913, "white slavery" narratives riveted the nation. Lurid tales of innocent country girls entrapped in big-city prostitution rings peppered the newspapers and magazines purchased by urban readers, and Hollywood exploited the topic in silent films. Plots were crystal clear—naïve virgins fell victim to the charms of conniving pimps and experienced madams—and played to the voyeuristic imaginations of readers. "Naive" meant white, typically middle-class, often native born, and sexually inexperienced, meaning that all other groups of girls carried some inherent promiscuity.[22] Although contemporary authors debated the realities of who descended into the trade and the depth of its reach, the scare incensed leaders of moral organizations, who launched intense campaigns to rid cities of vice districts. Brian Donovan explains, "The issue of coerced prostitution increasingly referred to as 'white slavery,' offered an unambiguous example of male cruelty and the need for the moral influence of women."[23]

In California, members of the Women's Christian Temperance Union immersed themselves in the issue by leading the fight to "amend the rape statute." Their agenda centered on raising the age of consent for girls from ten to eighteen years, thereby hoping to discourage men from sexual contact with girls, or from what reformers characterized as sexually preying on innocents. Starting their effort in 1887, WCTU members circulated a petition to reform groups, which warned that "the increasing and alarming frequency of assaults upon women, and the frightful indignities to which even little girls are subject, have become the shame of our boasted civilization."[24] In San Diego clergy solidified the efforts to stop the spread of vice by asking the city's board of trustees to increase regulation in the Stingaree and adopt a resolution refusing business licenses to "keepers of prostitution." The board agreed and passed its restriction on May 6, 1887.[25]

In support of the resolution, the *San Diego Union* published a series of stories detailing the ruin of young white girls at the hands of experienced female prostitutes. Rather than placing blame on male clients, the articles sided with popular understandings that carnal threats came from women.[26] One month after the resolution passed, nine women were arrested for allegedly enticing Gretchen Eisel, a fourteen-year-old runaway from San Francisco, into a known house of ill repute at the lower end of Sixth Street in the heart of the Stingaree. Gretchen's case highlighted to the public the absence of protective homes for girls, the increased efforts of the WCTU membership to monitor activities in the Stingaree, and the need for changing age of consent laws. The nine women who were part of the arrest had difficulty securing their $500 bail; however, the defendants agreed to leave the life of prostitution and enter private service, which probably influenced the court's decision to find them not guilty on the grounds of insufficient evidence. Gretchen revealed she had run away to escape an abusive home life in San Francisco and ended up in San Diego. After struggling to make ends meet on her dollar-a-week wages as a maid, she entered the disreputable house. After the trial, Gretchen and one of the nine arrested prostitutes were placed in Mrs. Watson's Home for Stray Girls in Los Angeles. Only Edna Russell, proprietress of the brothel, and one other prostitute connected with the case are known to have entered into private service.[27]

Two months later another story shocked the community and again featured a fourteen-year-old San Francisco girl. With all the makings of a gothic novel, the Julia Seiler case involved a family of means and featured bribery, adultery, and intrigue. Details kept readers captivated for months: Julia's boyfriend (a twenty-four-year-old man who was engaged to another woman) made arrangements for her to leave San Diego via steamer with Kate Clark, a known madam in San Diego. Clark had dyed Julia's blonde hair black as a disguise, but after only a week in San Diego, a detective hired by the Seiler family discovered her in Clark's house.[28] The Seiler family paid Clark to remain silent so as to minimize any publicity generated by their daughter's love tryst. But the plan backfired for the Seiler family when the sordid details appeared in the paper. The fiancé earned plenty of trouble too, as he was forced to "right his wrong" and marry Julia.[29]

Clearly, the ways the media communicated the perils of Gretchen and Julia are products of their time. The rise of sexualized pulp fiction published under the guise of crime pieces such as found in the *Police Gazette* and the attention of the WCTU consent campaign influenced the newspaper space devoted to these stories. Gretchen and Julia both ran away from their homes and had their privacy invaded, but class distinctions defined the outcomes of these girls' predicaments. Whereas Julia had the protection of her father's wealth to set her back on a moral path—marriage to the man who led her astray—Gretchen found herself protected by benevolent interests who provided her sanctuary from an abusive home. Of course, protective homes suffered from their share of abuse allegations, and authorities would eventually call for investigations of some institutions. But for fourteen-year-old Gretchen Eisel, Mrs. Watson's Home for Stray Girls offered the best chance for safe shelter from prostitution.[30]

Exaggeration typified reporting of the city's prostitution landscape. Whereas one reporter counted "at least nine houses of prostitution by April 1887," another writer claimed that "nearly 100 houses of prostitution, each containing from one to thirteen inmates," tainted the town. Editorials warned young men of the dangers they would encounter with a prostitute and listed the areas where one would find those prostitutes.[31] Yellow journalism at its best, these stories certainly advertised the zone as much as if not more than they issued caution. While some stories described prostitutes as prisoners trapped in the district with little control over their livelihoods, most conveyed little sympathy for the "dozen negro and thirty Chinese women competing with their depraved white sisters in the nefarious traffic." Race always figured into the descriptions, and writers made certain the readers knew the numbers of "negro" and "Chinese" prostitutes at work in the reprehensible trade. One unflattering description of a prostitute emphasized "her coarse and brutal face, the toddy blossom on the nose, the inellegant [*sic*] negligeé of the dirty mother hubbard which furnished but a partial concealment of her repulsiveness . . . a loathsome object," and young men who sought out female entertainment in the Stingaree would find only "the lowest class."[32] These were common descriptions for prostitutes in the late nineteenth century, and nonwhite prostitutes were considered especially heinous, because of their supposed ability to corrupt white men. Children born to prostitutes were "weak and doomed" to a terrible life, not only because of the poverty they likely experienced but because of an assumed inherited deviance.[33] Men had to be warned of the tainted bodies they would encounter in red-light districts, and the media obliged by feeding the fear.

In spite of the attention raised by Gretchen Eisler and Julia Seiler, police continued to find youngsters in the Stingaree. Since in California girls could legally give consent for sexual relations when they turned fourteen, most girls connected with prostitution in San Diego gave that number as their age. In February 1888 more complaints of child prostitution caused police to begin arresting suspected madams. One headline announced, "Police Declare War against the Owners of Houses of Ill-Repute," and the story reported on the city's Section 316 policy: "Every person who lets any apartment or tenement, knowing that it is to be used for the purpose of assignation or prostitution is guilty of a misdemeanor."[34] A misdemeanor offense hardly qualified as "war," but the regulation shook up the red-light district. Police arrested so many women in 1888 that court supervisors asked them to discontinue arrests after 10:00 p.m., because they could not keep up with the processing. While the Section 316 regulation offered some changes, it did not stop the activities in the Stingaree. Perhaps the cases of Jessie Dixon and Ethel Hunt influenced local WCTU advocacy. On October 22, 1889, police arrested Carrie Johnson on the charge of enticing a fourteen-year-old girl (Jessie Dixon, a name that proved fictitious) into her home for purposes of prostitution, and in 1890 authorities recorded the first charge of attempted rape in San Diego, against Charles E. Forsythe for abusing Ethel M. Hunt, who was "under the age of fourteen."[35] State lawmakers did not vote to raise the age of consent to sixteen until 1897, but the WCTU's age of consent campaign influenced how San Diegans understood rape and how they involved themselves in assigning criminality to certain actions.

Serial magazines and dime store novels used the "woman adrift"

trope to sell their stories, but a San Diego scenario proved the tragedy could be real. In November 1897 a coroner's inquest into the
death of Mary A. Monroe raised suspicion that the woman might
have ended her life by throwing herself in front of a streetcar. Monroe had been ill and out of work, surviving through the charity
of former employers and friends. Her brother, George Miller, was
an independent blacksmith who was "too financially oppressed"
to help his sister. A well-known African American man, Miller's
sibling connections also led to the discovery that Mary had been
passing for white during her three years in San Diego.[36]

Problems associated with crime in the Stingaree may also have
affected political directions taken by the community. In 1888 citizens
voted in a city charter form of government, which took effect the
following year and replaced the board of trustees with an elected
mayor (Douglas Gunn, editor of the *San Diego Union* and Anna
Lee Gunn Marston's brother), and included nine aldermen elected
at large and nine delegates elected by ward. Reorganization also
allowed for hiring a city attorney, city clerk, health officer, plumbing inspector, and superintendent of sewers, and establishing police
and fire departments.[37] Women could not vote or hold office, but
their connections to these new leaders through birth or marriage
helped position the group to attempt a moral overhaul of the city.

The Woman's Home Association remained connected financially and administratively to the WCTU and its membership, but it
focused on assisting sick, helpless, and unemployed women.[38] Established residents such as Anna Lee Gunn Marston worked alongside newcomers like Theresa Greenbaum Lesem, Haidee Goldtree
Blochman, and Anna Lee's second cousin Charlotte Baker, MD, in
the work of solving the city's social problems. These women were
all married and mothers of small children during some of their
most active service years, which challenges the model that some
historians of reform have emphasized of the single, childless activist known as the "social housekeeper" or "public mother" made
known by reformer Jane Addams.[39] They had been reared in an
era that expected women of their position to engage in charitable
works, and these women lived up to those expectations.

Anna Lee was born in 1853 in Sonoma, California, two years after her mother and brothers had joined her father in the state. Her father had moved west from Philadelphia, where he had been a teacher, printer, and antislavery activist to secure a new life for his family. In 1861 the family moved together to San Francisco and gradually migrated south to San Diego. Anna Lee's brothers arrived first in 1869, and she followed in the summer of 1875. Twenty-two at the time, Anna Lee met George Marston, and they became engaged in April 1876. George's parents and Anna Lee's mother hailed from the same town, Newburyport, Massachusetts, which surely helped in securing the marital match. The couple married two years later in May 1878 and eventually had five children. Their growing family and their department store kept them busy, but the Marstons always found time for public service. In addition to running the family home, Anna Lee involved herself in the Congregational Church, served as president of their Women's Missionary Society of Southern California, and became the first president of the wha.[40]

Physician Charlotte Baker, also from Newburyport, arrived in San Diego on January 2, 1888, with her husband, Fred (also a physician), and their two small children. The Bakers had met in medical school at the University of Michigan and married on Charlotte's twenty-seventh birthday, March 30, 1882. Within months, Charlotte finished her medical degree, and the couple moved to Socorro, New Mexico, where they tried their hand at ranching. The Bakers realized they were better suited to an urban environment, and they became attracted to San Diego. One draw was their familiarity with current residents, such as the Marstons. Another was the city's need for medical professionals. Charlotte had entered Vassar College in the fall of 1873, graduated two years later with a bachelor of arts degree, and worked as an assistant teacher for the Vassar gymnasium before moving to the women's reformatory prison in Sherbourne, Massachusetts, to teach physical education. That experience introduced her to obstetrician Dr. Eliza Mosher, who encouraged her to pursue a medical profession. In 1879 Charlotte entered medical school at the University of Michigan, which at the time was the only coeducational medical school in the United States. When they arrived in San Diego, the Bakers set up a private practice, and Charlotte soon became the medical examiner for the State Normal School. She immersed herself in community life by teaching Sunday school at St. Paul's Episcopal Church and providing free medical care to women and children she encountered through the WHA.[41]

Protestant in its origins but ecumenical in its outreach, the Woman's Home Association drew on its religious foundations to build a strong membership. In forming a leadership body for the Children's Home and Day Nursery, organizers invited area churches and Temple Beth Israel to each select one representative to serve as a vice president to president Anna Lee Gunn Marston, including several Jewish women. Theresa Greenbaum Lesem had been born, reared, and married in Chicago, and like Charlotte Baker moved with her husband and children to San Diego in 1887. Lessum would guide the CHDN as its president in the first decade of the twentieth century. San Franciscan Haidee Goldtree married into one of San Diego's leading Jewish families, the Blochmans. After graduating from the University of California, Haidee married Lucien Blochman on November 9, 1898. The couple's fathers had been business associates in San Francisco during the late 1850s, and Lucien's family had moved to San Diego in 1881, where they became involved in social and charitable organizations. Lucien was also active in politics, serving six years on San Diego's City Council (first in 1897 then in 1905). In addition to her commitment to the CHDN, Haidee would serve as a director of the College Woman's Club, a secretary of Neighborhood House, a Sunday school teacher for Temple Beth Israel, and president of Jewish Charities.[42]

Female reformers such as these women worked to educate the general public about the city's social welfare needs through their involvement with the WHA. As a result of problems with the vice district, WHA members created a Woman's Industrial Exchange in 1888. Exchanges operated as a way for women to support themselves or their families by selling products associated with maternal labor: baked goods, needlecrafts, and children's clothes. In an attempt to maintain anonymity among the makers, the group divided proceeds of the sales evenly, rather than makers receiving individual credit for their handiwork.[43]

The San Diego Exchange operated a bit differently, because of the general needs in the community. Instead of sponsoring a crafts market, the exchange established a lunchroom where women cooked and served meals, which erased anonymity. Annual reports for the exchange do not indicate the intended patron audience, but considering the connection to the WCTU, the lunchroom may have offered working-class men an alternative to eating in saloons or provided middle-class customers a respectable space to relax while shopping.[44] After a shaky start, within four years the group claimed a "self-supporting" status, with "a balance in the treasury twice as large as that of the last annual report." Those figures encouraged the group to continue its work, especially in light of the "general depression in business affairs, the decrease of population in our city, and the history of Woman's Exchanges in general."[45] Yet the Woman's Industrial Exchange movement would be short lived, and there is no evidence it lasted in San Diego beyond the 1892 report. The second agenda item of the WHA—to provide childcare for working-class parents—would be far more successful and long lasting.

Members of the WHA opened the CHDN in August 1888 as a resource for wage-earning parents and as a refuge for orphaned and abandoned children. An "oral tradition" recounted within the CHDN community traced its roots to when businessmen offered approximately $25,000 to the WHA in exchange for establishing a day nursery so as to curb absenteeism among their male workers.[46] City directories for San Diego County from the years 1885 to 1920 show a marked increase in the numbers of women entering waged labor, indicating that both fathers and mothers were leaving the household to earn wages.[47] With the encouragement of Bryant Howard (to whom the city had granted a deed of one hundred acres of park land), the WHA requested that the board of city trustees give them five acres of Howard's land to build a home for needy women and children. The trustees granted the request, and

FIG. 5. Women laundering at the foot of D Street at the waterfront, 1912. This labor-intensive and poorly compensated work was common among impoverished women, especially African American and immigrant women. © San Diego History Center.

the group embarked upon a fund-raising effort to acquire building funds.[48] Two years later it moved from rented cottages at First Avenue and Cedar Street (then Tenth Avenue and G Street) to its permanent site at Sixteenth and Ash Streets on the edge of the city park.[49] From the start, few parents used the facility as a day nursery, opting instead to board their children. Many mothers who used CHDN worked as domestics and probably lived in with their employers, thus leaving them no good housing options for their children. The CHDN gave these mothers a solution.

Initially, about thirty families with children ages six years and under turned to the CHDN, although organizers made some exceptions to age limits in order to keep siblings together. Within five years the facility cared for children from about fifty-five families. Typically, the child's family spoke English, and the parents had little to no formal education. Records indicate that most of the jobs held by the women in these children's lives were in the service sec-

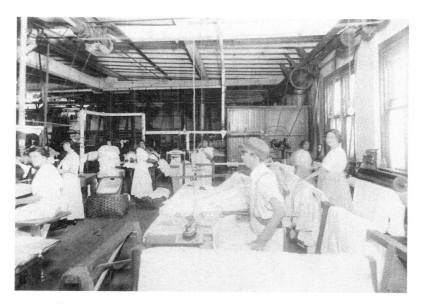

FIG. 6. The Electric Laundry Company in 1915, which employed primarily girls and young women, including Mexican American and Italian immigrants. © San Diego History Center.

tor, and the men worked in manual labor. The racial makeup of the children mirrored the town's demographics: most were white (some of whom were identified further as Mexican), and a few were African American. The Children's Home staff did not turn away any child in need of care; however, they took in American Indian and Asian children on an emergency basis only and quickly transferred them into private homes or facilities in other cities.[50]

Children who boarded at the CHDN likely benefited from the stability of the home's daily regimen. They awoke at 6:00 a.m., washed, dressed, made their beds, said morning prayers at 6:50 and ate breakfast at 7:00. The older children washed the dishes, swept the floor, and prepared for school at Lincoln Elementary. Every week they attended Sunday school at the First Methodist Church. The first and third Sundays were visiting days for parents, relatives, and friends, and children were allowed to visit at home on the second Sunday of the month. Every third Sunday, staff organized a birthday party for children born within that month. Insisting that their efforts invest a sense of individual freedom and responsibility in the children, personnel explained that residents did not wear uniforms, kept their own drawers, and had their own shelves on which to place rock, feather, and ribbon collections. As one account described, "Never a disciplinary institution, the home is just what the name implies: A 'home' for San Diego children."[51] Organizers emphasized that the children "have the appearance of being in a happy home watched over by a devoted mother to whom they constantly turn with zealous affection and confidence."[52] Indeed, as the local paper reported, the CHDN matron seemed "untiring in solicitude and affectionate regard for her varying flock."[53] To ensure a healthy environment, physicians Charlotte Baker and Bessie Peery checked each child for illness.[54] A nursery worker then acclimated the child to the home. Children discovered they ate three meals each day and wore clean clothes, and a kindergarten teacher from the Normal School taught them colors and the alphabet.[55]

Across the country advocates of day nurseries and short-term boarding understood the many problems associated with maternal wage earning. They tried to keep operational costs down so that even the poorest families could benefit from nurseries; plus, asking a mother to contribute to her child's care was an important feature of the day nursery movement. Advocates believed that evidence of mothers paying for childcare could counter opinions about working mothers neglecting their children or fully depending on charity for subsistence.[56] When critics suggested closing day nurseries and finding solutions that kept mothers at home, advocates highlighted the importance of mothers paying for their children's care. To ensure that mothers could afford care, some day nurseries took on the function of an employment agency that helped mothers secure day work. Jobs generally consisted of poorly paid and strenuous service-sector work, yet organizers believed employment helped mothers maintain some dignity within their poverty.

The motivation of CHDN staff and volunteers to help working-class families coincided with that of many clubwomen operating in the late nineteenth century: they hoped to both save children from disease and immorality thought to dwell in poor families and to help women out of troubled situations such as being abandoned by their husbands or falling into homelessness. They drew the line, however, at helping sick children or terminally ill women.[57] The medical involvement of Charlotte Baker in the CHDN challenges that limit a bit. Baker voluntarily examined the women involved with the Woman's Industrial Exchange, and all the children admitted to the CHDN, and her commitment represents a critical component of the CHDN programs. In addition to giving a thorough exam to every child who entered the CHDN, Baker visited it daily to ensure illness did not spread throughout the facility, which allowed the CHDN to provide a safe environment for children who had little access to medical care.

This type of advocacy offered maternalists a platform for effecting change in child welfare policy. Once the clubwoman's movement took off in the 1890s, maternalists used it to relay their messages.[58] Consequently, many day nurseries received substantial financial support and volunteer energy from members of these organizations. Clubwomen organized along strict racial and religious lines; likewise, the day nurseries at which they served accepted clients who shared similar cultural backgrounds. Indeed, Christian and Jewish children, even if they shared a national heritage such as German or Russian, often attended separate nurseries.[59] But the CHDN was the only facility in San Diego; thus, it accepted children of all faiths, at least on a temporary and emergency sheltering basis. Moreover, the county board used the CHDN to care for orphaned children, and those children who had been abandoned or lived in dangerous situations. In this way, the CHDN took on a dual agenda of providing custodial care to children whose parents paid a nominal fee for the service and to dependents of the county.

Boarding arrangements and payment schedules at CHDN seemed to be fairly loose. It cost more than three dollars per week to board a child, but no parental fee came close to covering that expense. Depending on the family's economic situation, a parent could pay from two to eight dollars per month for each child, although the organization charged nothing to those mothers they considered destitute, which contradicted their original dictate that payment helped preserve a mother's dignity.[60] Lizzie Burr began boarding her five-year-old son at CHDN in August 1896, continuing this arrangement for a few years. She originally paid them an eight-dollar monthly fee, but in February 1898 his board was reduced to only six dollars each month. We can only guess at the reasons for reduced fees. Burr worked in the home of a prominent San Diego official, so perhaps his influence played a role in the fee, or the boy grew into handling odd jobs around the facility to off-set his boarding expenses. Whatever the reason, the extra two dollars per month allowed this mother the chance to stay physically connected to his upbringing while earning wages as a domestic servant.[61] The CHDN also employed mothers as cooks and nurse's aides in exchange for children's board and a small stipend.[62]

Opening the CHDN to women who could not afford to pay fees for their children's board demonstrated its benevolent foundations, and Woman's Home Association leaders regularly added to and changed the home's guidelines to address mothers' needs.[63] Their philosophy carried into the twentieth century and, while admirable, did little to ensure an adequate cash flow for operations. The establishment of childcare and an employment agency, and the provision of medicines, cost more than association members anticipated. Budget deficits forced the organization into a continual mode of fund-raising to keep the programs equipped and functional. Flower shows and door-to-door campaigning during Christmas holidays generated some cash and positive publicity, but not enough revenue for the facility to run debt free, and it would eventually turn to the county for support.

Despite these drawbacks, CHDN provided a safe space for many children, including those who had been abandoned or orphaned, giving them a chance to be adopted into a loving home. Yet, as we learned with the case of Willie that opened this chapter, these adoptions were not always successful. Placing abandoned children could prove difficult, perhaps because potential parents did not trust the biological parentage. In her history of single pregnancy, Rickie Solinger explains that prior to World War II, society generally understood an illegitimate child as "the product of a mentally deficient mother," and therefore the child was "tainted and undesirable." Single mothers, no matter their race, were encouraged to keep their illegitimate children as a sort of penance for their sin of premarital sex. The development of agencies such as maternity homes began to change that thinking. Designed for moral redemption, maternity homes emerged in urban areas across the United States in the late nineteenth century and were typically built by religious groups such as the Salvation Army or the Roman Catholic Church. As such, these homes required mothers to repent for the sin of premarital pregnancy and accept that giving your child over to adoption completed the redemption.[64] The opening of the Girls Rescue Home in 1893 brought this thinking to San Diego.

Historian Regina G. Kunzel found this mandate of repenting one's sexual sins and embracing Protestant Christianity common in maternity homes across the nation, noting that "evangelical women conceived of maternity homes as primarily redemptive" and "set out to not only shelter but to reclaim and redeem their 'less fortunate sister.'"[65] But Charlotte Baker, who led the drive to open the San Diego rescue home, found this focus troubling and wrote in her diary in 1912 that she believed the program "too religious."[66] The CHDN offered single, pregnant women in San Diego another option: leaving their newborn child at CHDN to escape the shame of illegitimacy. The decision by some women to turn to CHDN points to the trust they felt in the facility. Willie's experience demonstrates this trust, as the mother, or someone closely attached to Willie's biological mother, knew the baby would be cared for if he were left at the CHDN. In another example, one woman gave birth at the CHDN, stayed there with her newborn for her six-week lying-in period, and then "gave" him away to "people at San Pasqual."[67] The record does not indicate why these people were chosen, but one hopes the boy did not become merely another pair of hands to labor on a ranch.

The success of the Children's Home and Day Nursery depended

on the WHA membership, especially in its initial years of operation. Every Saturday, WHA members brought baskets of food gathered from their own pantries and collected from church congregations.[68] The Catholic League and Ladies Hebrew Aid Society usually provided cash and groceries to families so that mothers could stay in their homes rather than work for wages; however, these groups also referred mothers to the CHDN.[69] Thus, the religious groups in San Diego seemed to collaborate when it came to finding childcare for a family. The WHA membership prided itself on giving mothers a chance to work and secure "the comforts of a home" for their families, believing the "aim" of their work was "to be helpful to the last degree, but at the same time to encourage self-respecting self-support."[70] Even though no WHA member had to earn wages, they accepted the reality that some women did labor outside the home and needed the CHDN.

Whereas many day nurseries and boarding homes in other parts of the country organized their facilities along religious, ethnic, and racial lines, CHDN did not officially turn away a child because of their parent's background; however, that background did appear to influence how staff responded to the care of a child. The CHDN records from 1888 to 1920 indicate that personnel opened the doors to nonwhite children, yet staff found alternate means of care for those children within a day or two. The CHDN staff called Fr. Ubach from St. Anthony's when American Indian children appeared at the facility, and they sent Asian children north to San Francisco, where two facilities had opened in the 1870s.[71] The Asian community in San Diego never exceeded 2.6 percent of the total population throughout the nineteenth century, and most of those residents were Chinese men.[72] The fact that no Asian children were cared for at the CHDN from 1888 to 1918 (and possibly to 1929) highlights the low demographic numbers and reveals how exclusionary practices directed at Asians, and particularly the Chinese, in California influenced their childcare options.[73]

Not all identities of the families using CHDN are crystal clear; however, Mexican-descent children seem to have first entered the facility in 1897. From that time to 1905, records note twelve other

Mexican-descent families coming into contact with the facility. These statistics gradually changed as more Mexicans arrived in San Diego, but like the Asian demographics, the Mexican population in these years never exceeded 3 percent of the total population. When the widow Leticia Ruiz approached CHDN in September 1898 with her one-day-old baby, staff accepted the child, although the interaction was awkward. The child is identified on the registration record only as "Mexican infant," as opposed to the usual full name of both mother and child, perhaps because the mother spoke Spanish and CHDN workers could not understand her. Ruiz agreed to pay three dollars per week and returned ten days later to collect her baby.[74] Ruiz and the child disappear from the historical record, so we can only imagine what arrangements this mother secured after she left the CHDN, but she probably found help among her neighbors. Ruiz's address fell in the heart of Barrio Logan, where Mexican families helped out one another, especially in 1898, when the Mexican population in San Diego remained small. The Chavez family is another example of how ethnic identity influenced the treatment some families received in terms of childcare. On January 20, 1902, police brought the Chavez children to the CHDN after they found them "in a destitute condition deserted by a drunken father, the mother having previously deserted the father about a year ago."[75] Comments like these did not appear in the Register for white children, even if they had been placed in the CHDN through a court order.[76] In another case involving Mexican families, the court committed the Sanchez children to the home and ordered their parents to each pay half of the care expenses accrued for their three children.[77] In rare instances, the court ordered white fathers to pay for board at CHDN but never demanded that of white mothers, so these examples bear out the prejudice that operated against Mexican-descent parents.

Unlike many white families, African American families who arrived during the boom era stayed in San Diego. Still, the 1890 census reported only 289 African Americans in the city. Most African American families lived in Logan Heights, and according to one account, these families experienced "racial antagonism" to the

extent they had endured in Texas or Oklahoma.[78] Few of these families used the CHDN during the period 1888–1905, as only two African American children entered the facility. The first child arrived
in November 1894, but CHDN personnel recorded only the cost of
his board, eight dollars per month.[79] Eight years later, an African
American mother brought her very sick three-month-old baby
girl to the CHD, and agreed to pay ten dollars per month for her
care, because she "worked out and [was] unable to properly care
for it." Costlier than the average board, the fee perhaps included
medicine; Dr. Baker, however, would have tended to the child
free of charge, no matter his or her race, so the fee may have been
intended to discourage the mother from continued use of CHDN.
Families of color had difficulty accessing good medical attention,
and this mother likely made the safest choice for her baby. Sadly,
the child died only ten days later.[80] The only other African American children recorded using CHDN were twin girls, whose father
admitted them in 1931 after their mother died in childbirth.[81]

In caring for abandoned children, no matter their race and
ethnicity, the CHDN protocol was to find a permanent placement
with a family of that same culture. For example, when personnel
found a two-day-old American Indian girl on their doorstep in
1889, they notified representatives with the Catholic Church, who
immediately removed her from CHDN and presumably arranged
for her care with a Catholic congregant. After receiving a one-
hour-old white abandoned baby boy in 1890, personnel called
the county supervisor, who turned the baby over to the care of a
white friend. And when a five-month-old child of a Chinese father
and an American Indian mother was left at the home in 1891, staff
arranged to send the baby to the Chinese Home for Girls in San
Francisco. The nursery became two-week-old Rebecca Rae's permanent home upon her delivery to the facility on December 16,
1890. Blind, abandoned, and white, she was cared for by CHDN
at the county's expense; but she lived only a few years, dying on
June 16, 1894. Her blindness prevented a successful placement in
an adoptive home, so the county turned to CHDN as a benevolent solution to the child's care.[82] These examples show that the

race and ethnicity of a child defined the actions taken by child-care workers, and CHDN staff dealt with orphaned white children in more personal ways.

Consider actions taken by Children's Home volunteers in 1906 regarding an orphaned white girl. A handwritten note to James Ross, chief of police for Santa Barbara, details the request to remove a former Children's Home resident from adoptive parents in the Santa Barbara area: "The people seemed to be decent, nice people, but it is another case of appearances being deceptive. It is the unanimous wish of the Board of Directors of the Children's Home that the child C.F. be returned to us. . . . We want to see the child well-placed, but not abused." The board offered to pay the child's steamer fare to San Diego, as well as other expenses incurred to secure her safe return. Signing only with T. L. (probably Teresa Lessum), the author made a conscious effort to keep confidential the identity of the adopted child by using only her initials and plain paper, rather than official letterhead or personalized stationery.[83] These local advocates played vital roles in saving other people's children and could do so because of the size of the city—but that intimacy would not last long.

Most contemporary references to CHDN highlighted the needs of poor mothers; however, from September 1888 through October 1905, thirty-five fathers turned to the CHDN to solve their childcare problems. Reasons included the death, desertion, or divorce of a spouse; a wife's admission to either the County Hospital or the "insane asylum"; or her imprisonment in the state penitentiary. Within one month's time, in the winter of 1892, two men made desperate decisions about the babies born to their families. One father gave his three-month-old son to a family in National City, who then brought the baby to the CHDN. Another man "left at the door" a five-day-old girl, then "drove away immediately." Healthy and white, the baby girl easily was placed by county Supervisors with an adoptive family two days after her mysterious arrival at the CHDN.[84]

Evidence from the CHDN shows that fathers regularly used the facility for both daily care and long-term boarding of their children.[85] While a few men released their children to adoption, most retained custody by making regular payments for their children's care. Widower Peter Wissner used CHDN to cope with the loss of his wife. On July 2, 1889, he took his daughters, Sara and Francine, to CHDN so he could look for work. A single father when he admitted his daughters, he returned two months later an employed, married man and collected the girls. Wissner died one year later, and their stepmother decided living at the CHDN proved the best short-term care option for the sisters. They stayed at the facility for four months, but their needs must have proved too great for the stepmother, because the next year she returned the girls to the CHDN, where they remained through their adolescence. Sara Wissner, nine years old when CHDN took her in permanently, left it upon her sixteenth birthday, in 1898, to enter domestic service. In 1900 her sister, Francine, also left the CHDN at the age of sixteen to live with a local woman, presumably as an employee. But just one year later, a CHDN worker noted that Francine "fell from bicycle in coming to the Home and unable to return to Mrs. Taylor. Later, employed in the Home."[86] Since the age of five, Francine had called the facility her home, and the staff did not desert her when she needed safe shelter in her adult years. In return, Francine gave CHDN her labor as their domestic.

The Wissner sisters disappear from the documentary record, so we can only guess if they married and bore children, continued as domestics for the CHDN, or moved to another community. The girls were among the few children in this era boarding at CHDN through their entire childhood. Like Peter Wissner, some men found new spouses to help them manage the children; other fathers temporarily used the CHDN until female relatives could travel from out of state to help manage the household. Such was the case with four-year-old Myrtle and twenty-month-old Fred, who lived at the CHDN for six months after their mother "left for parts unknown." They were admitted on March 15, 1889, and their father came for them on October 14 so he could take them to his mother in Illinois.[87]

Fathers regularly stepped through the Children's Home doors, but wage-earning mothers remained its primary users. The CHDN records show that many of the women who used it had recently migrated into the area, indicating that they probably lacked connections with neighbors or family who might have provided them with childcare. San Diego's female workforce did not congregate in one neighborhood or workplace; thus, these women had fewer opportunities to draw on sympathetic neighbors for childcare. Those kinds of relationships did not develop until the canning industry grew in the 1910s. Instead, mothers resorted to entrusting the care of their children to strangers (albeit benevolent strangers) at the CHDN.

Contemporary investigators found that mothers with small children and most married women who worked in 1900 (5.6 percent of all married women in the United States) did so because of family crisis; thus, "some families contrived to keep secret a working mother."[88] Mothers also contracted work in their homes—known as homework—as a strategy to balance wage earning and childcare. The ability to care for infants and small children, maintain one's domestic responsibilities, and earn wages fed a woman's drive toward homework. A homeworker might wrap artificial flowers, string beads, tie brooms, finish hems, sew buttons on shirts, or crochet or knit babies' clothing, all fine handwork that could lead to an early onset of arthritis and other crippling muscle ailments. Elderly women too infirm to stand or sit in factories for ten hours also used homework as an earning strategy. Homework was typically paid by the finished piece; thus, time spent on the job did not factor into a homeworker's earnings. Isolation from other workers kept these women naive to negotiations over wages and work environments. Employers preferred homeworkers, because they did not have to manage a jobsite and could exploit the homeworkers' productivity by paying them low wages.[89]

The jobs among mothers using the Children's Home and Day Nursery reflect the national findings on domestic day service and homework.[90] They worked as waitresses, seamstresses, or laundresses, or in private domestic service. Whether in personal homes or in public settings like laundries and restaurants, domestic service performed as day work allowed for mothers to work part-time and with more flexible schedules than they could find in a factory job. Often this meant a mother worked early-morning or night hours, which could give her some control over keeping her children in the household if she had an older child to help at home. If not, mothers used homework as a childcare strategy. Lydia Smithson boarded her eight-year-old daughter, Mabel, for only two weeks at the CHDN, opting instead to "sew at home" in order to keep her family intact.[91] In the spring of 1890, the mother of seven-year-old twins Joseph and Amelia Anderson chose to "take work home and keep children," after originally taking only Joseph to the CHDN. Two months later, the mother picked up Joseph and left Amelia behind. Perhaps she lived with a family who needed the labor of a boy, or Joseph may have found work as a delivery boy for downtown merchants or selling newspapers. Whereas boys could secure such jobs, young girls found it tougher to find employment that a parent would accept as respectable. Perhaps Mrs. Anderson found homework that both her children could help her with, such as broom tying. Whatever her reasons, within weeks Mrs. Anderson thought differently of her decision to board her daughter and claimed Amelia from CHDN. She paid nothing for her children's care, and in uncharacteristic fashion, staff made only the comment "No pay" on the record.[92]

Mysteries such as why the Anderson twins lived at the CHDN abound in the organization's documents. Considering the delicate situations faced by families who sought out help, and the social sensibilities of WHA members, such gaps in the record should be expected. Matrons did not turn away mothers and children who sought immediate care, and incidences of illegitimate pregnancy, interracial unions, abandonment, and divorce were more common than people wished to admit. Pregnant women knew to knock on the CHDN door when labor pains set in, and evidence of both married and single women delivering at the home indicates that medical care, adoption options, and confidentiality could be found at the CHDN.

In San Diego the deepening presence of immoral behavior and illiteracy among children and society in general continued to trouble reformers. By 1898, a decade after the opening of the CHDN, the state of California had completed its residential institutions for children deemed delinquent and in need of rehabilitation. The combination of licensing requirements and the opening of the state facility likely prompted CHDN organizers to change the ages of children who could be admitted. They were no longer willing to care for girls older than ten years and boys older than six years.[93] The WHA reported in 1899, "Their [the children's] moral training has been as much in our thoughts as their physical welfare. For the children of today will be the law-makers of the next generation; the children of today will also be the law-breakers of the next generation. The influences of youth mold the trend of character."[94]

The philanthropy of WHA members and their dedication to the CHDN allowed a safer life for the children of some families, yet the organization faced a number of challenges in addition to funding operations.[95] A chamber of commerce report in 1901 admitted finding "a general feeling of depression in San Diego, [where] glum faces meet one at every corner."[96] High unemployment, loss of competitive contracts to Los Angeles, regular flooding, an increase in immigrant populations, few social services, and the continual inadequacy of the city's infrastructure deepened the city's problems. Civic negativity, however, did not dissuade the WHA from issuing a citywide financial appeal to support CHDN, proclaiming, "Beyond all philanthropies those calculated to assist children appeal most strongly to humanity." Their optimism won out with the success of their house-to-house canvass, which raised over $1,100 in two weeks.[97]

By the turn of the century, facilities like CHDN needed to pass inspections by state investigators who evaluated the physical condition of buildings and the professional aptitude of providers. In California the push toward professional protocols started in the 1890s and became stronger over the next two decades, and both local and national organizations were influenced by the change. The mandate to license day nurseries shifted how the CHDN delivered care, and its personnel and volunteers embraced professional standards when state law demanded the change. Even though the implementation of standardized protocols took several decades to complete, social welfare professionals persisted in learning how to best accommodate the growing needs of the city. Benevolent reformers removed themselves from the daily operations and instead focused on fund-raising and public relations efforts.

Medical professionals and educators banded together to improve the social condition of the city. Directing their attention to adolescents and the fears of juvenile delinquency, a second generation of reformers implemented programmatic and institutional changes that reached beyond benevolent associations and into the legal system. Some parents turned to them for insight in managing the troubled behavior of their youngster, while others became the targets of reformers who claimed their parenting to be inadequate and in need of professional guidance. Reformers worked with the city's legal officials to assess a youngster's potential for rehabilitation. They also introduced vocational education into the school system as one way to curtail juvenile delinquency. San Diego was not the first or only city in California to embrace the ideas of child guidance professionals, but its embrace of juvenile justice methods helped reformers better manage the social unpredictability that arrived in the early twentieth century.

CHAPTER THREE

Court-Appointed Care

Interventions for Troubled Families

> In consequence of his bad behavior and incorrigible
> and vicious conduct.
>
> —Order of commitment for Frank Vasques, February 8, 1898

On September 6, 1902, Ellen Jones, mother of fourteen-year-old Russell, approached the local court in San Diego for help with controlling her "incorrigible and vicious" son. She reported that Russell earned wages from his gardening job but not enough to contribute any meaningful financial support to the family. He also used tobacco, was profane, and had already spent time in jail. Separated from a husband she described as "intemperate," and exhausted from raising her several other children, this mother pled with the court to take her son off her hands, as his behavior loomed "beyond [her] power and control." The judge agreed that Ellen could not handle Russell and stated he was "in danger of being brought up to lead a wholly idle, vagrant and immoral life." He sentenced the boy to seven years at the State Reform School for Juvenile Offenders located in Whittier, some one hundred miles north of San Diego.[1] By removing Russell from his home, the court intended to prevent further disruption in the Jones family and guide the boy toward a productive adulthood. Yet the decision brought Russell years of institutional care, distanced him physically from his family, and certainly influenced his familial relationships.

In turning to forces outside her family network, Ellen Jones risked the "moral condemnation" that accompanied parents and guardians who admitted they could not handle the youth in their home.[2] In San Diego, children removed from their households came from families who had few local contacts, struggled to find and keep steady employment, and had experienced some sort of disruption to the family. The Russell Jones case is one of only twelve orders of commitment executed by the court from 1897 to 1904 in San Diego County. While this small number cannot empirically show commitment patterns for the city, the cases demonstrate how legal authorities worked with adults to find solutions for managing their troublesome children. From building reformatories to establishing vocational education and social service oversight, San Diegans participated in juvenile justice initiatives as a way to curb delinquent behavior deemed an ever-growing problem in their city. The multifaceted agenda was not unique in the nation or even in California during the Progressive Era, yet it demonstrates how civic leaders and reformers embraced the strategies adopted by larger and more diverse cities. In San Diego's case, these decisions laid an important foundation for handling juvenile delinquency when the city faced tremendous population growth starting in the 1910s.

Through this agenda, authorities learned of three shortcomings embedded in the existing system. First, children who exhibited harmful behaviors needed to be kept separate from those children with no record of abuse, yet the city's limited resources prevented those separations from happening. Officials struggled with the realities of overcrowded spaces, and building a shelter for children in need of temporary care did not solve the problem; in fact, the new center was full the day it opened in 1903. Officials turned to the CHDN to help them shelter delinquent children; but that solution exposed children living at the CHDN to youth with troubled pasts, an irony that caused problems for families throughout the twentieth century. Second, during the early 1900s the population grew by the thousands, and segregation intensified as middle-class whites moved away from the bay and downtown area into neighborhoods touting new houses and schools.

These older neighborhoods and the families living in them were overlooked by civic officials, which led to a host of problems, from neighborhood blight to truant youth. Third, leaders realized that no one agency could be expected to serve the city's needs and took interest in how the reform community could solve social problems. Business leaders and politicians focused their attentions on attracting tourist and military revenue and left the work of developing a social welfare agenda to reformers.

These issues emerged in San Diego alongside a national juvenile justice agenda. Into and throughout the nineteenth century, children in the United States as young as ten years had served sentences for robbery, assault, or prostitution among adult offenders in penitentiaries designed for hardened criminals. Starting in the 1870s, society adjusted its attitudes about children and their capacity to learn, work, and establish relationships, and part of that adjustment focused on removing children under the age of sixteen from jails and prisons. Rather than subjecting children to sentences of hard labor within a penitentiary, reformers argued that society would benefit from children under the age of sixteen serving their time in separate reformatories. There they would learn vocational skills as a path toward becoming productive citizens. Additionally, criminal justice professionals like Denver judge Ben Lindsey recognized the traumas associated with adjudicating and incarcerating children with adult offenders. In the 1890s Judge Lindsey initiated a full-scale overhaul of the penal system that recognized the differences between children and adults, and insisted upon facilities with separate courtrooms, jails, and prisons for convicted youth. His work resulted in the establishment of juvenile courts across the country, which protected minors by sheltering them from the public eye as proceedings became sealed from the media and non-family-members.[3]

These actions were part of the larger agenda of social reformers who advocated for protecting children against physical and sexual abuses, especially incidences associated with child labor. Investigations included verifying exploitation in circuses and theater troupes, in textile factories and coal mines, and that boys as young as five years were selling newspapers on street corners. Members from a number of women's groups—such as the Women's Christian Temperance Union, the General Federation of Women's Clubs, the National Association of Colored Women, and the National Council of Jewish Women—involved themselves in the fight to eliminate child labor, change age of consent laws, and initiate juvenile justice proceedings.

Their efforts gained support from psychologist G. Stanley Hall, who introduced in 1904 a new life stage for children ages twelve to eighteen years. When Hall formally assigned "adolescence" as a critical period in the human life cycle, his findings helped change how law enforcement, educational professionals, social workers, and parents dealt with this age group. Hall recognized that adolescents experienced tremendous changes in their physical growth and social development, and because of adolescents' undeveloped physical and mental capabilities, he cautioned experts and parents alike on placing them in situations that demanded them to act as adults. His findings encouraged the separation of youth offenders from adult criminals, removal of adolescents from the adult workforce, and providing youth with more educational opportunities. The advocacy of Judge Lindsey and psychological findings of G. Stanley Hall led to the formation of juvenile justice practices across the country, including a separate penal system. These practices accomplished several items in the juvenile justice reform agenda: they protected juveniles from adult offenders; recognized that adolescents did not act with a fully developed awareness or consciousness of their actions; and helped parents and guardians who struggled with raising unruly children. The agenda also defined troubled youth as "incorrigible" and "vicious," which became qualities thought to be embedded in poor or working-class families.[4]

"Incorrigible" became a useful adjective among authorities and parents to characterize children who experimented with sexuality, rejected family and school responsibilities, and seemed bent on damaging their own or others' reputations. These behaviors always fell into gender-specific categories: for girls, incorrigible actions included sexual experimentation and promiscuity or out-of-wedlock pregnancy (acts of a private nature), whereas for boys, incorrigibility meant truancy, vagrancy, and crimes against people and property such as robbery or assault (often but not always a crime acted in public). Immigrant parents often complained that their children rejected their family culture by embracing American or "white" culture, with its more relaxed expectations of chaperoned dating and fashion styles. They worried about young people spending time together in leisure zones like the beach or amusement parks instead of helping around the home, and these parents welcomed the supervision advanced by reformers. However, in the spirit of protecting adolescents, specific groups became targets under these agendas.[5]

Unmarried mothers, families with absent or intemperate spouses, adolescents loitering in leisure zones, and children caring for infants all attracted reformers' attentions and garnered their oversight of the family. Authorities perceived parents who allowed their children to work or roam the penny arcades and theaters as unaware of or nonchalant about the dangers associated with these adult settings, and they used this supposed ignorance to justify their increased scrutiny and regulation of these families. One result, removing children from the household to a reform school, often led to uncomfortable consequences for these families. They lost several things when their adolescent child entered a reformatory: earnings of an adolescent worker, assistance with childcare, language translation, and respect from their adolescent children. Complicating these outcomes was the original intent of juvenile reform agendas. Because they were often tied to Americanization campaigns, and implemented in public schools or community centers, juvenile reforms danced around cultural stereotypes of people living in poverty, such as defining mothers who labored as absent, thus unloving, parents.[6] To deal with these complex relations, states across the country turned to reforming the court system.

Illinois implemented the first juvenile court of law in 1899 and is often recognized as the leader in the juvenile justice movement because of that action. California began dealing with juveniles in the mid-nineteenth century, but in different ways. From 1850 to

1879, children found guilty of a crime were sent to the state penitentiary, San Quentin. Most of those children were American Indians, *Californios*, and Mexicans, and, starting in the 1860s, Chinese youth would also be sent to San Quentin. Children served their time in forced labor alongside adults in the laundries, brick foundries, and fields.[7] The addition in 1858 of the San Francisco Industrial School (SFIS) and Magdalene Asylum in San Francisco, and Marysville Industrial School in 1859 shifted their incarceration at an adult prison toward rehabilitation at a reformatory. Children and youth from across the state who led an "idle and immoral life" were committed to SFIS as a reform strategy. Funded through a collaborative effort between the state and private citizens, SFIS originally focused on vocational education but then shifted its focus toward a purely correctional agenda in the 1880s. The Catholic Church operated Magdalene Asylum, and organizers likely hoped to address the growing prostitution trade in the city by housing girls who were identified as sexually experienced in the asylum. State government operated Marysville Industrial School. Set in a rural area, Marysville also used vocational education, but it lasted only six years, closing in 1868 because of expenses. The majority of youths admitted to these institutions were white, with between 10 and 20 percent of the forty to fifty youngsters being of Mexican origin.[8]

State officials acknowledged the tremendous need for facilities dedicated to this age group by approving, in 1889, funding to build and operate two juvenile reformatories: Preston School of Industry (Preston), located in Ione, a rural community just south of Sacramento; and the State Reform School for Juvenile Offenders (Whittier) some thirty miles southeast of Los Angeles. Both opened in 1891 and served different populations of offenders. The state Board of Prison Directors managed the six-hundred-acre Preston for males between the ages of sixteen and twenty-one years who had been convicted of a capital offense.[9] Its physical structure could house 550 juveniles, but an average of 391 youth served their sentences at the facility. Sixty-eight "regular employees" kept Preston detainees in line through harsh discipline, military-style drilling, and the threat of incarceration at an adult prison.[10]

Whereas the prison board operated Preston, an outside board of trustees managed Whittier.[11] Intended to rehabilitate both male and female nonviolent delinquents, staff still used corporal discipline and a military regimen to maintain control, which drove some of the detainees to attempt escapes from the facility. If caught, they incurred harsh punishments, including having their ankles shackled in a ten-pound weight known as an "Oregon Boot" and serving extended time in solitary confinement with limited food and water.[12] The facility could accommodate four hundred juveniles, but the usual population was about three hundred detainees. Female delinquents were housed in segregated cottages clustered about one mile from the administrative buildings and boys' dorms, but from the start of Whittier's opening, authorities recognized they needed to better separate girls from boys. Girls suffered terribly at Whittier. As early as 1896, Whittier School trustee Adina Mitchell uncovered physical and emotional abuse, describing staff actions as "outrageous," with girls being "brutally punished and neglected," from shackling, whipping straps, confinement to isolation cells, and their hair being shaved off. Mitchell called for separating girls and boys in different campuses as a way to provide more equitable treatment and eliminate physical abuses. However, lawmakers did not authorize a separate facility for females until 1913.[13]

The State broke ground one year later in Ventura, making the California School for Girls its third juvenile institution. It opened in 1916, and seventy-five girls were moved from Whittier to the new facility. Ventura could accommodate one hundred girls, but the average population was fifty-five girls and twenty-three regular employees.[14] Reports of abuse followed the girls from Whittier to Ventura, and investigative reporting in 1914 and 1919 by the *Los Angeles Times* confirmed such abuse. Clothing, residences, access to medical care, and training opportunities for girls proved deficient compared to those provided to boys, and the move to Ventura seemed to escalate the ill treatment. The paper documented allegations of girls being subjected to ice bath punishments and drug injections, but unfortunately, no clear reforms came of the stories.[15]

A fourth juvenile institution opened in 1902. The Sherman Institute, located in Riverside, was a federally operated off-reservation boarding school for American Indian children. Federal authorities did not design or intend for it to reform youths; rather, it functioned as a manual training school for children ages six to fourteen years, from reservations in California, Nevada, Oregon, and Washington. Most of the children had been orphaned or half orphaned and were thus vulnerable to the persuasions of federal agents who insisted Sherman Institute could best provide for them. Despite its purpose as a school, Sherman Institute also housed children deemed by federal agents as uncontrollable and in need of intense supervision, and administrators relied on local authorities to monitor which children should be sent to Sherman.[16] Records from the early years of Preston and Whittier do not indicate American Indian youth among their census, and a 1932 study of Indian groups in San Diego noted, "Reports of delinquency among juveniles are rare," and that "no Indian boys" lived at either Preston or Whittier.[17]

Sherman adopted vocational education as a key strategy to acculturate Indian children into Euro-American society. In addition to farming on the facility's forty acres, boys could choose carpentry, painting, blacksmithing, tailoring, printing, steam heating and fitting, electrical connections, or plumbing. Girls' training focused on dressmaking, cooking, and general housekeeping for service in private homes. Typically, forty to sixty children out of three hundred remained at Sherman year-round. Officials believed a Sherman education presented youngsters with amenities usually reserved for white, middle-class children, and they emphasized the facility's beauty as a positive force in the educational process.[18]

Sherman monitored students with an eye to erasing Native culture: students could speak only English at the school, and boys and girls could not speak to each other.[19] Children from San Diego made the trip north to Sherman, but not always voluntarily. The same 1932 study that noted the rarity of juveniles living at Preston or Whittier found that many adults living on the reservations requested that their children have better access to on-reservation day schools or the local public school, because they did not want their children leaving them for a boarding school experience, even if that school offered vocational education. Many of these parents had attended Sherman for at least one year in their childhood, and the experience stuck with them, usually in a negative way.[20] Not intended as a reformatory, Sherman evolved into a vocational high school, a process that started in the 1930s by eliminating one grade level from the elementary school each year. Consequently, some students who attended in the 1930s returned to the reservation with only a sixth-grade education.

The three state reform schools gained authority as the century progressed. Preston and Whittier had been built to remove children from adult prisons, yet for several years after these opened, youth offenders still faced trials in adult courtrooms and holding cells. In an unprecedented act of reform, legislators passed a statute in 1903 empowering all superior, justice, and police courts in California to act as sites where authorities heard juvenile cases. This statute shows the investment of California in juvenile justice reform, since this became the first statute to include local authorities from smaller communities in this work. California differed from states like Illinois, which allowed only communities with a population over five hundred thousand to hold a juvenile court. In practice, that translated to Chicago being the only city in Illinois authorized to hear juvenile cases, which gave it control over the development and maintenance of the Illinois system. California's statute enabled juvenile courts and the management of juvenile probation to exist across the state, meaning that authorization to provide a juvenile court existed from the largest city in 1900 (San Francisco with 342,782 persons) to the smallest city (Santa Rosa with 6,673 persons).[21]

Few people contested the need for separate juvenile and adult courts, but it took California a few years to establish successful practices, especially since the costs to implement and maintain these systems far exceeded the capacities of state and local budgets. To alleviate these types of budget constraints, officials expected the relatives of committed children to reimburse their county for expenses related to their transport to and boarding at Preston,

Whittier, or, later, to Ventura. But that expectation was completely unrealistic, and counties were forced to assume these operational costs. This led to the judicial practice of sentencing minors to prison rather than a reformatory as a way to reduce county budgets. This ironic twist to the spirit of reformatory action caused the California legislature to pass an additional act in 1904 stipulating that juveniles could no longer be imprisoned, and it assigned new age parameters for commitment and incarceration to adult prisons: boys seven to sixteen years, and girls seven to eighteen years *could not* be sent to adult prisons. This act demonstrates the wider influence of the age of consent campaigns, as the ages coincided with older consent ages. Once committed to a juvenile facility, boys could be held until age eighteen, and girls until they turned twenty-one. The age differences clearly show the gendered bias attached to commitment practices. While boys were cited for violent crimes, they were freed earlier in a nod to their being ready for employment, but also because they could without question be incarcerated to adult prison if they again committed a crime. The ruling "protected" girls from sexually promiscuous activity until an age at which they could suitably marry; if they committed a crime upon their release, they would find themselves incarcerated in adult prison, but their longer juvenile sentences seemed to be a preventive from such recidivism.

Whittier superintendent Fred Nelles initiated some changes, such as discontinuing harsh discipline, but he also implemented IQ testing that targeted certain boys for skills training. This vocational education strategy helped some detainees, but the tests inevitably categorized African American and Mexican-descent boys as feeble-minded and incapable of learning certain skilled jobs. The method ignored language and cultural differences among non-white boys and essentially eliminated them from any meaningful vocational education during their time at Whittier.[22]

San Diegans accommodated the juvenile justice movement by initiating the order of commitment process in 1897 and then by organizing the Boys and Girls Aid Society (BGAS) in 1903. That organization immediately built a shelter for children awaiting foster-care placement or transfer to state reformatories. Known by most San Diegans as the Detention Home, the facility was never intended for long-term housing, and unlike the state institutions, it was overcrowded from its start. Because of problems with transport, many children spent months, not days, in the Detention Home, which exacerbated overcrowding and caused children to miss school and other rehabilitative programs.[23] This was not unusual for local facilities, and it led California legislators to pass the Juvenile Court Law of 1909, which gave judges discretionary oversight as to where a neglected or delinquent child could be placed and for how long.[24] The intent of the law was to alleviate overcrowded conditions and to address issues surrounding child abuse and neglect—essentially, to protect children with no criminal history from children who did have such a history. It also encouraged judges to assign children to local facilities rather than send them out of the county. For San Diego, this meant using the Detention Home and the CHDN, named the Children's Home (CH) by the twentieth century.

The CH was included as a site for obvious reasons: it had a good reputation for child caring and had the space to house additional children. Wards of the court could bring financial stability to an operational budget, since the county paid for their care, and personnel managing the CH budget understood this as a path toward financial stability. Those factors led to them increasingly accepting court-appointed children into the facility. Additionally, caring for court-appointed wards demonstrated the successful execution of the CH mission to provide care for some of the city's most vulnerable children. But problems emerged with the new system. Children with no record of delinquent or criminal behavior often shared a room with a youngster jaded by several years of petty street crime.[25] For some children, the trauma attached to losing parents through sickness or accident became multiplied by the fear of close quarters with someone who might have been crude, cruel, and even violent. During the 1920s, children whose parents needed day care stopped using CH for that purpose, and by the 1930s it had developed into a residential space for troubled children and youth.

Court authorities intended for commitments to reformatories to both rehabilitate unruly youth and release their families from the burden of raising the difficult child, and some parents initiated commitment proceedings as a way to protect other children in the household. The orders of commitment in San Diego between 1897 and 1904 illustrate this point. California established its juvenile court in 1903; however, between 1897 and 1904—the time prior to mandated juvenile court hearings and the opening of the Detention Home in San Diego—twelve families approached the county court to request an order of commitment to Preston or Whittier. Albeit limited, the data suggest that parents and guardians approached the court for help when children in their care exhibited "incorrigible" behavior.

In 1900 carpenter J. H. Harper approached the court because of his "incorrigible and vicious" fourteen-year-old son, Howard, who was "beyond [his] control and power." The commitment hearing included an unusual appearance by a police officer, George H. Cooley, perhaps because of Howard's criminal history. Having already spent five days in jail for stealing shoes and wire cutters, Howard confessed to profane behavior but balked at the charge of intemperance, stating to his interviewer, "I hardly ever drink anything." Stealing shoes and wire cutters is an odd combination, but these items point to a level of poverty in the Harper household or at least to rebellion on Howard's part. For a father to admit he could not control his son must have proved embarrassing for Harper but worth the outcome, as the court ruled that Howard's behavior justified committing him to Whittier.[26]

While it may not be immediately apparent when considered alongside traditional forms of childcare, public reformatories served a childcare function, and the act of committing one's troubled child to such an institution was a childcare decision. By asking the courts to remove these "incorrigible and vicious" children from their home, parents and guardians accepted that they would not see the child for several years, yet their request may have been the only way to bring stability to their households. Middle-class reformers and working-class parents did not always agree on family culture, but when faced with how to control children deemed incorrigible, vicious, and out of control, they came to similar conclusions. Using detention homes and reformatories offered one of those common grounds, especially as a strategy in controlling violent sons, and daughters believed to be too sexually free. Immigrant adolescents seemed particularly vulnerable to being committed to an institution, as their behavior went against their cultural traditions. The changing behavior among girls especially troubled society.

Parents and guardians witnessed their daughters resisting cultural traditions that expected the girls to live at home until marriage, turn over their wages to their parents, care for younger siblings, perform household chores in addition to wage earning, and remain sexually chaste. Many parents began blaming their daughters' rebellious, ill-mannered, or promiscuous behavior on city life, Americanization, and the growth of leisure activities. Young women in the workforce willingly participated in exchanges their parents deemed inappropriate, such as chats about sex on their lunch breaks, flirtations with passersby and coworkers, and laughter over raunchy jokes. Workers also learned the tough lessons attached to unprovoked sexual advances, as the workplace could expose them to harassment by male coworkers or supervisors, and they had little recourse against or ability to fend off these sexual advances.[27] Immigrant young people working in the Progressive Era city dramatically changed urban demographics and altered family life. Services in urban areas, such as laundries and restaurants, allowed for young men to postpone marriage or to not marry at all, which affected the marital opportunities for young women in their social station. Working-class parents worried their daughters ignored the "external methods of control that operated best in relatively small, close-knit communities" now that they had entered the urban waged labor force.[28] Instead of relying on the forms of monitoring behavior that had worked into and throughout the nineteenth century—patriarchal authority, religious doctrine, neighborhood gossip, community shaming—some parents now turned to the judicial system for help in controlling their children.

A common feature among the committed adolescents in the

San Diego orders was their lack of a meaningful relationship with a parent or guardian. Several of the youths could not recite the name of a parent, because they either never knew the individual or had never lived with the person, and they disrespected the parent they did know. Poverty also ruled their lives. Several families had moved to the area during the economic turmoil of the 1890s, and only two of the youths were born in San Diego.[29] But those moves not only did not solve the families' problems but perhaps heightened them, as they landed in a city with no job, no housing, and probably no familial contacts. Clearly, children had no control over these decisions, and that lack of control could act as an accelerant to troublesome behaviors.

The commitment of Virginia Ybarra demonstrates this dynamic. Virginia's aunt, Mexican national Charlotte Ybarra, initiated San Diego County's first order of commitment on September 8, 1897, when she asked the court to remove her fifteen-year-old niece from her home because she was "incorrigible and beyond [Charlotte's] control." Charlotte's decision to turn to the court must have been a difficult one, since she had pledged to her dying sister fifteen years earlier that she would care for one-month-old Virginia like a mother. These promises transpired in Mexico, where the Ybarras continued to live for some time, and the records do not indicate when they crossed into San Diego. Charlotte saw to it that Virginia had a bit of education, which amounted to only three months of formal study. She requested Virginia's commitment the same year that San Diego public schools began integrating vocational education into the high school curriculum, but Virginia likely did not benefit from this effort. Literacy among poor rural Mexican girls grew in the late nineteenth century yet remained unusual, and most Mexican youngsters living in California had few opportunities to move beyond a second- or third-grade level of education.[30] Consequently, many of these young people found themselves in the workforce in poorly paid jobs. If a girl had family members who would vouch for her respectability, she could marry, but that choice might only exacerbate her poverty through early motherhood and economic dependency on her husband.

In Virginia Ybarra's case, the court seems to have feared that the girl had inherited an assumed promiscuity from her mother, and it interpreted her sexual awakening as criminal. It is not surprising that authorities saw a Mexican-born adolescent as sexualized and in need of taming, as Mexican women were included in the long list of nonwhite women stereotyped by the white majority as hypersexual, thus deviant. Virginia's incorrigible behavior prompted Judge E. S. Torrance to side with the aunt and commit the girl to the State Reform School in Whittier. His decision came two days after Charlotte Ybarra approached the court and left no room for appeal. Upon delivering his decision, Torrance directed the court chaperone to take the girl immediately into custody to serve her three-year sentence.[31]

When the Ybarras came before the county court in 1897, they faced a justice system that recognized differences in adult and child behaviors but had just started separating the two groups of offenders. The fact that the court sent Virginia Ybarra to Whittier rather than to the Girls Rescue Home hints that Virginia was not pregnant but was indeed rebellious, and her ethnicity as a Mexican-born girl would have worked against her admittance. The Girls Rescue Home insisted that its boarders embrace Protestant Christianity and admit their sins of foul living, including engaging in premarital relations and disobeying parental authority. The Home also admitted adult women, and the court may have not wanted Virginia to taint the redemptive spirits of these women. Moreover, Virginia may have been baptized as a Catholic. But Virginia's Mexican roots most likely secured her fate to the Whittier sentence.

Within months of the Ybarra case, the court dealt with its second order of commitment. Again, the circumstances involved an "incorrigible" Mexican-born adolescent whose mother had died. But unlike Virginia, sixteen-year-old Frank Vasquez demonstrated a steady pattern of delinquent and profane behavior. He chewed tobacco, smoked, and had been jailed twice: twenty-five days for stealing and then forty-five days for vagrancy. The court learned that Frank had attended his neighborhood school, Sherman Heights

Elementary, for four years, where he learned to read and write; and he had worked in watch and soap factories, where he earned wages that probably helped in the support of his three sisters.[32] In spite of his job history, Frank was brought before the court "in consequence of his bad behavior and incorrigible and vicious conduct," and Judge J. W. Hughes sentenced him to Whittier.[33]

Racially and ethnically biased stereotypes influenced many decisions by criminal justice officials, and the cases of Virginia Ybarra and Frank Vasqúez show how Mexican youth suffered from these biases.[34] Authorities believed that criminality was inherited and that poverty, race, and ethnicity contributed to those inherited characteristics. But they also believed they could control criminality by committing at-risk youth to reform institutions for a several-year term. In the case of eleven-year-old Royal Stark—a white boy who had been removed from the street in 1899—commitment to Whittier for two years perhaps saved him from a host of ills: living on the streets, entering prostitution, or a life of hardened crime. Royal told his interviewer that his father, Fred Stark, was a railroad switchman, "intemperate," and maybe lived in National City; he thought his mother, Lizzie Underhill, lived in Los Angeles. Royal's homeless state would have sent him to the Children's Home, but his age and uncertainty about his parents' whereabouts guided the court's decision to send Royal to the state institution. Because his parents were separated, the court judged that his parents were incapable of properly supporting and caring for their son, so it stepped into Royal's life to save him from future harm. What the file does not reveal is Royal's reaction to the decision. Perhaps he had run away from abuse at his home and found life on the streets tolerable. But he was silent about that environment. Ultimately, Royal had to pay for his homeless state by entering Whittier. The records do not indicate that Royal used prostitution to survive, but if he had, the authorities likely kept it out of the official documentation because he was male. They were not this discreet with girls.[35]

Concerned parties believed that young girls were lured into prostitution, and by the twentieth century, the fear of white slavery pertained only to white girls and young women. White slavery narratives conditioned readers to fear men, especially nonwhite men, who interacted too intimately with white women, and these tales heightened anxieties about the type of immigrants moving into the United States. But a new issue emerged with increased immigration and migration of nonwhite youth: the "girl problem."[36] These girls troubled society because of their independence, especially in terms of their sexuality. Whereas the "woman adrift" issue had sparked the age of consent campaigns, the girl problem elicited greater authoritative oversight of working-class families with adolescent girls.

Through the efforts of female advocates and assisted by the passage of the Mann Act, ages of consent would be raised throughout the country to fourteen, sixteen, or eighteen years of age by the 1920s.[37] But prior to these legal changes, societal norms placed much of the responsibility for preserving one's virtue on girls, even when they had endured abuse by adults. Thus, society expected girls like Virginia Ybarra to wholeheartedly protect themselves from ill repute. If a girl exhibited tendencies toward immoral acts, a parent, guardian, or legal authority could turn to the juvenile court system as a way to control her sexuality. Four of the commitment cases dealt with girls—two thirteen-year-olds and two fifteen-year-olds—and while only thirteen-year-old Bessie Henry had a previous run-in with the law (she served ten days in jail for petit larceny), the court defined all four girls as "incorrigible," "vicious," and "uncontrollable." Bessie told the court she had been employed in nursing and chamber work, but none of the other girls had earned wages.[38]

The youth in the twelve commitment cases in San Diego embodied a number of disquieting characteristics: poverty, absence of a strong parental figure, youthful wage earning, connections to vice, familiarity with sexual activity, and limited ties to the community. Most of the adolescents came from households overburdened with domestic disorder. Bessie Henry's father lived and worked in Texas, which left her mother alone to care for Bessie and her six siblings, likely the reason Bessie earned wages at such a young age. Seventeen-year-old Clarence Eaton had been born in Vicksburg, Mississippi, but reported to the court during his commitment hearing that he did not know the name of his father or mother and did not know if he had any brothers or sisters. Charged with the crime of embezzlement, Clarence ended up in Preston "for the term of his minority," which would be four years later. The court assumed that the absence of a strong family unit and proper parental supervision resulted in the behavioral problems. Surprisingly, all of the youths were literate in English, except for Virginia Ybarra (although she could tackle basic reading and writing in Spanish), despite their being of a range of cultures that included African American, Mexican American, and Mexican national, native-born white, and white immigrants. All of the boys could read and write to some extent, and several had either worked or apprenticed into a trade.[39]

California had passed its compulsory education law in 1874 to keep children out of the workplace and prevent loitering in adult spaces, and, starting in the 1880s, communities adopted vocational education as a deterrent for juvenile delinquency.[40] Factory inspectors discovered that wage-earning children preferred the workplace to school, and in an attempt to return children to school, educators suggested adding vocational training to school curricula. Completely gendered in its implementation, vocational education courses taught boys to operate and repair machinery, and girls to clean, sew, and cook. Programs also linked students with potential employers.[41]

In 1883 Oakland became the first school district to integrate cooking and sewing classes, mechanical drawing, and woodworking into the grammar school curriculum. San Diego's public school system followed Oakland's direction in 1891 by adding woodworking for boys and sewing for girls to curricula in grades six through eight, and within a couple of years these courses were also offered at the high school. By 1897 (the same year as the first order of commitment), San Diego's public schools formalized their vocational education curriculum by extending the school day to accommodate courses in woodworking, cardboard work, sewing, and indus-

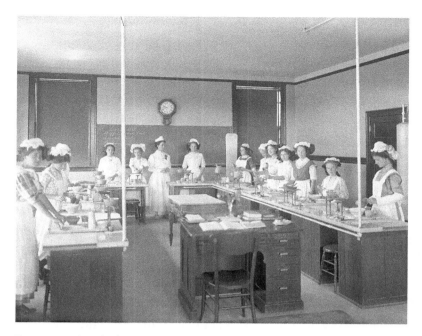

FIG. 7. Vocational education was introduced into the curriculum in San Diego schools in 1897. This domestic science class for girls in City Heights, c. 1913, demonstrates the gendered nature of courses. © San Diego History Center.

trial drawing.[42] Reformers agreed that adding vocational education to the curriculum provided children, their families, and the community at large with a number of benefits that centered on preventing children from the moral dangers of an idle life. It allowed middle-class values of temperance and restraint to seep into children's minds and promoted the importance of learning a skilled trade. The end result, educators believed, would be a reduction in crime and a decrease in the number of families who were dependent on both public and private relief.

The development of San Diego's Free Industrial School (FIS), established in 1894, fits with these reformist directions and represents one of the first vocational alternatives in the country. Woman's Home Association members, especially Mrs. J. F. Carey, championed the building of the school as a solution for unemployment in the city.[43] With the FIS coming on the heels of the

1893 depression, the motivation driving FIS volunteers is easy to understand; its initial success as a magnet site for poor youngsters makes sense coupled with the movements by state educators toward manual training. FIS was located in a neighborhood dominated by newly immigrated families, primarily Italian, Portuguese, and Mexican. Designed to decrease the school dropout rate of non-English speakers, the program taught boys to use tools for a variety of trades, and girls learned domestic skills, especially cooking and sewing.

Most youngsters who attended FIS came from families whose lives were dictated by the fishing industry, where men worked the water for weeks at a time, leaving mothers alone to care for the household. Many of those mothers also worked in the fish and sardine processing plants, adding another burden to their day, as shifts lasted ten to twelve hours and kept them on their feet and away from their households. Rose Zolezzi noted that tuna fishing took her husband away from their family for long periods of time (up to a month). While her experience refers to a later era (1930s and 1940s), the basic parameters of the fishing industry's effect on a family did not change from an earlier generation. Zolezzi married in 1932 and had three children under the age of twelve by 1941. She had to care for and discipline the children because her husband saw so little of them, and consequently she did not want them to remember him in a negative light.[44] FIS supporters worried that the absence of paternal authority in the house led to a weak family order, and FIS structured recreational activities not so much as a function of the school but as to counter the perceived chaos in the lives of fishing families.[45] While FIS operated for three years prior to the first order of commitment, there is no indication that the committed youngsters attended the school. It offered some respite to these families, but its overall impact was limited to that specific neighborhood and did not consistently draw youth to its program. Thus, by the 1910s the FIS organizers were looking for alternate uses of the building. They would find one with the opening of Neighborhood House, San Diego's first settlement house program (whose history is assessed in chapter 5).

When California passed the juvenile law of 1903, vocational education in the state served as a preventive measure to keep young people in school and remove them from the workplace. It fit with the national movement of eliminating child labor and allowed for many college-educated, female activists to use their professional expertise in a reformist environment.[46] On a national level, concern over children laboring in mills led to the organization of the National Child Labor Committee (NCLC) in 1904. High accident rates, missed school, poor health, and vulnerability to abuses by adults heightened the attentions of NCLC members, five thousand strong by 1909.[47] In addition to millwork, the NCLC took a keen interest in one of the most popular but controversial jobs for boys, selling and delivering newspapers.[48] In noting that newsboys could be as young as five, the NCLC reported that "corner newsboys worked outside for long hours in unsupervised environments" and documented "at length what they believed to be the physical, emotional and educational toll of such work."[49]

This energy at the national level influenced state and local authorities to launch their own investigations. California's State Bureau of Labor report of 1911–1912 found 171 minors under the age of eighteen working in San Diego's manufacturing, wholesale, and retail establishments. Minor girls typically worked in the laundries and the fish and vegetable canneries. Boys found work at the pier and in construction, in soap and leather factories, and as delivery boys. School authorities could issue work permits to minors between the ages of twelve and fifteen, but the NCLC had set a standard whereby no child under the age of fourteen could work in "ordinary gainful occupations."[50] The NCLC recommended that boys under sixteen not be permitted to work at street trades between 8:00 p.m. and 6:00 a.m., but California regulators set work parameters between 10:00 p.m. and 5:00 a.m. Those times probably had more to do with the rhythms of the agricultural, fishing, and growing cannery industry and less to do with any conscious effort to exploit child labor.

To ensure these standards were being followed, in 1914 San Diego's key female reform body, the College Woman's Club, conducted a systematic study of local conditions. Their study, *Pathfinder*

FIG. 8. Newsboys for the *San Diego Sun*, 1925. © San Diego History Center.

Social Survey of San Diego: Report of Limited Investigations of Social Conditions in San Diego, California, reported forty-three work permits issued to children, thirty-two of which were held by children who had not completed the eighth grade. But that hardly illustrates a trend toward wholesale use of child labor. More important were those children not reported in any survey, particularly farm and homeworkers, and the undercounted newsboy population. An estimated four hundred newsboys delivered newspapers in San Diego,

FIG. 9. Girls and women packing cherries at Rancho Cereza Loma in Mesa Grande, San Diego County, c. 1905–7. © San Diego History Center.

and twenty-five messenger boys worked in San Diego's downtown. These messenger figures made reformers nervous, because the investigators had it on "good authority that 'they are acquainted with almost every apartment that is questionable in San Diego.'"[51]

Pathfinder investigators also found that few accommodations existed in schools for laboring children to complete their educations. The school district did not run continuation or night schools, and by 1914 San Diego could no longer boast of its leadership in vocational training, since by then few children attended programs at the FIS. The little training that existed in the city did not come near to filling the needs, plus they tended to serve only white youth. The YMCA had a "small enrollment in a commercial and a drawing class"; girls could find classes in domestic science, sewing, and millinery at the YWCA; and only two stores offered continuation classes.[52] The advances made in vocational education during the 1890s affected only enrolled public-school students, so adolescents could leave school and enter the workplace at the age of twelve. Where they ended up haunted reformers.

The Dentention Home (DH) had become one resource for this population. From its opening in 1903, San Diegans used the DH as a stopgap measure for handling youngsters at risk of falling into criminal behaviors, including children admitted because of a parental death or illness. Associated Charities records from 1914 show how thirteen-year-old Josephine Pearce (a pseudonym) rebelled when authorities placed her in a foster home because her mother took ill. Health professionals and social workers had convinced her parents to send Josephine (the eldest of seven children) to a foster home. There she could earn her keep as a domestic and save the family from further poverty. But after less than one week in the foster home, Josephine ran away when her foster mother disciplined her for "being naughty." The Pearces then learned that authorities were removing the rest of their children from their home. The probation officer placed their two young boys in the Children's Home, and the other four children at the DH. The Pearce children, however, had other ideas about who would care for them and adopted their elder sister's strategy of running away. The boys twice ran away from the Children's Home, and the siblings at the Detention Home escaped three times.[53]

This episode is a rare look at how children made themselves heard. The Pearce family appeared in the records throughout the winter of 1914, as the parents persevered in retaining parental custody and the children fled from their foster homes. But it seems the authorities reconsidered their original strategy of separating the children only after the continued dramatic actions of the Pearce children to reunite with one another and with their parents. By running away, the Pearce children made obvious to the adults in their lives that they wanted their family to live together, even if that meant going hungry some days. Several months after committing to outside intervention, the Pearce couple struggled to regain their parental rights. Josephine's mother was discharged from the hospital, and her father secured a job where he earned a daily wage of $2.50, but child welfare authorities agreed to a reunion only after the children's third flight.

Sometimes the behaviors of parents, not the children, initiated authoritative contact with a family. Widowed, divorced, or never-married mothers always prompted an investigation of home life by authorities, as did evidence of single fathers managing the household. Children's Home records show how the death, desertion, or incarceration of a mother prompted swift action to remove children from the care of a father. The exchange in September 1915 between Children's Home personnel and Frederic Kallenberg, a father of six whose wife had abandoned the family when he became sick, illustrates the trauma faced by some men who approached reformers for help. Personnel expressed sympathy for Kallenberg's situation and exhibited an initial willingness to work within the financial means of the family, but eventually they removed his children from his care. Kallenberg's wife had left him with nothing, having taken over $300 from their home stash, as well as $25 from the bank, and she sold the horse and wagon Kallenberg used to peddle fish. The father committed to paying the Children's Home "whenever he [could] get work," but his situation represented all that could go wrong with a family if the maternal influence had been a negative one.[54] Kallenberg never seemed able to fully provide for his children after his wife deserted him. While the records are unclear for three of his children, the youngest three fell in and out of the system throughout their childhood, going from juvenile court, to a private home placement, then to the Children's Home Society of California in Los Angeles, and finally, to adoption.[55]

The act of removing these children from their loved ones certainly created more turmoil than provided custodial help for Kallenberg. The case records cite only the mother's desertion, so one can assume the staff did not observe any moral failing (such as intemperance) by Frederic; but unfortunately for the Kallenberg children, authorities did not trust the ability of their father to care and provide for them. That distrust by social work professionals had traumatic consequences for all of the children and their father. Kallenberg turned to the Children's Home for help with caring for his six children but in the end lost his custody rights.

Charles and Henry Scott fared better. The record is sketchy

as to how he cared for his four-year-old son after his wife died on New Year's Day in 1911, but by September 1918 Charles Scott decided to board his then eleven-year-old son, Henry, at the Children's Home. Charles worked at a lunch counter in San Diego and lived in Tijuana, Mexico. For three years he made fairly regular monthly payments of ten dollars for the boy's care. On September 18, 1921, the CH discharged Henry (now fourteen years old) to his father.[56] Why Scott lived in Tijuana remains unknown, but the Mexican Revolution was in full swing, and Tijuana's vice district took off in this era when Prohibition in the United States restricted legal alcohol consumption in San Diego.[57] Scott may have boarded Henry at CH to remove him from this element, or perhaps he used it so the boy could attend American schools. Once Henry turned fourteen, compulsory education ended, and the boy could enter the waged labor force to earn his own way. That Scott allowed CH staff to rear his son obviously worked in his favor. He accepted the constraints of his life as the single father of a young child, voluntarily boarded Henry at CH, and responsibly paid the boarding fees for years. That decision saved him from the watchful eyes of social workers, and his son from placement in the Detention Home.

Leonard Martin also sought help with childcare, when his wife was admitted to the state mental hospital in the fall of 1917. He approached Associated Charities for help in "securing a housekeeper in order that his home may be maintained," which included two young sons. According to policy, the Charities called the probation office and placed the children in foster care, advising Martin that a mature couple would offer the boys an example of domestic stability. But the decision scared Martin and pushed him into swift action. He had approached the organization for help in finding a woman to clean his house, put a meal on the table, and watch his children while he worked during the day. Instead, he found himself and his sons caught in a whirlwind of regulatory actions that removed his boys from his household and his care. Within a week of contacting the agency, Martin found a new home and employed a neighbor woman to care for the children. The Charities agreed his home needed to be regularly investigated, and it kept a close eye on the Martin family.

Surveillance by the Associated Charities, Martin's own realization about his situation, or a combination of the two certainly figured into the father's decision to make yet another move and arrangement for childcare. This time Martin engaged a husband and wife to watch his children, but the wife soon reported dissatisfaction with the deal, and the Martin family again moved. One month after doctors committed Mrs. Martin to the state mental hospital, the children had lived in four different homes with four different care arrangements, and more than eight strangers handling them in their daily lives. The probation officer stepped into the case and agreed with the AC that the boys needed to be permanently removed from their father. The situation with their mother signaled just cause for removal, but additionally, Martin waited tables at three different restaurants and presented "no definite plan" for the future of his children. Clearly, Leonard Martin did not represent a model head of household. After an investigation found conditions in their home "deplorable," the probation office prepared to make the Martin boys wards of the court. Martin desperately sought to retain custody of his sons. He solicited the aid of a long-lost cousin who owned a small store near Logan Heights School. The woman willingly took the boys in, promptly burned their clothing, and outfitted them with fresh clothes. Soon after, the AC reported that Martin lived downtown and the cousin had started "real training of the boys." By the first of the year, the children were "getting along very well," and investigations among neighbors found the children healthy and safe.[58]

Parents rendered single through the incarceration, commitment, or abuse of a spouse concerned society, and when the remaining parent was a father, the trouble became compounded in the minds of all involved. Obviously, the trauma in the Martin household dates back further than the point at which Mrs. Martin became institutionalized, and their children had long experienced serious disruption in their daily lives. Leonard received little credit from the authorities for his attentiveness to his children, and instead, they recognized his cousin as the key influence in turning around this family. In the eyes of authorities, the Martin family redeemed itself only through the intervention of a woman with maternal instincts. Reformers found maternal death particularly tragic, because they often viewed the home as running smoothly prior to a mother's death. Death victimized children and husbands through no fault of their own. Reformers worked to save the family from further tragedy by dividing children into homes with a woman's influence, even if that meant separating siblings from their father and each other. But in the case of the Martins, mental instability proved the culprit in attempts to separate Leonard from his sons.

Frederic Kallenberg and Leonard Martin represent men who resisted boarding their children; however, single fathers like Charles Scott recognized that boarding allowed them to retain their parental hold. Fathers who voluntarily boarded their children received respect from social workers and legal authorities, because they were viewed as admitting they could not handle the domestic duties. The Marino family case shows this view. Men like Anthony Marino expressed their fatherhood through earning wages and not in direct childcare. When his wife, Helena, died in March 1915, Anthony tried to care for his four children, ages two to thirteen years, but after five months he boarded them at the Children's Home. The elder children remained there for several years, but the two-year-old left just three months later, possibly going to an aunt who lived in the neighborhood and kept a grocery store; however, the record is unclear about these specifics. Marino made monthly payments of $6.25 per child, plus he sent extra money for new shoes and clothing throughout 1915 and 1916. In 1917 his monthly payments increased substantially, to $8.95 per child. Existing records reveal Marino's financial commitment to the care of his children, but we don't know about the extent of his emotional attachment. Did he visit them regularly or send them letters and gifts? Did the younger children recognize him as their father, or did he fall into the background? Whatever the scenario, the childhoods of the Marino children all ended differently. The eldest boy lived at the CH for three years, leaving when he turned sixteen; the CH discharged the other son at the age of fourteen; and all we know of Josie, the eldest daughter (six at the time of her entry to CH), is that on September 2, 1922 (when she would have been thirteen), authorities sent her to the Detention Home, probably because she had aged out of living at the CH.[59]

Juvenile courts listened to parental concerns, assigned children the label "delinquent," and ordered them into reform institutions so as to both teach the juveniles respect for elder authority and relieve society from such ill-mannered young people. Court actions, however, could and did backfire on parents. Single parents depended on elder daughters and sons to tend to the younger children, prepare meals, and help with wage earning, either through homework or day labor. Once the court ordered a child to an institution, the parent lost a valuable childcare provider and contributor to the family economy.[60] Rebellious daughters posed severe domestic problems for households, because they tainted the family image and denied parents their labor. As noted by Mary Odem, daughters of immigrants often pushed the boundaries of what their parents expected of them.[61]

The pattern of young, first-generation American girls trying to break away from the traditions of their parents holds true for Josie Marino and may be the reason for her commitment to the Detention Home. We can only infer from their case history typical scenarios facing the Marino family, but some possibilities can be identified when looking at their situation alongside other families using the Children's Home. Anthony and Helena Marino had traveled the country in search of work: their sons were born in New Jersey, their eldest daughter in Tacoma, Washington, and the youngest child was born in San Diego. A brick mason, Anthony Marino may have sought steady employment working on buildings for the Panama-California Exposition due to open in San Diego's city park in 1915. The Marinos had migrated south to California in 1913, where soon after, on March 16, 1913, Helena delivered their youngest daughter. Two years later Helena died, leaving her husband alone to care for four small children.

The Marino family had settled in the heart of San Diego's "Little

Italy," which possibly played a role in Anthony's ability to keep his children at home for a short while.[62] Records indicate that other widowers turned to the Children's Home immediately after their wives' deaths and used it to board their children, but Anthony's female neighbors likely helped him tend to domestic duties. Language may have also been a factor. In Little Italy residents mainly spoke Italian; however, the elder Marino children most likely had picked up English in their travels and may have been better positioned to understand CH personnel.[63] Marino never missed a payment, which would have worked in his favor toward retaining custody. Most parents who used the CH had good intentions to pay regular board fees but seldom fully met this obligation. Self-sufficiency was an important component in judging the stability of families, and Marino proved his ability to financially support his children. Yet the children's moral training loomed large, and they had already experienced periods without significant maternal influence. His sons posed no problem; however, popular thinking encouraged the fear that his daughter could fall into promiscuous behavior, and living at the DH could keep her from that trouble. Anthony Marino had not cared for his daughter since she was six years old, and he did not start when she turned thirteen. His parenting decisions may also have been influenced by the 1915–1916 Panama-California Exposition.

The exposition altered the physical, cultural, and social landscapes of the city. Historians recognize it as a force in San Diego's urban development, as its presence launched a cleanup campaign to rid the city of a large vice industry and improve public health services.[64] Since its expansion in the 1870s, police had turned a blind eye to vice activity and rationalized that little harm came to the city when the activities remained within the Stingaree. San Diego police were not alone in this thinking. Historian Neil Shumsky explains: "In American cities between roughly 1870 and 1910, the segregated red-light district served as another form of boundary maintenance—literally as well as figuratively. Nearly every advocate of segregation emphasized the need to avoid contaminating respectable neighborhoods and to separate moral from immoral behavior, just as traditional public health proponents had fought for the quarantine of biological plagues."[65] Civic leaders in San Diego followed this line of reasoning until they began planning for the exposition. Because the Stingaree, business district, and exposition site were in close proximity to one another, leaders changed their thinking about their acceptance of a red-light district.[66]

To address these issues, in 1912 activists Charlotte Baker and Ellen B. Allen formed the Purity League. Their efforts followed the achievement of female suffrage for California women in 1911, and their activism joined other reform groups across the country—indeed, throughout North America—in extinguishing red-light districts. The San Diego group understood the linkages between tourism and vice, and knew they needed to address how to block vice activities from the exposition. But they did far more than work with exposition planners to ensure the moral purity of amusements. The Purity League developed an educational campaign for the general public as to the health risks attached to risky sexual behavior, offered vocational training to prostitutes as an avenue for ensuring their shift to respectable labor, and built municipal recreation centers as healthier alternatives to saloons, gambling games, and theater amusements currently lodged in the Stingaree.[67]

The group renamed their organization the Vice-Suppression League to emphasize its expanded reform plan and used the research skills of its members to pursue its goals. Baker's diary indicates the league corresponded with cities that had closed their red-light districts, and they learned that San Diego should hire a policewoman to deal with female prostitutes and child delinquents.[68] But Mayor Charles O'Neall and Police Chief Keno Wilson questioned the practicality of the league's agenda and were not convinced that a female police officer could handle the job. Further, they wondered where these prostitutes would live once the city shut down the vice district, and who would provide them with viable work. League members reported they planned to send violators to the Girls Rescue Home, but locals challenged that plan. It was one thing to have rescued girls in the residence, but an entirely different issue to accept the presence of known prostitutes in their neighborhood. League members believed if they gave women options for a cleaner life, they would jump at the chance to remove themselves from prostitution. Not so. One prostitute stated, "Every woman in this district is just where she wants to be. We don't need anyone to reform us."[69] The league persisted, and on November 10, 1913, police launched a raid on the Stingaree, which resulted in the expulsion of dozens of women from brothels. League representatives offered the women transport to the Girls Rescue Home, but most of the women refused the help. Police tightened their monitoring of known brothels, but those actions simply pushed the prostitution trade underground.

Baker's involvement in the project subjected her to ridicule and death threats, but the attacks did not shake her commitment.[70] The overall effect of the 1913 raids dissipated when the exposition closed, prompting Baker and Allen to reinvigorate the effort four years later through the Women's Civic Center (wcc), a group originally organized in 1903 under the name Committee of Nineteen, and a legacy of the wha. Their goal was to "lend a helping hand to those unfortunates who desire to lead a clean life."[71] In addition to being part of the original Vice-Suppression League, many of the wcc members were highly involved in other reform projects, such as the 1911 state suffrage campaign and launching a Travelers Aid Society in the city. To jump-start their effort, the group invited the mayor, members of the common council, the city attorney, and delegates from women's organizations to a luncheon on June 15, 1917, to discuss city affairs. Luncheon organizers hoped to attract around fifty women, so they were ecstatic when the numbers approached three times that. The healthy attendance proved women's interest in civic affairs, but more importantly, wcc activism helped retain and advance funding for vital services in the city. For instance, when the city council considered closing the Mission Valley Hospital in 1919, the wcc protested the action. The hospital was known for treating venereal disease, and purity campaigns still figured prominently in the wcc mission. In order to preserve funding, wcc members contacted the Women's Welfare Commission, the San Diego County Medical Society, the Social Workers Association, the College Woman's Club, and all other women's clubs to encourage their attendance at a public hearing on December 17, 1919. Women turned out in strong numbers and successfully lobbied the council to retain funding for the hospital.[72]

Writing about a visit to San Diego's Mission Valley Hospital, philanthropist and reformer Ethel Sturgis Dummer reflected on the poor treatment of girls who had fallen victim to sexual promiscuity or abuse: "The stupidity of our past intolerance quite overwhelms one when one visits the venereal disease hospitals and finds these 'wild' women to be pitiful children, sadly in need of help."[73] Dummer challenged the prevailing notion that these patients were "feebleminded," believing instead that societal scorn and condemnation for their situations had produced shell shock similar to soldiers.[74] Dummer's view is an alternate perspective of the problems facing some women and girls, and important because of her work in transforming the juvenile justice system throughout the nation. Throughout her life Dummer devoted herself to child-help causes. As a volunteer at Chicago's Hull House and Juvenile Protective League, she learned the stark differences between how she lived and the material realities of those using these services.[75] Ethel married Frank Dummer, the vice president at her father's bank, in 1888, and the couple raised four daughters. The Sturgis family had traveled to Coronado since the 1880s, and the Dummers built a home in the coastal enclave in 1905.[76] They spent their summers in Coronado, where they quietly supported the work of San Diego's Associated Charities by providing waged work to unemployed men and women.[77] Dummer's wealth and social position could have allowed her to offer her service in name alone, but she threw herself into the work in both Chicago and San Diego. She did not hold a college degree or ever earned wages; however, she certainly worked in the fields of social hygiene, contraceptive concerns, educational access, and juvenile justice. She regularly visited Chicago's juvenile detention home and court proceedings, and offered her home as a gathering place for advocates to discuss how to better help juvenile offenders. In San Diego the Dummers quietly financed welfare programs and asked that their philanthropy be kept "invisible."[78] Dummer did not shield her daughters from the realities of how most Americans lived, and she encouraged them to pursue professional training so that they could engage in finding solutions to these issues.

Administrators depended on financial support from families like the Dummers, and they began taking a public stance on issues involving childcare, education, and child labor. Public school educators took a vocal role in monitoring children's actions by declaring their opinion on procedures and activities that brought children into precarious situations. For example, Guy V. Whaley, superintendent of San Diego City Schools, declared in 1919 that he and his principals were especially concerned with the consequences of activity in the public created for girls, explaining that "selling on street corners and in busy storefronts robs our girls of the modesty and retirement, which should characterize childhood, and has a tendency to make them bold and forward."[79]

Reforms in juvenile justice, childcare, and education took shape over several decades. The successful lobby to keep open the Mission Valley Hospital shows the continued strength of the female reform network in San Diego. When women secured the right to vote, their advocacy took a political turn, and they moved into the domain earlier reserved for men. Their activism resulted in professionalism coming to childcare agencies such as the Children's Home, involvement in the juvenile justice system, closing the redlight district, and advocating for changes in the public schools. A new group of activists, characterized by their university educations and experiences with Progressive Era reforms, changed the direction of family care programs in the interwar era.

State and national law forced San Diegans to pay attention to delinquent children, but the entry of professionally trained child advocates changed the focus of childcare. Through their involvement in the College Woman's Club, these advocates built a comprehensive social welfare program that addressed the multiple childcare needs of working and impoverished families. The development of local branches of national programs such as the Visiting Nurse Association and the Travelers Aid Society allowed reformers to offer specialized care. The acknowledgment by civic leaders that their city needed to depend on professionals to deliver care came later to San Diego than to other cities in the United States; however, it did not come too late.

CHAPTER FOUR

Professional Care

Expert Protocols for Childcare Programs

Our distance from the centers of social work led us to become our own training school.

—Evelyn Lawson, president of the Children's Home, 1913

In the spring of 1914, a visiting nurse for San Diego's public schools inspected the home of an elementary student to learn why she had missed so much school. The girl lived with her tubercular, alcoholic, and pregnant mother and a man who presumably had no biological connection to the girl. The nurse found the girl to be suffering from malnourishment and general neglect, prompting school officials to admit her to the Children's Home. The girl lived there for two years, and even though officials had blamed her ill health on the man they found in the house, the mother may have been the real abuser. The man was a deckhand for the U.S. tugboat *Harris*, which took him away from the house for week-long stretches, but he met all financial responsibilities for the care of the girl during the two years the girl spent at CH.[1] Yet this man's working-class status and intimacy with a woman to whom he was not married made authorities nervous.

School officials knew they could depend on the professional judgments of staff to care for this student and others like her, because by 1914 an organized network of protection agencies operated in the community. Between 1900 and 1910, San Diego's population grew by nearly 22,000 people, and by 1920 it numbered

74,361. That demographic included professionals trained in health, social welfare, and education, as well as thousands of workers in search of stable employment.[2] In San Diego mining and construction jobs attracted men from every corner of the country, and a vibrant canning industry employed workers of all ages. The city also housed the largest tobacco plant on the Pacific Coast. Inventions in aviation created jobs for both the middle and working classes, and city officials paid special attention to the interests of its new military partners.[3] In the midst of this growth, business leaders focused on supporting middle-class residents. They organized the Civic Association to develop the waterfront, while the San Diego-California Club focused on marketing and promoting the city's benefits to neighboring states such as Arizona. Military ties, especially with the U.S. Navy and Marine Corps, brought noncommissioned, single military personnel as well as married officers with families to San Diego. They recognized that good housing and schools for the families of officers and enlisted personnel would secure military connections and generate important revenue for the city. Throughout the Southwest, for example, in Houston, Phoenix, and Albuquerque, civic leaders began depending on the power of their chambers of commerce.[4] Unlike those other southwestern cities, San Diego's chamber of commerce did not fully separate itself from the political persuasions that accompanied the military into San Diego, because the military drove the economic growth in this era.

Many of these newcomers had young children, but few ties to the city, so they found themselves struggling to find childcare. Just like the people they assisted in their agencies, reformers came to the city for a variety of reasons, but a common theme emerges from agency documents. Professionals saw San Diego as a growing city that needed and responded well to their expertise. This chapter assesses how professional protocols surrounding childcare influenced the formation of local oversight bodies. The Associated Charities (AC) initially led that oversight. Established in 1909, the AC provided organizational direction for the professional implementation of court-mandated programs and encouraged collaborations among private and public entities. Federal immigration policy also influenced how agencies interacted with certain families, such as when and how refugees from the Mexican Revolution sought assistance. Then, in 1920, county officials created the San Diego County Welfare Commission (SDCWC) as a central authority to oversee how residents used the public funds assigned to them. The combination of the private AC and the public SDCWC allowed advocates and residents to benefit from diverse avenues of assistance and tightened connections between public agencies and private organizations.

Opportunities to earn wages in the many novelty shops, restaurants, and domestic services that catered to an unmarried male clientele, and continued movements of young, single women into the area, prompted the start in 1900 of the Travelers Aid Society of San Diego (TASSD). The city would soon house a King's Daughters Home chapter, and in 1907 the YWCA opened its San Diego branch.[5] TASSD, like its sister units in other cities, worked to protect unattached young women and adolescent girls from the evil forces lurking in big cities by offering them safe escort to respectable boarding homes.[6] TASSD guides focused their attentions on women and children who appeared at the train station and boat docks, and found them temporary beds through cooperative arrangements with the Children's Home and YWCA; thus, TASSD also provided parents with another resource to sort out their childcare situations.

The AC returned to the city in the midst of these changes. In describing the reformatted AC, reformer Daisy Lee Worthington Worchester did not exaggerate when she wrote, "I doubt that any program was ever begun with the advantages of wider experience."[7] That experience came from a tightly knit cadre of Progressives who had cut their reform teeth in factory investigations of cotton mills and as resident workers in urban-centered settlement houses. Similar to other areas affected by Progressive action, San Diego changed with the emergence of the female reform network, who immersed themselves in developing a social welfare plan for the city and saw it through implementation. Both married and single, some of these women were new to the city, while others had been born into San Diego's elite families.

In addition to Charlotte and Fred Baker, married Progressives included the Hills and Worchesters. Archibald and Mary Anderson Hill moved to San Diego to restore Archibald's health. The couple had married after Mary graduated from Vassar College, and they then helped establish settlement houses in New York City and Louisville. Daisy Lee Worthington also graduated from Vassar and then taught there for two years before joining the 1907 National Child Labor Committee (NCLC) investigation of cotton mills. During that work, Daisy met attorney Wood F. Worchester, and the two soon married. They honeymooned at the New York School of Philanthropy and then led a settlement house in Pittsburgh. The couple moved to Colorado Springs, where Wood ran that city's Associated Charities. In both Pittsburgh and Colorado Springs, the Worchesters worked with Alice Adams Robertson, San Diego's "first official caseworker," who encouraged them to move to San Diego.[8]

Some reformers, like Edith Shatto King, had been raised in San Diego, and as with the Worchesters, the NCLC mill investigation in 1907 was an early professional assignment.[9] She then assisted in collecting data for a national study of the living and working conditions of department store clerks. In 1909 she returned to San Diego with her husband, Fred, to help cure his tuberculosis. The Kings knew the Hills, and Mary persuaded them to help her organize an AC in the coastal community. Even though he was sick at the time, Fred accepted the challenge and became San Diego's first Charities secretary; however, his illness forced him to resign. Alice Adams Robertson recommended Wood Worchester as his replacement, even though he was not living in San Diego. Doctor's orders for Daisy Lee to "rest at sea level" solidified the Worchesters' choice to leave Colorado and join the growing professional reform community in San Diego. Wood served as the new secretary, but the day-to-day grind of operating an AC fell to Mary Hill.[10]

Activists in the Progressive Era embraced a broad spectrum of ideologies and circumstances, and in San Diego it took a combination of longtime residents (like Drs. Fred and Charlotte Baker), native-born San Diegans (like Fred and Edith Shatto King), and eastern transplants (like Wood and Daisy Worchester) to infuse social reform into the city. That infusion had been percolating since the start of the College Graduate Club (CGC) in 1896. The CGC began as a social group for young professionals to generate intellectual conversation and debate over current themes in the country, all the while serving as a social center for San Diego's elite, college-educated community.[11] The CGC flourished for a decade; however, sexism affected the membership, and by 1907 some of the men reorganized the club as a male-only association, renaming it the University Club, even though members did not need to hold an academic degree. Instead, initiates needed only to prove receipt of an honorary degree, at least two full years of attendance or graduation from a professional school, or military commission. In this way, the University Club shifted from an intellectual exchange to a fraternity network where the city's elite businessmen, politicians, and military officers could secure deals, change law, and decide politics.[12]

Segregating women from the community's business, political, and intellectual connections can be linked to statewide and local decisions surrounding the female suffrage movement, which likely concerned those men who had opposed universal state suffrage.[13] CGC members Charlotte Baker and Ella B. Allen had led the suffrage campaign in San Diego with an exhilarating range of activity that included summer parades, touring the county by auto, and giving speeches in all kinds of public settings.[14] When in 1911 California voters accepted the amendment allowing for the female vote, women in San Diego took that right and immediately asserted their expertise in the realm of social welfare. In an interesting twist, the exclusionary policies of the University Club ultimately led to the establishment of an organization with a longer-lasting influence on the direction of professional advancement, and San Diego's social welfare and public policy directives. No longer welcome in the group they helped found, in 1911 Baker, Allen, and Mary Anderson Hill launched the College Woman's Club (CWC).

They organized the cwc as both professionals and women seasoned by years of sexual discrimination. Coeducational universities and colleges guided female students toward courses in teaching, early childhood education, or home economics but balked if they showed interest in scientific or mathematic studies. Some, like Cornell University, grudgingly allowed women into the classroom, but male students made life rather unpleasant for the few women who entered the programs. Such attitudes helped generate the growth of all-female colleges whose faculty encouraged students to pursue all manner of study and occupation. But these institutions were the exception in a society that accepted job and occupational segregation.[15] Much of the scholarship that reviews the challenges by women to these gendered barriers assesses the involvements of women engaged in national and international organizations. Conflicts like the University Club's exclusions point to the importance of city-specific actions. The Republican Party was deeply embedded in San Diego, with all of its mayors in the early twentieth century aligning with that party. The Progressive Era ideals of leaders such as President Teddy Roosevelt and Republican governors of California likely allowed the city to embrace certain reforms, but it was the city's women who tackled the difficult work of social welfare reform.

Many of San Diego's reformers involved in this era were married, but plenty of single women also engaged in social reform. Helen Marston represents a key example of how young, single, college-educated women devoted their time and talent to social reform. As the youngest daughter of George and Anna Lee Gunn Marston, Helen had grown up with the city's movers and shakers, and was educated at the Episcopalian Bishop's School. She followed her sisters to Wellesley College, where she met activists like Jane Addams and Emily Greene Balch who enacted national reforms in labor and immigration law, compulsory education, and social welfare.[16] After graduating from Wellesley in 1917, Helen returned to San Diego and joined her sister, Mary, in the work of San Diego's first settlement house program, Neighborhood House (NH).[17]

These reformers knew the city could benefit from a settlement house, but first they needed to handle the diverse needs of a changing demographic, and that could be best accomplished through an Associated Charities. As central coordinator for all relief-giving agencies, the AC worked to improve communication between and distribution of resources among charitable organizations. Its staff also encouraged organizations to replace volunteers and missionaries with nurses and "friendly visitors" trained in public health practices and social work procedures.[18]

Religious leaders represented one group that was receptive to learning professional methods. They often knew personal details of a family that proved helpful in devising a care plan; thus, in the spirit of collaboration, the AC invited local clergy to serve on its Advisory Council. This collaboration is seen at the final AC meeting of 1909 when the friendly visitor for the AC reported her plan to keep the children of an Anglo father and a Mexican mother with their parents, rather than removing them from the home. She convinced their oldest son to return to school and quit his night job so he could help his Spanish-speaking mother with childcare. That arrangement, the visitor believed, would keep the baby in the home, rather than placing her in a boarding home. Father McNellis, the Catholic Church's representative, agreed with the plan and pledged that his church would send $5 per month for several months to the family to help with expenses. He also promised to "send a young lady from his church who speaks Spanish to call on the family" to explain the proposed assistance.[19] The council's effort to accommodate the mother's language shows they understood the need for bilingual personnel and the trouble that language barriers could cause for parents.[20] The integration of the Roman Catholic community provided critical funding for the family and the personal touch of a bilingual advocate. In the end, the children remained at home with their parents, and the family weathered the unemployment of the father with their dignity intact. Yet one needs to also recognize that a very different outcome would have occurred if the family's gender dynamics had been different. If the husband had been Mexican and the wife Anglo, the Associated Charities may have removed the chil-

dren, claiming this marriage walked the borders of miscegenation. Whereas Anglo men had been marrying Mexican women
since the early nineteenth century, reverse relationships were not
so welcome among the general population.[21]

Connections to the diverse groups working with families allowed
the AC to immediately prove its value to the San Diego community. It moved away from a volunteer-driven operation to a program with paid staff, and in 1911 Mary Dietzler became its first paid
registrar. The organization also hired a visiting nurse to investigate its charity cases.[22] That combination of expertise helped the
AC address the legal mandates associated with the juvenile court
system. Yet it is important to emphasize that the AC had no legal
authority to assert certain actions; rather, it operated as a coordinating body that oversaw how legally mandated authorities implemented the laws.

AC staff also worked with public officials to find solutions for
disabled individuals to lead more independent lives. State law provided that deaf children between the ages of three and twenty-
one years could receive eight years of public instruction if five or
more deaf children resided in an area. The city's board of education could also establish a school for the deaf at its discretion. In
1910 the district attorney found twelve deaf children of school age
living in the city, and members of the Charities' advisory council
decided to seek further information about the services these children needed. In the same council meeting, members discussed the
possibility of establishing a center for the twenty-four blind men
and six blind women in San Diego and "securing for them the
services of someone to read to them regularly."[23] The AC also kept
an eye on the environment at the Detention Home, and in a January 1911 meeting, council members discussed rumors that neither Sunday school nor elementary instruction occurred in the
facility. Charities head Fred King raised the issue with Judge Guy,
who seemed surprised and agreed to investigate the issue. Perhaps
he did so with Senator Wright, who was in San Diego working
on legislation to hire two more probation officers, a man and a
woman, for the juvenile court. Three months after Wright's visit,

the county found a resolution and began providing the Detention Home with an elementary school teacher.[24]

An area of change that did not meet with the approval of the Associated Charities concerned the 1909 juvenile justice law that allowed local boarding homes to care for delinquent juveniles and county wards. Their discussions included how to integrate young people into the community, rather than commit them to a detention center. For instance, members wanted to locate a "home-like place" for eighteen-year-old Gladys Turner to work and serve out her probation, and were concerned that George Miller had been taken to the Detention Home after an unsuccessful placement with a couple living in the country. Apparently, the boy was "unreliable and indolent," had "pronounced atheistic views," and refused to go to his aunt's home, so the probation officer housed the boy at the Detention Home until they found a suitable vocational program for him.[25] AC concern over placements in the Detention Home made sense, given the facility's overcrowded condition. The Detention Home ran on county and state funds and typically fell last on the long list of governmental budget demands. Congressional lobbying had successfully swayed politicians to support commercial tourism and military spending, but not social welfare programs. Perennially understaffed, the Detention Home's skeleton crew of only four people worked overtime just to provide basic custodial care to the children and youth under their watch.

For fifteen years, the Detention Home operated with only four staff: a superintendent, a matron, an assistant matron, and a cook, with the matron making the same $30 monthly salary as the cook. Additionally, allegations of abuse plagued the staff. The Boys and Girls Aid Society (BGAS) investigating committee in 1919 found no credible signs of severe abuse; however, they did dismiss the superintendent and matron, and added another assistant matron and a babies attendant. The dismissals resulting from the three-week investigation were not explained in the society's report, but it did note that the forty-four children currently at the facility appeared well clothed and nourished. The facility was clean, heated, and furnished with warm bedding, but it lacked adequate closet space, washbowls, and bathtubs, and no space existed for a needed isolation ward. The committee recommended the obvious: that the home be enlarged, since too many beds crowded the dormitory. Unfortunately, it took money to follow these recommendations, and none existed for such an expensive building project.[26] The role of the Detention Home was to house children temporarily, but authorities simply had not anticipated the city's population growth and of children subsequently needing the Detention Home.

Instead, judicial officials turned to the Children's Home for help with housing children. Head matron Miles regretted that more children could not be placed at her facility, but they also had run out of space. Disease prevention practices created another wrinkle, as CH required all residents to undergo a physical exam certifying their good health. If a child exhibited any sign of a contagious virus or infection, medical personnel had to deny them a bed.[27] Unfortunately, children most in need of shelter were usually also the sickest and ended up in the County Hospital, which had a notorious reputation for making patients sicker rather than healing them.

After the 1909 juvenile law changes, CH changed its protocols for interacting with families. Prior to 1909 the matrons recorded general characteristics about the family in the facility's register when a child entered and left CH. These notes included basic demographic information, but each entry differed a bit depending on who processed the child's entry. Starting in 1909, staff used a standard charting card to record case histories that included physical, medical, economic, and demographic information about each child. Shifting to a standard process required the coordination of all aid programs and was intended to highlight a family's path through the social welfare system. Standardization also required parents who sought services for their family to reveal personal details of their lives, especially why they needed to board their children. Some parents justifiably balked at the intrusion into their family concerns, but that lack of privacy became the price for receiving public assistance. By the 1910s mothers sometimes faced embarrassing screening questions that supposedly ensured that women using the CH worked out of economic necessity and not because they had rejected motherhood. Screening questions also allowed for staff to address a key objective among the institution's board members: to emphasize the expectation of financial responsibility of parents and guardians for the care of their children.

Because some families could not meet the fees, CH staff reached out to privately funded organizations for assistance with paying for care. Along with the continuing, albeit smaller, aid of the juvenile court and county supervisors, agencies such as the AC, Navy Relief, Jewish Hebrew Society, and the Silver Gate Lodge paid the board for some children.[28] These fiscal decisions originated in part because the CH could no longer rely on the good nature and plump pocketbooks of generous volunteers. It gained the expertise of credentialed advocates when it began hiring professionally trained women, but CH personnel did not possess the same economic standing as those earlier volunteers who had generously given of their time and money to run CH. Personnel found themselves in the uncomfortable position of raising money for their own salaries. By 1922 the budget committee of the Welfare Council understood this predicament and noted it in a memo to the council's directors, but this realization would not benefit staff.[29]

Judicial actions also changed the demographic makeup of the children who lived in the facility, as it shifted to a space for children judged dependents of the court by the 1903 and 1909 laws. These rulings pushed judges to remove children from single-parent households and place them in a facility, like San Diego's CH. Evidence also shows single parents—mothers *and* fathers—perhaps used the CH to maintain parental custody by showing the juvenile court that they had made good choices about childcare in not leaving their children unattended or in other dangerous situations. For the years 1909–18, two-parent households were the minority of those families using the CH. Out of 196 households, only 42 families, or 21.5 percent of those using the facility, represented two-parent households, and among those 42 households, seven parents did not live at home due to an incarceration or hospitalization for "insanity." So those families realistically lived as one-parent households. Most of the children, 78.5 percent, or

154 children, came from households with only one parent present. Another thirteen children (6.5 percent) had no parent in the home, and those parental losses came equally through death, desertion, and legal separation. Twenty-four fathers and nine mothers had deserted their families; eighteen households had undergone divorce; and twenty-four couples were separated. Seven mothers were too sick to tend to their children. Six unmarried women, twenty-four widows, and twenty-one widowers used the facility, and staff defined thirteen children as orphans and two children as half-orphans.[30] Clearly, children staying at the CH suffered from familial loss and needed the stability it could offer. More importantly, their parent or guardian trusted CH staff to provide that stability, and the AC acknowledged that trust as a deciding factor in its decisions to recommend use of the Children's Home over the Detention Home.

Some families had been affected by the Panama–Pacific Exposition. In their attempts to clean up the city for the exposition, officials found many people without access to clean water, preventive health care, and sanitary housing. Noxious smells and waste, particularly from the fish canneries and soap factories, flowed directly into the harbor and created health risks and squalid living conditions for those living in or near the industrial area.[31] In 1909 the city health department's plumbing inspector, Walter Bellon, found dilapidated buildings with open privies, rat colonies, and standing sewage throughout the Stingaree. He ordered a full-scale demolition of problem structures, which helped physically clean up the vice district but unfortunately did little for other neighborhoods troubled by poverty.[32] People living in other areas, like Barrio Logan, made due with a woeful infrastructure and housing that reformers described as "some old house or unsanitary shack."[33] A significant number of children who ended up in either the Detention Home or the CH lived in the areas affected by the cleanup campaign.

Citizenship requirements represented another change from the pre-1909 protocols that childcare advocates had to address. In October 1913 CH matron, Mrs. Miles, informed the AC, "The Home does

FIG. 10. Mexican women and children, refugees of the Mexican Revolution, being escorted down a San Diego street by a soldier from Camp Kearney, 1916. © San Diego History Center.

not want to take too many Mexican children," and that "applicants for admission must have been born in the United States or parents must have been naturalized."[34] This policy was certainly driven by the federal immigration quota system and the state of affairs in Mexico, as its violent revolution displaced hordes of people. Two years earlier concerned San Diegans had raised funds for Mexican refugees by canvassing the city with a door-to-door appeal. The Charities had approved of the relief effort, stating, "The refugees are now among the poor of this county," and agreed to help the Red Cross in purchasing tents for a Tijuana relief camp.[35] But within two years sympathies toward Mexican nationals waned, and even their American-born children seemed suspect. In discussing the fate of four young Mexican American children, the AC decided the best arrangement would be for a neighbor to care for them until their tubercular mother recovered from her illness and their unemployed father began earning enough wages to support the family.[36] The Mexican Revolution had pushed families north into the United States, and international borders tightened. Those political realities influenced the fates of children and affected the childcare choices available to their parents.

Immigration stipulations also influenced public policy in the region, and San Diego's close proximity to the vice industry in Mexican border towns (like Tijuana and Mexicali) concerned reformers. Across the country working-class, immigrant parents elicited much attention from childcare specialists, as these reformers believed this group held good promise in adopting new parenting strategies. Their interest came in the midst of nativist calls to curtail immigration as a panacea to stem the spread of disease. Intemperance and ignorance, nativists argued, justified tightening international borders, especially with regard to certain women. As early as the Immigration Act of 1875, federal policy targeted immigrant women. The act excluded from entry into the United States any woman "who had been convicted of and was serving a sentence for committing a felony and women imported for purposes of prostitution." Martha Gardner argues that this action "ushered in an era of restrictive legislation that would, by the early decades of the twentieth century, proscribe a long list of immoral behaviors, physical defects, mental deficiencies, and racial characteristics," and women bore a significant share of these restrictions.[37]

In 1882 the federal government passed another Immigration Act, and the Chinese Exclusion Act, which together declared race and class characteristics as appropriate parameters for denying entry into the United States. As a result, mothers, pregnant women, and girlfriends attached to men judged as having immoral or suspect backgrounds were often refused entry into the United States. Any hint of association with prostitution, gambling, or domestic service in a boarding home raised official suspicion and denied a woman access to work or uniting with their family members in the United States. Officials could take a further step by deporting women they suspected of "immoral conduct."[38] Communities along the Pacific Coast experienced immediate effects, as these federal actions tightened all borders to immigrants, especially to women.

Women were also the focus of a 1907 congressional provision

that allowed for deportation of any individual designated a public charge within three years of entry into the United States. Border authorities characterized pregnant women and mothers immigrating without their children as immoral, assumed the women to be public charges, and denied them entrance into the U.S.[39] In *United States v. Bitty* (1908), the Supreme Court ruled that an immoral woman—one caught in fornication, premarital sex, adultery, or homosexuality—posed a severe threat to families and sanctified marriage, and she could be deported for her behavior.[40] The release of the forty-two-volume Dillingham Commission report in 1910 and 1911 solidified deportation strategies by shifting fear away from the border to women who had already passed immigration criteria and were living in the United States, especially women assumed to be engaged in prostitution. Commission findings validated thinking that women who prostituted themselves could never regain respectability or raise morally healthy citizens and thus should be kept from securing citizenship.[41]

These rulings directed decisions in San Diego when officials tightened the San Diego–Tijuana border because of the Mexican Revolution. Upon her husband's death in the spring of 1914, one Mexican mother of eight refused to return to her husband's native Ensenada, insisting San Diego's AC help transport her to relatives in La Paz, because its location in the southern Baja Peninsula made it "more remote from the dreaded Revolution." The AC, however, feared subversive activity in the family and simply wanted them out of San Diego. Where the family ended up was of little interest to the group.[42] Likewise, in June 1914, authorities refused to support a young widow of the revolution, who had also lost her baby ten days earlier, and advised her to return to friends in Tijuana.[43] The decision to deny this woman any support seems particularly callous given her traumatic loss and suggests that the fear of potential contact with insurgents of the Mexican Revolution trumped humane action. By spring 1916 San Diego police reported regular arrests of Mexican men, and continued surveillance of the Mexican American community. Prior to the revolution, charitable organizations like the Woman's Home Association would have reached out to the mourning mother and found transportation and lodging for the widow. But the war across the border, continued expansion of vice, and federal immigration law persuaded some people that these women brought trouble to the area.

Throughout this era, the Associated Charities took on greater responsibility in monitoring the types of children admitted to the Children's Home and the Detention Home, especially Mexican immigrants. We see this in the González family case. Widower Jorge González asked the Charities to help with "securing a home or housekeeper" for his three children, so he could work at the Santa Fe Freight Depot. Within days, agency workers had separated the children into two different households, the baby and four-year-old with an "American" family, and the oldest boy with foster parents in another house. González did not have this in mind when he asked for assistance, and within two weeks the father gathered his children and secured his own day care arrangements with two young women in his neighborhood. With the children in a familiar place chosen by González, he could retain control of his children's welfare and keep them together. The agency seemed wary of this situation and thought it "advisable to try to secure a home for this baby other than a public one of this sort."[44] To their mind, single fathers should use boarding homes or adoption, and Mexican-descent men especially needed to turn over the care of their children to personnel or families who presented a better model of the American family.

Other Mexican families received similar treatment from the AC. In September 1920 the Charities decided that unless the newly migrated Hernandéz family became self-supporting "very soon," they should return to Calexico.[45] Their situation came before the association when the attendance officer for the public schools reported that the fifteen-year-old Hernandéz girl worked instead of attending school. Her parents insisted they needed their daughter's earnings in order to survive, but the AC held firm on its decision that unless the couple withdrew their daughter from paid employment, they would be forced to return to Calexico. As Mexicans, the Hernandez family had little recourse. Once their daughter had been reported absent from school, they became defined as bad parents and targets for supervision. Ironically, San Diego public schools invested little energy in educating Mexican and Mexican American youngsters; but once authorities became aware of the girl in the workforce, they issued a warning for the parents to abide by American standards of parenting and keep their teenaged daughter in school.

Such warnings were not unusual and often stemmed from adolescent girls earning wages in areas considered dangerous. For instance, in 1910 AC officials took notice of young girls working in various laundries owned by Chinese men. Their concern over a "white girl" working at Jim Lee's Laundry at 364 Sixth Avenue (the heart of the Stingaree) prompted probation officer Reed to question the Chinese proprietor, who reported a girl "comes to the door at intervals asking for work." Reed learned the girl was Mexican, had been employed at the laundry, "but not for some time," and the proprietor did not know her name or address. Concern for the girl's safety dissipated upon learning her ethnicity, as they fully expected Mexican youth to be present in the area and were comfortable with a Mexican girl asking for work, although as we saw with the Hernandez family, the work should never remove her from school.[46] The real worry was in the ethnicity of the laundry owner. Asian men who employed non-Asian girls worried authorities, as racist stereotypes of opium-infested, sexually charged Chinatowns made Asian-owned laundries and restaurants off-limits to young, white girls, and women looking for respectable work. If a girl worked for a Chinese man, people generally believed she had fallen victim to white slavery.[47]

AC actions point to this attitude in San Diego. Two years after the incident at Jim Lee's laundry, the Charities discussed the situation of a young Italian girl, Maddie Cantero, found ironing for a Chinese laundry located near her home. She earned $1 per day and worked three days a week. They suggested she take a position as a domestic in a private home, but Maddie wanted to work near her mother, who apparently was "satisfied" with the laundry. However, AC members remained nervous about Maddie's workplace. Interestingly, they worried more about where she worked than her truancy. The AC recommendation for the "mother to be warned of danger and [Maddie] urged to find other work" showed that their apprehension stemmed from who employed her, the kind of work she did, and where she spent her day.[48] Laundries fell on a list of workplaces condemned by the National Child Labor Committee as unfit spaces for young girls.[49] The Canteros, however, were not going to have strangers dictate how they made a living. The Charities retracted its position, but its members were uneasy with Mrs. Cantero's seeming nonchalance about her daughter's safety. This interaction highlights an important limitation of the Charities: it had no formal or mandated authority over families. Members of their committees were professionally trained in social work or education, but they had no legal authority to control familial decisions.

AC staff could, however, assess agency operations, suggest changes toward professional standards, and monitor the custodial conditions at local agencies. The Helping Hand Home (HHH), established in the 1890s as a shelter for homeless men, is one example. The HHH never expected to be used for child placement, but the county turned to them to house children caught in the overcrowded conditions at the Detention Home. HHH methods came under scrutiny after the passage of the juvenile court laws made certification to care for children harder to attain. In order to secure a license, a boarding home had to pass annual inspections by professional service providers who evaluated educational curriculum and violations of health and safety codes. The State of California had passed legislation in 1903 requiring all boarding homes to secure licensure, but the law had little effect until 1913, when a second law established the Board of Charities and Corrections (BCC) as state supervisors of licensing issues. In California licensing was aimed at eliminating "baby farms" and regulating maternity homes rumored to be mistreating unmarried mothers, but the act achieved sporadic change. Responsibility for inspecting and licensing homes lay with county health departments or health officers, but since no statewide system existed to coordinate this

FIG. 11. Boys working in the yard of the Helping Hand Home as girls observe, c. 1920. © San Diego History Center.

work, few officials found time to fully investigate homes.[50] In San Diego, however, the HHH fell under BCC scrutiny.

In 1910 HHH had opened a day nursery, and a rare inspection five years later by the BCC produced an unsatisfactory report. HHH made some improvements in its operation over the summer, and the BCC issued a license, but only on the condition that boys living at the home stop selling newspapers on the street. NCLC had been working since 1904 to remove children from the workplace, and they had highlighted the particular vulnerability of messengers and newsboys to disreputable environments. The presence of children laboring in these situations must have proved frustrating for the BCC and led to its ultimatum. But HHH could not come up to proper standards. For the next several years, the staff regularly dealt with threats by the BCC that it would have to close its operation. Some issues concerned lack of professional practice— "records poorly kept" and "low standards in management and housekeeping"—while others applied to direct care of children, such as overcrowded dormitories. A February 1917 report concluded the facility was "unsatisfactory in a great many ways": a poorly constructed building with rooms in disrepair, poorly furnished and emotionally cold, neglected grounds, and ineffective house-keeping throughout the facility. Investigators were shocked to find HHH still using a "long table, oil cloth table covering, benches and enamel dishes" to feed children, missing or worn window screens, fences in disrepair, and "almost no playground equipment." BCC gave the association several months to improve conditions, but by December it ordered HHH to discontinue its day nursery care. The facility abided by the order and within the week sent the children to the CH.[51] Such incidents helped convince officials in San Diego that professionals needed to play more critical roles in the administration of child-help agencies, institutions, and programs. One important step in this direction was San Diego's embrace of state-supported mothers' pensions.

As one of a set of reforms designed to remove mothers from the waged workforce, mothers' pensions provided monthly stipends to women rearing their children without the aid of a husband's earnings. Championed by maternalist reformers, the concept of "paid motherhood" fit with their philosophical beliefs that mothers were the best care providers of their children.[52] They advocated for mothers' pensions so as to encourage women to embrace motherhood as a right rather than a maternal burden, and advocates believed aid to qualified mothers would ultimately reduce the incidence of delinquent, physically unhealthy, and ignorant children. In 1911 Illinois became the first state to adopt a mothers' pension law. By 1913 eighteen states followed suit, including California, and by 1920 over three-quarters of the states had enacted some form of a mothers' pension.[53]

State commissions approved mothers for a pension, and only mothers who upon investigation were found to be morally sound qualified for one. In general, mothers who had been widowed or abandoned by their husbands fit the definition of a "worthy" woman, and only three states (Michigan, Tennessee, and Nebraska) allowed unmarried mothers to even apply for a pension.[54] Recipients, no matter where they lived, were usually white and native-born, since authorities managing the pension program often embraced cultural stereotypes about certain mothers. Political scientist Gwendolyn Mink explains how many pension reformers believed African American mothers possessed an innate ability to juggle the dual responsibilities of earning wages and mothering, and "defined Black mothers not as women but as workers," because of their long history of laboring for whites, with some of that labor in raising other women's children. Most white Americans believed stereotypes depicting the "naturalness" of single motherhood among African American women, rationalizing that black women did not need a mother's pension. Exclusion from the program extended to Mexican American mothers, although for different reasons. The stereotype of Mexico as a "feudal" society that encouraged lifelong dependency on government aid drove the decision-making process for blocking Mexican American mothers, especially in the Southwest, where the Mexican American and Mexican immigrant populations were more pronounced. Instead of understanding the program as temporary assistance for these women, pension administrators feared that mothers' pensions were a conduit to permanent government dependency. Thus, pension administrators dismissed the value of mothers' pensions for Mexican-heritage families and focused instead on establishing Americanization projects.[55] No matter the racial or ethnic ties of a family, a mothers' pension rarely covered a family's expenses, and many recipients continued to work at jobs that took them away from their mothering responsibilities.

Staff at the Children's Home seemed to bridge the two beliefs. Childcare resources had not grown with the population, and until 1914 the CH remained the only facility that passed licensing requirements. In 1913 Justine Oake used it when her husband died. He had made a good living as an electrician at the Electrical Equipment Co. and had purchased a Metropolitan Life Insurance policy. Yet for reasons not recorded, by December 1916 four Oake children aged seven to thirteen years, lived at the CH. A ledger notation,

"Turns over to us money she received from State," suggests Justine received some public funds, probably a mothers' pension, but the evidence of the type of aid is not clear. Not all of her children seemed content with the living arrangements; her thirteen-year-old son, Theodore, left the facility on his own accord after only a one-month stay, and staff decided to permanently discharge him to his aunt on February 9, 1917. The two youngest stayed at the CH until October 14, 1918. It took Justine Oake five years to stabilize her family, and without the help of her sister, the CH, and state funds, it probably would have taken her much longer. The records do not indicate so, but her older children probably began earning wages and helping their mother meet expenses.[56]

Parents who entrusted their children to the facility expected CH staff to protect their children throughout the day and night, which included separating their children from youngsters the court had ruled delinquent. Parents also fought to maintain custody and resented what they perceived as heavy-handed control over their family. When the AC learned that an anxious mother, Mrs. Hedrick, reportedly "visits her children at the Children's Home and upsets them by talking about wanting to take them away," the Charities agreed a worker should meet with the upset mother. They directed the staff member to "influence [Hedrick] to leave children in the Home unless investigation shows that she is able to take care of them in her own home. If State aid can be secured for children, woman should choose an alternative and not worry the Home any longer."[57] Two weeks earlier Hedrick had left her three children at the Children's Home but could not come to terms with her choice and appeared at the facility at all hours wanting to see them.[58] Personnel knew that an anxious parent could disrupt the operation of their busy facility, and the unorthodox visitations likely upset both the Hedrick children and the routines of other children.

Hedrick kept up this behavior for another four months. Perhaps because of this mother's persistence, the Charities agreed the children should be reinstated to the mother's care and supported with state aid.[59] One of those steps, state aid, occurred, but social workers did not believe Mrs. Hedrick could adequately and safely care for her children. The children remained at the CH while the state paid $6.25 per month for each child's custodial care. Tragedy struck, however, when one of the Hedrick children died in the CH on March 6, 1914. No documentary record exists to indicate Mrs. Hedrick's reaction to her child's death, but it must have been horrified. One can imagine the chaos when the child died, as well as the strained meeting between CH matrons and AC staff to rehearse the best way to break the news to the nervous mother. Whatever conversations transpired must have satisfied Hedrick, as her two other children continued to live at the CH throughout the summer.

As the Hedrick case shows, once parents released custody or were forced to do so by authorities, they lost their right to assume care, even in the face of tragedy. In the spring of 1914, another mother, Mrs. Walling, found herself on the brink of losing her children to adoption because of a terrible miscommunication between herself, the CH, and the AC. Having fallen ill and unable to care for her children, Walling asked the home to take in her children; but apparently, they had no room, especially for a woman who could not pay the boarding fees. AC staff suggested to Walling that the county supervisors could provide her with an allowance equal to the amount spent if the children boarded in the home. But Walling did not see her problem as a financial one. The AC office reported that she called, "protesting that she is not in health to take care of her children even if the means should be provided; she expressed gratitude for the provisions sent by the County through this office but insisted that she wants the children placed in a home."[60] AC staff believed Mrs. Walling had released her children for adoption, whereby they proceeded to find permanent placement for the children. Livid when she discovered what the AC meant to do with her children, Walling flatly refused to give her children over to adoption proceedings. She had pestered the AC for several months, fighting to retain her parental rights, and did not intend to let her efforts fail. Within two weeks of learning about the adoptions, Walling found work and a place to live, thereby demonstrating to authorities her ability and desire to care for her children.[61]

In another case, Mrs. Fiedler allegedly allowed her young daughter to "run wild in the streets," and AC staff recommended she use the CH. No husband was present in her life, but the records do not indicate why. Fiedler agreed, but nearly one year later, she asked the AC to send her home to New York, where, she believed, more institutions existed to help in the care of her children. Mrs. Fiedler peddled wares on the corner of the plaza in the downtown, but police citations forced her to sell only at night, which proved deadly for business and likely subjected her and her daughter to the suspicion of prostitution. Anxious to get her out of their jurisdiction, the AC agreed to look into resources in New York.[62]

Fiedler, Walling, and Hedrick fought with authorities over losing their parental rights and their children to strangers and were deemed problem mothers by those involved with their cases. Read one way (the mothers'), the evidence suggests that personnel from the CH and AC misinterpreted the mothers' actions. Read through a reformer's mind, the mothers had admitted their failures at parenting. Operating under the Juvenile Court Laws of 1909 and 1913 (which clarified definitions of "neglected, dependent, and delinquent children"), the AC, county supervisors and CH staff worked toward finding long-term and permanent care for the children.[63] Hedrick and Walling, while viewed at times as hysterical or unrealistic, persisted in having authorities hear their voices so as to retain custody of their children. These single mothers had few resources available to them in San Diego to both earn wages and care for their children. The one option that existed, the CH, had become by the 1910s a boarding home and not a day nursery. Mrs. Fiedler recognized that reality and returned to New York, where she had access to several day nurseries. Existing records do not indicate that authorities recommended or denied a mothers' pension to these women, but one thing is clear about these mothers: they fought to retain their parental rights and even moved out of the city and state to do so.

Essentially, professionals in the decade after juvenile justice laws were enacted encountered a different generation of mothers than those who turned to the CHDN in 1890. Matrons now faced women who were savvy about securing relief, more experienced in working for wages, and more knowledgeable about the existence of day nurseries. Perhaps these women had heard how their children could be adopted away from them. One woman, Claire Decker, insisted on finding a job where she could take her baby girl, despite promises from the AC that the Children's Home would find room for the child. But Decker refused to cave in to agency pressure to board her daughter and turned to the Methodist Social Services, which helped her find housekeeping work for several men on a ranch in East County where she and her daughter could live together. Decker looked to a religious organization for assistance when she believed the secular AC threatened her parental wishes.[64]

Over time, the AC turned to the CH, knowing the children would benefit from nutritious diets, inoculations, regular schooling, and a disciplined schedule of activities. Their matron, Mrs. Miles, told a *San Diego Union* reporter, "This is a home in every sense of the word, and there is nothing that we abhor so much as the institutional idea."[65] The home's 1913 report credits the child-study movement for making its work possible. Personnel were excited about playing a role in "correcting theory by practice," yet board president Evelyn N. Lawson admitted that the shortage of trained workers affected their work. "Our distance from the centers of social work," Lawson explained, forced the Children's Home to become its "own training school, paying for the privilege of being so, because young children cannot be neglected while we make deliberate choice of attendants."[66] By the 1920s Children's Home policy dictated accepting "only those cases where admission ... seems the only alternative." That meant screening out parents who, "tired and discouraged, turned to an institution such as the Children's Home as an easy way of shifting their responsibilities."[67] This attitude was a far cry from the benevolence of the 1890s.

Childcare workers across the country no longer applauded attempts of wage-earning mothers to support the family, and they

FIG. 12. A boy who resided in the Children's Home, 1921. © San Diego History Center.

viewed many of these mothers as unfit.[68] Social workers in this era tried to fully assess a family's situation before suggesting any action; volunteers, on the other hand, tended to handle problems immediately, with little attention to the possible mitigating circumstances causing disruption in a family. In her analysis of family casework standards in Minneapolis, Beverly Stadum found that by the 1920s families were less likely to receive immediate material relief when social workers investigated the situation under question, as the process of adhering to professional standards became more important than providing aid to desperate families.[69]

Removed from the centers of professional study, San Diego's social workers could and did focus on material relief. In their attempt to emulate professional standards, CH matrons worked to "persuade the parents to reconsider" putting their child in the facility, thereby "maintaining their home and a united family."[70] Yet they understood that most of the mothers who approached them

FIG. 13. The Children's Home was recognized as a safe boarding home for children whose parents or guardians needed long-term childcare, and for wards of the court. © San Diego History Center.

were forced into boarding their children because they worked for the survival of the family and not for pin money. Aid included arranging for adoptions or temporary board, and moving families back to their original homes in other states or countries. Because of the transient nature of San Diego's population, advocates often dealt with trying to reunite lost family members, including locating a child's father, mother, or other blood relation. Judgments about families regularly entered into case records when San Diego workers tried to connect children with appropriate guardians. Comments such as "Father intemperate," "Mother incompetent," "Unstable house due to divorce" pepper the case records from this era. They also believed the round-the-clock socialization of a boarding home offered a more effective tool for training children who desperately needed the attention.

Social workers in San Diego also learned to accept that volunteers could be their first line of defense in stabilizing families, especially with helping newcomers to the city. The Travelers Aid Society of San Diego is a good example of this association with volunteers and novice social workers. From its inception TASSD recognized the importance of casework experience, but it also operated on a skeleton staff under the umbrella of the local YWCA and the goodwill of volunteers. For instance, when Mrs. Mirabel Riley took over for the vacationing Ella Thomas, the office admitted that Riley was "inexperienced as a Travelers Aid worker," but because she had "some experience in Welfare and Survey work," the woman "did very nicely for a beginner."[71] Charged primarily with securing a safe environment for travelers entering the city, Aid guides discovered that the situations they faced became far more complicated than simply meeting a family at the dock and delivering them to a home. Young women arrived with wrong or nonexistent addresses for relatives, unattended children had been put on trains with no instructions for finding a parent upon arrival, and bewildered young mothers needed acclimation to the strange city.

The city's hosting of the Panama-California Exposition in 1915 posed a special challenge for TASSD. In 1915 the TASSD assisted 13,766 persons; that year only chapters in San Francisco, New York, and Philadelphia claimed more assistance calls (and the presence of a competing exposition in San Francisco certainly affected those numbers). Among its U.S. chapters, the San Diego branch gained first place for minimum per capita expense for fieldwork and for maximum number of persons assisted per agent. With only five agents responsible for covering the railroad depots, steamer docks, streetcar exchanges, and investigations of homes, Aid guides averaged helping 2,753 people each year, or 230 persons each month, proving that aid work was a daily commitment for staff.[72]

The experience of a Travelers Aid guide in helping reunite a mother and child illustrates the complexities of that work. On the afternoon of September 3, 1915, the worker found four-and-a-half-year-old Forrest Holmes "wandering around aimlessly" at the Santa Fe train station. She learned he had traveled alone from Los Angeles to San Diego and was waiting for his mother to retrieve him, but after a two-hour wait, it became clear to the guide that Forrest's safety rested in her hands. Hoping for the best but depending only on the memories of a small child, the two left the station in search of Forrest's mother. The guide "suspected domestic troubles" for a number of reasons. First, in her mind, no decent mother would set a child alone on a train without a note to explain his destination. Secondly, Forrest's parents no longer lived together. She teased out of the boy that months earlier his mother had sent him to live in Los Angeles with his maternal aunt, and his sister to friends in Redlands. To the guide these arrangements proved family instability rather than maternal responsibility. Lastly, she learned the mother worked at the Lower California Fisheries Company, and the guide did not trust that a maternal wage earner could properly care for her child. With few leads to trace the boy's family, the guide phoned the Fisheries Company, and within the hour the assistant manager appeared at the station. After questioning the boy, the manager replied that "it was a shame that a bright boy like that should be thrown out on the world," confirmed the parents' separation and that the mother had not worked at the cannery for several weeks, and offered directions to where he thought the woman lived. With little concrete information, the guide knew she might not find this mother. But that evening she did find the woman.

Solid detective work by the Travelers Aid guide led to a happy reunion. "A tall, fair and rather pretty woman" answered a knock at the door, and "the boy impulsively said 'hello mama!' [The mother] grabbed him and kissed him over and over again," with "no signs of him not being wanted." The guide seemed satisfied that Forrest's mother could properly care for the boy despite living in "poor surroundings," losing her job at the tuna cannery weeks earlier, and now purchasing groceries "on credit." The woman "looked clean and neat," was "rather pretty," and showed "no signs" of not wanting her boy. Forrest may have returned to poverty or continued trouble in the home, but the Travelers Aid guide felt confident he had his mother's love to help him through the rough times. Admitting she had believed the manager when he described the mother's character as questionable, this advocate's observations of the woman and environment made her reassess the demeanor of a wage-earning mother. Despite her obvious poverty, Versa Holmes "did not have any look of dissipation as [the manager] had led her to expect," and the guide believed the boy had found a welcome and loving home with his mother.[73]

A social worker appointed by the Associated Charities probably would have handled the assignment differently. The boy would have been taken to the Detention Home until the juvenile court could hear the case. After perhaps a week, a judge may have assigned him to the Children's Home as a temporary ward of the court, and a court-ordered investigation of the mother's home would have confirmed hers to be an unstable environment. Securing county payment for his room and board, the social worker would try to find the mother employment at a job with wages sufficient to maintain the boy's board at the CH. However, under Travelers Aid direction, emotional stability weighed more than economic security, so reuniting mother and child proved decisive. Racial ideology must also have figured into the guide's assessment. The worker emphasized Versa Holmes's pretty, fair, and clean appearance, likely because she was white and young. The guide probably would not have paid this level of attention to an African American or Mexican boy, and American Indian or Asian families would not have contacted or received help from the TASSD.

Travelers Aid guides did not work in isolation, and like members of the AC, they often connected with associates in other organizations to find appropriate resources. In November 1921 TAASD guide Anna Speer showed this networking ability by securing lodging and food for an "anxious and bewildered but very determined little Mother" and her two young children. A Mexican national, the mother had immigrated to San Diego in search of work but had no resources lined up upon her arrival. Speer arranged for the elder child to live at the Helping Hand Home, the baby stayed with the mother at the Rockwood Home in Pacific Beach, and Catholic Charities provided the family with "gifts of clothing and money." Speer's supervisor admitted the case proved trying, yet rewarding, and recognized the involvements of local organizations in stabilizing the family. She praised Speer in stating,

"What our Mrs. Speer has done for this little Mexican woman would fill a small volume. The fitting of square pegs into round holes is always attended with considerable labor."[74] The attention Mrs. Speer gave this mother is unusual given the problems facing Mexican and Mexican American people during this era. The persistence of the revolution deepened prejudices against these groups, but perhaps the mother's small children helped to sensitize Speer to the problems facing this family.

But the mother must have thought differently about the outcome of the guide's "considerable labor." After all, Mrs. Speer's actions divided her family. The TASSD removed the family from the street and potentially dangerous scenarios yet seemed unaware of the full consequences of these actions. They had placed the older child in a home that had failed licensing criteria several times and was located miles away from his mother. We can only hope that Mrs. Speer placed him in the home because he spoke English and was not surrounded by strangers with whom he could not communicate. The TASSD had done its job—secure the family safe housing—and that's how it reported the interaction, but no foreseeable plan as to how to round out those "square pegs" existed to reunite this family. It is understandable that it could not find lodging for the family to remain together, but it is less clear why the TASSD placed the woman in the Pacific Beach home. That arrangement removed the family from Barrio Logan, the downtown neighborhood where in 1921 most Mexican-heritage families lived and where the settlement Neighborhood House was located. By 1921 NH had developed into an important resource for Mexican families, and it's unlikely the TASSD did not have connections within the settlement. The distance between HHH and the Rockwood Home assured sporadic contact between the boy and his mother, as travel would have involved an expensive streetcar ride. Unfortunately, the sources do not elaborate on the future of this family, but one hopes that Catholic Charities, NH, and the Mexican American community stepped in to find a more reasonable solution for their long-term needs.

The TAASD guides treated families whom they encountered differently, and racial and ethnic backgrounds seem to account for these differences. Consider the interactions between the TAASD guide and Versa Holmes alongside the Mexican family assisted by Mrs. Speers. The guides necessarily treated Holmes and the "little mother" from Mexico differently—after all, their needs were quite different—yet they seemed ignorant of the potential damage that separating young immigrant children from their mother would incur. The eldest boy may have spoken English, which made his placement at HHH easier; however, he most likely also helped his mother with translations and the care of the baby, so their separation put her at a new disadvantage. The divorced, white, and American Versa Holmes gained control of her son, while the Mexican mother lost control of her child, demonstrating that citizenship and ethnicity certainly factored into the TASSD actions. The Mexican–U.S. border was unstable due to the persistence of the Mexican Revolution, and the fears associated with smuggling alcohol, drugs, and people were all factors that likely influenced the actions taken by Mrs. Speers.

Earlier in 1921 Thomas and Speer had submitted a report outlining the benefits of their work: "One young woman of education and refinement who had learned of her child's whereabouts through the AC said that she had previously hated all charities but now [held] the attitude that the thoughtfulness and courtesy of the little woman in charge of this work has completely changed her mind. She had found such ready sympathy and cooperation."[75] But not all of the TASSD clients liked the organization's collaborations. A disgruntled father learned that Travelers Aid was more than a social network when he approached the Los Angeles Society for assistance in locating his wife and youngest children, who were supposedly in San Diego. The father "made his story seem very pathetic to the worker," but after investigating the case, TASSD learned the woman had left her husband because of his "sex perversion." They notified Los Angeles of their findings, concurred that the woman's excuse for leaving was certainly legitimate, and advised their colleagues to keep silent on the whereabouts of his family.[76]

Evidence from agencies like TASSD point to how advocates oper-

FIG. 14. Women at a San Diego County Welfare Commission meeting, 1921. ©
San Diego History Center.

ated through the lens of their white, middle-class, heterosexual
lives. They saw their actions as saving immigrant and working-
class families from the misery of poverty, single motherhood, or
family separation. The focus on custodial needs was admirable, but
they did not always recognize loving connections between parents
and children. In a case involving a divorced couple, TASSD guides
described the family of an eight-year-old boy as "very pathetic,"
because his divorced parents lived in two different cities. The boy
split his time between living in San Diego and Vallejo in the northern part of the state. Although both parents had remarried, the fact
that this couple arranged for and could handle joint custody held
little weight for the society. While they believed no home should
be broken, the guides did accept the assignment of securing his
rail passage, because the boy's mother had entrusted them with her
son's safety. Despite their beliefs about family unity, they understood that a child's immediate safety was always most important.[77]

In San Diego the transition to professional standards proved difficult for some organizations that relied on volunteers to staff programs. TASSD staff understood and even accepted the theories of family casework, yet when it came to problem solving, many of them believed "Americanization plus Christianization" remained the best "remedies" for problem cases.[78] That philosophy probably figured into Mrs. Speers's work on finding housing and a Catholic connection for the young Mexican mother, and her actions brought praise from her superiors. But by the 1920s the city's needs had grown beyond these types of theories. To address these limitations, the Board of Supervisors passed an ordinance in 1919 creating the San Diego County Welfare Commission. Effective January 1, 1920, supervisors noted that social welfare "should not be relegated to private philanthropy and thus be made merely a matter of charity, but a function of the government with ample room for the work of private agencies." The commission intended to abide by professional standards when assigning aid and emphasized structured operations that included "constructive" casework, public education, investigation follow-up, and "co-operation of all the social agencies throughout the County."[79] One area it surveyed involved the county-ordered dependent children who were assigned to seventy-eight homes, either licensed or awaiting license by the Board of Charities and Corrections.

In spite of efforts to coordinate care, breakdowns in the system resulted in some youngsters being shuffled numerous times to multiple places. Investigators cited the mishandling of a fifteen-year-old girl who spent time at four facilities—the Door of Hope, the Detention Home, the County Hospital, and County Jail—as she awaited transport east to live with relatives. Because one of her stays included the Door of Hope, one can surmise she was pregnant and that the situation led to her being labeled delinquent and possibly spending time in jail after she delivered her baby at the County Hospital. The same report criticized the Detention Home, characterizing it as "by no means a credit to the city and county." Investigators were troubled by girls and boys sleeping "under the same roof" in overcrowded dormitories. They also discovered the practice of holding children under sixteen at the city and county jails, explaining, "they are kept from older prisoners . . . but if the county jail is crowded, this is difficult to accomplish."[80] By the 1920s the national reforms that had put in place the Detention Home did not operate smoothly in San Diego, and in some cases the children most in need of professional attention were the least served by the reforms.

Problems also occurred at the Children's Home. It took in many of the county's wards, but its bed capacity did not match county need, and by the 1920s the children assigned there seemed better suited for placement at the Preston, Whittier, or Ventura reformatories. Consider the case of eleven-year-old Bobby Joe Carter. On January 8, 1920, the juvenile court placed Bobby Joe in the CH, citing him as "delinquent" and his home as "unfit." His mother earned $55 per month as a maid for a missionary couple and was in good health. But a cloud of immorality hung over this mother and son: she gave birth to Bobby Joe just eleven days after marrying his father, was now divorced, and did not know the whereabouts of Bobby Joe's father. Bobby Joe ran away from the facility only six days after the court admitted him, demonstrating that for some children, the CH served as a detention center rather than the comfortable abode promoted by organizers.[81]

Despite these problems, the county focused on budgetary concerns by establishing the SDCWC in 1920. Commissioners handled a wide spectrum of issues among the increasingly diverse community that included benefits to Catholic, Jewish, and Protestant families. Their fund approvals sent several children to the federal boarding school for Indians, Sherman Institute; dealt with immigration issues; and decided where dependent children should live. A July 1920 meeting proved typical for the commission, as it decided who would receive aid: two Italian mothers of small children, one abandoned by her tubercular husband, the other left dependent on the county when law enforcement caught her fugitive husband and returned him to prison; a newly delivered Mexican woman struggling to care for her newborn and her invalid mother; two elderly men, an "old Indian" born in 1840 and an eighty-six-year-old Episcopalian widower, described as a "superior old man" riddled with eczema; and several orphaned children made wards of the juvenile court.[82] Throughout the summer, concern surrounded applicants with ties to Mexico and several tubercular patients who came to the attention of the commission as well as one family known "for years" to commissioner Mrs. Palmer, who described them as "a disgrace to San Diego; they have interbred until all are thorough degenerates." Palmer was exact in her advice to the commissioners: "The family should not be aided, and every agency used to break up this household and correct conditions." She reported, "This is nothing but a house of assignation."[83]

Reformers had long voiced concern over these kinds of issues; however, it took state investigations to professionalize decisions and assistance. A task of the commission was to oversee standardization among programs, and on August 31, 1920, representatives from twenty-three agencies met to consider implementing the Community Welfare Council. Nine of the agencies represented local chapters of national organizations such as the YWCA, the Salvation Army, and the WCTU, and the other fourteen representatives spoke for San Diego–specific organizations like the CH, the BGAS, and NH. Their involvement highlighted the concerns of a diverse group led by representatives from four administrative associations: the Charities Endorsement Board, the chamber of commerce, the merchants' association, and the Manufacturers' and Employers' Association. Charity workers and professionals alike attended the meeting, and they voted unanimously in favor of launching the Welfare Council, which would develop into San Diego's Community Chest (and subsequently the city's United Way chapter).[84]

In spite of this unity, religious differences began to influence social welfare decisions. Minutes from meetings in 1923 show a growing angst over the handling of relief among Catholic relief recipients. At issue was the reality that most of the city's philanthropy came from Protestant benefactors and that Catholic Charities did not do its share to replenish the fund. The council decided to withhold funds promised to Catholic Charities, perhaps thinking it would spark fund-raising in Catholic parishes. But the action only irritated the Catholic Charities leadership. To try to calm tensions, the council invited Catholic Charities director Father Michael Sullivan to a meeting as an act it certainly understood as benevolent. Sullivan, however, charged the council with behaving badly, calling "attention to the extensive charitable work undertaken in the city by the Catholic Charities, and to the large percentage of Catholics among the Mexican and Italian population of the city which groups are the people most needing relief." Citing discrimination against Catholics, the priest believed a Catholic should sit on the council's board of directors, and he announced Catholic Charities intended to "discontinue participation in the Community Chest in 1924."[85] Sullivan's threat was serious, but so was the council's response: it deleted all requests from and grants to Catholic Charities in its 1924 support. Instead of aiding Catholic Mexican and Italian families, the Welfare Council decided to give its attention to the Community Music Association ($3,500); County Parent Teacher Federation ($300); La Jolla Free Hospitalization ($500); and the upkeep of the Community Welfare Council building ($3,500).[86] Whereas the Welfare Council proclaimed to be concerned with the health and welfare of all San Diegans, the budget clearly indicated otherwise, as Catholic Charities was nixed from its budget. The documents do not indicate a prejudicial mind-set in their budget deliberation; however, the reality of discrimination against Catholics throughout the country cannot be overlooked as influencing the Welfare Council decision. Certainly, Fr. Sullivan believed this to be the case.

Transitioning to professional practices was not easy for public or private institutions in San Diego. Travelers Aid personnel admitted it took several decades for their organization to fully adopt standardized practices, stating in their 1937 report, "It is a longtime planning for the good of less fortunate children."[87] While the CH had implemented professional admittance standards with the juvenile justice laws in 1909, it did not employ its first social worker until 1930. This step moved it along in re-envisioning its purpose in the community.[88] By 1938 it had refined its mission to care for children who "did not fit into the accepted pattern of behavior. . . .

Boys and girls, particularly adolescents, who have not been able to adjust to the complex pattern of life as we know it today. Not the delinquents ... but the misfits."[89] The shift from day care and boarding of adjusted children to the expansion of court-appointed care of "delinquent" and "misfit" children occurred gradually and with the collaboration of other agencies. The Children's Home could make this shift because reformers recognized the need for more day nurseries located near the worksites where parents labored, and they worked to establish these resources.

The expansion of day care shows the effort by professionals to provide families with more than charity. Parents reacted positively to the growth of day nurseries but balked at reforms that challenged parental custody rights, and finding the balance between assisting and controlling families would be a constant struggle for childcare advocates. The creation of a settlement house program helped ease the strain of limited social welfare resources for Mexican-descent families. Reformers established Neighborhood House because of the Mexican Revolution and the growing anti-immigrant sentiment in the region. Whereas the Children's Home balked at taking in children whose parents were not citizens, Neighborhood House embraced this group of children and adolescents.

CHAPTER FIVE

Neighborhood Care

Localizing the Settlement House Movement

> I do not believe anyone on the border can guess what a gen-
> eration of Mexican children might become were they properly
> taught not only English and the three Rs, but also skilled hand
> work, offering a real opportunity to earn a decent living.
>
> —Edith Shatto King, "My Mexican Neighbors," *Survey*, 1917

In 1917 Wood and Daisy Worchester returned to San Diego with their fifteen-month-old son when Wood was offered the position of chief probation officer. They had lived in San Diego for a short time when Wood ran its Associated Charities, and they looked forward to new opportunities; but when they arrived, they learned the position had gone to another man with more local connections. Their situation soon changed, when the reform community asked Daisy to become the head worker at Neighborhood House (NH), San Diego's first settlement house. Daisy described their year at NH as one "of increasing horror," as World War I gave everything they did "a strange, nightmarish sense of futility," and measles, pneumonia, tuberculosis, and the "terrifying epidemic of influenza" caused heartache for people of all ages and social positions. According to Daisy her family made "no artificial effort to 'share the life' of our neighborhood during that year," as measles took hold of Wood and bronchial pneumonia settled into their baby's chest.[1]

This chapter examines how reformers involved in San Diego's

settlement house movement immersed themselves in the challenges of the area. Through Daisy Worchester's memoir, the writ-
ings of NH residents Edith Shatto King and Helen Marston, and
reports from organizational leaders, we see how settlement life
changed the perspectives of these white, middle-class reformers.
They began their work at NH with preconceived notions about
Mexican culture, but after spending intimate time with the families
who used NH resources—especially mothers and their children—
these reformers developed a deep respect and affection for their
Mexican neighbors in the Barrio Logan community. We also see
how people in the community responded to these reformers.

Historians of the settlement house movement have noted how
it laid the foundation for women to secure a "female reform network" through which they introduced child labor laws and protective labor legislation, participated in city beautiful campaigns,
and led debates in favor of female suffrage.[2] In San Diego that
female reform network operated through the College Woman's
Club (CWC). Several members had gained social welfare experience as residents in the nation's most influential settlement houses,
namely, Hull House in Chicago and Denison House in Boston;
and through their citywide investigation of San Diego's social welfare landscape, they became keenly aware of the absence of a settlement in San Diego. Published as *The Pathfinder Social Survey*, the
CWC study originated as part of the larger cleanup campaign associated with hosting the Panama-California Exposition between
1915 and 1917, and the findings quantified the types and extent of
day care, recreational options, public health access, and vocational
training programs in the city. The survey also noted the existence
of job, housing, and educational discrimination toward immigrant and newly migrated families, and identified Barrio Logan/
Logan Heights as a community with great need. Neighborhood
House emerged in 1914 as a result of the CWC survey.[3]

These reformist women recognized the political and economic
benefits that came with their social positions as white, middle-
class, educated professionals and used that status in their advocacy.
Women in California had secured the vote in 1911, and CWC mem-

bers utilized their political rights in local, state, and national elections to advance their reform agendas. *The Pathfinder Social Survey* quantified that agenda by providing the group and the city's leadership at large with a template for how to develop a social welfare program. CWC members residing in NH also made an impression on those who lived in the community, for most upper- and middle-class whites stayed far away from Barrio Logan. Experienced in settlement work, very little in the way of visual poverty surprised these reformers, but the friendships they made with residents of the area did surprise them. Laura Rodríguez grew up in the *barrio* and remembered CWC member Helen Marston as one of a group of young settlement house workers who walked the neighborhood to get to know the people who lived in "the midst of the cruelest kind of poverty,"[4] yet she found other reformers too focused on an Americanization agenda that emphasized U.S. patriotism, holidays, food menus, and middle-class housekeeping standards.[5]

Living in settlement houses and interacting with people outside their class status demonstrated the commitments of reformers to solving problems associated with poverty. In some instances, reformers learned the languages spoken and cultures practiced in those neighborhoods, and strong bonds formed between them and their working-class neighbors. Agendas differed by region, but all settlement houses included some kind of Americanization project. Objectives often focused on converting immigrants from their supposed peasantlike, "Old World" heritages to "American" methods modeled on white, middle-class ideals of homemaking, child rearing, and paternal support.[6] Because of their location in close proximity to industrial worksites, settlements usually provided day care and kindergarten programs to the children of workers. Consequently, day nurseries in settlement houses often took on larger cultural agendas of Americanization for immigrant children and racial uplift for African American children.[7]

Regional ties certainly influenced settlement house relationships. In San Diego some Mexican-descent neighbors had recently immigrated to the city, while others could trace their connections to the area through several generations. The same is true for resident workers, as some had been born and raised in San Diego, and these common roots may have kindled a positive relationship despite their cultural and class differences. Both groups understood the geographic and cultural space where NH operated, and perhaps that knowledge allowed them to better navigate prejudice and discrimination. Whatever the backgrounds of those visiting NH, they benefited from the resources and programs offered at the site. The settlement house movement touched San Diego twenty years after most cities of its size, and stayed limited to NH until 1929 when Casa de Salud opened about five miles south of San Diego's downtown district in National City.[8] But its positive effect on the people in the area cannot be overstated. Medical attention, nutritional advisories, bilingual education, day care, recreational activities, and civil rights advocacy flowed through NH to the families living in Barrio Logan.

Alongside the Associated Charities, the juvenile court system, and the Children's Home, settlement house programs expanded social services to Mexican-descent families during a time when they faced overt discrimination. African Americans also began using NH services in the 1920s and experienced similar assistance from programs. Well into the 1950s, NH held separate and distinct programs for adult African Americans, such as dances for young people and cooking classes for mothers held on nights when no other group would be visiting the center. However, children's programs, especially sports teams for boys, were racially mixed.

Prior to the founding of NH in 1914, the CWC and some church congregations, primarily Catholic parishes, advocated for bringing basic services to poor Mexican and Mexican American families. But the CWC became the first organized group to do so in a professionally informed manner. Two central themes developed from their *Pathfinder* research: a need for coordinated oversight of social programs, and the need to direct aid toward underserved groups, such as families who had recently immigrated from Mexico.[9] Fighting from the Mexican Revolution added traumatic weight to the region experienced by few other American communities during the same period.[10] Anti-immigrant (especially anti-Mexican) and anti-union policies allowed for a hostile climate to grow in the city, and CWC members believed a settlement house would help calm some of the prejudices.

According to one history of the CWC, members of its social service committee initially voted on sponsoring a dance hall or working with the probation court to address concerns about the spread of juvenile delinquency. Despite reform programs such as vocational training at the Free Industrial School (FIS), young people had limited options for age-appropriate leisure activities, and they found that truancy among children from the working class continued to be a problem. Adolescents could leave school at the age of fourteen to work, but not all adolescents earned wages, choosing instead to loiter in downtown streets and neighborhoods. The CWC voted to focus their efforts on this population by developing a dance hall for young people, to keep adolescents off the street, occupied, and supervised.[11] This focus fell in line with the national concern over offering young people safe and chaperoned options for heterosexual engagements.

While some CWC members began work on the dance hall, other members set their sights on the larger population in the area and began planning for a settlement house. The *Pathfinder* provided the data for targeting which services should be offered at the future settlement, as well as the work already accomplished in the city. For example, out of five hundred places inspected in 1912–1913 by the Department of Public Health, officials had ordered two hundred closed to residential living. Many of the condemned dwellings were located along the waterfront and grossly overpopulated, such as one tenement that "housed twenty-three persons in four rooms."[12] Survey authors, Fred and Edith Shatto King, underscored that such attention to cleaning up the city was admirable but that the problems did not cease with demolition.

In addition to the rank physical spaces, city physician Francis Mead had concluded in 1910 that the infant mortality among "Americans" was low, but "high among Mexicans who are hopelessly ignorant."[13] The *Pathfinder* echoed Mead's conclusions regarding mortality numbers, citing that out of 1,191 documented births in 1913, eighty-five babies (or 7 percent) died before reaching the age of one year. Additionally, 135 children under the age of five died that year. The Kings explained: "This is perhaps not large compared with the infant death rate in eastern industrial cities, but it is far too large for a city whose natural advantages and size should make ideal conditions for babies." The investigators argued that while the city relegated large sums of public money to educating school-age children, "irreparable injury" to many of these children had already occurred due to a general lack of care and proper nutrition. Dr. Mead's comment regarding Mexicans and ignorance demonstrates that prejudice among authorities influenced health care delivery and likely contributed to the high infant mortality. Some milk inspections were in place, but the *Pathfinder* authors pointed to poor maternal education, stating that "it is safe to say that at least half, probably more [deaths], could have been prevented if mothers had been taught the proper care of their children, and if there had been a safe milk supply." The survey authors also chastised the women and doctors of the city for not entering into public debates about the purity of the milk supply, charging, "If they do not personally come before the Council in support of proper ordinances, these conditions will continue to exist."[14]

The *Pathfinder* authors were likely referencing the activism by women's clubs in major cities regarding tainted milk supplies. In Los Angeles ordinances moving dairy cows out of city boundaries met heavy opposition from farmers and did not pass until 1908.[15] As in Los Angeles, a vibrant women's club collective existed in San Diego. Club news had been distributed in San Diego since 1900 through the monthly magazine the *California Club Woman*, whose subscribers tended to be white and wealthy or middle-class, and typically well educated. Like many women's club magazines, the publication included a healthy dose of articles on art, literature, amateur poetry, community happenings, and musings of its members. It also offered updates on clubwomen conferences and events from around the country, and editorials on international news.[16] CWC members were part of this readership, but they differed significantly from most of its subscribers by taking a critical view of the city's political leadership. Professionals like the Kings and Worchesters mistrusted San Diego's politicians and political structure, comparing them to the "machines" they had encountered in eastern cities. They also wanted to motivate clubwomen to take a more active role in the public forums attached to policy making, such as implementing an agenda to secure safe milk.

Perhaps the struggles by the Los Angeles advocates influenced the direction offered in the *Pathfinder*. It included two suggestions for curbing infant mortality: first, that the city establish a visiting nurse program whose professionals would train mothers in the proper care of infants; and second, to create a free day nursery for the babies of working mothers. Ultimately, the *Pathfinder* underscored an important reality: "The greatest need of the community in its present undeveloped state of social consciousness and unconcern of many of its citizens for the needs of the whole, is a coordinating of social interests."[17] Their study supported the ongoing work of the AC but also emphasized the need for a social settlement in order to bring San Diego in line with other communities of its size.

CWC members followed through with its suggestion, and within months of publishing the survey, opened NH on Fourteenth Street near Market, two blocks north of the FIS. Edith Shatto King accepted the job as head resident, a position she would keep for only one year, resigning in December 1915 because her husband took ill. But her leadership guided the settlement's opening and expansion into the FIS building. The Barrio Logan location promoted the goals of both the FIS and the CWC to reach out to the immigrant communities of Mexican, Portuguese, and Italian families, but the FIS had fallen onto difficult times. Having built a new facility in 1912 at Sixteenth and Beardsley Streets, FIS volunteers discovered by 1914 that the school suffered from too few students and financial contributors. Because vocational education had been fully implemented in the public-school curriculum in 1897, the FIS really had no business expanding into a new building. As a solution its board invited NH to share its building, and on August 15, 1915, CWC's executive board agreed to move NH to the larger space. The move offered a solution to the financial problems of the FIS and connected NH residents to young people already involved with the industrial school program.[18]

Within a year of opening its doors, NH programs influenced the area, especially by bringing quality education to underserved children. Probation officer Blair explained in the house's 1916 annual report that the children lived ten blocks from the nearest public kindergarten, and that many attended only to the third grade, so they missed out on vocational education. He emphasized, "The houses of the children (sometimes mere hovels) offer them nothing. We find them idling in the street and on vacant lots; the girls marry young with no preparation for life. Much lawlessness, such as petty thievery and destruction of property, exists and our juvenile court *is kept busy in this district.* The largest number of our juvenile court cases come from this district" (asterisks in the original).[19]

To change these neighborhood dynamics, the organizers of NH implemented a full range of social programs that included a day nursery, kindergarten, recreational activities for children and youth, instruction in English language, and education in parenting and hygienic housekeeping. Mothers who brought their children to NH's day nursery typically worked in the area's laundries, olive works, and fish canneries. Fathers also labored in the canneries, as well as on the wharf and in the lumberyards. Attendance figures for the earliest years of the day nursery have been hard to track, but in 1915 thirty children filled the NH kindergarten. Settlement leadership had employed Miss Alice Andrews, a former teacher from La Jolla's Episcopalian private school, the Bishop's School, "on a very small salary" to teach kindergarten; and the full class was "all that [Miss Andrews] could handle alone," but it offered a partial remedy for the "many neglected-looking children playing in the streets."[20]

Additionally, in its first year of operation, sixty children were enrolled in the Saturday sewing classes; "swarms" of boys used the playground in supervised recreation; about one hundred young men and women attended Thursday-evening dances (closely chaperoned by the Kings); and an average of thirty adults attended

FIG. 15. Women preparing sardines at the Normandy Company, 1924. Cannery work provided women from the Mexican, Italian, and Portuguese communities opportunities to earn wages. © San Diego History Center.

English-language classes held at night. One can imagine the bustling atmosphere generated by so many programs. Organizers also reported high attendance at cooking classes for women and children, the day nursery, a folk-dancing class, a club for young girls, and "a large club of young Mexican men for the purpose of discussing civic questions." A few Greek men attended the adult English-language classes, but nearly 90 percent of attendees at NH programs were of Mexican descent and spoke only Spanish.[21] These programs were certainly not unique to those offered in settlement houses across the country, but the convenience of these programs operating out of one location was new to San Diego and proved successful.

NH staff also addressed the problems with impure milk and a general absence of affordable medical services. In 1916 the Public Health Department had to admit, "It is now a well-established fact

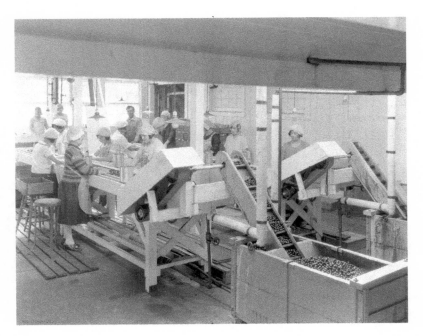

Fɪɢ. 16. Women of diverse ages pack olives for the Old Mission Olive Factory, 1928. © San Diego History Center.

that San Diego offers little to the tubercular, in fact such cases frequently do poorly here."[22] Whereas the department was referring to the city as a whole, many of the people who lived in the NH service area were afflicted with troubling illnesses such as tuberculosis and influenza. One preventive solution came that year when the city's Board of Health made the settlement the site of a free milk station. NH residents also opened a free health clinic on Thursday afternoons and adopted the classic Progressive strategy of using visiting nurses to extend care to the neighborhood.

Neighborhood House provided services for families who would otherwise be denied assistance because of their citizenship status or ethnicity, but it was not a panacea for ending discriminatory practices in the city. When the Worchesters lived in NH during 1917, Daisy committed much of her day to dealing with the women and children who came to the settlement's milk station, health clinic, and English-language classes. In her role as head resident, she observed the intense prejudices directed at Mexican families and desperately tried to end the discrimination, but with little success. Daisy related the scenario of a mother of four very sick children being denied adequate medical attention because they were Mexican. The mother, Mrs. Garcia, appeared at the settlement one night, desperate for help. Worchester followed Garcia to her home, where she saw a baby "lying on the only bed in the house," sick with pneumonia, and three other children "tossing about, all broken out with the measles," atop a pile of gunnysacks. She explained to Garcia that the children needed hospitalization, but Garcia had already sent for a doctor, because she feared her children would die in the County Hospital. Daisy soon discovered, however, that the "well-known baby specialist" who had endeared himself to her because of his "kindness and skill" in caring for her son treated Mexican patients differently. The doctor demanded a $5 payment before he would even look at the sick baby. Worchester ran the two blocks to the settlement, gathered some money, and immediately returned to the Garcia household. The doctor collected his fee, listened to the baby's chest with his stethoscope, and coldly pronounced the baby dead. To Daisy's shock, he left the home without attending to the other three children, who were obviously in serious condition.[23] The physician's callousness stuck with Worchester and strengthened her resolve to help women like Mrs. Garcia. Some of that assistance came through the growth of NH programs.

Some mothers also began requesting information about birth control. In recalling her interaction with Mrs. Ortega, a mother of eight, Worchester recognized the limitations connected to talking about birth control in a public setting. Mrs. Ortega wanted to know why Worchester could bring "milk to babies," "school to children," and "English to Mexican men" but did not share with the women the secrets of birth control.[24] Worchester expressed her frustration about the episode but did not admit to any further conversation with the woman. In 1917 it would have been illegal for Worchester to pass on any product to the mother, but perhaps she shared with Mrs. Ortega in private how to access and use douches, condoms or diaphragms.[25] Yet these products were hard to find, expensive, and seldom available to working families. Questions about birth control methods show the personal connections made across class lines, but they also demonstrate the vast social distance between the two women. Access to goods and services that could improve the material condition of families simply did not exist for someone like Mrs. Ortega. The settlement house movement allowed for women from diverse backgrounds to interact in private spaces over private concerns, and birth control enthusiasts targeted the settlement house as a logical site for hosting maternal clinics. But there is no evidence that in this early phase of settlement work in San Diego, Worthington and other NH residents distributed birth control information or products.[26]

cwc member Helen Marston also recognized incidences of discrimination toward Mexicans and believed her involvement in NH programs helped her overcome cultural "preconceptions" of Mexicans as lazy thieves and liars. In an article for the mouthpiece of social reform, the *Survey*, Helen pointed out that women in Barrio Logan carried "the double burden of home with its many babies and of work in the fish canneries, whither they go, day or night, at the sound of the whistles." Regarding the presumed idleness of Mexican men and boys, she explained, "Some of them work for desperately long stretches. . . . The idling which we so resent is sometimes merely the result of spurts of night work, followed by a few hours of sleep in the adjacent lumber yards."[27] But she did not always think this way.

Helen Marston's advocacy for the people of Barrio Logan strengthened with her settlement house life. As a native San Diegan born to one of the city's most prestigious couples, Marston admitted, "I grew up to think all Mexicans lazy people, with a carefree philosophy that put off doing everything until tomorrow."[28] Experiences during her years at Wellesley College and in eastern settlement houses, and interactions with people she met at NH, influenced her ideological shift. She embraced "public motherhood" as described by her mentor Jane Addams, learning at Hull House that settlement residents should immerse themselves in the neighborhood culture(s) by mingling with people at their church celebrations, shopping at nearby marts, playing with the children, and helping mothers tend to their babies. Marston did all these things and hoped her efforts at NH showed the people living in Barrio Logan that she sincerely cared about their wellbeing.

CWC members had initiated programs at NH to address a lack of resources among Mexican-descent families; however, these families were not alone in experiencing discriminatory practices in job hiring, access to medical attention, housing, and good education for their children. Only a few hundred African Americans lived in the city when the settlement opened in 1914, highlighting their minority status and marking them for racial persecution. In fact, African Americans in San Diego understood the city to be a sundown town. Their numbers increased during World War I to about a thousand people, or 1 percent of the total population, and many of these families lived in the segregated Barrio Logan known to them as Logan Heights.[29] Evidence from the AC and TASSD indicates that advocates working in those organizations had little knowledge of the needs of black families, let alone possible resources for them. A complaint in 1918 by W. D. B. Mead of the YMCA to the AC suggests the racial dynamics at play in the city. Writing about a "colored man ... soliciting funds and obtaining credit for a YMCA in San Diego," Mead insisted the man had "absolutely no authority" from his organization to launch such a campaign and asked for the Charities to investigate matters. Informal inquiries by AC agents (who were white) led them to learn about a growing African American community in the Logan Heights area, and its need for a YMCA that accepted nonwhite visitors. The man proved his authorization by Southern Baptist authorities in Los Angeles, but whites in San Diego did not want to admit that a "colored man" could be an authorized and legitimate solicitor.[30] Their ignorance of this man's legitimacy and task highlights the deep segregation present in San Diego.

Racial bans in the city led the black community to bitterly refer to it as "the Mississippi of the West."[31] Most restaurants denied seating to African Americans, theater owners directed them to bal-

cony seats, and cab transportation for them was limited to the
one black-owned cab company in the area. That company could
not accept fares outside the boundaries of Logan Heights.³² The
"racial ban" at restaurants, hotels, and dance pavilions continued
into the late 1940s and caused one post–World War II study on
race relations to proclaim: "The opposition to the patronage of
negroes and other colored minorities in San Diego's places of public resort seems to be tighter and more extensive than in almost
any of the other major urban communities of the Pacific Coast.
Although these discriminations are in violation of the Civil Code
of California, some proprietors appear to make a practice of set-
tling such cases out of court. In other cases, the payment of fines
seems to be regarded by proprietors as a routine expense of doing
business in San Diego."³³

NH advocates understood the critical nature of services provided
by the settlement, and while they could not do much to address
job and housing discrimination, their health programs improved
maternal and infant health in dramatic fashion. NH residents began
their engagements with mothers and children in the era when the
federal government established a separate unit to address maternal, infant, and child health. The Children's Bureau, established
in 1912 as a division of the Department of Commerce and Labor,
represents one of the most influential expressions of maternalism, as female reformers used it to assert a national foothold in
developing maternal assistance and child-saving programs. Federal programs launched in this era included the Smith-Lever Act
of 1914, the Smith-Hughes Act of 1917, and the Sheppard-Towner
Maternity and Infancy Act (STMIA) passed in 1921. Taken together,
these actions helped address the health and welfare needs among
impoverished people and infused money into areas previously
ignored or overlooked by political initiatives as in San Diego.³⁴

Female-led agencies like the Children's Bureau strengthened
the provision of health education among pregnant, new, and nursing mothers as a strategy to improve infant health. Mothers contacted the Children's Bureau for any kernel of advice on pregnancy,
infertility, birth processes, postpartum healthcare, and infant care,

writing over I25,000 letters each year. Reformers realized women needed more personal contacts, so they began campaigning for federal funds to initiate preventive health care across the country, and the STMIA allowed for this kind of public intervention. STMIA gave federal money to states to develop educational programming, which included instruction on nutrition, hygiene, and general maternal/infant care. It also funded child-health clinics and visiting nurses who specialized in the care of pregnant and newly delivered women.[35]

STMIA moneys were distributed to communities on a matching-fund basis so as to promote state involvement with the federal government. The STMIA became "the culmination of long-standing efforts to get the government to take responsibility for child welfare," and it became the program in which clubwomen, settlement house residents, and public-health workers collaborated in their maternalism.[36] As the first legislative victory after national female suffrage was secured, STMIA represents the strength of maternalism.[37] Unfortunately, partisan politics and fear over a suffragist push for an equal rights amendment led to the demise of the STMIA in I929, but during its eight-year tenure, funds from the STMIA dramatically improved the health of pregnant and postpartum women, and newborns and infants.

NH residents designed programming to address maternal and infant health by first using private funding, then Smith-Hughes and STMIA funds. Through both the milk station and its open-air school for tuberculosis-ridden children, NH residents encountered many more children afflicted with communicable and treatable disease. In an effort to prevent further outbreaks of measles, diphtheria, and influenza, settlement residents took advantage of the federal grant money offered through the Smith-Hughes Act of I917. Intended to bring health services to areas isolated from quality medical care, these grants emerged from the "rural crisis" noted by politicians, government officials, reformers, and academics. All agreed that vocational education designed to improve "family farmers' productivity and physical health could help remedy inequities perpetuated by racism and ethnic prejudice" in rural areas.[38]

Communities negatively affected by industrial change could also apply for Smith-Hughes grants. NH primarily served families who either farmed or labored in agriculture-related industries, such as fruit, vegetable, and fish canning, making the settlement grant-eligible. NH secured funding and used it to establish in 1918 the Little Mothers Club, led by registered nurse Mary Hart Taylor, who was in charge of the city's child hygiene division. A strategy to develop good mothering for future generations, the program trained young girls in the care of pre- and postnatal babies. Hart Taylor also implemented the testing of Mexican children for "subnormal mental and physical development" as a way to diagnose possible learning problems and intervene with specialized care during a child's formative years.[39] By 1921 Hart Taylor took charge of supervising visiting nurses in providing medical examinations for babies, distributing pure milk to families, and teaching hygiene classes to mothers and daughters: all programs that had been suggested in the *Pathfinder* and partially funded with Smith-Hughes grants.[40]

Beyond accessing federal grant opportunities, settlement staff established collaborations with existing city programs, such as its book loan program with the public library.[41] The settlement also hired a teacher who held a weekly cooking and sewing class for local mothers. The popularity of these classes prompted volunteers to build large ovens in the settlement's backyard, along with donating material for the sewing classes. These experiences gave women a chance to gather socially while fulfilling their domestic responsibilities.[42] Many lifelong residents of the neighborhood fondly remember their mothers using those ovens and noted that the settlement created an important community space for their mothers.[43]

Despite these advances, the first few years of operation proved troubling for both NH residents and those they helped. When NH opened in 1914, the Mexican Revolution and the U.S. entry into World War I contributed to suspicious thoughts about immigrants or citizens who did not regularly speak English. The development of NH needs to be viewed in light of nativist agendas spreading throughout the country but particularly in Southern California, where concerns about border security heightened long-standing tensions between Anglos and Mexicans. As Mexican laborers ventured north, their presence strengthened the Americanization movement in California.

Supporters of Americanization also found favor among California's reform community, including some settlement house workers. Governor Hiram Johnson acted on this nativist energy by creating in 1913 the California Immigration and Housing Commission (CIHC). These supporters argued that home visits and settlement house education could teach Mexican families Anglo standards of food preparation, hygiene, and familial ethics. Writing for the CIHC in 1915, home teacher Amanda Mathews Chase minced no words in her justification for why Californians benefited from Americanization programs: "Mexicans lack social mobility because they are shiftless and thriftless. . . . These people are *not* a hopeless proposition. But they need education of a peculiar sort—education that shall be a disciplinary tonic—that shall give them standards—that amounts to evolution."[44]

Most NH advocates agreed on the importance of providing medical attention and safe gathering spaces to children and adolescents; however, they debated the extent to which the settlement should engage in Americanization. In an interview regarding the history of NH, Helen Marston "spoke with disdain" of those volunteers and staff dedicated to Americanization. She recounted how a woman from the Daughters of the American Revolution complained that children spoke Spanish at the settlement, and then stopped visiting the settlement when learning that NH residents had no problem with the children naturally falling in and out of Spanish.[45] Marston believed NH had room for both American and Mexican cultures.

This incident is a reminder of how reformers' actions reflected the societal ideas of their time. Settlement house workers were long familiar with cultural barriers between themselves and their largely immigrant neighbors. Despite their university degrees and professional experience, some reformers looked to racial and ethnic stereotypes when deciding an individual's worthiness to participate in social programs. These choices controlled how the poor

could organize their daily lives, often requiring them to free themselves of Native customs and adopt American standards. Considered more healthy and efficient, American methods included shifts
in diet (pasta to potatoes), medical care (physicians instead of mid-
wives), and emphasizing the importance of biological family rather
than extended networks of fictive and familial kin. These changes
became managed in the settlement house, a space where reformers
typically maintained power by controlling who accessed programs.
Yet historian Elizabeth Rose found that some programs bent their
rules to incorporate customs familiar to neighborhood families,
such as in Philadelphia, where Jewish immigrants claimed their
neighborhood center as a place where cultural heritage could be
preserved and residents engaged in an "ongoing dialogue" about
the role(s) experts should play in their lives.[46]

Mexicans engaged in a similar cultural dialogue in San Diego.
In the most public examples of support, Edith Shatto King and
Helen Marston publicized the organization's activities by writing
articles for the *Survey*. The publication drew an international audience of reformers and was recognized in the social reform arena
as the most influential and widely read professional journal of its
time.[47] Shatto King's essay "My Mexican Neighbors" appeared in
1917, when the city's anxiety over border issues had reached a high
pitch. Three years later, in 1920, the journal published Marston's
"Mexican Traits," which shows a keen intellectual understanding
of the area's intercultural environment. Their articles were not
the first essays on San Diego to appear in the *Survey* during the
1910s–1930s, but the few others about the city reflected the booster
tone of trying to attract people to the city for leisure and tourism, rather than the activist bent of Shatto King and Marston.[48]

Contrary to the zealous nativism shown by Amanda Mathews
Chase, the messages penned by Shatto King and Marston noted
an inherent loyalty and industry among Mexicans. They believed
providing Mexican immigrants with better health care and housing represented a humane and just action, and they highlighted
how learning English could improve job opportunities for Mexican laborers. Both women admitted that their time spent with

Mexican people through their settlement house work ran counter to what they had learned during their San Diego childhoods, and they encouraged other whites to look beyond stereotypes that depicted Mexicans as a lazy, ignorant group of people.[49]

Shatto King explained how Anglo prejudices against Mexican families, especially toward Spanish-speaking children attending the public schools, confined them to a life of poverty. She chastised teachers who provided special classes for Norwegian immigrants who did not speak English but ignored the educational needs of Mexican children in the same situation. In describing the importance of literacy and vocational education in a child's life, Shatto King emphasized, "I do not believe anyone on the border can guess what a generation of Mexican children might become were they properly taught not only English and the three Rs, but also skilled hand work, offering a real opportunity to earn a decent living."[50]

In her essay Helen Marston focused on reconciling the gendered stereotypes of Mexican couples that she had learned while growing up in San Diego with what she observed in her daily interactions with Mexican families. She entered Barrio Logan believing that Mexican wives and daughters earned wages and performed all domestic duties because Mexican men were lazy, but living at NH changed her mind. She realized her perceptions of an innate laziness among Mexican men could not be proved by experience, noting the problem lay in their "lack of ideas rather than an unwillingness to work." She realized that the ethnocentrism informing her childhood could not be authenticated by her adult interactions with Mexican families. But such a change in perspective did not come immediately, even to someone as devoted to social justice as Helen Marston. She recognized the "distinct effort" made by some Mexican fathers to attend English classes offered at NH, yet Marston also admonished those fathers not in attendance for not trying hard enough to learn technical skills and English.[51] But she also admitted she did not know Mexican fathers as well as mothers, thereby opening the door to understanding how gendered roles proscribed one's opportunity to work, and that racial and ethnic identities compounded these restrictions.

Marston was not alone in her revelations. Recalling how her father blamed Mexicans if anything was missing about the garden, Edith Shatto King admitted, "As a child, I was never taught to fear or hate the "dirty" Mexicans, only to despise them." Mexican and Anglo children did not play together, and it was that segregation that eventually shook Shatto King's thoughts on Mexicans. She recounted an incident from childhood in which a group of Mexican children had grown angry at not being able to play in the favorite spot of Anglo children, and their anger confused her.[52] But she realized as an adult the role this incident played in her social reform, setting her on a path that eventually led her to implementing English classes at NH so the children could perform better in the public schools. Shatto King's actions had little to do with Americanizing or control. Rather, she wanted to remedy some of the past hurt her family and friends had inflicted on their Mexican neighbors.

Stereotypes learned in childhood were well imprinted on the two women and sometimes made their way into the essays. Both women romanticized the poverty of Mexican migrants and offered their readers a sanitized view of crude conditions. In "My Mexican Neighbors," Shatto King wrote, "On moonlight nights one rarely passed by without hearing the soft tones of La Paloma from a guitar or a violin, and sometimes laughter and gay Spanish words, coming from the shadows under the pepper trees. [Others] liked the open starlight better than shack or garden. They traveled in groups and camped about the country wherever work was to be found ... their fat brown babies close by, naked in the sun."[53]

Civic leaders had long been using a romanticized Latino culture to entice newcomers to their communities. The 1915 Panama-California Exposition exploited the beauty of a Spanish past, popular fiction embraced the stereotypes, and advertisers painted festive Latin American scenes on fruit boxes to entice buyers.[54] But the reality of life for those who came to NH looking for clean milk and free health checks was far different from these marketed versions. Shatto King failed to explain that Mexican migrants had no other choice than to keep their babies in the field while they labored through twelve-hour days, often in the hot sun. Likewise, living under the open sky was their only option, not one of choice. Surely, King as NH's head worker understood these realities, so her decision to paint an idealistic picture is curious and perhaps was used to appeal to readers' visions of San Diego as a southwestern paradise.

Marston also romanticized living conditions, writing that the Mexicans' "primitive ways of living help" their situation, because "cracks let in air, sunshine is sought for its heat, and there is little furniture to make cleaning hard." Her characterization of their poverty belies her devotion to ending their poverty, and one is reminded of the strength of stereotypes. Also puzzling is her belief in an inherent dishonesty among Mexican people, especially men and boys. She wrote, "Everyone knows that the Mexican does not have the same standards of honesty [as] the American," claiming nationalism and gender had much to do with the trait.[55]

What, exactly, can we make of this woman who turned her back on society's coming-out parties to face the grit and grime of poverty? Marston embodied the characteristics of the New Woman—young, white, upper- and middle-class, college-educated, enthusiastic, and energized by the possibilities of change—and she found likeminded women at Wellesley, in visits to Hull House, and upon her return to San Diego. Publishing in the *Survey* proved the strength of these connections. Like many of her contemporaries, Helen Marston rejected marriage and childbearing upon graduation, focusing instead on advocating for increased social welfare in her hometown. Her parents taught her the stance that with wealth came responsibility to help those less fortunate. The Social Gospel—the responsibility of the wealthy (and thus most capable) to provide for those less fortunate—had informed her parents' philanthropy and certainly influenced Marston's work in elevating the status of Mexican families.[56] The steadfast philanthropy of her parents nurtured her social activism from the time she was a young girl. Her Wellesley education and subsequent training as a settlement worker may have intensified her convictions to help the poor, but George and Anna Lee Gunn Marston gave her their blessing to throw herself into San Diego's under-world. In fact, when Neighborhood House fell short of operating funds in the summer of 1925, Marston's father stepped in with a $700 donation to get them through the year.[57] Her sister, Mary Marston, joined her in volunteering at the settlement and ended up embracing it as her life's work. Thus, NH became a critical program for the Marston family's philanthropy.

Marston took a different path than most women of her social position, but she first had to come to terms with long-held stereotypes informing her attitudes about why certain men and women remained oppressed. Marston unwittingly reveals that in some areas she clung to irrational stereotypes of her Mexican friends and believed women using the milk station needed to understand and adopt American ways in order to better preserve the health of their children. We see Marston's humanness in this contradiction: some reformers did not set out to control those in their care, but in their attempts to improve lives, they, in fact, did issue a fair amount of control over people's lives.[58] Interestingly, Marston posited that political injustice had influenced Mexican poverty, noting, "Is it not possible that these descendants of the Mayas are a backward people today, because for centuries they were deprived in their own country of the proper soil in which to develop?"[59] Land reform in Mexico harkened back to Mexico's independence from Spain in 1821 and continued into the twentieth century. Marston's comment was simply acknowledging her engagement with the larger social issues at work in the lives of Mexican immigrants, although few in San Diego's elite sympathized with the plight of landless peasants. In fact, many San Diegans became angered with the jump in immigration that resulted from the outbreak of the Mexican Revolution in 1910. Marston opened herself to criticism from her contemporaries by acknowledging Mexicans had been unjustly denied property, for this was truly libelous thinking for a southwestern Anglo in 1920, and especially for an elite woman.

Marston's activism strengthened over time as she led the formation of the San Diego chapter of the Women's International League for Peace and Freedom and joined the American Civil

Liberties Union (ACLU). As a member of the ACLU, in 1934 Marston made six trips to the Imperial Valley to support Mexican migrant farm workers striking against the lettuce, melon, and pea farmers. These acts were truly defiant, since the strike ultimately hurt her father's business when lettuce growers threatened a boycott of the Marston Department Stores. At the age of forty-three, Helen settled into a more traditional life by marrying and having a son; however, her husband, John Beardsley, a deputy city attorney in Los Angeles and an ACLU member, was devoted to social justice. A widower, Beardsley found in Marston a partner equally devoted to social justice. Coming to marriage and motherhood later than most women of her generation, Marston hardly gave in to the expectations of her race and class privileges but merely tempered her activism during this part of her life.[60]

Some San Diegans believed Mexican families were inherently communist, thus subversive. Political fear entered all circles of the city, even among those groups committed to helping the underserved, like the Associated Charities. They realized the need for stepping up assistance to Mexican families but thought others might be better equipped. In March 1916 the Charities noted: "The police have recently been arresting a number of Mexican men. Three of the families have had to come to us for assistance. They felt that just as far as it was possible to do so, these families should be turned to the county for help."[61] This decision came four years prior to the formation of the SDCWC, so the source of the county aid is not clear.

San Diegans also worried about the dangers of sickness, as soldiers stationed at Camp Kearney transmitted influenza, measles, and pneumonia throughout the area. The influenza epidemic of 1918 hit Barrio Logan particularly hard, but nervous whites saw only that these life-threatening illnesses would harm their families.[62] From 1918 through 1919, about 7 percent of the city's forty thousand residents caught the flu, and 7 percent of those cases died from the virus. Many victims lived near the waterfront or in Barrio Logan, two areas known for poverty and exposure to transient people. The first official reactions to the flu developed from reports in October 1918 that the virus had attacked soldiers and sailors training in Camp Kearney, located between the city and the international border. Within days, authorities quarantined military sites (Camp Kearney, the naval training camp in Balboa Park, Fort Rosecrans on Point Loma, and the naval air station on North Island) and closed all public amusements and facilities, including churches, schools, libraries, and auction sales. Even women's club meetings were banned. Consequently, the influenza epidemic caused economic hardship, as owners and employees of movie houses, restaurants, pool halls and saloons, and shops lost customers to mandated closures.[63]

In addition to these citywide problems, organizational disarray within the Neighborhood House leadership stunted its effectiveness in its first five years. From 1916 to 1919, leadership shifted every six months or so, few residents signed on for the work, and volunteers found themselves teaching classes as well as doing the heavy house labor.[64] When Marston recruited Daisy Lee Worthington Worchester to take over as head worker in 1917, NH needed "reviving," having suffered from the "blight of war, [and] the disorganization of every form of social work which dealt with foreigners." Worchester described NH activities as "usual" for a settlement program but she also remembers her year in residence as nightmarish and blamed a "corrupt" Board of Supervisors for the lack of concern toward the needy. She charged that they made "certain that every dollar which was spent would do a dollar's worth of good for them and their political aspirations."[65] San Diego's labor organizers also voiced critiques about the city's business practices and jobs moving from San Diego to Tijuana. The San Diego Labor Council reached out to Mexicans living in the city as one way to strengthen the labor movement, yet their efforts provided little sustaining change for an equitable work environment.[66]

Into the 1920s a nod toward Americanization directed settlement programming, but its focus on bringing health resources to the community produced far more influential results.[67] From 1919 to 1929, Mary Snyder directed the settlement, and her ten-year appointment brought stability to the operation. Under Snyder's guidance NH programs and facilities grew, including the purchase of land to enlarge the recreational areas.[68] In its review of 1921, staff counted 340 different people attending its activities, a figure that did not include kindergarten students, the milk station recipients, or health clinic clients. Advocates remained primarily female—its thirteen-member board of directors and four-person staff included only one man, Stanley Millar, boys' assistant—and all staff members were unmarried, as were half of the board members.[69]

One noticeable change in the 1921 report was in its listing of "Clubs for Boys and Girls—American, Mexican, Colored."[70] Social services for African Americans remained minimal into the post–World War II period, and the few resources that did exist derived from the leadership of black community members dedicated to social uplift. In 1929 a group of African American women organized a "colored" branch of the YWCA in Logan Heights, which offered vocational classes, health education, and housing for African American women in need of a temporary home.[71] But when in 1937 a young African American woman arrived at San Diego's Santa Fe train depot and requested directions to a "YWCA for colored women," a white Travelers Aid worker had to make numerous calls to locate appropriate housing. Seemingly unaware of the YWCA branch, the worker explained, "We managed to place her from our list of private places for colored people. She was advised where to go to secure employment."[72] She did not indicate these "private places" for housing and employment, but likely they included the home of African American Rebecca Craft, who in 1934 had founded the Women's Civic League. It provided educational scholarships for children and adolescents as well as distributed food, bedding, clothing, and household goods to African American families living in Logan Heights. The League also took on the battle to hire an African American schoolteacher, a fight it would not win until 1942.[73]

Settlement residents included African American children and youth in programs, yet in a segregated manner. Across the country, settlement residents often separated visitors by race and ethnicity, and usually did not mix cultures within the same dwelling. NH did not officially operate race-specific programs, events, or classes, but it did intentionally segregate individuals within the function. The 1920 Christmas party divided its entertainment into Mexican and "colored," and by 1922 the settlement devoted Saturday-night space to the "colored people," with a mothers and girls culture club meeting in the evening, followed by a social hour for boys and men, especially sailors in port.[74]

Despite these actions, NH advocates succeeded in improving the health among families living in the community, and particularly in lowering the rate of infant mortality among Mexican children. In 1921 the American Child Hygiene Association gladly recognized San Diego as having the third-lowest infant mortality rate among cities with a population of fifty thousand to one hundred thousand. The Public Health Report for the City in 1921 credited nurse Mary Hart Taylor with much of this success. It also noted the cooperation between several organizations and individuals—Women's Federated Clubs, Women's Civic Center, College Woman's Club, Parent Teachers Association, Associated Charities, church aid societies, school nurses, and the Metropolitan Life Insurance Company nurse—as critical elements in lowering infant mortality.[75] Service projects by teen girls from the economically privileged Francis Parker School also lessened the tremendous workload in the NH clinic. The girls helped weigh and measure the babies at NH, sewed baby layettes, and made special food baskets for neighborhood families to enjoy at Thanksgiving and Christmas.[76]

Mary Hart Taylor refused to accept full credit for the program's success, attributing much of the progress to Mrs. Charles Brackett, whom she described as an "untrained assistant" at the NH milk station, who spoke fluent Spanish and possessed an "intimate knowledge of the home life of the Mexican."[77] Professionals like Hart Taylor realized the importance of bilingual interaction even if that communication came from "untrained" personnel. For her, it was critical that Mrs. Brackett served as more than a translator of language and could communicate why a mother would be nervous to take her child to the County Hospital and would call in a *curandera* (community healer) or *partera* (midwife) instead of coming to the settlement's clinic.[78]

For the year 1924, the infant mortality rate declined in San Diego from 59 to 54.7 deaths for children under the age of one year per 1,000 children born alive. This compared to a national average of 79.3 for cities 50,000 to 100,000 (San Diego had an estimated population of 96,445 in 1924).[79] Yet while the infant and maternal mortality rate for the general population declined, it rose among Mexicans. Between 1922 and 1932, only 28 percent of Mexican women in San Diego delivered their babies in a hospital, as opposed to 68 percent for all other groups. The Mexican community feared the County Hospital, because typically one entered the facility when death seemed inevitable. Consequently, pregnant women preferred to deliver at home under the care of a *partera*. Dilapidated housing and their required waged labor denied these women a quiet and restful lying-in period, making it difficult for them to properly heal. Puerperal septicemia (infection related to childbirth) caused 44 percent of deaths among Mexican mothers, a figure two and one half times greater than for any other racial or ethnic community living in San Diego. Infant deaths among Mexicans were double that of any other group in the city. During the ten-year period, Mexican babies represented 27.5 percent of all infant deaths, even though they constituted only 14 percent of all local births.[80]

However, Hart Taylor's focus on maternal education, especially in regard to milk, helped keep these figures lower than if no attention had been paid to Mexican women. Her advocacy also touched the larger San Diego community. To safeguard against communicable disease, educators taught mothers that breast milk provided the healthiest nourishment for newborns and that mothers should try to breastfeed throughout their babies' infancy. They also introduced hygienic procedures for using formula and storing food. Hart Taylor's program to test the physical and mental abilities of children seemed to "increase interest in the clinic" and helped draw "foreign mothers" to lectures on health care given by NH personnel.[81] But ethnic prejudices persisted among authority figures, such as the assistant superintendent of San Diego schools, Edwin B. Tilton. For his fieldwork series on the economic health of California, University of California economist Paul S. Taylor interviewed Tilton in 1928. When asked about the capabilities of Mexican-descent students, Tilton responded: "He is inferior; and inferior race no doubt. The Japs and Chinese shot past him. They are superior. The Mexicans are slow to learn." Tilton emphasized, "The Mexicans at Sherman school [where the bulk of Mexican children attended] have bad social habits and are not clean."[82] Sentiments like those held by Tilton certainly worked against Mexican American youth; however, scholars from outside San Diego began studying the situation in San Diego and influencing some change.

Two studies, *Mexicans in California: Report of Governor C. C. Young's Mexican Fact-Finding Committee* (October 1930) and *How Mexicans Earn and Live: A Study of the Incomes and Expenditures of One Hundred Mexican Families in San Diego, California* (1933), offered state and local authorities important data about Mexican-heritage families. The latter study, *How Mexicans Earn and Live*, demonstrates the power of professional networks and their effectiveness in delivering services to San Diego. Researchers with the Heller Committee for Research in Social Economics at the University of California secured San Diego as a study site through a personal contact with NH director, Constantine Panunzio. A graduate of Berkeley's School of Sociology, in 1929 Panunzio took a position with the Sociology Department at San Diego State College and replaced Mary Snyder as the head of NH. Leadership renamed his position "director" and hired his wife, Lenore, as the associate director of the settlement. Her position is an interesting example of cooperation, networking, and negotiation, as it called for half of her time to be on loan to the San Diego City Schools to direct adult education among immigrants.[83] The director and associate director positions were new to the organization, and the Panunzios' scholarly goals shifted NH for a short time away from its origins as a resident-driven settlement guided by female professionals and volunteers to an academic laboratory led by a male university scholar.

Rather than directing the provision of basic services, the Panunzios focused on gathering research by inviting the Berkeley-directed committee to survey the NH community in 1930. They included San Diego Public School personnel who taught English to adults at the settlement and the primarily Mexican-descent families who used NH programs.[84] The surveyors clarified an important feature of their methodology: that their study did not necessarily represent the "average" or even the "typical" Mexican-descent family in San Diego or California, because study subjects held a personal connection to NH and its director. Perhaps that is why their findings pointed to the high level at which Mexicans in San Diego assimilated into American culture and did not use government relief. This study was also used in comparison to a set of Detroit families whose head of household worked in industrial settings, and those findings were published in a 1930 *Monthly Labor Review* (MLR) article.[85]

Both the Detroit and Heller researchers selected control families who fit Anglo-American standards of family composition, which they defined as households consisting of a father and mother raising their biological children. The Detroit control group included only those families whose earnings came solely from a male head of household who worked at least 225 days in 1929 and earned at least $7 per day. Households could not include boarders or extended family, and children living in the household had to be less than sixteen years of age. Ethnic allegiances included Catholic, Jewish, and Protestant families from Poland, Italy, Syria, and Germany. The Heller study opened its controls to including interethnic families, as only one of the parents needed to be of Mexican origin, but both parents needed to be alive at the time of the interview. In addition, the family needed to have resided in San Diego only for the twelve months preceding the investigation. These parameters may have reflected intermarriage between Anglos, some immigrant groups (like Filipinos), and Mexicans in San Diego, and the regular movements in and out of the city; but the study does not spell this out.[86]

The Detroit research eliminated from its control group female-headed households and did not consider the effects of wages brought to the table by a mother in a male-headed household.

The Heller report, on the other hand, included households where women either earned the primary wage or contributed to the family income. Nearly half of the women in the San Diego households (forty-four) earned wages to supplement the family income. Most of this work was "irregular" and "part-time," but it still represents a dramatic departure from the families in the MLR report. Fish canneries employed most of the women in the San Diego study (thirty-two); five worked as shop clerks; two labored in laundries; one woman was a cigar maker; and another sewed for a living. Only one woman listed clerical work as her occupation, while one woman assisted in "her husband's store" but was not paid for her time.[87] The Heller Committee found that Detroit families lived better than Mexican-descent families who lived in San Diego, primarily because of access to higher-paying manufacturing jobs. Canneries in San Diego provided an important source of income for many Mexican families, as well as Italian, Portuguese, and Japanese immigrants, but their hourly earnings were far less than those of workers in Detroit's manufacturing sector.

The Heller report legitimated the much earlier findings of the College Woman's Club and affirmed the need for continued social programs offered by NH, but in 1930 the city began experiencing more-widespread poverty. The Panunzios joined NH prior to the city's economic downturn and the country's acceptance of repatriation of Mexican peoples. As one strategy to free up jobs for white men, some cities began repatriating Mexican-descent residents who worked in manufacturing, construction, and food-processing sectors (including those people who were U.S. citizens). Historians have shown that repatriation occurred in regions with small populations of Mexican-born workers. For example, the steel and meatpacking industries in the Midwest used repatriation, but Mexican Americans in New Mexico escaped the policy because of its large Mexican-origin population. Yet repatriation also operated in areas with both a large number of Mexican Americans and a history of intense racial animosity, like Texas and Arizona.[88]

No evidence exists of NH taking a leadership role in preventing *or* in cooperating with San Diego officials on its repatriation policy, but authorities did employ the practice across the county. Starting in 1929, San Diego County officials repatriated 1,893 people, 49 percent of whom listed Baja California as their destination. Welfare authorities justified its repatriation practice by insisting it saved the county from abusers of public aid. However, according to *Mexicans in California: Report of Governor C. C. Young's Mexican Fact-Finding Committee*, released in October 1930, only 165 Mexican American and Mexican immigrant families received county aid in 1928; by 1931 that number had not dramatically changed.[89] Mexicans simply were not approved for state-sponsored resources.

The Panunzios resided at NH for only one year. Anita Jones joined NH as its head resident on October 1, 1930, bringing an era of bilingual leadership to the settlement. Jones arrived in San Diego with impeccable credentials and experience for the NH position. Having earned a bachelor of arts degree from the University of Texas, she secured a master of arts in social work from the University of Chicago. Jones spoke fluent Spanish and for two years had directed the Mexican Immigrants Protection League program at Hull House.[90] Those Hull House connections continued once she took over in NH, as renowned figures Jane Addams and Dr. Jane Robbins both visited the settlement in the early 1930s.[91] Under Jones's leadership, the federal government selected NH for the primary site of San Diego's emergency nursery school program, which further cemented its connection to federal assistance. In addition to the emergency nursery school, the settlement maintained a strong connection with cannery operatives through its other programs such as English language instruction, baby health stations, community ovens and baths, and recreational activities for young people. It also introduced a Marital Relations Clinic, where women could find birth control advice.[92] NH provided a full-day program—7:00 a.m. to 6:00 p.m., Monday through Saturday—thus maintaining a day-nursery schedule but infused with nursery school ideals.[93] This practice extended the advocacy of the Progressive Era leaders into the Depression so that by the mid-1930s, NH resources served a second generation of Mexican American families. Jones encouraged the development of these programs, and because she spoke Spanish, she could communicate directly with the dominant cultural group who used the home. The successes in improving the overall health and education of clients at NH made it a natural site for national and state programs to invest funds.

When the Great Depression hit San Diego, WPA officials appointed NH as an emergency nursery school (ENS) site. Its connections to federal grants made it the likely candidate, and it straddled the worlds of education (nursery schools) and custodial care (day nurseries), unlike other day care programs in the city, such as the one opened in 1927 by the Junior League of San Diego (JLSD).[94] The JLSD had developed a decade earlier, and members tended to be from elite households, college educated, and members of sororities during their university years. In some ways, their involvement in the league became an extension of that collegiate sisterhood. They opened their day nursery at 736 Seventeenth Street in October 1927. Organizers described the location as "in a tenement district of poor dwelling houses, near the edge of the Mexican section" and said that they intended to help families who labored in the canneries and small factories southeast of downtown.[95] Parents paid fifty cents a day per child. The center opened with only four children in attendance, but within the first years, those numbers expanded to an average of twenty-two children each day. Volunteers operated the day nursery, Monday through Saturday, and the facility could hold thirty children.[96] All children received physical examinations, and smallpox vaccinations and diphtheria immunizations were arranged in cooperation with the County Health Department. The league also paid special attention to "postural defects" and fitted children with proper shoes when they discovered problems of the feet and legs.[97]

Other groups also took an interest in public health concerns. In 1932 the General Federation of Women's Clubs (GFWC) commissioned a study by the Metropolitan Life Insurance Company to survey community health in San Diego. Three clubs—La Mesa Women's Club of the City of La Mesa, the Progress Club of the City of El Cajon, and the San Diego County Federation of Women's Clubs—entered into the cooperative endeavor with the San Diego Chamber of Commerce and the San Diego County Hospital. The GFWC study indicated that during 1931 the County Health Department in cooperation with women's clubs and Parent Teacher Association (PTA) groups held sixty-nine baby conferences. Also in 1931 the county conducted 1,068 preschool examinations of children ages one month to six years. Additionally, county services included a pediatric clinic for indigent children every Tuesday morning at the County Hospital on Dickinson and Front Streets, where "defects may be treated free of charge."[98]

This information may have led to the opening of a prenatal clinic in the spring of 1932. Services reported at a Visiting Nurses Bureau meeting in April included free pre- and postnatal care, hospitalization for a nominal fee, pediatric advice up to the baby's ninth month, and contraceptive advice "to those requesting it." Whereas in 1917 Daisy Worchester could not provide contraceptive advice, by 1932 the Comstock Act had been successfully challenged by birth control activist Margaret Sanger, which cleared the way for some clinics to provide information on preventing pregnancies. The clinic would "fulfill the need where the County cannot take part pay patients and neither County nor Mercy Hospital can arrange to give contraceptive advice." Clearly, medical professionals understood the importance of, *and* the controversy over, contraceptive use (especially among its Catholic clients) and worked out a compromise to cover patients cared for at the Catholic-managed Mercy Hospital.[99] This clinic (the Hoffman Memorial Hospital Mother's Clinic), and three subsequent clinics, addressed maternal and infant morbidity; unfortunately, these clinics could not sustain operations, and all had closed within five years of opening.[100]

The women's club study did not dedicate itself to an examination of Mexican-origin families, but the findings indicated that Mexican children suffered from poverty in ways not experienced by white children. The study cited the area referred to as Old Town in National City for "health and social problems," which were "frequently inextricably combined." To address these concerns, the Community Chest (a fund-raising arm for the city) assigned a settlement worker to the area, thereby creating the region's second settlement house program, Casa de Salud (CS), located at 1833 Seventh Avenue in National City.[101] Thus, by the depth of the Depression, some San Diego families could benefit from the programs offered at two settlement houses, NH and CS. Neighborhood House made its bath facilities open to the public as a way to improve hygiene and general health conditions, and as mentioned earlier, its community oven became a popular gathering place for women as they prepared meals for their families.[102]

Interestingly, the club conducted its study shortly after the Mexican community in Lemon Grove (an agricultural community about ten miles east of downtown San Diego) won its petition for a writ of mandate to the school board blocking the attempt to segregate their children from district schools.[103] The study and legal activism came in the midst of repatriation agendas.[104] Scholars of migrant farm labor have emphasized how whiteness did not guarantee a privileged position when it came to securing work, benefits, or respect during the Depression era.[105] In San Diego's citrus groves, vegetable fields, and canneries, newly migrated whites worked alongside Mexican, Asian, and European immigrants. A relatively open international border excused the need for a firm repatriation policy, yet violence attached to racism flourished in the area.

San Diego's Mexican community learned to fear assaults, which included lynching and gun violence by the local chapter of the Ku Klux Klan, the Exalted Cyclops, No. 64.[106] In the early 1930s, Latino activists formed El Congreso del Pueblo de Habla Española (the Congress of Spanish-Speaking Peoples) as a protective organization against such mob violence. It established chapters across Southern California and the Southwest, but its influence was tempered by political challenge.[107] In the 1930s San Diego resident Mercedes Acasan Garcia was a maid for a prominent white family in San Diego. She heard about Klan activity in the rural areas and made sure she used caution when taking the back roads into Mexico to visit relatives. Garcia explained that "laborers in rural areas had their homes or barns burned. Several growers patrolled their fields to calm their sad and worried field hands; their crops were worthless without Mexicans."[108] Families who had migrated north from Baja during the early years of the Mexican Revolution or had lived in the region for several generations might have escaped repatriation, yet racial segregation and job discrimination by school districts and employers continued to control these families.[109] However, in the face of repatriation and discrimination, some Mexican American men secured employment through the county's Work Relief Program, including constructing the clinic building for Neighborhood House by making the adobe bricks and tiles for the eight-room, two-bath facility. The finished product stunned relief personnel, who marveled at the skilled craftsmanship, including the building's inside, "neatly finished in white with rustic woodwork."[110] But access to this kind of work in the city was rare for Mexican American men.

By the late 1920s, reformers throughout the city noticed new childcare concerns, such as a marked increase in children traveling without adult supervision or approval. Travelers Aid guide Alice Byrd Hoskins remembered aiding "two little black boys from way down south who had hiked" to San Diego and observed that "everybody was hiking."[111] Reformers also heard of parents increasingly leaving their small children home alone when they went job searching, because they could not afford even the nominal fee asked at day nurseries. The development of the WPA emergency nursery schools served as the primary remedy for these childcare problems. The combination of public resources like the emergency nursery schools and community services offered through national organizations like Travelers Aid helped stabilize the shifts occurring in the city's social infrastructure. In spite of its rocky start, in only twenty years the people and programs associated with Neighborhood House had created significant influence on the city and its people. NH residents utilized their national, state, and local connections to access governmental and philanthropic funds, and forged collaborations between public agencies and private organizations to develop a network of emergency nursery schools and to provide safer environments for young people. The additional resources needed in the 1930s benefited from the foundational programs and helped disadvantaged families survive the turbulent times.

CHAPTER SIX

Emergency Care

Collaboration during Economic Recovery

We have never known anyone even in San Diego who could live on blossoms and sweet perfume.

—Travelers Aid Society of San Diego greeter

On August 27, 1929, the Children's Home released nine-year-old Darlene Callahan to her mother for what the staff hoped was the last time. Her father worked for the U.S. Navy, which took him away from San Diego for months-long stretches, and her mother waitressed at a local restaurant. CH staff designated as "Broken Home" cases that involved parental sickness, work-related absence, or divorce, which is how they defined Darlene's situation when she first entered at the age of three. The third and final admittance entry for Darlene on October 11, 1928, recorded that the girl had suffered through smallpox, measles, scarlet fever, whooping cough, and chickenpox. These childhood illnesses may have pushed her mother over the edge of what she could manage as a single parent, and the CH became a ready refuge for her child. By the summer of 1929, Darlene's mother informed CH staff that she had recently married and no longer needed their assistance.[1]

No more entries appear for Darlene. Certainly, Darlene's poor health would continue to pose challenges, but her mother did not continue using the CH, perhaps because Darlene had aged out of the facility or because the marriage solved the family's childcare problems. By the 1920s three day nurseries operated in San Diego—ones in the Neighborhood House and Casa de Salud settlements and the other managed by volunteers of the Junior League of San Diego—so the CH shifted toward boarding children with long-term needs such as being orphaned, sickly, or with parents forced to work out of town. Along with the Detention Home, it also cared for children needing specialized attention because of delinquency. These facilities received a combination of public and private resources, which allowed them to stay afloat and provided working-class parents help during the Great Depression.

This chapter reviews how childcare needs influenced the ways in which San Diegans dealt with the effects of the economic instability in the 1930s. County health and welfare reports indicate the Great Depression had settled into the city by 1929, causing increased reliance on assistance from public and private programs. Several factors contributed to this dynamic: the doubling of the city's population from 74,361 in 1920 to 147,995 in 1930; haphazard civic planning that overlooked the vast disparity of wealth in the city; the propensity among business leaders to grow low-waged, part-time jobs that attracted transient workers, rather than full-time, permanent jobs backed by organized labor; and a dependent relationship on the defense industry to stabilize San Diego's economy. One report by the San Diego County Department of Public Welfare and Emergency Relief Association documented that unemployment in the early 1930s contributed to an increased usage of NH services, with nearly seventy-five thousand persons visiting the settlement from October 1, 1932, to May 31, 1933.[2] National decisions, of course, influenced the economy in San Diego, but the decision by local authorities to allow the military to dominate the city's urban footprint produced unexpected consequences.

In 1917 the U.S. Navy broke ground on its advance marine base forty miles north of San Diego's downtown (commissioned in 1921 and now known as Camp Pendleton) and secured an air station on the Coronado inlet. In 1919 city officials transferred land to the navy, so it could erect a first-rate naval hospital, and by 1921 the navy had also built a supply depot and a submarine repair base, declaring San Diego its Eleventh Naval District Headquarters. This divided the leisure community of Coronado into part resort town and part naval stronghold. It also solidified Coronado's socioeconomic divides, as white elites hired African American and Asian domestic servants to help tend to their children, homes, and lawns. Throughout the county, planners, entrepreneurs, and city officials catered to the diverse needs of military personnel, from services for young and single enlisted men to the comforts of commissioned officers who transplanted their families to San Diego.[3] They required housing beyond barracks, their children attended local schools, and they helped grow the middle-class culture in the area. Country clubs, social associations such as the Junior League, churches, and civic organizations benefited from officers' families joining them and volunteering for service projects. Fashionable restaurants, boutiques, and salons emerged alongside architect-designed homes and innovative private schools that catered to the new clientele; however, this segment of the population constituted a small part of the city's demographic.

A November 6, 1934, story in the *San Diego Union* reported the community had benefited from $28 million in capital investments devoted to naval establishments, and the navy's $30 million payroll connected to the county represented 10 percent of the total annual naval payroll appropriation. The story intended to educate readers to the importance of the navy and to intensify that relationship as one way to combat the Depression.[4] Yet most of the city's job growth came from the lower-paying service sector and did little to alleviate poverty; in fact, once the navy dedicated its buildings for the city's second world exposition (California–Pacific International Exposition in 1935–1936), the building expansion in the city slowed, and men associated with construction—both skilled and unskilled workers—found themselves unemployed or underemployed.[5] As in earlier decades, women contributed to family economies by working in domestic service and the canning industry, but their wages seldom fully compensated for the loss of a skilled man's earnings. So, while the growing presence of the military generated an increased revenue stream for the city, it also expanded an already large community of transient workers laboring in poorly compensated service jobs.

This era tested the effectiveness of San Diego's social welfare system, as it grew to rely more on outside funding. The combination of local, state, and nationally funded programming helped shield many San Diegans from the worst effects of the Great Depression and cemented the turn to professional care providers for the management and organization of childcare in San Diego. Since governmental requirements included using trained educators and healthcare providers, involvements from nonprofessional volunteers (such as members of the Junior League) became a liability for securing and retaining eligibility. Thus, funding secured through the federal government's New Deal programs further professionalized the city's social welfare network.

During this era familiar figures like physician Charlotte Baker and social activist Helen Marston remained engaged in the work of helping impoverished people through their involvements with the YWCA, the Visiting Nurses Bureau (VNB), the Associated Charities, and Neighborhood House. They were joined by transplants from the Midwest, like Anita Jones and Ann Seeger, whose social work and public health training in industrial cities served them well in San Diego. As the director of NH from 1930 to 1941, Jones provided an important bilingual voice among the city's social welfare leadership and connected the city to the social work profession through the National Federation of Settlements.[6] Ann Seeger, a registered nurse, caught the attention of social welfare leaders because of her experience with public health nursing in Detroit and at the San Diego County Hospital. That combination of nursing positions made her the top choice to lead San Diego's fledgling Visiting Nurses Bureau.[7]

Medical professionals seeking opportunities to establish practices also moved to the city. Physician Rieta Campbell Hough moved to San Diego in 1927 ready to launch a career in pediatrics. After completing medical school in 1919, she interned in San Francisco and assisted a doctor in San Jose for two and a half years. Encouragement from other physicians who touted San Diego's growing wealth led her south, where she connected with another female physician, Martha Welpton. But instead of healing the bumps, bruises, and broken bones of the city's elite children, the two treated many people whom other physicians would not consider for care. Hough explained that she and Welpton saw the worst cases in the region, including "a good many drunks" suffering from overindulgences in Tijuana, patients sent to the isolation hospital because of tuberculosis, and individuals too poor to pay for their care. Once the Depression hit the area full force in 1930, Hough spent considerable time at the County Hospital, where the sickest and often poorest patients lived out their illnesses. The female physicians also treated immigrant families who suffered discrimination, including the Chinese community and the Russian émigrés living in Ensenada.[8]

Reports from community organizations support Hough's comment about the lack of care for indigents and from 1930 to 1934 show a rapid growth in people too poor to pay for their medical care. NH programs helped improve the survival rates of mothers and infants through clean milk and immunization programs, but they reached a small portion of people in need of medical care. Another solution for increasing the delivery of public health was the expansion of the Visiting Nurses Bureau.[9] In June 1930 the Associated Charities recommended hiring Seeger to lead the unit because of her experience with Detroit's VNB in the early 1920s and her success at the San Diego County Hospital. Detroit's often miserable weather and dense population of a million people had presented daily challenges to Seeger—for instance, language and other cultural barriers marred the type of care she hoped to give to recent migrants from the South or to Eastern European immigrants. But her move from the country's fourth-largest city to one a tenth of its size proved unexpectedly exhausting. San Diego's temperate weather made travel and the stench of diseased bodies easier to stomach, but nursing along the southwestern international border brought Seeger into contact with new types of patients, like transient workers, servicemen, and tourists who unwittingly exposed the area to tuberculosis and influenza.

Seeger marked six months on the job when she signed her name to the VNB monthly report for December 1930. During that time, the number of free patients served by the Bureau had increased dramatically, from 22 people in July to 278 people in December; 113 people paid what they could, and only 15 patients paid in full. Seeger reported that 118 of those calls were maternity related, producing 173 children, meaning that many of those calls involved births of twins and added an uncomfortable weight to an already struggling family. During those six months, Seeger documented that 54 "American" and 44 "Mexican" mothers had used the VNB services. She grouped another 20 mothers who were Indian, Japanese, Hawaiian, or Filipino under a category "Others." To these women were born 72 Americans, 68 Mexicans, and 33 Others, indicating that in every category twins and/or triplets were born. African American mothers or newborns must have been included in the "American" category; or these women may have been denied assistance, however, that seems unlikely, considering that by 1930 Neighborhood House, the Children's Home, and the Travelers Aid Society assisted the African American community. Chinese women and children also were not indicated in the report, which fits the history of the Chinese community being excluded from using public resources.[10]

San Diego's VNB consisted of three nurses: Seeger, its director, and two very competent nurses she had recently hired, Katherine Tuttle and Esther Shong.[11] But the VNB was still sorely understaffed, and finding ways to relieve her overworked and underpaid staff became Seeger's main concern. Seeger was the only nurse qualified to take maternity and newborn cases, and the other nurses' workloads intensified as the decade wore on. In January 1931 the nurses made 459 calls, but just three months later they clocked 708 visits, and only 12 of those constituted "pay-calls." A record month in August 1932 saw the nurses handle 826 calls; out of those, 554 were listed as "free," and another 142 as part-pay.[12] A June 19, 1931, memorandum by Seeger to the members of the Board of Supervisors and the members of the city council reveals her need to justify the staff's hard work. Seeger explained how the VNB helped

FIG. 17. The Associated Charites in San Diego expanded the Visiting Nurses Bureau in 1930, due to the great public health needs in the city. Maternal and infant care was a critical resource provided by nurses like this one taking a baby's foot impression, c. 1928. © San Diego History Center.

wage earners who could neither afford a hospital or private duty nurse nor qualify for indigent care at public clinics or the County Hospital. She emphasized the importance of education done by the nurses giving bedside care and reducing the dangers of an epidemic.[13] Nurse Katherine Tuttle reported in January 1933, "Many of our patients required intensive care," and she listed the cases of two women who required daily two-hour visits. The plight of eleven-year-old Bernice, who cared for six younger siblings because of a sick mother, had also caught the nurses' attention. They were happy to report that after several conversations with the father about the harm this caused the girl, Bernice was resting and "gaining rapidly."[14] But the stresses of the job pushed the VNB staff to their limits. By May 1933 Shong had fallen ill with a "severe attack of influenza," and Seeger scrambled to find a replacement.

The overworked VNB represents one example of how population shifts took city leaders by surprise. Day laborers, skilled craftsmen, personal service workers, educators, clerical workers, artists, and white-collar professionals vied for the same jobs and waited together in the same relief lines. Caseworkers at the county's Public Welfare Department worked round-the-clock to keep up with the surge in people requesting assistance. By 1934 the understaffed office was handling 800 to 1,000 new cases each month, with the average caseload per field worker at 163.[15] The overwhelming numbers caused terrific confusion in the offices and unprecedented relief lines, where people found themselves waiting for three to four hours in lines stretched around buildings. The chaos led observers to complain that "the office staff [was] so tied up in office routine that it was practically impossible to do a consistent piece of field work."[16]

These statistics tell only a part of the story. Reports from state and county government bodies show the heightened desperation of both residents and transients to secure steady work and reunite their families. San Diego carried some weight in state budgetary concerns, but not enough influence to compete with California's three larger cities, Los Angeles, San Francisco, and Oakland. After all, over one million people lived in Los Angeles and 630,000 in San Francisco; and nearly 300,000 people called Oakland home.[17] As centers of commerce and Pacific immigration, those cities provided jobs to a more permanent workforce with the potential to increase state and local tax dividends. Their sheer numbers engendered more attention from state and national politicians. Yet the Depression did not bypass San Diego, and concerns over how to manage the growing homeless and underemployed population worried city leaders and social welfare professionals.

People arrived in the city convinced of the certainty of jobs and affordable housing, like the man who hitchhiked to San Diego from Cleveland in the winter of 1932 only to find himself selling newspapers on a street corner. He approached the TASSD for help in sending his family on to him, insisting he earned "four dollars per week and about seventy-five cents on the side," an income he believed sufficient to care for his family. The TASSD workers did not agree and notified the Cleveland Travelers Aid office that no assistance in travel should be given this family, because "we have never known anyone even in San Diego who could live on blossoms and sweet perfume."[18] Author Clyde Parker wrote of his frustration with not being able to provide adequately for his family. Forced to survive "almost entirely on beans, with milk for the child and . . . usually . . . day old bread," the Parkers benefited from county aid, but that assistance came with a terrible stigma. Knowing little about relief programs, Parker learned from his local grocer that the county could provide him with food, so he investigated the option. According to Parker, "the case worker, after a long talk, said 'Well, since you've gotten yourself in a position where you can't support your family, we'll have to do it for you.' I was so deeply ashamed that I refused to return to her when my grocery supplies were gone, but after several weeks, I was forced to apply again. This lady did apologize to my wife later, saying that she was ordered to be harsh with new applicants for food."[19]

The embarrassment experienced by people like Parker did not go unrecognized by county relief supervisors, who took steps to eliminate caseworker abuses. In spite of a tremendous caseload in 1934 of 9,510 families and limited staff resources—a supervisor, an assistant supervisor, a coordinator, three district case workers and several field visitors—the county Case Work Department implemented several changes "directed toward preserving a helpful, sympathetic attitude on the part of all persons representing the office toward all clients served." Public welfare supervisors insisted abuses lay with untrained personnel. To repair the problem, they developed mandatory training sessions for all case workers and friendly visitors on how to interact professionally and respectfully with families. They now used the term "clients" rather than "indigents," and first responders met clients in the home to save them the long wait times. Emphasizing its role in benevolent terms, public relief officials underscored that "when all is said and done, the one and only reason this entire office exists is because of the need of relief

for employable unemployed," and supervisors insisted caseworkers adopt a similar attitude.[20]

The Depression also made life tougher for families who had
long struggled to survive, such as Indians living on reservations
and employed by local ranches. Some Anglo professionals felt
"Mission Indians" depended too much on government aid and
needed to learn skills to make them self-sufficient. To that end, C.
F. Fine, assistant county agent of the State Agriculture Extension
Service, recommended in a 1932 study "intensive work" in moving "Mission Indians" toward subsistence farming.[21] That same
study explained an interaction between a federal case worker and
a family living on the Santa Ysabel reservation (about sixty miles
northeast of the city) about its poverty. The family of five consisted of a thirty-year-old man, his wife, and their three children.
The husband could not find work even though he was a skilled
carpenter. Anglos characterized him as a "steady worker and fairly
reliable," a "pretty decent man, good worker, does not bother any-
body," and an "apparently rather earnest Indian." Yet his potential
employers and the caseworker agreed that his obese wife created
a serious problem for the family. Drawing on stereotypes that an
overweight person was lazy, ignorant, and even disreputable, the
report concluded she must be a bad mother and was holding back
this seemingly productive man. The government allotted them $5
for clothing, and $5 for blankets, and their six-year-old son received
a hot lunch through the reservation day school. The couple's goat
and chickens provided enough milk and eggs to keep their four-
year-old daughter and one-year-old son from starving. But as the
Depression drained government coffers, families defined by federal
rules as dependent found fewer resources flowing in their direction. Public officials viewed a white man's inability to secure work
as a tragedy, yet understood the Santa Ysabel man's unemployment
as a condition brought on by a marriage to an ill-kempt woman.[22]

A variety of reformers began using San Diego as a case study
for social conditions in the state, county, and nation (such as in
the Governor Young and Heller reports), but their findings generated little concrete change at the local level. In the case of "Mission

Indians," experts' studies only reinforced the long-held stereotypes of self-imposed dependency among American Indians. One agent posited that American Indians "have demanded assistance without being willing to exert a maximum of self-help. They have failed to appreciate that they have advantages, which many of their white neighbors do not have. Land to cultivate, free garden seed, grain advanced without cash payment; free wood to use or to sell; hot lunches and clothes for the children; free medical and hospital service, and no rent or taxes to pay."[23] This agent's frustration is clear, but so is his prejudice. His belief that people should not complain about their survival when so much federal money had been designated for their use ignores the historical foundations of their dependency and the federal government's complicity in that status. In 1932 "Mission Indians" lived on land with poor soil, endured drought conditions, and lacked sufficient tools to make a go at a subsistence garden. But the federal agent believed they brought it on themselves and concluded that families had been deficient in using the wealth of resources provided to them by the federal government.[24]

The study also advised the county Board of Supervisors to assign a public health nurse to travel the reservation as a remedy for over-burdened physicians, and for parents to bring their children to the Indian Health Bureau facility in Riverside County. Investigators argued that a visiting nurse posed a more efficient use of slim resources, but parents did not want to subject their sick children to a half-day, rut-filled drive over mountainous roads to the nearest health facility. White officials insisted, however, that the patient needed to come to the physician, and not the other way around.[25] The problem was twofold, in that the lack of physician power kept medical personnel tied to the facility, and the remoteness of reservation homes hindered physician house calls. Moreover, white physicians assumed Indian families had access to transportation and enough gas to drive the vehicle. The missing factor in doctors' presumptions was parental concern and protection for the sick child. Unfortunately, San Diego reservations remained isolated and physician-free for several more decades.

Fig. 18. By the 1930s, schools like the Mesa Grande government school allowed children to remain with their families on reservations, 1931. © San Diego History Center.

Federal aid assigned through New Deal programs began flowing into San Diego County by 1934 but went largely to white families in urban areas. Consider the way ethnicity defined budgetary distinctions in the designated State Emergency Relief Administration (SERA) food budgets for San Diego County. SERA recommended a budget of $2 per week for "active men" and $1.61 per week for "active Mexican men." Those budgets accounted for diet preferences in terms of bread vs. tortillas, but it also expected differences in terms of protein; it recommended meat for whites but beans for Mexicans. Further, Mexican family budgets did not include money for cod liver oil (considered a required cost for all other children up to five years), cocoa, and various vegetables (spinach, carrots, potatoes).[26] Perhaps SERA believed Mexican women kept kitchen gardens, but no evidence of this exists in the report. Despite these differences, Mexican families survived on their smaller appropriations and even garnered praise from some relief officials for their wise expenditures. According to a study made of one hundred San Diego County families receiving relief in 1934, "the mother who got the greatest caloric value per dollar was an illiterate Mexican woman."[27]

One problem facing workers in the city was the closing of the canneries in 1932. Technological advances in preserving catches at sea and packaging for long-term consumer use invigorated the fishing industry in the early twentieth century. Fishermen caught yellowfin tuna and skipjack all year, and large schools of albacore through the summer months. Consequently, the canneries buzzed with activity year-round and in heightened fashion during some of the hottest months in San Diego, September and October.[28] These exploitive catch practices depleted fishing pools by the 1920s and caused a total shutdown of the canneries in 1932, forcing many fishing families to turn to public relief and private charity. The industry rebounded in early 1933 when the National Recovery Administration helped it experience a small comeback. But within the year, relaxation of tariffs allowed an influx of Japanese tuna into the American market, exacerbating the plight of the fisherman's family. A December 6, 1933, story in the *San Diego Sun* reported that the "dumping of hundreds of thousands of cases of tuna on the American market . . . struck a virtual death blow at a once-lucrative market" and dramatically affected the way fishermen could survive. All canneries planned to close down indefinitely on December 10 when the tuna boats tied up, negatively influencing women's wage-earning opportunities.[29]

Female labor dominated seafood cannery production. Older married and widowed women completed the first stage of production by scaling and deheading fish and sardines, which required a good deal of skill in handling knives but was one of the lowest-paying positions. Single women, the newly married, and mothers of young children worked together on the lines, doing jobs such as packing and labeling the product, jobs that earned a higher wage. Men did not wholeheartedly condone their wives and daughters leaving the home to work but reluctantly conceded that the income provided an important contribution to the family. Shifts lasted up to twelve hours; workers knew to report to their stations when the cannery whistle blew, and often that sound awoke them from deep slumber in the middle of the night. Tuna and sardine preparation was cold, wet work, and most jobs entailed standing throughout one's shift.

Fishing families also faced uncertainties because of irregular finances and work routines. Caterina (Katie) Asaro entered the canneries at age sixteen, packing tuna at the Westgate starting in 1927. She remembered hard work that carried into the night when a catch came in. Unprotected by union contracts, workers did not openly complain, because they could go for weeks-long stretches of only two or three hours of work. Asaro noted that during the summer, packers could expect steady work from eight in the morning until five, six, or seven in the evening, but the hours of employ always depended on the size of the catch. Asaro married in 1929 and continued canning for another year and a half until her son was born. She recalled tough times for her fisherman husband, Andrew, during the Depression. He secured a job through the WPA working at Balboa Park, but Katie remembered them not qualifying for any other form of aid. She returned to the canneries in 1933 to survive the Depression, working until 1935. The Asaros had another child in 1936, and after an appendix surgery, Asaro admitted that her health, not her children, kept her home. If not for the operation, she probably would have continued working in the cannery to help support her family.[30]

Asaro's labor represents a typical action among Italian, Portuguese, and Mexican families in San Diego. Caterine (Caty) Brigante Ghio entered a sardine cannery at the age of sixteen, like many of her friends. Her father grudgingly gave his consent for her to work, perhaps because the cannery manager lived across the street from them and kept a close eye on his neighbor's daughter. In her chronicle of cannery life in California, historian Vicki Ruiz explained how male relatives and friends "often assumed a protective role over their women kin."[31] While Ruiz referred to Mexican families, her point is relevant for other ethnic groups in the cannery. Ghio's father permitted his daughter to venture into the work world only when he knew she would not fall into an unwanted romance or meet up with girls whose families let them roam the neighborhood. Ghio left her position on the floor of the cannery after a few years when she married. She remembered most of the younger workers as "San Diego born girls," and "the older women were Italian."[32] Ghio lost her husband in 1938 and opened a fish restaurant, Anthony's Fish Grotto, which she would develop into a landmark spot on the harbor.[33]

Several generations of women labored in the canneries, but they did not always work alongside one another. When the whistle blew, sometimes at 2:00 a.m., workers were expected to head down the hill to the wharf. The Asaros lived at the top of Hawthorne Street, a steep trip for anyone, let alone a tired mother dragged out of bed by the canneries' whistle. Asaro remembers, "My mother used to walk all the way down, straight down, that's where the cannery was. Steel was first, then came Neptune, and then came Del Monte cannery on Juniper Street."[34] As hard as the trek to work, the mile-long return up the hill to their homes must have tried the strength of even the sturdiest of women, as backs, necks, and legs ached from standing at their stations for over twelve hours.

Cannery families lived in the same neighborhoods and helped each other with maintaining their households by sharing childcare, produce from their kitchen gardens, and friendship. Ruiz found that childcare needs united Mexican female workers with their Anglo co-workers in "various efforts to secure suitable babysitting arrangements," and this "cross-ethnic bridge" became the most significant interaction between female operatives in the canneries.[35] Often several generations lived in the same house, as female workers needed their mothers and in-laws for childcare, especially when the family included an infant or a toddler. These older women knew their role in caring for their grandchildren stabilized the family, especially during lean months when no boats fished the waters. Sometimes older children accompanied their parents to work and played outside near the wharf or in the drier areas of the plant. Luis Alvarez grew up in Barrio Logan in the 1930s and remembered, "People were very united, very friendly;

you could leave your home without having to . . . lock it down and feel pretty safe that no one would bother you. There was more respect between people, especially the younger people toward their seniors."[36] Luis's father was a painter, and his mother worked at one of the fish canneries. But for those households without an elder, or in times when coordinating care with a neighbor proved futile, the NH and JLSD day nurseries served them.

Seafood cannery owners knew workers needed childcare. When the industry rebounded in 1934, a consortium of canneries asked NH to devote day nursery space for its workers' children and supported it financially. Local advocate Ethel Dummer Mintzer explained that "owners of the two canneries gave the rent for a small house next to the [NH] kindergarten," unemployed parents "scrubbed the house and cleaned the yard," and volunteers painted the space with donated paint.[37] As with its inception twenty years earlier, NH also received money from the College Woman's Club and the Community Chest, and then secured WPA funding to operate as a federal emergency nursery school (ENS).

ENS moneys became an important conduit of federal intervention throughout the country and in the state of California. By 1937 seventy-one emergency nursery schools serving 2,176 children operated in California, which represented the fourth-largest number in the country.[38] Implementation of the schools served a fourfold purpose: first, to hire unemployed teachers, nurses, nutritionists, clerks, handymen, physicians, and psychologists; second, to relieve distress and raise morale among parents of young children; third, to reduce malnutrition among the nation's youngest children; and fourth, to raise behavior standards and practice among those children.[39] Early childhood educators understood the ENS program as an opportunity to assert the benefits of a nursery school curriculum and to fully separate their programs from the more familiar day nurseries.[40] Nursery school educator Christine Heinig recalled, "No one wanted [the emergency nursery schools] to be simply child-minding or baby-sitting centers"; thus, educators set out to design intellectual engagements that awakened and fed children's natural curiosities and talents as a supplement to their home environments.[41]

San Diego's leadership came from Ethel "Happy" Dummer Mintzer, who devoted her time and talent to exposing children of all backgrounds to the nursery school method. One of four daughters of philanthropist and social welfare advocate Ethel Sturgis Dummer, she was raised with every advantage available to a wealthy family in Chicago, including private teachers and holidays at their two summer homes in Lake Geneva, Wisconsin, and in Coronado, and an education at the privately funded Francis W. Parker School, located in San Diego's prestigious Mission Hills neighborhood. Happy's maternal aunt Clara founded the school in 1912 with her husband, renowned architect William Templeton Johnson. The school's mission embraced innovative teaching and learning methods with an interdisciplinary approach. The Johnsons financially supported the school until the early 1930s, when their divorce and the shock of the Depression necessitated the development of alternate budgeting. Happy began teaching at the school upon her graduation from the University of Wisconsin in 1918. She taught until 1922 and then became its principal. In 1930 she became the school's director, and she appointed then-teacher Irene F. Thuli (a University of Chicago alumna) as principal, which freed her from the daily responsibilities of running the school so that she could lead the implementation of WPA-funded emergency nursery schools in San Diego.[42]

Happy Dummer Mintzer understood some of the issues that working women navigated. She married L. Murney Mintzer, a naval officer stationed in Coronado, in 1923, and had three children. Economic stability allowed the Mintzer couple to hire a nanny so that Happy could continue her work at Francis Parker School. They also lived in a Mission Hills home near enough to the school, which allowed Happy to breastfeed her children as needed. Family lore has it that when a Mintzer baby needed feeding, their nanny would raise a flag up the pole, which would be visible to Happy in her school office, and the young mother would scurry home for a feeding. Happy also benefited from a husband who honored her intellect and professional ambitions, accepted her family's long history of engagement in Progressive reform, and encouraged her to continue her leadership roles in the community. Happy served as director of Frances Parker School until 1938, when she unexpectedly died from cancer at the age of forty-one.[43]

Prior to her untimely passing, Mintzer involved herself in implementing nursery schools throughout the city. Nursery school theory emphasized parental involvement in a child's learning and had been devised as a tool for white, middle-class parents (especially those mothers who had earned a college degree) to learn the science of parenting and to encourage their investing time in their children's early education.[44] Mintzer believed that working-class parents would also benefit, and that they wanted to be involved but were overwhelmed by their multiple roles of wage earning, housekeeping, and child rearing. Mintzer explained in a 1936 article, "Modern psychology has demonstrated the importance of the earliest years of childhood; now it is for those of us who see and understand the needs of little children to interpret the work of the nursery schools as widely as we are able."[45]

Mintzer advocated for a broad application of nursery school theory through her involvement with the ENS. She encouraged staff to include parents and siblings in the curriculum and did not shy away from opportunities to interact with families, both in the classroom and in their homes. In describing her daughter's devotion to nursery schools, Ethel Sturgis Dummer noted, "My daughter was asked to speak to a group of Mexican mothers. She told them that children were very much like little puppies . . . who follow positive suggestion, not negative command." When Mintzer made a home visit to a Mexican household, she learned her message had reached beyond the classroom, as "the father greeted her with, 'Oh Nursery School! The woman who says 'not to say don't.'"[46]

Nursery school education emerged as an important resource for wage-earning families in San Diego thanks to Mintzer's advocacy. In a series of articles published in the mid-1930s for the *San Diego Teacher's Association Bulletin* and the *Parent Teacher Association Council*, Mintzer outlined the intent of nursery school education and its implementation in San Diego. She explained that in order to secure funding, cities had to demonstrate community interest in and public-school cooperation with implementing a site. San Diego proved its viability as a locus for four schools, and administrators selected eight "well qualified unemployed teachers" to train at a two-week institute course at the University of California, Los Angeles. They completed their training in March 1934, returned to San Diego, and began preparations to introduce one hundred students to the program in just two weeks. Plans had outlined that the WPA would remodel or repair rooms and build the necessary equipment, but by the time the ENS organizers came to California and selected San Diego as a funded site, the WPA unit had closed. Instead, cooperation between public school personnel and the community in general allowed for the nurseries to open. Public schools offered space in three of the targeted districts and rounded up extra furniture. At night, teachers, parents, and older siblings of the nursery school children cleaned, painted, and built furniture. The American Red Cross donated blankets, federal sewing projects made pajamas and sun suits, and concerned citizens bought toys for the schools. Mintzer directed the operation and explained, "It was a herculean task but on the morning of April 2, 1934 four nursery schools opened: at Washington, Brooklyn and La Jolla Elementary schools and at Neighborhood House."[47]

The ENS program brought parents into the classroom in cooperative roles. To accommodate working parents, the San Diego programs used a nursery school pedagogy, but its hours of operation fell along the lines of day nurseries. From its start the ENS program proved extremely popular, and all four sites had waiting lists; the Washington school waiting list was forty families long. A physician authorized a child's health for initial entry to the school, and then a nurse inspected children every day. Following the typical nursery school regimen of recording health conditions, nurses kept weekly records of height and weight, and with parents' help monitored a daily sleep chart and adjustment records. Children received a "hot balanced lunch" of "carefully planned menus." Mary Hart Taylor reported that most of the cases of enlarged tonsils, constant colds, and skin troubles seen at the

NH clinic were "infinitely improved" because of the proper food, rest, and care given to the ENS students. Moreover, Hart Taylor explained, the exposure in the ENS helped students build immunity to illness. Mintzer attributed the success of the program to the "experienced, well trained teachers" and believed that "all sorts of emotional difficulties straighten[ed] out. Temper tantrums, feeding problems, shyness and such anti-social behavior fade[d] away under the friendly but quiet and steady atmosphere created in the Nursery schools."[48]

In the summer of 1936, the oversight for the ENS was transferred to the State Emergency Relief Administration. Teachers experienced scheduling reductions and pay cuts from one-fifth to one-half of their initial loads, but their dedication to the children persisted in spite of these conditions. Noted one teacher, "You can't treat two-year-olds like a load of lumber or a building project which can stand idle between hours of work." Instead, teachers worked on reduced pay and supplemented classrooms with supplies and food from their own homes. Mintzer emphasized that many parents appreciated the teachers' efforts and hoped the city would expand them.[49] Perhaps the closing of the Junior League's day nursery that summer prompted this response.

The voluntary nature of the league's commitment, to arrange for, manage, and supervise their day nursery (open since 1927) required financial, physical, and emotional devotion from a large team of women. The league did not turn away children if their parents could not afford the fee. In fact, the group established a policy of bumping children who could afford the nursery in order to make room for those families in desperate situations. Since the nursery seldom reached its capacity of thirty children, the league never resorted to dismissing children; still, that policy led professionals to criticize the league and its work. By the 1920s social workers believed clients should accept the responsibility of paying for all or at least part of the cost of caring for their children; otherwise, the day care became a form of relief and contributed to a family's dependency rather than its independence.[50] However, JLSD entered the childcare arena as a way to assist dependent mothers and did not harbor ideas about the women gaining independence. This position frustrated the league's national arm and led it to chastise the San Diego chapter for using untrained volunteers who had little to no understanding of family casework. National league reports indicate it had been encouraging chapters to expand membership and activities beyond social networks among elite women so as to immerse themselves in the full life of their town.[51] JLSD strove to achieve that goal by recruiting women with professional and/or university allegiances, but that did not necessarily include social workers. Shortly after the headquarter critique, Junior League members received expert guidance from University of California sociologist George Mangold, who had studied the day nursery as part of a citywide assessment he conducted and published in 1929. In that report Mangold outlined several changes the league should adopt to improve its nursery: expand recreational facilities, maintain better supervision of the children, and increase medical attention to help isolate communicable disease. Mangold also recommended that day nursery attendants make home visits.[52]

Part of a larger critique of social services in San Diego, Mangold's suggestions proved too far reaching for JLSD. Still, Mangold's critique gave them pause, because by 1932 league members questioned the need for their nursery, even offering their building to the city as a possible ENS site. The federal government "turned them down," claiming it did not want to "set up a nursery in an already existing agency."[53] Sonya Michel explained in her history of childcare that New Dealers "preferred innovation over the tried (and what they considered failed) forms of charity of the past." Rather than using voluntary day nurseries to set up emergency nursery schools, policy makers turned to nursery schools "whose star was newly risen in federal policy circles." The federal decision to use nursery schools "pushed the day nursery even farther to the margins of the realm of social policy, spelling disaster for voluntary day nurseries, whose numbers fell by one-quarter between 1931–1940."[54] The Junior League's day nursery was part of that declining statistic.

Federal officials likely objected to the lack of professional input at the JLSD day nursery. Since 1930 officers from the league's national headquarters had been recommending that the nursery hire a professional supervisor, and for a period of months in 1935, a trained social worker did oversee the San Diego operation. But she could not repair the damages of several years. Chapter members complained of rising costs, low attendance, and the resignation of their supervisor. They cited parental negligence as one reason for the facility's weakening state, noting it had "become a parking place for the children and as such is much too expensive an agency ... the average daily attendance is nineteen and costs about $365 a month."[55]

JLSD members explored turning the facility over to the Community Chest, but that body seemed reluctant to take on a program in financial despair. In August 1935 JLSD asked Dr. Edna Hawley, faculty member at San Diego State Normal College, to study the nursery's caseload, but it rejected her findings as "absolutely worthless" and employed Mrs. Lucille Marshall to reevaluate their program. There are no indications as to why JLSD saw no value in Hawley's report, but perhaps personalities proved the barrier. Hawley was not a league member, whereas Marshall appears to have been a Junior League insider. One year later, upon recommendations from Marshall's study, the league's nursery committee advised their group to close the nursery. JLSD had just raised $3,700 for the day nursery, a remarkable sum considering their effort occurred at the beginning of the economic recovery. Feeling an obligation to the public, they paid off the building mortgage of $2,500, made necessary repairs and improvements on the building, and "ran the Nursery with an efficient staff until provision was made for all the cases." While families in the neighborhood still needed day care, JLSD could no longer afford to operate their nursery in the red. The facility closed on August 15, 1936. With ten children still attending the nursery, JLSD "assumed responsibility for working out under professional direction" alternative provisions of care. In the case of two children, it paid for the children to live in boarding homes.[56] Their care and attention to finding safe spaces for these children is unusual and shows how devoted these women were to a nurturing custodial care, in spite of the criticisms they faced from professional critics.

On January 3, 1938, the regional director of the Associated Junior League of America, Mrs. Bradner W. Lee Jr., arrived in San Diego for a two-day observation of local programs. She had little positive to offer the group. Lee opened her report by questioning the logic of San Diego even hosting a league chapter with only 102 members (50 of whom were active). Lee held "both sympathy and admiration" for the San Diegans as they worked through a transitional period of older members believing younger members incapable of sustaining the group. Lee noted, "I feel that there should never have been a League there. The population is too transient, the city is small, and it is primarily a resort (Coronado) and a Naval Base." This shows how many members belonged to the military community, living in either Coronado or Pt. Loma. Lee's report documented the obvious effects of the Depression, citing the closures of the day nursery and its source of income, the League Thrift Shop. Lee understood that shuttering the day nursery was essential but noted the project was "endeared to the older members" who "considered [the nursery] indispensable, contrary to professional advice that it was unnecessary to the community." As with many voluntary day nurseries across the country, the JLSD program suffered from the success of ENS. Parents who qualified financially to use an ENS stopped needing the services of the JLSD day nursery, where they would have to pay, even if only a minimal amount.[57]

By 1938 the JLSD seemed willing to listen to advisors such as Marshall, Lee, and even Hawley. They eliminated any social service hands-on activities and instead funded the salary and expenses of a children's case worker. She managed the caseloads at five different children's agencies in the area and received her paycheck and supervision through the Associated Charities. The chapter paid $175 each month to cover the salary and $50 annually for supplies. Thus, JLSD stepped away from direct childcare and moved toward creating adolescent programming by starting a recreation program for disadvantaged girls from Memorial Junior High School. Every week JLSD members met with the girls at the league building to teach them dance, music, art, and "deportment." But they devoted most of their energy toward fund-raising.[58] That legacy carried through the rest of the twentieth century as the Junior League of San Diego grew to 190,000 members and raised hundreds of thousands of dollars for charitable interests.

The demise of the JLSD day nursery seems to have signaled a transition from volunteer-driven organizations offering childcare to professionally regulated childcare and nursery school education provided by trained teachers and managed with government oversight. Neighborhood House residents, all of whom were trained professionals by the 1930s, had identified cannery families as particularly vulnerable and able to benefit from emergency nursery school intervention. The advocacy of these professionals helped families living in the southwest neighborhoods of the city locate and secure childcare. In 1934 it appeared as though San Diego would lose the canning industry, but fears of the canneries abandoning the city never came true; in fact, Anita Jones commented to the National Federation of Day Nurseries on how the steady cannery work throughout the summer and fall of 1935 brought "more income than usual" to those using NH services. Jones noted how the 1935–1936 California–Pacific International Exposition contributed to this situation, and she worried that its close would bring a dreaded slump to the city.[59]

Launched in the midst of the Great Depression, the California–Pacific International Exposition generated solid income and goodwill for the community, and it displayed educational innovations in a time when Progressive ideas had waned. It also provided temporary work in constructing exposition structures and servicing the grounds, and further cemented the city's relationship with the navy. The military was ever-present throughout the new exposition, and one booster commented in 1935, "One thing that San Diegans should realize is that the officers and men of the fleet represent virtually every city and hamlet in the nation. These 4,000 officers and 55,000 men will write home about San Diego and the Exposition, one of the greatest and most effective forms of advertising that any city or Exposition ever enjoyed."[60]

FIG. 19. Workmen on the buildings for the 1935–36 California–Pacific International Exposition run to receive their paychecks, 1934. © San Diego History Center.

As with the 1915 Panama-California Exposition, San Diego's reputation as a coastal paradise helped draw visitors to the 1934–1935 fair. Organizers also recognized the growing partnership with the military and massaged their relationships with New Deal Democrats to secure funds necessary to repair Balboa Park buildings and erect new structures. San Diego's natural gift of temperate weather allowed tourism to continue generating revenue for the city. Thus, another strategy used by civic leaders to counter the Depression involved the familiar tactic of hosting a World's Fair. The two-year event showcased the botanical beauty and architectural splendor of Balboa Park, promoted educational innovations, and emphasized amusement park entertainment. Physician Rieta Hough remembered the exposition as "one of the biggest fun things" she'd ever attended in her life: "I'm sure that it did a great deal for the economy, but even more, it got people acquainted with San Diego. Always before it was San Francisco or Los Angeles, and San Diego was a step-child."[61] Visitors to the exposition spent their money on midway games and foods, and much was made of the adult zones, where a nudist colony, striptease acts, peep shows, and fan dances remained some of the most popular attractions and generated the most revenue.[62] The exposition also emphasized scientific and educational innovation such as astronomical technology developed by the California Technology Institute and instructional methods like the demonstration nursery schools. One of the first large-scale promotions of nursery school learning appeared at the exposition when the Brooklyn Street ENS moved into the Palace of Education in Balboa Park. Through large panes of one-way glass, exposition visitors could watch the goings-on of the nursery staff and children without disrupting the classroom experience."[63]

Isabella Hammack supervised the demonstration project. She personified an early childhood educator who helped set a professional tone for San Diego's childcare program. Hammack had strong ties to San Diego before being selected to lead the project. After graduating from San Diego's Normal School, she taught in El Cajon (a town on the eastern border of San Diego County) for one year and then moved to the San Diego city school district, where she taught for twelve years. In 1925 she entered the University of California to pursue an advanced degree in parent education, child development, and child teaching. With her master's degree in hand, Hammack taught child development and supervised students at the nursery school at Mills College in Oakland. She then returned to San Diego and the nursery school at Francis Parker. San Diego State Normal College hired Hammack in 1931 with the specific assignment of organizing a child development program. Her expertise guided the inclusion of the Brooklyn Street program at the exposition and its transfer to State College upon the exposition's closure.[64]

Just as promoters of the Columbian Exposition in 1893 and San Francisco's Exposition in 1915 had done, San Diego boosters used the nursery school to attract middle-class parents to this exposi-

FIG. 20. Vegetable and seafood canneries provided important wage options for women in San Diego. These women sort peppers for packing, c. 1935. © San Diego History Center.

tion. The Brooklyn Street nursery school shared exhibition space with models of the Palomar Observatory designed by scientists from the California Institute of Technology as examples of educational innovation.[65] Ethel Mintzer noted how the exposition proved the value of childcare and parent education in an unprecedented way.[66] Touted as an educational advance, the demonstration nursery school continued well after the exposition closed, through its transfer to the newly built San Diego State Normal College.[67] The exposition also strengthened the military's commitment to the community and introduced the city to hundreds of newcomers who otherwise would not have dreamt of moving to San Diego.

Yet cannery workers, not middle-class parents, had been the primary users of both the day nurseries and the nursery schools in San Diego. Poorly paid and subjected to long hours, workers moved to unionize through the efforts of international labor organizer Luisa Morena. Her visit in 1937 stirred up hopes for the United Cannery, Agricultural, Packing, and Allied Workers of America to unionize the canneries, and El Congreso expanded its civil rights activism to counter repatriation.[68] But the military, not labor or tourism, took over San Diego. By the decade's end, military preparedness forced the city into round-the-clock production, pumping its population to over two hundred thousand. Traveling to the city for work rather than pleasure, people arrived with barely one week's worth of food supplies and no prospects for permanent housing. Their bedraggled states did not go unnoticed by permanent residents. In-migrants from the Midwest, South, and East Coast, no matter their race or ethnicity, found themselves targets of hurtful slurs, housing segregation, and job discrimination. As the fear of a U.S. entry into World War II percolated across the country, San Diegans faced their biggest challenges yet in securing housing, jobs, childcare, and enough rations for permanent residents and the thousands of hopeful transient workers who descended upon the community starting in 1939.

Most people who arrived in 1939 and 1940 were poor, unemployed, and dislocated from their immediate kin networks. In its annual report for 1939, TASSD reported assisting several "families and individuals hired for the aircraft industry coming to San Diego without sufficient funds," with some of those people forced to return to their home cities after losing those jobs. Other families ended up in San Diego by accident rather than design. One man showed up in the Travelers Aid office with two children, seven and eleven years old, claiming they had all hitchhiked from Ohio after he lost his WPA job. The man believed he could find work along the way, but nothing had solidified and "he found himself without food or shelter." The agency fed the trio and referred them to the Salvation Army. The TASSD guide reacted to their dilemmas with exasperation: "So many people think California and San Diego in particular is abounding in jobs. They hear of this and that job waiting for somebody to come and take it. The result is that they arrive with only enough money to live on for a few days.... Someone suggests seeing the Travelers Aid and lo, here they come." Others traveled to San Diego in search of a lost friend or lover connected with the military. The Red Cross asked Travelers Aid to assist a young pregnant woman, hoping to convince the father of the unborn child to marry her. The TASSD guide described her as "attractive with a fairly good education," whose growing belly had forced her out of a waitress job. She now supported herself with domestic work and realized there was no future with the marine; thus, she asked TASSD to help her with transport back to her mother in Indiana.[69]

Some pregnant women who connected with TASSD insisted on staying in the city, despite the fact that the fathers of their babies would not admit to paternity.[70] For these women, in particular, city shortages made a bad situation worse, as pregnancy or newly delivered status would affect the kinds of work they could secure. On Christmas Day 1940, Eleanor Mead, executive secretary of San Diego's Associated Charities, wrote to the national Charities general director, Linton B. Swift, to reveal some of the problems facing San Diego and her organization. She explained: "Agencies, city fathers, city and county departments, federal agencies are all going to it and we are trying not to let it run away with us completely. The aircraft industry is one of our biggest problems, and the families coming for work, no homes for them, and traffic is terrific for our little town. But we still have our sunshine, our poinsettias, fifteen-feet high—and hope that eventually there will be some peace for this world."[71] Mead's letter ended with optimism, but many issues afflicted residents in this new decade.

Troubles with securing quality housing and day care coupled with severe rationing, regular blackouts, daily air raid exercises, and dealing with the constant rumors of enemy attacks kept San Diegans on edge for several years. While not in a war zone, San Diego's designation as home to the Pacific Fleet made it a target and almost overnight further militarized the city. Sailors, marines, fliers, and soldiers descended upon the county, and the downtown and harbor areas burst with activity. Everyday activities shifted toward making life more pleasant for off-duty servicemen, but at the same time ensuring national security. Servicemen and civilians could catch movies all night and day at the Fox Theater or take in a revue at Eddie's, where "continuous entertainment" included Fran Ross and her All Girl Band. Roller rinks, dance halls, and diners filled with enlisted men and their dates. Downtown's Hollywood Theatre on F Street between Fourth and Fifth Avenues boasted packed houses seven days a week. Famous for its "Big Girl Revue" that included male and female dancers, singers, and striptease acts, the place was packed mainly with sailors. Massive blankets of chicken wire covered in feathers hung over entire streets to camouflage defense factories, partially built battleships, and service automobiles. The eerie canopy disguised production sites from the air but caused rashes, headaches, allergic reactions and anxiety for the workers passing beneath.[72]

San Diego's economy pumped into overdrive starting in 1939, altering life for all residents in ways that further stressed the limited housing, social services, and medical resources. As in the 1930s, federal intervention offered some relief, but the needs far exceeded what federal resources could provide. Nevertheless, San Diegans came to depend on public services as their city became more closely tied to the federal government. The federal programs implemented from 1930 to 1935 provided a foundational structure for services expanded during World War II. San Diegans began experiencing economic recovery by the late 1930s, and tremendous demographic change. Fifty thousand people arrived in 1940 alone, and the number of San Diegans working specifically in defense-related jobs grew to ninety thousand.[73] Many of those workers were married women with small children, a group that constituted 40 percent of the workforce by 1945. By 1941 the federal government had included it on its list of "war impacted" areas, which opened access to federal assistance for housing and childcare programs. That assistance did not fully solve the problems facing San Diego's leaders and residents, but it did cushion some of the toughest falls during the war years.

CHAPTER SEVEN

Wartime Care

Navigating the San Diego Home Front

> It is possible for San Diego children to attend child care
> centers as long as eighteen hours a day and be with their
> own parents only while they are asleep!
>
> —Child Welfare League of America, 1944

When Kay Hill arrived in San Diego in July 1941, she expected to find housing that would accommodate her family. As a condition of employment with Consolidated Aircraft Corporation (CAC), her husband had relocated to San Diego several months earlier, and Kay was anxious to reunite their family. But instead of easing their children into new school patterns, she found herself dealing with landlords who refused to rent to them because of their children. They were not alone. Housing shortages and discriminatory practices against couples with children left many families in the cold. The Hills resorted to renting a hotel suite, an expensive solution, but one made possible by an engineer's salary. Companies like CAC smoothed the transition into San Diego for some of its recruits, giving them guidance on where to send their children to school and how to navigate the housing shortage.[1] Most people moving into the area, however, did not benefit from similar resources. Otis Porter from Pawnee, Oklahoma, secured a CAC job, making sixty-four cents an hour as a line worker. He sent for his wife and six children but had terrible luck in finding affordable housing that accommodated them all. The Porters made due with a one-room efficiency in an auto court for eighteen dollars a week and were thankful to be together.[2]

Families like the Hills and Porters represent typical experiences of people moving into San Diego from across the nation or other parts of California. Newcomers to the area—referred to in the media as "Aviation Okies" or by governmental census takers as "In-Migrants"—faced exasperating searches for adequate and affordable housing because of the incredible population boom in San Diego. Its civilian population soared in two years from 192,486 in 1940 to 276,000 in 1942, and by 1944 the city's population had grown to 286,050 (a 41 percent growth in four years); and the military population skyrocketed from 38,075 in 1939 to 193,296 in 1944.[3] Business and civic leaders had been recruiting the military and manufacturers like CAC for several decades, and they knew the city's services needed an overhaul, but the war economy accelerated those concerns and caught leaders off guard. Urban historian Christine Killory explains how in 1940 "San Diego suddenly achieved national prominence as an urban problem—a congested war production area where the demands of mobilization threatened to stretch municipal resources to the point of collapse."[4] In fairness, few people would have predicted the unprecedented consequences of war production.

This chapter expands the analysis of the wartime crisis by highlighting how families with young children struggled to secure affordable housing, access to medical care, and options for safe childcare.[5] The population change created by in-migrants and casual transients cast a troubling mark on the city. Affordable housing, safe childcare, and room in school classrooms concerned parents, and all residents faced problems associated with rationing, security precautions, curfews, and a widely fluctuating economy. Cost of living in San Diego rose nearly 12 percent from October 1939 to October 1941. The acting commissioner of labor statistics reported that "the increase in living costs in San Diego over the two-year period has been considerably greater than the average increase in the larger cities of the country, where costs rose 9.1 percent over the same period." In 1941 from mid-July to mid-October, the cost of living in the city increased by 4.8 percent, with retail food prices jumping by 7.6 percent, "considerably more than the increase in the country at large."[6] Federal authorities had based wartime food allotments on the 1940 population figures, which resulted in severe shortages. Residents competed for commodities of sugar, coffee, fresh meat, flour, milk, and gasoline, and shop owners reserved food for longtime regular customers. Women on the adventurous side smuggled coffee, sugar, cigarettes, and silk stockings out of Tijuana, but one needed transportation across the border, and the risks deterred most people from taking such actions.[7] Unlike in earlier decades, childcare concerns affected a broad spectrum of residents, as women from the working and middle classes entered the job market for the first time.

In San Diego, foster care homes, parent–child boarding homes, and licensed family day care homes emerged in the early 1940s in an attempt to alleviate this childcare crisis. Additionally, reformers at the federal, state, and local levels collaborated to establish a statewide collective of childcare centers, California Child Care Centers (cccc). These were designed specifically for workers connected to defense operations; however, the needs far outweighed the resources, particularly the absence of infant care. The combination of these services offered relief to a good portion of working families, and some parents relied on their own families, but the war drew thousands of mothers from all walks of life into the workforce. According to figures from the federal government's Women's Bureau, the number of female workers in the combined San Diego County/City region expanded from 23.7 percent of San Diego's workforce (or 18,546 workers) in April 1940 to 38.1 percent (or 53,610 workers) by March 1944. In-migrant women represented just over half of the new laborers.[8] Across the nation the war economy accounted for greater numbers of women workers over the age of thirty-five entering the workforce, but the *opposite* occurred in San Diego, as more younger women than older women entered waged labor. Fifty-four percent of San Diego's female workforce had been under the age of thirty-five in 1940 and increased to 57 percent by 1944. From 1940 to 1944, women workers with children under the age of ten remained constant at 10 percent, meaning these women needed some sort of childcare.[9] From 1939 to 1944, some 51 percent of San Diego's total labor force (or 78,675 women) had migrated into the city, and these in-migrant women represented 80 percent of the city's new female workers. Their presence changed the city dynamic by infusing a decidedly youthful element into the area's working-class sector. By 1944 some 46 percent of all in-migrant women over the age of fourteen worked in waged labor, compared to 34 percent of local women. In-migrants were younger than either the local San Diego or national female worker, and a greater percentage were married.[10] Those figures translated into this group needing affordable, reliable, and stable childcare, because they could not rely on family networks to help them with this responsibility.

In-migrants moved to San Diego to fulfill a work or military obligation or for the promise of employment. Some couples, like the Johnstons, took in stride their living conditions, but they were unusual. Luise Johnston recalled being oblivious to the city's over-population and associated problems because she was so in love with her husband. The Johnstons arrived from Oklahoma in late 1940, found a small apartment in the North Park neighborhood near Thirty-second Street and El Cajon Blvd., and quickly made friends with other young couples renting in the complex. Her husband's college education secured him an engineering position at CAC, and Luise also took a job with CAC as a file clerk, despite having earned a college degree. She trained as an international telephone operator, a position that "thrilled" Luise with the "thought [she] was helping to win the war." Luise remembers the company treating her and her husband very well: when she became pregnant, they allowed her to work through her eighth month and gave her time off to have the baby; and they helped the couple secure a housing loan so they could move into one of the new homes being built in Pacific Beach. Their son was born in 1943, and Luise decided not to return to work. Her husband's middle-class salary proved adequate to support the family, and their connections to loan assistance and newly built homes gave them a stable life. Their racial identity as whites allowed them wide access to secure employment and safe housing, and because Luise removed herself from the workforce, the Johnstons did not suffer from the lack of childcare in the city.[11]

The majority of the female workforce did not work for companies that offered housing referrals, loan assistance, or professional salaries. Transplanted companies like CAC helped improve San Diego's economy by providing hundreds of well-paying and stable jobs, but most of these jobs went to white men. Unlike other war-impacted areas, such as Oakland and Los Angeles, in-migration did not diversify San Diego's population: the 1940 census designated 96.9 percent of the population "White," 2.0 percent "Negro," and 1.1 percent "Other" (primarily Filipino, Chinese, and Japanese). This differed significantly from the national average of 89.9 White, 9.8 percent Negro, and 0.4 percent Other, although it is important to recognize that the census categorized Mexican Americans as "White." Local San Diegans, however, did not collapse these categories, and the long-standing prejudices against Mexican-descent people continued into the 1940s. The March 1944 census showed figures of 97.2 percent White, 2.5 percent Negro, and 0.3 percent Other, which exacerbated the racism existing in the city.[12]

Census statistics reveal the demographic weight of the war, and oral histories of women living in San Diego highlight the cultural responses to these changes, especially the differences between local and in-migrant mothers.[13] Most women workers believed they would become a "Rosie the Riveter" in the defense industry, collect a hefty paycheck, and make exciting new friends, but to their surprise, most of them ended up in low-paid, service-sector jobs.[14] Racial and ethnic barriers also prevented African American, Mexican American, and non-English-speaking women from accessing the higher-paying jobs found in defense factories or commercial businesses. The Pacific Parachute Company was an important exception. African American Howard "Skippy" Smith owned the company and insisted on hiring a diverse workforce that included mostly women from African American, Mexican, Brazilian, Filipino, West Indian, and white communities. The fac-

FIG. 21. The Pacific Parachute Company employed a diverse group of women, which included white, African American, and Mexican American women of various ages, c. 1943. © San Diego History Center.

tory produced fifty thousand small-sized parachutes during its first year, earning Smith the National Negro Business League's Spaulding Award for achievement in business in 1943. By 1944 and the end of the war, contracts diminished and the company closed its San Diego operation and moved to Los Angeles.[15]

Most women in San Diego, no matter their identity, worked in non-defense jobs. They labored in the canneries, candy factories, and various shops, and in a variety of service jobs, from washing dishes, cooking, and waitressing to domestic work in private homes and businesses. African American women labored as domestic servants in private homes, cooks and maids in hotels, restroom attendants in department stores, or operators in laundries. A young woman could also earn money as a movie theater usherette or in the dance clubs and bars that catered to servicemen in the downtown area and along the midway near the naval base in Point Loma. Women from the Japanese community had worked in the fish canneries, and their forced removal in 1942 due to Executive Order 9066 opened their positions for others to fill. Some Filipino women (immigrant and native born) also worked in the fish canneries along with (but seldom alongside) immigrants who spoke little to no English, such as Mexican, Italian, and Portuguese women. Mexican and Mexican American women also worked at smaller factories that processed pickles, olive oil, and lemon juice for national distribution, helped manage family grocery markets and cafés, or sewed in tailor shops. Others worked as seasonal laborers in the citrus and olive groves, tomato fields, and other vegetable farms.[16]

Importantly, Mexican-descent mothers tended to have familial help with childcare through their daughters and nieces. Several residents of Barrio Logan remember the girls in their neighborhood as being responsible for the care of the home and children while their mothers worked in the canneries. The Piña sisters, Armida and Obdulia "Tulie" Trejos, recounted how their mother depended on them throughout her childbearing years but especially so when she entered the cannery in the early 1940s. Their mother gave birth to fourteen children (sadly, two died in infancy), and Tulie remembers taking her siblings to the NH clinic for immunizations. Their father worked but did not allow their mother to do so; the war changed that for a time. Their mother's employment gave the family a respite from the deep poverty they endured throughout their childhoods, as her earnings purchased a stove, an icebox, and new beds for the family. Unfortunately, her brothers got into trouble and had to appear in juvenile court for their actions. The judge agreed to release them to the Piña parents if Mrs. Piña quit her job so as to better supervise her children. She complied with the judge's orders but hated to do so. Tulie believed her mother found freedom from her abusive husband while working, and Tulie admits that despite the responsibilities of caring for her siblings, she enjoyed her teen years because the strict rules of their household became far more relaxed when her mother entered the cannery.[17]

Moves across the country as a result of military service or work transfers usually severed ties to extended kinship networks that could help parents manage childcare, wartime rations, and limited housing options. Loneliness, isolation, overt racism, job discrimination, and unfamiliarity with Southern California living created additional stresses, especially for in-migrant women. For female heads of households, the possibility of losing their husbands as a result of his military service compounded their problems. Some women had married immediately prior to their husbands being shipped overseas, and these women often found themselves newly married and pregnant but alone in a strange city.[18] Or, like Ruth Martin, they followed their husbands to San Diego, which left them estranged from their home network.

In 1944 Ruth Martin and her three small children came to San Diego to be nearer her husband, Frank, a petty officer first class, who was stationed in the city. Resources were at an all-time low, and rationing kept grocery, gasoline, and housing prices at a premium. In order to secure a rental, the Martins lied about their religion. Ruth described their year in San Diego as "miserable," as terrible housing conditions and high food prices made caring for her children extremely difficult: "No toilet, no sink. Used a big bucket and buried it in the back yard. At night the rats ran around. Had to sterilize everything before use. Weren't allowed yard privileges so sat on a stoop. Went to Zoo every Sunday for peace and air. All 3 children got whooping cough, one polio also. I lost weight caring for them and not the proper food for them and decent housing. Couldn't get diapers, had to use anything that was white. Scrubbed everything by hand." Ruth's description is a hygienic nightmare, and it is no wonder her children fell ill. She wrote of enduring taunts from locals and emphasized that she never experienced a single kindness the entire time they lived in San Diego.[19] Another white woman reported her desperation in finding housing that accepted her children, exclaiming, "What do they want me to do with my kids, drown them?"[20] Beyond insufficient childcare, these mothers found numerous barriers to stabilizing their family life.

Many mothers often had to deal with these problems alone, due to their husbands' working in other states or being stationed abroad. In-migrant women who had expected to be full-time homemakers found themselves entering the workforce in order to make ends meet. Some companies, like CAC, played an important yet reluctant role in hiring women, especially white women, for the sewing, wiring, and assembling of small parts. Since moving its operation from Buffalo to San Diego in 1935, the CAC payroll catapulted from 3,170 employees in 1940 to 45,000 in 1943, providing jobs from design engineers and electricians to welders and upholstery fabricators. During the 1940s CAC was the second-largest employer in San Diego (the navy being the largest) and used its influence to convince officials to build the city's airport at the harbor so as to accommodate the growth of its business.[21] Starting in 1941 the company began hiring women to compensate for its loss of men to military service. Concerned by so many unskilled and female workers handling production quotas, the company implemented the "first mechanized assembly line for heavy bombers in America."[22]

Kettenburg Boat Works, another company that experienced tremendous wartime growth, shortened its five-year apprentice course to two years to accommodate the need for skilled labor. The city public school district also changed its curriculum by dedicating resources to vocational education. At the height of the war (1942–43), 29,500 students received vocational training in the public schools, and more than 125,000 students were trained throughout the war years. American Indians at the Sherman Institute were one group who benefited from this focus. By 1942 six Indian Service boarding schools, including Sherman, offered vocational training in skills needed in the defense industry. Sherman courses prepared men and women in acetylene and electric arc welding and various machine shop jobs. Only men could enroll in heavy arc-welding courses, and only women took business courses such as typing and stenography. Solar Aircraft employed many Sherman graduates, and seeing female welders at the plant was not unusual. One such was Mrs. Elizabeth Ortega, a "Mission Indian" who had been schooled at Sherman, and who received the "highly prized Army–Navy 'E' pin" for her skill and efficiency on the job.[23]

The experiences of Japanese and Japanese American families in San Diego County offer another important perspective of how the war changed life for people in San Diego. In 1940 some 2,076 Japanese-heritage people lived in San Diego County, and another 828 lived in the city. They earned a living by farming vegetables, working in the fishing industry, or keeping small shops.[24] Executive Order 9066 dramatically changed the culture of their community. As a result of the Japanese attack on Pearl Harbor, on December 7, 1941, President Franklin D. Roosevelt signed and issued on February 19, 1942, the order to remove all persons of Japanese ancestry from military areas, and San Diego was identified as such an area. On April 8, 1942, fifteen hundred Japanese-descent residents voluntarily gathered at San Diego's Santa Fe Depot for rail transport north into Orange County to the Santa Anita Assembly Center, a racetrack converted to a military-style barracks. They hoped to show other San Diegans through their peaceful and orderly assembly that they were law-abiding citizens. But San Diegans turned against the quiet group, forgetting the positive contributions to the economy and community that the Japanese had made since arriving in the late nineteenth century. Other Asian groups, especially residents from China and the Philippines, feared possible backlash from the Executive Order and kept their distance from all involved in the issue. For months prior to the evacuation, local editorials proclaimed ugly sentiments against the Japanese community, and their livelihoods disintegrated with Executive Order 9066. Most Japanese in San Diego lived out the remainder of the war at the Poston Internment Camp in the Arizona desert.[25] Upon the end of the war, detainees were released from internment camps, but they remained isolated from the majority of San Diegans through job and housing segregation.[26]

A surreal silence on the evacuation and internment of Japanese-ancestry people enveloped the city. Simultaneous to the implementation of the Executive Order, national magazines instead touted the city's pleasant weather and plentiful jobs. Recognizing the incredible population surge, the *Saturday Evening Post* characterized San Diego as a "Blitz-Boom" city, and a *National Geographic* advertisement promoted it as the perfect vacation spot where one could ski, surf, and experience war preparations firsthand.[27] In linking defense preparedness with leisure fun, the advertisements normalized the militarization of San Diego. Yet aside from the weather, little about San Diego in 1942 signaled a vacation paradise.

Poor access to affordable housing compounded economic and social problems for San Diegans. Housing space expanded, but not nearly enough to meet the need, leaving some people forced into uncomfortable situations like living in tents, converted garages, drafty trailers, or their cars. To prepare for an expected increased workforce in San Diego, Congress authorized in 1940 the building of the largest planned community in the United States, the Linda Vista Housing Project. Federal architects envisioned the three-thousand-family unit project, located atop a canyon plateau northwest of Mission Valley, as a self-sufficient neighborhood with schools, hospitals, shopping centers, and parks within walking distance of the homes. The project became possible because of funds available through the federal Lanham Defense Housing Act, and its operational jurisdiction fell to the Public Buildings Administration. The federal government broke ground on March 5, 1941, and contracted for it to be completed within three hundred days. But the grand designs never materialized, and the project became a terrible eyesore. The residences looked more like barracks than private homes, and residents soon overtaxed the rudimentary sewers, electricity, gas, and water delivery lines that had been quickly installed.[28] Historian Mary Taschner explained, "From a construction standpoint, the plans for Linda Vista worked perfectly. But from a planning point of view, the project served as a horrible example of what can happen when the local community is not considered in any way."[29] The Linda Vista project never achieved the efficiency standards envisioned by federal planners. One ten-inch water pipe connected to San Diego city water supplies, and residents entered the development from a single narrow winding road.[30] Isolated from the hub of the city, the neighborly feel envisioned by its architects never materialized.

Housing continued to be a problem in spite of additional federal projects such as the Frontier development in Point Loma near the naval base, and authorities were most concerned about low-cost options for workers. Rental rates remained a problem throughout the war era. Locals understood the rental bonanza as a rare opportunity to earn a little extra money and rented their garages, sheds, and extra bedrooms to desperate in-migrants as a way to counter inflation and food shortages. Self-described land-lords charged exorbitant rentals and discriminated at will by using religion, race, ethnicity, and familial status to ban certain people from renting their properties. As we saw with Ruth Martin's situation, these practices could have devastating effects on a family. By 1942 the city council passed an ordinance structuring rental fees, but locals found a way around the rulings and continued to overcharge.[31]

In spite of these problems, San Diegans saw a bit of relief by January 1943 with the completion of several federal housing projects, like the Linda Vista and Frontier projects. Employees who worked at certain companies that built or supplied materials for weapons and other military supplies (such as Campbell Machine Company and Tavares Construction Company) were eligible to live in the projects. In San Diego, twenty-eight companies or governmental units were included on the eligibility list, allowing for some families to move from tents and trailers into homes.[32] Substantial help could have arrived earlier if San Diego's leaders had accessed funding through the newly established National Housing Authority; San Diego's boosters, however, did not wish to pursue government subsidies for federally subsidized low-income housing, because they believed the buildings would stain the beauty of its coastline.[33] Politics likely figured into the decision as well, since San Diego continued to be a staunchly Republican and non-union city. Federal subsidies helped workers in machine cities like Detroit, but leaders from western cities like fast-growing Dallas and San Diego distanced themselves from lobbying for nonmilitary-related federal funding. Even though workers came to the city because of the war economy, it took four years of chaotic social dynamics for San Diego's business leaders to understand housing as a military issue. San Diego eventually established an office in Washington for lobbying purposes, but not until April 1943.[34]

In-migrants experienced the majority of the housing problems, but some locals also struggled with finding affordable housing, especially if work or military service separated family members. Native San Diegan Mary Jane Babcock's experience demonstrates problems some local young couples dealt with because of the wartime conditions. Like so many young women of her generation, Babcock married her high school sweetheart months after they both graduated from high school in 1942 and soon became pregnant.[35] The young couple could afford only a converted garage, and when her husband was shipped overseas, Mary Jane had to deal with the challenges of their housing alone. Termites swarmed out of the garage walls, but when Mary Jane notified the landlord, he simply shrugged his shoulders. Pregnant, alone, and disgusted by the bug-infested rental in University Heights, Mary Jane moved to a small cottage in a safe, quiet neighborhood close to the bus line in Ocean Beach. She delivered a healthy baby, and when her son was just three months old, Mary Jane began work at the telephone company. The third-shift job presented a childcare problem for the new mother, but the solution came in the form of a boarder. A woman from South Carolina whose husband had been assigned to the North Island naval base answered an ad Mary Jane had posted on the company message board. Because the South Carolinian had a five-year-old daughter, housing had been difficult for her to find, and living with Mary Jane solved her problem. The women divided housework, childcare, and shopping duties, and since their schedules did not overlap, they seldom had to share the living space of the small one-bedroom house. The arrangement worked for about a year, until the husband was transferred out of state, and the woman and daughter followed him. Mary Jane's budget limited her options, but her parents lived in the area, so she moved home and enrolled the baby in a nearby day care center.[36]

Thousands of women in San Diego dealt with situations similar to Mary Jane's by turning to a tried and true method of pooling their resources. They developed networks within their neighborhoods to ensure the safety of their children and shared childcare, shopping, cooking, and cleaning responsibilities as well as friendship. The decision to take in a boarder was a common choice for wage-earning mothers of infants in San Diego. These women typically returned to work in order to supplement an enlisted man's meager pay or to fully support their families if recently widowed, abandoned, or divorced, or if their husbands had been wounded in the war. Connections to a workplace often helped women find resources, even if an employer did not offer benefits to its employees. Mary Jane's entry into the workforce gave her an added network to navigate problems with housing and childcare. Both Mary Jane and Ruth were white and working-class, and experienced the downside of property owners playing loose with definitions of "room for rent." But Mary Jane entered the workforce and used that network to help her find a boarder, and then she could turn to her parents for help. One will never know if the Martins' neighbors ignored or mistreated them to the extent believed by Ruth, but the fact that she remembers it being because of her in-migrant status and religion is important. Mary Jane benefited from being a local San Diegan with family ties in ways that Ruth Martin did not.

So much of Ruth's trauma derived from her not knowing her way around the community, being isolated in her "home," and overwhelmed with the care of three children under the age of four. With an absent husband and no friends or family to take the toddlers so she could nap with the baby, Ruth became exasperated with this stage of her life. It seems unlikely that a property owner would ban children from a yard, but Ruth asserted "yard privileges" did not come with the rental agreement. She insisted locals treated them poorly and that only her husband's service buddies helped them. She depicted a barren environment that lacked access to public transportation and basic amenities. It must have been extremely tiring to shop for groceries with three small children and a baby in tow. Ruth does not mention utilizing social services or even being aware of their existence, but perhaps these programs could have provided her with some respite or at least introduced her to a friend she so desperately craved. Add to her problems the fact she had no indoor plumbing, and it's no wonder she hated her life in San Diego.

As with housing, the medical needs of the community expanded, and practitioners fought to keep up the frantic pace of providing health care to all who needed it. Dr. Rieta Campbell Hough noted that her practice quadrupled during the war years, requiring her to put in sixteen-hour shifts. Those hours took a toll on her body, and after the war ended, she was ill for two years trying to recover from the exhaustion. Recalling this time in her life, Hough bitterly explained, "I always thought about what one of my pediatrician friends wrote me during the war. He was sitting under a tree in Australia and he wished he were home helping us. All these doctors who went to war and have wonderful retirement pay—I thought that I did more work than many of them did, and I really think that I should have had a pension, a pension for service beyond the call of duty."[37] Hough points out an important issue about military service: the discriminatory nature of its recruitment and hiring that denied most female and nonwhite male professionals participation.[38]

The many physicians and nurses sent into war zones left a limited number of medical personnel to deliver, immunize, and treat sick babies. A decision by the navy to deny servicemen's wives and other female dependents access to the Naval Hospital stressed an already taxed healthcare system and pushed these pregnant women to the Sisters of Mercy Hospital. That situation cut the normal ten-day maternity stay to four days for insured women with high-risk deliveries, and to as little as two days for women who delivered a healthy baby and appeared healthy enough to recover at home. Hough remembered Mercy Hospital delivering as many as eight hundred babies a month during the war years, noting that the Lying-In Hospital in Chicago was the only obstetrical unit in the country that delivered more babies. Hough stated, "Our quarters were so limited that many of our patients were delivered and then had to be sent home in about five or six hours by ambulance after they felt there would be no complications."[39] But once a woman left the hospital, she faced the dilemma of how to care for her baby when she returned to work.

San Diego's birthrate situation reached crisis mode by 1941. Interviews with mothers, reports from local service organizations, company assessments, and national surveys pinpoint the care of infants as the number one problem facing parents in San Diego during the war years. Parents without familial connections in the city could board children with foster families, but this was not a popular measure among mothers. Many women balked at the idea of living apart from their children, especially if their children were not yet school aged. Instead, like Mary Jane Babcock, they arranged to share housing with other mothers, with whom they traded housekeeping and day care responsibilities.

As with housing and medical care, existing childcare resources simply did not match the need. The baby boom made infant care necessary, but solutions eluded the authorities. Boarding homes and foster care homes seldom took children younger than two years and rarely accepted infants under the age of six months. Moreover, many people believed mothers should enter the workforce only after they had weaned their breastfed-baby or the baby ate solid foods, and preferably after the child entered elementary school. One option included the holdovers from the emergency nursery schools established in the mid-1930s, but those programs focused on educating children aged two to six. Additionally, the working population had expanded from the city's center, and none of the existing nurseries were located in the new housing developments.

Problems associated with finding childcare for all ages of children dominated the caseload of the Family Services Association of San Diego (FSASD), the renamed Associated Charities. According to the FSASD, in March 1941, eighteen parents requested placement of their children in boarding homes due to the war situation. In only four months, those numbers tripled to sixty-seven in July, increasing again in September to eighty-three. A slight decrease came in the fall, with seventy-eight parents requesting assistance in October, and another seventy-four in November.[40] While these numbers from 1941 are only a fraction of the parents in need of childcare,

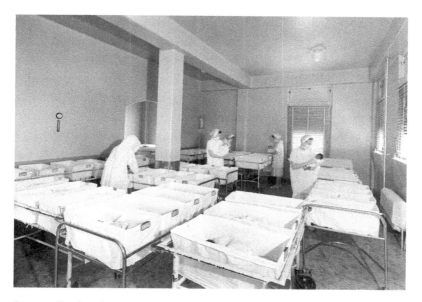

FIG. 22. During the war years, as many as eight hundred babies a month were delivered at the Sisters of Mercy Hospital, 1942. © San Diego History Center.

these 320 requests for boarding assistance represent the most desperate situations and typically involved an in-migrant family.

Even when resources became available, agency officials ran up against how to convey to parents the realities of childcare solutions that would separate children from parents. FSASD director Eleanor Mead explained that her agency focused on families who had one parent working in defense (generally the mother) and seldom extended assistance to families in which both parents were present and earning wages. In those situations her organization encouraged the mother to stay at home to raise the children. She emphasized: "We believe strongly as an agency and as individual workers in the importance of our American family and home and we encourage its maintenance wherever it is possible. We do recognize, however, that there are times when it is necessary for children to be away from their parents and in those cases which we accept, we try to find the best substitute home for the children."[41]

According to a state report in August 1942, San Diego planned "to lean rather heavily on this type of care [foster day care], and the County Welfare Department is busy inspecting new homes."[42] FSASD made eighty-seven different placements of children in foster boarding homes in 1943, demonstrating the reality of separating families as a childcare option, but both agency and parent used it as a last resort.[43] Most mothers and childcare professionals did not see foster care as a good solution, because they believed it dramatically interrupted maternal bonding. Additionally, the national office of the Family Welfare Services Association of America (FWSAA) reported in 1942 that social agencies in San Diego made "no effort" to establish consultation centers for women considering paid employment. That oversight, the study documented, created the unfortunate situation of mothers overlooking the needs of school-aged children and using poor-quality care for their young children. The study pointed out that many mothers had placed their children in unlicensed homes, and San Diego had not developed any systematic care for school-aged children. As a result, women were leaving their jobs in the airplane factories specifically because they could not find childcare.[44] Studies like those conducted by the FWSAA helped convince the San Diego community that coordination between governmental bodies, social welfare agencies, and private businesses could create childcare solutions.

In addition to foster boarding homes, a large system of family day care homes had emerged in the city. Yet most of these providers reserved their spaces for older children, since many of these newly licensed providers were themselves mothers of infants or toddlers and did not feel comfortable caring for multiple children under the age of two. Counts on March 1, 1943, showed 118 licensed family day care homes in San Diego, but only ten of those homes were licensed to care for infants and/or children aged one year to preschool. Six of those homes could care for up to ten preschool-aged children, indicating how authorities allowed for licensed homes to be crowded beyond usual capacity so as to meet the demand.[45]

These figures underscored the enduring need in the city for childcare and spurred agency workers to devote significant time to recruiting and training foster day care providers. Within two months of the March census, the community had managed to recruit more women to open their homes and pass through licensure procedures for operating a day care home. In May 1943, 156 licensed day care homes listed vacancies. But infant care spaces remained a problem.[46] Consequently, nurse supervisors of federally funded child care centers in San Diego began openly discouraging mothers of infants to earn wages.[47]

United States Employment Service recommendations that women use boarding home care for children under the age of two primed several organizations to advocate that San Diego provide more infant care.[48] Some parents found affordable housing and childcare in a system of "parent–child homes" created in the city, but they catered to white families. The women who sought out parent–child homes tended to not have ties to the area, could not afford to wait for an opening at a nursery school, and did not want to be separated from their children. Often these mothers were in positions to settle in a parent–child home because their husband's military service was not located in San Diego. Mrs. Douglas faced this predicament in 1943. Recommended by the FSASD to use a parent–child home, Douglas agreed the arrangement would fit her needs but had questions the agency could not answer. She appreciated the requirements for a "stated agreement between parents and guardians" concerning such common issues as how and when to discipline, deciding which items the guardian should purchase with parental money, customs of the guardian home, and the acceptability of giving treats between meals. But the home entry requirement list—twelve stipulations in all—did not cover a critical issue in Douglas's eyes: "parents' feeling about sex education." She wanted it clarified that only she had the authority to guide her children in such personal matters.[49] Mrs. Douglas's questions and requests for clarification underscore how wage-earning parents negotiated with care providers to ensure their children remained emotionally connected to them. The city's development of the parent–child home illustrates that authorities wanted mothers to live with their children and shows how the community devised stopgap solutions to problems that were overwhelming the social network system.

The federal government provided some funding for these efforts, but as in the past, philanthropic campaigns, local businesses, volunteers, and parents paid the bulk of expenses. Even though public child care resources increased, many parents did not go through city services, opting instead to (or perhaps forced to) make arrangements themselves with neighbors, friends, and family, or in exchange for help with childcare and domestic service.[50] This is likely how most African American and Mexican American families survived, since they often were not approved for parent–child boarding homes due to the persistent racial discrimination in the city.

Another problem area was the city's lack of before- and after-school programs for adolescents. San Diegans, along with most of the nation, believed that adolescents whose parents worked away from home or served in the military needed closer monitoring to reduce incidences of sexual experimentation, alcohol use, and truancy. As a tonic for such activity, organizations like NH and the YMCA as well as city schools made sure it included this age group in its recreational programming. Dances and socials for servicemen were regular occurrences in the city's downtown, and these events made parents, school officials, and social workers nervous about adolescents posing as independent adults and mingling with far more socially experienced men. Immigrant parents were typically very strict with their daughters (especially the Italian, Mexican, and Portuguese families) and seldom let them attend dances without a chaperone. But most in-migrant parents did not have the same kind of established social network to guard against problematic encounters, so NH stepped in as a parental substitute.

Neighborhood House also expanded recreation and sports activities geared toward boys as a deterrent to juvenile delinquency. In 1943 Merlin Pinkerton joined the NH staff as the boys director, replacing Frank Galindo, who moved into a teaching position at Memorial Junior High. Pinkerton's hiring is linked to the Sleepy Lagoon murder trial and the zoot suit riots that troubled Los Angeles in the summer of 1943. Juvenile justice authorities hoped to prevent a similar situation in San Diego by dedicating more attention to boys and male adolescents, especially those from families who faced societal discrimination. At first the community complained that Pinkerton did not speak Spanish and did not understand the cultural expectations of the boys he would interact with; however, those complaints soon quieted, as "Coach" Pinkerton's devotion to helping the boys at NH became clear. Pinkerton's involvements included testifying as a character witness for boys called before the juvenile court, intervening when local business owners acted in racist ways (such as denying a group entry into the Fox Theater), and helping them find employment. He worked at the settlement into the 1970s.[51]

Despite these local efforts, national authorities from the FWSAA criticized San Diego officials for their poor handling of childcare resources.[52] Some relief came in 1943 with the development of the California Child Care Centers (CCCC), but hindsight shows us that the centers offered too little too late. Subsequent to the FWSAA report, the aircraft industry, the Public Welfare and Board of Education Departments, the Civilian Defense Council, and the War Manpower Committee collaborated in 1942 to apply for and secure Lanham Act funds. California's Committee on Children in Wartime produced a twelve-point policy statement on November 21, 1942, setting in place standards for the *emergency* (thus temporary) care of children due to the war. Committee members emphasized that the war created unusual conditions, so any measures implemented by the state should not be permanent programs. The committee focused on how best to provide day care for children ages two years through sixteen, assuming along with most authorities that mothers with children younger than two years would not enter the workforce.

California legislators grudgingly agreed to the plan but made clear that their vote resulted from the temporary status of women working because of the war. In her analysis of the state-funded CCCC program, Natalie Fousekis notes that legislators never intended to hold public meetings on the need for childcare but reluctantly did so upon the insistence of childcare advocates. Public hearings in Los Angeles, Oakland, and San Diego drew participation from working mothers alongside agency directors and early childhood educators to impress upon government officials the dire need for childcare. In San Diego, speakers at the hearings included the president of a local PTA and the director of Catholic Charities, both of whom reported on nursery schools filled to capacity. The director of Catholic Charities, Ellen Sweeney, noted, "Bayside Center, our nursery school, is taxed beyond capacity," which required her on a daily basis to turn away parents who worked in the defense industry.[53]

Signing off on the program in January 1943, the California legislature assigned school districts the authority to develop a comprehensive program. They understood operating funds would come from the Lanham Act, parents' fees, and support from industries affected by worker absenteeism. Only after these sources had been accessed would State War Council funds be made available to the program.[54] The Committee for Children in Wartime worked toward provision of standardized programs that integrated educational components with custodial care services.[55] Then, through the passage of the Child Care Center Act of 1943, the state guarded any liability to fully funding the centers. This act allowed for some state funding, but only to supplement federal monies budgeted through the Lanham Act.[56] California's program emerged as one of the most important and successful childcare solutions in the state and nation. Funded federally (through the Lanham Act of the Federal Works Agency), managed regionally (by the California State Department of Education), and operated locally (through public school systems), the centers demonstrate how diverse bureaucracies came together during the crisis and developed an efficient and quality childcare program.[57]

California's program was one of five in the nation and enrolled more children than any other state; in May 1945 more than 25,500 children received care at the centers, which "represented 18 percent of the nation's enrollment at the height of the Lanham Act program."[58] School districts immediately applied to the Federal Works Agency for funding, and implementation operations began within two months. The San Diego School District received a $906,568 allotment on April 1, 1943; only the Los Angeles School District had received a larger nursery allocation, $1,873,237.[59] With that federal funding, San Diego established twenty-one extended day care centers in conjunction with the public school district to address the concern of school-aged children roaming the community. Each center offered care for before and after school, on Saturdays, and during the summer for children ages five to sixteen years. Additionally, eleven government nursery schools, fifteen state-licensed nurseries, and eight privately operated nurseries opened in the city with the purpose to care for younger children.[60]

By 1945 sixty-one centers operated in five public school districts. Combined, average active enrollment at the nursery centers reached 1,015 children and 1,125 students at extended day care centers. Another 474 children were cared for at combination centers. In 1945 centers opened in districts from the southern tip of the county in National City to the northern boundary of Oceanside. Private organizations, such as the San Diego PTA, also provided care through the program. It operated one of five non-school programs in the state to receive Lanham funds and was the last non-school program to be awarded funds ($29,044 from July 1, 1944, to October 31, 1945). Crucially, the PTA program devoted its care to infants. Guidelines called for centers to operate from 6:00 a.m. to 6:00 p.m., Monday through Saturday, with some exceptions made for certain communities and industries. San Diego's centers fell into the latter category and operated around the clock.[61]

A 1943 report by childcare advocates discovered that communities with several factors in place prior to the war were better able to deal with the "bureaucratic nightmare" of federal dictates: "a strong tradition of civic activism, a structure of facilities and service capable of supporting a program, an educational establishment committed to the possibilities of public child care, and the willingness to take the initiative when federal aid proved belated, insufficient, or completely unavailable managed to come the closest to success."[62] California as a whole fit these parameters, as did San Diego. In San Diego, there were never enough spaces to match the need, and societal beliefs by politicians took center stage, pushing the warnings of childcare advocates aside. Historian Emilie Stoltz-fus explains in her analysis of these debates in the years following World War II that "even as they enacted a permanent program, California lawmakers remained deeply suspicious of non-maternal care for young children."[63] These suspicions arose in spite of the advocacy from early childhood educators and the statewide Parents' Association, which understood and tried to define the cccc program as an educational rather than a social welfare resource.

Moreover, the ccccs did not address care for children under the age of two years. In an attempt to solve the infant care problem, the state Department of Social Welfare licensed the Family Services Association of San Diego as a unit with authority to place children in facilities (including boarding homes) rather than operating only as a referral agency. Responsibilities for nursery center care also shifted to the FSASD, and by May 1943 only three of the previous government-operated nurseries remained under federal control. Additionally, the public school systems of San Diego and Chula Vista (a south bay community) took over eight facilities and opened a new site in the Pacific Beach area.[64] These moves shifted authority from regional to local oversight, with the FSASD handling that responsibility. Another solution to the infant care problem came in 1944 when the city helped aircraft carrier plant Ryan Aeronautical establish experimental care centers for babies at least six months old to two years, but the center had a limited effect on the citywide problem.[65]

There is no question the ccccs provided quality day care. Yet most female workers in San Diego did not benefit from the ccccs or the Ryan center, because they worked in businesses or service areas *indirectly* connected with defense contracting. In addition to the public schools that were adapted into childcare centers, five centers were built in San Diego County with Lanham building funds; combined, those centers accommodated only 270 children.[66] Factories operated around the clock; however, not all of them manufactured munitions or processed supplies for military consumption. Many people, but especially women, worked in San Diego's service sector, which included laundries, restaurants, lunch counters, and cafeterias. Some women (primarily white, English-speaking women) were hired by businesses like the San Diego Electric Railway Company, which filled its bus and street-car driver vacancies with women. Local businesses depended on literate, white women for secretarial and clerking jobs, and stores like Walker's Department Store hired single white women in their sales positions. None of these businesses fit the parameters for CCCC eligibility, so mothers who worked at these establishments or ones similar in nature were on their own for finding childcare.

A report in 1944 by the Child Welfare League of America (CWLA) criticized how the city was handling childcare, stating that "situations which threaten children appear to have increased in even greater proportion." These included: "family disruption due to fathers absent for long periods due to military service or wartime employment; mothers employed outside the home; extremely congested housing; children employed at high wages and frequently emancipated from parental control; the emotional tensions which accompany worry over members of the family in service, long hours of work, and changed environment." The report also found that "educational, health, and recreational facilities in San Diego appear to have been better developed prior to the war than the child care agencies," with "some serious liabilities in the existing community pattern for child care."[67] CWLA researchers declared that the "staffs of the agencies in San Diego responsible for child placement include too few social workers, and those staff members who have had some specialized training in social work frequently lack the necessary training and experience in children's work."[68] The CWLA was likely referring to the shift to local FSASD control. In hindsight it is clear that the agency took on far more than its staff could handle. The state unit allowed for the shift but did not offer the local agency any financial assistance to hire additional staff, which it sorely needed to handle San Diego's complex problems.

National agencies asserted their authority, and local agencies worked to adapt those policies, but practical solutions also came from the working mothers.[69] Mothers like Mary Jane Babcock could not wait for the FSASD, the CCCCS, and the CWLA to work out its plans. She singlehandedly took in a boarder, then hired a sitter, moved in with her parents, found a private nursery, and budgeted her earnings so as to pay for her baby's child care, food, diapers, and clothing. Babcock's family network, not a government agency, helped her. In-migrant, white mothers had no network and needed the assistance offered at the cccs, the parent–child homes, the foster boarding homes, and the licensed family day care homes. cwla estimated in its 1944 study that "in San Diego more children are cared for outside their own homes because their mothers are employed than in any other city of comparable population. . . . It is possible for San Diego children to attend child care centers as long as eighteen hours a day and be with their own parents only while they are asleep!"[70]

Early childhood educators with the cwla had emphasized in 1939, "The day home is a supplementary service to the parental home and not a substitute for it," so the statistics they found in San Diego several years later did not sit well with the organization.[71] While by 1944 a combination of public and private collaborations operated in the city, the cwla was not impressed with the work done by San Diegans to stabilize the childcare crisis. Instead, the association was concerned about the reality of so many children being cared for by someone other than a family member. They counted 2,400 children in "group care outside their homes because their mothers are working; over 1,000 children are wards of the Juvenile Court of San Diego; . . . almost 1,000 children are receiving care in foster family boarding homes; and between 350 and 400 children are receiving care in children's institutions." Their numbers did not include those children and adolescents in the Detention Home or city or county jails. Perhaps most troubling were the 110 children under the age of sixteen arrested during May 1944 and housed in city or county jails. As cwla emphasized, these figures "point to community situations which seriously threaten the well-being of children."[72]

On May 16, 1945, cwla sent a report to "federal officials having responsibilities for day care or known to be interested in it," outlining six "specific suggestions" to "account for the whole child."

First on their list—the local administration of day care services— acknowledged the reality of a worker's daily routine where one had no time, energy, or personal connection to dealing with the federal bureaucracy. The league also called for cost-sharing arrangements between "public and private funds including parents' fees." They separated themselves from nursery school educators by insisting "the promotion and administration of nursery schools naturally lies in the field of education. Its development should not be contingent upon the needs of mothers who require for their children the daytime care and service of a foster mother or the staff of a day care center.... Day care requires planning which accounts clearly for the welfare of the child and his family, and consequently should be administered primarily as a welfare service."[73] Their report recognized the reality that parents needed day care so they could work. If that care included an educational component, they were grateful, but they did not look for or need a nursery school model. Rather, CWLA argued that parents needed basic day care to keep their children safe. Importantly, CWLA defined day care as a "welfare service" and did not include employers in the list of units that should be responsible for seeing that day care existed for workers. Clearly this points to the ideology in the twentieth century that families should remain the responsible parties for raising their children, and if they could not fully handle that responsibility, then a welfare source had to step in. It also emphasizes a gendered separation of responsibility, with men providing the financial support and women handling the domestic care for the family. This philosophy supported the foundation of the CCCCS being a temporary need due to wartime employment. But by 1945 it became obvious that childcare needs had not diminished with the end of the war.

One result of San Diego's childcare problem was the firing of FSASD executive director Eleanor Mead, which shows an example of laying blame for the complex problem at the feet of one person. The CWLA review influenced FSASD board members to take radical action against Mead, as they believed her lack of leadership had led to the city's childcare problem. Citing Mead's exhaustion as a major problem, the board agreed that she needed professional medical treatment, and in May 1945 the board had her committed to a sanitarium. During her stay they completed an executive search, and when she returned to work, Mead was met with a request to resign and an offer of two months' severance pay. Mead had little recourse: while she had courted the Family Welfare Services Association of America national office for years as a professional, the local board believed she had failed in carrying the organization through the tumultuous World War II era.[74] Certainly, Mead should not be held responsible for such an immense and complicated problem of providing childcare in the war-impacted city, but the FSASD board used her as its excuse for failing to fully serve San Diego's families.

The expectation in 1945 that servicemen and their families would leave the city at the conclusion of the war never materialized.[75] They stayed, along with the thousands of civilian inmigrants. The problems with housing and childcare also stayed. In association forums community relief workers noted their concern over how to handle these issues, but no system came together to deal with the large numbers of children and youth in need of attention.[76] Authorities were also concerned with the deviant behavior that seemed to follow the troops, making San Diego a breeding ground for the spread of illicit business. No longer called the Stingaree, the downtown district continued to host its share of bars, strip clubs, and nightclubs with seedy reputations. A 1945 study by the city's TASSD documented too many uncomfortable situations. It pinpointed numerous pregnant and unmarried newcomers (suspiciously, these women all gave twenty-one as their age at the time of their interview) and an uncomfortable increase in runaway girls. TASSD also showed its bias toward compulsory heterosexuality in its citing of a fifteen-year-old "seriously disturbed homosexual boy masquerading as a girl." TASSD concluded that the war had led to these individuals falling into precocious and dangerous behavior, which caused grave consequences for all involved.[77]

Childcare woes continued to plague the city into the 1950s. Daycare needs would not be solved for this generation of parents, and the expectation that mothers would remove themselves from the workforce to care for children was not realized. Families chose to make San Diego their permanent home, partly for the promise of continued employment in the defense industry or an expanded tourism trade. They also became used to the temperate climate and possibility of home ownership in the many tracts under construction in the city. Business leaders and government officials at all levels continued to see day care as a "welfare service" rather than a critical labor issue. That thinking proved deadly for the passage of a national childcare program. Yet California did successfully extend its child care centers, becoming the only state government to do so. But just as during the war, not enough spaces existed in San Diego for the children who needed the care. A report in 1956 by San Diego's Community Welfare Council estimated that as of January 1, 1956, sixty thousand women were employed in San Diego County, with approximately fifteen thousand having a child or children under the age of eighteen. Their figures did not distinguish which of the fifteen thousand children were young enough to need adult attention, but it did provide figures on day care spaces (2,042), all of which were filled. Potentially, thirteen thousand children still needed care. Since waiting lists existed at half of all the city's facilities, surveyors reminded the community of its need for day care space and the ever-increasing number of working mothers in San Diego.[78]

These workers faced little to no support from their employers in how to secure childcare, as it continued to be recognized as a social welfare concern rather than a condition of employment. Both the number and diversity of people entering the city in the early 1940s created different demands on the city's small but effective childcare structure, and because of parental advocacy, the ccccs stayed open and workers also found flexibility with licensed family day care homes.[79] Whereas government funding allowed for these operations to keep running, they also endured beyond the war because of the efforts of advocates and workers at the local level. Unfortunately, the problems associated with San Diego's lack of childcare did not end with the war.

Conclusion

The community should be concerned with the need to provide adequate day care facilities for the care of children in view of the increasing number of working mothers in San Diego.

—Mrs. M. M. Clancy, Chairman of Day Care, Community Welfare Council, June 1956

In a 1944 survey of child welfare resources in San Diego, Miss Mary Keeley of the Child Welfare League of America reported, "The protection and care of the children of any community is too big a job for social agencies alone. In a community as greatly pressed with serious problems as San Diego, continuous exploration and use of all services available to children is an urgent necessity."[1] The survey listed the various agencies and units of government that attended to children, many of which had been providing childcare to San Diego's children for decades. Missing from the list of responsible entities were employers.

Immediately after the war, the severe problems with finding childcare dissipated for families in the city. Boarding children in foster homes changed dramatically, from 228 children being served in 1945 to 33 children in 1946, and to 47 in 1947. Yet thrice the number of families in that same time period received relief: 368 different families in 1945, some 892 in 1946, and 1,100 by 1947.[2] The combination of the foster home boarding figures with relief provision statistics indicates that families no longer needed to board their children out, perhaps because a parent had been removed from the workforce and could care for the children; however, that workforce removal also put the family in economic jeopardy. The protocol of removing women from gainful employment to make room for men exacerbated the economic struggles of families in San Diego.

City leaders counted on mothers voluntarily leaving the workforce, but many families depended on the earnings of mothers, so childcare again became a concern. A 1956 report to the Community Welfare Council made clear that San Diego's workforce required day care services, with the care of preschool-aged children continuing to pose concern. Facilities in operation were filled to capacity: six of the fifteen day care centers operated through the San Diego City Schools had waiting lists, and so did sixteen of the thirty privately owned nursery schools (that were licensed and supervised by the state Department of Social Welfare). Those forty-five resources already cared for 1,070 preschool children. Another fifteen nursery schools supervised by San Diego City Schools served 480 children. No good solution had been found for the problem of infant care, and the city needed more trained childcare personnel.[3] The report showed that social service agencies had been wrestling with how to provide day care to its wage-earning families for over a decade but could not seem to look beyond governmental programs for solutions. Strategizing with business leaders to implement employer-sponsored childcare could have made a difference. After all, that is how the Children's Home and Day Nursery (CHDN) started in 1888. But employers, most politicians, and much of society in general understood childcare as social welfare and not as a benefit of employment.

From the 1850s through the 1940s, San Diegans established daily or long-term care options at a variety of sites and for a wide array of reasons, including parental wage earning, death, disease, or desertion, and one or both parents choosing to or forced to give up their parental rights. Each type of childcare—from indentured service, apprenticeship, day nurseries, settlement houses, and vocational centers to reformatories, maternity homes, foster care, and boarding homes—offered a solution for some families, but the results were not always in the best interests of both children and parents. Program organizers often depended on philanthropic dollars and volunteer labor to initiate and sustain operations, which jeopardized the professional development of childcare in the city. When early childhood educators, social workers, and visiting nurses and physicians entered the region, programs became regulated and thus more professional. These resources elevated the health and welfare of San Diego's weakest residents, but the success of these programs depended on political favor, economic stability, and philanthropic generosity.

At the start of this research, I believed that the quest by San Diego's business leaders for a strong tourist trade, military connections, and entrepreneurial energy canceled the concerns of advocates hoping to provide working-class families with safe childcare and healthy living conditions. I learned that leaders did focus on building a coastal paradise and promoting its appeal to wealthy investors; however, many also recognized the need for implementing social reforms in the city and chose to care about how those programs developed. These leaders (most of whom were men) listened to advocates (most of whom were women) as to the most effective ways to establish social reforms. They learned that children of wage-earning residents were some of the most vulnerable people in the community, and while these leaders often did not interact with the parents who needed assistance, they trusted advocates to develop programs that would ensure a safer environment for impoverished people. The programs and projects that emerged in San Diego's first one hundred years of American rule were certainly not perfect, but they did provide a foundation for improving the lives of the city's poorest residents.

Social reform in San Diego emerged alongside national agendas to monitor and guide children whom professionals considered at risk for deviant and harmful behavior, and often encouraged the further stigmatization of children who lived on the margins of society. As a community that developed simultaneously with control of indigenous populations, immigration woes, and anxiety

over the expansion of slavery, San Diego's residents allowed segregation, discrimination, and prejudice to influence the development of childcare resources and social reforms. In its first decades,
Anglo children might spend their childhoods in boarding homes,
while American Indian children worked on isolated ranches or in
private homes located in town. Children from other communities
of color, such as Mexican-descent, African American, and Asian,
were often segregated into culturally specific spaces.

In the 1850s reformers focused on "assisting" American Indian
children, who many local citizens believed were uncivilized and
needed "Americanized." These children and their families fell victim to a cruel system of indentured service to Anglo property
owners, which had been sanctioned by California's political, legal,
and business authorities. Reformers sat on both sides of the issue:
some hoped that working for Anglos would alleviate homelessness among Indian children, while others emphasized that indenture cruelly separated Indian children from their families and clan
networks. By the 1870s Californians had controlled Indian nations
and increasingly ignored the dilemmas facing Indian children.
Missionaries and benevolent associations stepped in by offering
education through boarding schools, but San Diegans as a whole
adopted an attitude of removal of all American Indians from the
town to reservations in remote areas.

City leaders turned their attentions to immigrants and poor
Americans who began migrating into the area. In the 1880s they
initiated vocational training and expanded the public school district in an effort to educate a growing illiterate workforce. When
the CHDN opened in 1888, reformers in San Diego had already
immersed themselves in the national campaigns to address sexual
abuse by elevating the age-of-consent laws. To that end, reformers
in San Diego focused on impeding the growing prostitution trade
by passing a series of laws that regulated city spaces and allowed for
sexually active girls to be committed to institutional care. By 1914
reformers established a settlement house for families in the Logan
Heights neighborhood, most of whom were Mexican or Mexican
American. They also developed public health screenings, expanded

county aid programs, and connected with national authorities as ways to energize funding for childcare projects. These connections proved important for establishing a network of emergency nursery schools during the 1930s, offering San Diego a national platform for the implementation of laboratory nursery schools, and launching federally directed day care in the 1940s.

Feminist scholars remind us that women forced into negotiations with people of greater socioeconomic power faced constant threats to their right to mother.[4] In their attempts to protect their children, some mothers lost their parental rights for significant periods of time or even permanently. It is important to remember that wage-earning and unemployed mothers in San Diego did not easily turn over their parenting rights and responsibilities, and the evidence is clear that these mothers used every available option to keep their children in their households. They resorted to decisions like boarding at an institution only when that choice proved the safest environment for the children.

I was not surprised to read the reactions of mothers who were separated from their children because of workforce issues, but I did not expect to find so much evidence of fathers attempting to care for their children in the face of heartache and trauma. Widowers and abandoned husbands struggled to maintain custody of their children in their homes, and to communicate to social workers and other childcare professionals that they were worthy and capable of caring for their children. Societal expectations of fathers providing financial support but not the custodial and nurturing functions of child caring worked against these fathers in their fights to maintain custody. The records show valiant attempts by fathers to convince agency personnel that they could properly parent their children. But they also show that agencies seldom sided with the father and often removed children from the home and the father's custody. The efforts by fathers to care for their children push against the prevailing notions of fathers being disconnected from their families in this era. Instead, we see deep bonds between parents and their children, especially within working-class families who struggled to survive in uncertain economic times.

The evidence in San Diego also shows how many advocates found themselves confronting long-held notions that characterized breadwinning in solely male terms or child rearing within the bounds of white, middle-class parameters. Visiting nurses and social workers from Neighborhood House, the Associated Charities, or volunteers with the Travelers Aid Society entered homes to understand how the working poor organized their lives and endured troubled times. They discovered that most mothers earned wages so that their families could eat, and not for "pin money." These reformers learned a good deal about how working-class families adjusted their lives to accommodate the family's needs, and they shared their findings with civic leaders.

Unfortunately, the provision of quality childcare was and continues to be an expensive venture. Programs depended on the philanthropy of San Diego's elite households. Public funds grew with urbanization, yet public officials always struggled with balancing how to pay for dire city improvements, such as sewer and water lines, with the growing social welfare needs of the community. At the turn of the century, legal regulations required San Diego's officials to direct funds toward juvenile justice reforms. Those funding decisions created a dilemma for organizations in how to handle diverse groups of children. Some children boarded at facilities for childcare reasons, while others had been removed from their parents because of a delinquency conviction. Because the city or county reimbursed an institution for the care of a ward of the court, they shifted toward caring for publicly funded children. The Children's Home made this shift in the 1920s when it changed its focus from a day nursery that cared for the children of working parents to a facility that focused on the care of the city's most troubled children and youth. They could make this shift because of the growth of other childcare programs like the day nursery opened by the Junior League and those offered in the Neighborhood House and Casa de Salud settlement houses.

In the new century, changes in regulations led to organizations in San Diego adopting more professional oversight for their childcare programs. It also led to increased conversations with parents about the kinds of care they needed or wanted for their children. Officials learned to negotiate with parents and listen to family histories, perhaps because of the increased presence of professionally trained social workers and educators in San Diego. For some, that meant orders of commitment, but for the vast majority of those seeking help in San Diego, it meant using a day nursery or boarding home on a temporary basis.

Childcare professionals—physicians, teachers, nurses, and social workers—also engaged in conversations with politicians and business leaders to encumber public dollars in support of childcare programs, especially during the turbulent 1930s and 1940s. During the Great Depression, city leaders and child advocates used federal funding to respond to workers' and employers' pleas for more child care resources in San Diego. From the 1920s government funding proved vital to offering services in San Diego. Neighborhood House secured grant moneys for public health; the passage of the Federal Emergency Relief Act in 1933 provided many workers—professional and unskilled—assistance with securing food, housing, employment, and day care; and the Lanham Act secured childcare space during World War II. The emergency nursery schools funded through the relief act formed the foundation for explorations in early childhood education, and this innovation was promoted at the 1935–1936 world exposition. Yet childcare programs could not keep pace with the population growth in the 1940s, and many workers were forced to use boarding arrangements that separated them from their children. While those decisions prompted the ire of nationally situated advocates such as the Child Welfare League of America, the reality was that local advocates worked around the clock to devise better solutions. Care providers like Family Welfare Services director Eleanor Mead and pediatrician Dr. Rieta Campbell Hough literally worked themselves to poor health that required several months and even years to fully recover from. Publicly funded programs like the California Child Care Centers offered some remedy, but not a full-scale solution.

San Diego's female reformers implemented programs that allowed for flexibility and honored the livelihoods of working people. But they did so in a gendered environment that marginalized childcare as women's work and a women's issue. In general, male civic leaders did not involve themselves in the daily operations of childcare, and postwar manipulations of the family ideal further gendered childcare agendas. Immigration policies also isolated many workers from accessing social programs, and they continue to do so. The increased militarization of the border by the federal government and self-directed militias makes it difficult for advocates to provide care to families in a trusting environment. Stepped-up patrols and heightened physical barriers send powerful messages to individuals outside the protection of U.S. citizenship. Yet, like so many of the advocates highlighted in this study, present-day advocates continue to work toward lessening the strains on working families.

Situated on the busiest international border, San Diego's explosive demographic growth throughout the twentieth century has led it to become the eighth-most populated city in the United States, and the second-largest in California. With this size comes a host of complex problems, with the disparity of wealth heading the list. Data from kids.data.org for San Diego show that in 2016, some 15 percent of children live in poverty. While this is an improvement from the 21.8 percent over the years 2006–2012 (the recession years), this figure is still the fourth-highest in the state.[5] Childcare costs can contribute to these figures, as they come close to half of an impoverished family's annual income. Advocates continue to use a combination of federal, state, and local resources, but in the United States, childcare programs and the personnel who run them remain underfunded and underequipped to meet the growing needs among families.[6] A February 2011 report by Human Rights Watch found that the "United States is an extreme outlier in the area of work–family policy," as 97 percent of 168 countries studied offer paid maternity leave, but the U.S. is not one of them.[7] The U.S. Department of Labor National Compensation Survey found that in 2010 "only 10 percent of private sector employees had access to paid family leave," and that "access to paid leave is more likely if an employee is well paid, works in managerial or professional occupations, or is employed by a company with at least 100 employees."[8] Whereas the federal Family and Medical Leave Act was signed by President Bill Clinton in February 1993, it does not apply to employees of companies with fewer than fifty employees and is not a paid-leave benefit; thus, it offers no benefit to the most-vulnerable workers.

California was the first state government to offer its employees another option: the Paid Family Leave Insurance Program (PFL), also known as Family Temporary Disability Insurance. Introduced in 2002 through Senate Bill 1661, the PFL program was "specifically built on top" of an "important foundation in California," the temporary disability insurance program in place since 1946. California is one of five states and one territory (Hawaii, Rhode Island, New York, New Jersey, and Puerto Rico are the others) that offer a state disability insurance program. The programs are fully funded through a payroll tax paid by employees; thus, all employees who pay into the State Disability Insurance Fund are also covered by PFL. Eligible workers may use up to six weeks of benefits for time taken off to care for a "family member," which is defined as a "child, parent, spouse, or domestic partner."[9]

In 1998 California voters also passed Proposition 10 to increase state excise taxes on cigarettes and other tobacco products as a way to fund health and childcare services to children prenatal to age five. Known as the Children and Families First Act, the legislative mandate has funneled nearly $700 million per year toward early childhood development programming, with 80 percent of the revenues allocated at the county level. In San Diego the "First 5 San Diego" measure was approved in November 2010 to provide $2.25 million in bridge funding to maintain childcare assistance for wage-earning parents previously on government assistance and adversely affected by "welfare-to-work" decisions. It also identified the Black Infant Health program as a funding priority to improve the dramatically high mortality rate for African American babies in San Diego County.[10]

The entrepreneurial skills and tenacity of parents to find solutions to childcare continue to stabilize families, because programs for children continue to fall last in line of public and private budget priorities. In San Diego the strong foundation of programs cemented in the late nineteenth and early twentieth centuries continues to provide childcare resources. Neighborhood House, the San Diego Center for Children (which was the Children's Home), the Polinsky Children's Center (the county's emergency shelter for abused and neglected children), and the Salvation Army's Door of Hope all started their programs in the Progressive Era and continue to provide critical services for families in San Diego.

For much of the twentieth century, the expertise and personal dedication of health and education professionals, social welfare and labor advocates, and concerned neighbors have made safe childcare possible for marginalized families. In San Diego these groups often melded together, but just as frequently socioeconomic positions maintained separations among these individuals. Advocates who had connections to national reform leaders and agendas offered avenues for San Diego to move out of the realm of localized support and toward collaborations with state and federal projects. Infused with "expert" advice, city educators opened the doors to experimentation and academic analysis at the same time that city boosters paved the way for federalization of the community. The expanded urban footprint included new schools, but few childcare options for infants and toddlers. Contrary to projections by urban planners, people did not leave the city when World War II ended. Instead, people continued to migrate into the area and influence the need for housing, schools, and childcare. San Diegans have chosen to care about children, but it is an expensive proposition that cannot be ignored. Collaborative, affordable, and comprehensive solutions that benefit the majority of families remain to be implemented, but the history of San Diego's first one hundred years shows us that people do choose to care.

Abbreviations

AJLA	Associated Junior League of America
CSDE	California State Department of Education
CWLA	Child Welfare League of America
FWSAA	Family Welfare Services Association of America
FSASD	Family Services Association of San Diego
NFSNC	National Federation of Settlements and Neighborhood Centers
NH	Neighborhood House
OC	Order of Commitment
OHHC	Oral History Historical Collection, SDHCRA
PR	Public Records Collection
PWERA	San Diego County Public Welfare and Emergency Relief Association
SDCC	San Diego Center for Children Records
SDCCUW	San Diego Community Chest Records/United Way of San Diego
SDCWC	San Diego County Welfare Commission
SDHCRA	San Diego History Center Research Archives, Casa de Prado, Balboa Park
SDPH	San Diego County Department of Public Health
SDCL	San Diego Central Library, California Collection

SDSU   Malcolm A. Love Library, Special Collections &
            University Archives, San Diego State University
SDSUOH   San Diego State University Oral History
SWHA   Social Welfare History Archives, University of
            Minnesota Libraries
TASSD   Travelers Aid Society of San Diego
UWSD   United Way Archives, Headquarter Office of
            San Diego

Introduction

1. The Children's Home and Day Nursery (CHDN) records are located in the San Diego Center for Children Records (MS227) in the Documents Archives at the San Diego History Center. Because these records are from a private institution, I created pseudonyms for the parents and children found in these records to protect their privacy and developed a catalog system for the cases I reviewed, which I explain in chapter 2. Details regarding how "Marie O'Malley" made her decision to use CHDN are based on a composite reading of cases 42/43/44, SDCC.

2. In February 1889 the *San Diego Union* and *Daily Bee* published word of a gold discovery in Mexico's district of El Alamo, about sixty miles southeast of Ensenada. Within a month, packed steamers, chartered schooners, and trains full of hopeful goldminers left San Diego for the area. The rush lasted into 1890, and during that same time, opportunities for women to earn wages also existed at a number of small interests in Ensenada, including soap and textile factories, flour mills, fruit canneries, and a brewing company. See Flanigan, "The Baja California Gold Rush of 1889," 11–20; Bonifaz de Novelo, "Ensenada," 14–28.

3. The group operated in a rented cottage on Cedar and First with Miss Marah McClun as its first matron. *Review, 1899*, p. 1 in Box 5, Series IV—Scrapbooks, SDCC.

4. The children, Mary Gilman Marston, Elizabeth Marston Bade, Harriet Marston Headley, Arthur Marston, and Helen Marston Beardsley involved themselves in the local chapters of civic programs throughout their lives. See Gregg Hennessey's articles cited below; Marston, *George White Marston*; Starr, "Philanthropy in San Diego, 1900–1929," 227–73; Ciani, "Revelations of a Reformer," 102–23.

5. Hennessey, "Creating a Monument," 136–63; "George White and Anna Gunn Marston," 96–105; "George White Marston and Conservative Reform in San Diego," 230–53; Ports, "Geraniums v. Smokestacks," 50–56; and Stephens, "The History of Social Welfare Agencies in San Diego County," 10.

6. The classic work on true womanhood is Welter, "The Cult of True Womanhood," 151–74. See also Jameson, "Women as Workers, Women as Civilizers"; Blair, *The Clubwoman as Feminist*.

7. The "trans-border urban system" of Southern California–Baja California demonstrates how "several central cities and adjacent communities on or near an

international border share a high degree of economic and social integration." The Southern California-Baja California transborder system includes the *municipios* of Tijuana and Ensenada in Baja California and the counties of Santa Barbara, Ventura, Los Angeles, Orange, San Diego, Riverside, and San Bernardino in Southern California. *Municipios* in Mexico and counties in the United States are analogous political jurisdictions. Baja California comprises four *municipios*: Tijuana, Ensenada, Tecate, and Mexicali. In 1990, 45 percent of the total population of Baja California lived in Tijuana. See Rubin-Kurtzman, Ham-Chabde, and Arsdol Jr., "Population in Trans-Border Regions," 1020–45 (quote from 1021). See also Lim, *Porous Borders*.

8. Delgado, "Border Control and Sexual Policing," 157–78.

9. Corporate interests drove many historical accounts of San Diego's development, such as Richard F. Pourade's seven-volume series published in the 1960s by the San Diego Union-Tribune Publishing Company. Boosters' visions of a coastal paradise always competed with the real-life dramas of economic downturn, health epidemics, vice district expansion, and military dominance. Mike Davis, Kelly Mayhew, and Jim Miller make this point in *Under the Perfect Sun*.

10. In her overview of this complex historiography, Elizabeth Jameson complicates the "national U.S. narrative" by arguing "such histories must recognize analytic categories and narratives divided and erased by social and national borders, and the unequal power inscribed in androcentric, ethnocentric, and nationalist narratives." See Jameson, "Dancing on the Rim, Tiptoeing through Minefields," 1–24, quote from page 1. Moreover, Neil Foley reminds us that "whites are raced, men are gendered, and women are marked by class," in *The White Scourge*, 11. Some early challenges to the western myths include Butler, *Daughters of Joy, Sisters of Misery*; Limerick, *Legacy of Conquest*; Limerick, Milner, and Rankin, *Trails*; White, *"It's Your Misfortune and None of My Own."*

11. Kevin Starr's masterful multivolume history of California from Oxford University Press is an exception, although he pays more attention to San Diego from 1950 onward than to the earlier era. See *Americans and the California Dream, 1850–1915* (1973), *Inventing the Dream: California through the Progressive Era* (1985); *Material Dreams: Southern California through the 1920s* (1990); *Endangered Dreams: The Great Depression in California* (1996); *The Dream Endures: California Enters the 1940s* (1997); *Embattled Dreams: California in War and Peace* (2002); *Golden Dreams: California in an Age of Abundance, 1950–1963* (2009). For Los Angeles, see Deverell and Sitton, *California Progressivism Revisited*; Chávez-García, *Negotiating Conquest*; González, *This Small City Will Be a Mexican Paradise*; Haas, *Conquests and Historical Identities in California*; Koslow, *Cultivating Health*; Molina, *Fit to Be Citizens?*; Odem, *Delinquent Daughters*; Simpson, *Selling the City*.

12. Tomás Almaguer highlights the "racial fault lines" embedded in national and, specifically, Southern California culture in *Racial Fault Lines*; Allison Varzally reinforces this point in *Making a Non-White America*.

13. Boris, *Home to Work*; Broder, *Tramps, Unfit Mothers, and Neglected Children*; Cameron, *Radicals of the Worst Sort*; Cooper, *Once a Cigar Maker*; Hewitt, *South-

ern Discomfort; Hunter, *To 'Joy My Freedom*; Kleinberg, *The Shadow of the Mills*; Pleck, *Black Migration and Poverty*; Ramey, *Child Care in Black and White*; Rose, *A Mother's Job*; Tentler, *Wage-Earning Women*.

14. Boydston, *Home and Work*, 81.

15. Roediger, *The Wages of Whiteness*.

16. Fraser and Gordon, "A Genealogy of *Dependency*," 309–36.

17. See Deutsch, *Women and the City*; Enstam, *Women and the Creation of Urban Life*; Flannigan, *Seeing with Their Hearts*; Hickey, *Hope and Danger in the New South City*; Putnam, *Class and Gender Politics*; Spain, *How Women Saved the City*; Turner, *Women, Culture, and Community*; and Wood, *The Freedom of the Streets*.

18. Muncy, *Creating a Female Dominion in American Reform*; Pascoe, *Relations of Rescue*.

19. The scholarship on these reforms is voluminous. For excellent overviews, see Koven and Michel, *Mothers of a New World*, quote on page 2; Michel, *Children's Interests/Mothers' Rights*; Skocpol, *Protecting Soldiers and Mothers*.

20. Anderson, "Changing Woman," 149; *Changing Woman: A History of Racial Ethnic Women in Modern America*. See also Deutsch, *No Separate Refuge*; Gordon, *The Great Arizona Orphan Abduction*; Jacobs, *White Mother to a Dark Race*; Schackel, *Social Housekeepers: Women Shaping Public Policy in New Mexico*.

21. These sources helped me to tease out the thoughts of people with limited literacy (or illiterate people), but I am cautious in attributing an emotion or action to a parent based on the observation of a reformer. Other historians who have used court proceedings and institutional case records to hear the voices of women in the United States with little power include Alexander, *The "Girl Problem"*; Gordon, *Heroes of Their Own Lives*; Kunzel, *Fallen Women, Problem Girls*; and Schoen, *Choice and Coercion*.

22. See Robens, "Charlotte Baker"; Sexton, "The San Diego Woman's Home Association," 41–53; Shelton, "The Neighborhood House of San Diego"; Stephens, "The History of Social Welfare Agencies."

23. Population figures from *San Diego County and First Annual Report 1888, City of San Diego*; and Lorey, *United States-Mexico Border Statistics since 1900: 1990 Update*.

24. Bokovoy, *The San Diego World's Fairs and Southwestern Memory*; Bridges, *Morning Glories*; Kropp, *California Vieja*; Lotchin, *Fortress California 1910–1961*.

25. Lorey, *United States-Mexico Border Statistics since 1900: 1990 Update*.

26. Gochenaur, *Health Department First Annual Report of the Board of Health of the City of San Diego for the Year Ending December 31, 1888*, 34.

1. Indentured Care

1. Rancher Cave Couts described the problems in his November 1862 correspondence to Abel Stearns: "Small pox is quite prevalent—six to eight per day are being buried in S. Juan Capistrano—Indians generally. One case in San Dieguito and two in San Mateo is [*sic*] the nearest to us. I vaccinated the whole *rancheria* at San Luis some six weeks since, & hope they may escape, thus saving our com-

munity of the terrible disease." Cited in Pourade, *The Silver Dons: The History of San Diego*. See also the Office of the Board of Trustees of the City of San Diego, Ordinance No. 1, March 16, 1869, Section 1, which established the Pest Hospital to contain smallpox and other contagious diseases, noted in Kelly, "First Annual Report of the San Diego County Hospital and Poor Farm to the Board of Supervisors, for the Year Ending June 30, 1889," 362–89, note 19.

2. Chandler and Quinn, "Emma Is a Good Girl," 34–37.

3. Almaguer, *Racial Fault Lines*; Moore, "'We Feel the Want of Protection,'" 96–125; Chan, "A People of Exceptional Character," 44–85; and Sandos, "'Because He Is a Liar and a Thief,'" 86–112.

4. Scholars studying how isolation from their cultures could radically alter childhoods include Adams, *Education for Extinction*; Child, *Boarding School Seasons*; Lomawaima, *They Called It Prairie Light*; Trennart, *The Phoenix Indian School*.

5. For studies on the social conditions associated with indentured servitude in the colonial era, see Block, *Rape and Sexual Power in Early America*; Fischer, *Suspect Relations*; Sundue, *Industrious in Their Stations*; Tomlins, "Indentured Servitude in Perspective," 146–82.

6. Hackel, *Children of Coyote*, 281.

7. The historiography on conquest in the Spanish Frontier is vast, with attention to a gendered analysis offering a key shift in understanding how colonizers used matrilineal authority to engage their agendas. See Barr, *Peace Came in the Form of a Woman*; Bouvier, *Women and the Conquest of California*; Brooks, *Captives and Cousins*; Chávez-García, *Negotiating Conquest*; Gutierrez, *When Jesus Came, the Corn Mothers Went Away*; Monroy, *Thrown among Strangers*; Weber, *The Spanish Frontier in North America*.

8. González, *This Small City Will Be a Mexican Paradise*, 124–130, 142. González admits the difficulty in exacting numbers of captives for the Mexican era, 1821–1846.

9. James Rawls highlights how "this law and related acts of the legislature were an attempt by the state government to legalize the peonage system that had existed in the Mexican period. Rawls, *Indians of California*, 87.

10. Eliot West explains the effects of such statutes in "Reconstructing Race," 7–28. For Southern California nations, see Carrico, *Strangers in a Stolen Land*, 38–39; Fernandez, "Except a California Indian," 161–175; Rawls, *Indians of California*; Shipek, *Pushed into the Rocks*, 39.

11. Rawls, *Indians of California*, 90.

12. Rawls, *Indians of California*, 101–8.

13. Moore, "'We Feel the Want of Protection,'" 103.

14. Nancy Fraser and Linda Gordon argue that "signifiers" such as race and ethnicity have influenced how a citizen can interact with the state and can trigger or define "registers" of access to the systems in a state. An economic register occurs when "one depends on some other person(s) or institution for subsistence"; a sociolegal register is a "status" with "the lack of a separate legal or public identity, as in the status of married women created by coverture"; a political register appears

when "subjection to an external ruling power" exists, and it "may be predicated of a colony or of a subject caste of noncitizen residents"; and a moral/psychological register acts as "an individual character trait like lack of will power or excessive emotional neediness." See Fraser and Gordon, "A Genealogy of *Dependency*," 312.

15. Figures on forced labor in California have been difficult to pinpoint. Historians have analyzed how the increased Anglo-American presence in the mid-nineteenth century altered life for American Indians in other parts of California, but effects on communities south of San Luis Rey mission have received less attention. James Rawls explains that to ensure an accurate estimate, all county archives in the state would need to be researched, since no central archive holds the copies of all indentures. To my knowledge such a search has not yet been made. See Almaguer, *Racial Fault Lines*; Haas, *Conquests and Historical Identities in California*; Heizer, *The Destruction of California Indians*, 219; Hurtado, *Indian Survival on the California Frontier*; Monroy, *Thrown among Strangers*; and Rawls, *Indians of California*, 91.

16. Cook, *The Conflict between the California Indian and White Civilization*, 57; Rawls, *Indians of California*, 96.

17. Kropp, *California Vieja*, 9–10. According to cultural historian Phoebe Kropp, for Anglos the "term Indians referenced a regional past more than a group of residents." Kropp explains the "national tendency to distance whites from nonwhites" contributed to the use of two racial labels common in Southern California—Anglos and Mexicans—and "concealed the great diversity within and between these groups." Further, "white Americans learned to use the moniker *Anglo*, for which *America* seemed to be a close synonym, to differentiate themselves from *Mexican*, conflating racial and national identity on both sides. . . . Southern Californians remained attached to the term *Anglo* as a salient social identification. The term neither referenced individual ethnicity nor implied the lack of one, it simply signaled *not Mexican*."

18. Anthropologist Diana Bahr discovered from oral interviews with women representing four generations of a "Cupeño" family that Native peoples learned to accept European descriptions of their nations as a survival mechanism. One woman "recall[ed] that although her mother told her the family was Cupeño, she also advised her: 'Just say you're Mission Indian. That way then everybody won't foul it up.'" See page 76 of Bahr, "Cupeño Trail of Tears," 75–82. Starting in the mid-twentieth century, Indian peoples have been reclaiming their language and culture, such as the "Luiseño" identifying themselves as "Poyomkawish." *Kumeyaay* is a term applied by anthropologists to the Tipai-Ipai language group, who had previously been called Diegueño by European Americans; yet not all "Kumeyaay" refer to themselves in this manner. On names, see Carrico, "A Brief Glimpse of the Kumeyaay Past," 115–39; Shipek, *Delfina Cuero*; Jeffredo-Warden, "Expressing the Sacred."

19. My thinking on looking within familial spaces has been informed by the work of Stoler, "Tense and Tender Ties," 829–65. See also Fischer, *Suspect Relations*; Hurtado, *Intimate Frontiers*; Pascoe, *Relations of Rescue*; Van Kirk, *Many Tender Ties*.

20. Frémont, *A Year of American Travel*, 77, 91, and Frémont, *Mother Lode Narratives*, 102–3, as cited in Rawls, *Indians of California*, 115.

21. Historian Margaret D. Jacobs has emphasized the gendered components of conquest, noting "unlike more masculine terrains of colonialism, removal and institutionalization of indigenous children was largely a feminine domain, defined primarily around mothering, particularly targeted at indigenous women, and implemented largely by white women," in "Maternal Colonialism," 456, and Jacobs, *White Mother to a Dark Race*.

22. With the entry of Anglos, many *Californios* also lost their land when Anglo men began marrying into their families and did not recognize rights to property enjoyed by *Californio* women. See González, *Refusing the Favor*; and Monroy, *Thrown among Strangers*.

23. As Douglas Monroy explains, "*Californios* not only worked the Indians but enjoyed themselves as well; they gave things away to ensure status instead of accumulating them." Monroy, *Thrown among Strangers*, 168.

24. For biographical details, see Flannigan, "The Ranch House at Warner's," 208–39. *Californios* had already taken land and water access from American Indians who had farmed in the area for centuries.

25. I explored how San Diego's burgeoning commercial interests depended on the growth of gambling, prostitution, and saloons further in Ciani, "A 'Growing Evil' or 'Inventive Genius,'" 249–84.

26. Quoted in Monroy, *Thrown among Strangers*, 189.

27. See, for example, the narrations of soldier José María Amador, who lived at the San José mission, and Father Junípero Serra's account of abuses occurring at San Gabriel mission, analyzed in Bouvier, *Women and the Conquest of California*, 101–3. On the sexualization of American Indian women and Anglo perceptions of that phenomenon, see also Castañeda, "Engendering the History of Alta California," 230–59; Chávez-García, *Negotiating Conquest*; Hurtado, *Intimate Frontiers*, and *Indian Survival on the California Frontier*, 169–92.

28. A corrective to this misreporting is Sandos, *Converting California*, 51–59.

29. The Anglo push to own land in San Diego intensified after statehood, but commercial schemes—the "New Town" venture in 1849 and building a wharf in 1850—failed and made little immediate impact on the region. See Crane, "The Pueblo Lands," 104–27; Garcia, "Merchants and Dons," 52–80; and Hughes, "The Decline of the *Californios*," 1–31; Phelps, "'All Hands Have Gone Downtown,'" 113.

30. Darnall, "Letters of Thomas Ryan Darnall," 58.

31. Those population totals were tiny compared to other communities in the region, for example, the northern Mexico mining town of Sonora (1,960 in 1860); the interior port city of Sacramento (6,820 in 1850 and 13,785 in 1860); and San Francisco, the largest urban center in California, with 34,776 in 1850 and 56,802 in 1860. Figures taken from Table 5.1: Major Urban Centers in California by Population and Function, 1850–1860," on page 21 of Phelps, "'All Hands Have Gone Downtown.'"

32. Monroy, *Thrown among Strangers*, 193.

33. Monroy, *Thrown among Strangers*, 192–93.

34. I thank Michael Magliari for offering his insights on unfree labor to me. See Magliari, "Free Soil, Unfree Labor," 349–89, quote on page 373.

35. Sandos, "'Because He Is a Liar and a Thief,'" 97.

36. As Florence Shipek explained, the Minority Report represented prevailing interests in San Diego that "Mission Indians" should "be allowed to remain on small home sites because they supplied an excellent, indeed the only, source of labor in Southern California." Shipek, *Pushed into the Rocks*, 30; see page 214 for full citation of the report.

37. For instance, Rebecca Schiller bore and reared nine children in a town with few services, so "Mission Indian" women likely helped her through her labors. See Karsh, "San Diego Pioneering Ladies," 21–32. On American Indian labor, see Carrico and Shipek, "Indian Labor in San Diego County," 205; Shipek, *Lower California Frontier*, 7; May, "Dog-Holes, Bomb Lances and Devil Fish," 73–91.

38. Sandos, "'Because He Is a Liar and a Thief,'" 97–100.

39. Carrico and Shipek, "Indian Labor in San Diego County," 205.

40. The coexistence of what Maria Lugones defines as "logic of purity" (where oppressive systems consume victimized peoples) and "logic of curdling" (where "oppressed subjects resist systems aimed at disciplining, violating, and erasing them") helps explain how children and parents could have negotiated the multiple oppressions and personalities they faced in San Diego. Lugones, *Pilgrimages/Peregrinajes*, 121–48.

41. Ephraim Morse's biography reads like a typical Argonaut in the early pioneer years of California. He left his home in Amesbury, Massachusetts, to seek his fortune in California gold, first joining a group of investors who sold merchandise to prospective miners, then as a prospector on the Yuba River. Poor health ended his mining attempts, and he headed south to San Diego in search of temperate weather. He and his partner, Levi Lack, arrived in San Diego in April 1850 and set up shop in the short-lived development Davistown. In 1853 Morse moved his venture to Old Town, where he entered and ended another partnership. He left the mercantile world for farming in 1859 but returned to Old Town and storekeeping two years later. See Smythe, *History of San Diego 1542–1907*, 280–82; Knott, "Reading between the Lines (of a Business Ledger)," 206–20.

42. Chandler and Quinn, "Emma Is a Good Girl," 34–35.

43. Chandler and Quinn, "Emma Is a Good Girl," 35; Knott, "Reading between the Lines," 213.

44. During the mid-nineteenth century, Anglo Protestants and Hispanic Catholics clashed in the territories of New Mexico and Utah over conversion tactics for Indian children. See Jones, "'Redeeming' the Indian," 220–41.

45. Chandler and Quinn, "Emma Is a Good Girl," 36–37.

46. Chandler and Quinn, "Emma Is a Good Girl," 34–35.

47. For an overview of Jewish residents in the American period, see Schwartz, "The Uneasy Alliance: Jewish Anglo Relations in San Diego 1850–1860," 53–60; Karsh, "San Diego Pioneering Ladies," 21–32.

48. "Ramón Culfa to Andres Scott. July 12, 1884. Document Files, Indentures, Document Archives, San Diego History Center (SDHC).

49. On Kumeyaay migration, see Cuero, *Her Autobiography*; Shipek, *Pushed into the Rocks*.

50. *San Diego Union*, July 1, 1884; November 14, 1884; November 22, 1884; and November 30, 1884. On sundown towns see, Loewen, *Sundown Towns*.

51. *San Diego Union*, November 22, 1884 and November 30, 1884.

52. McNeil, "St. Anthony's Indian School in San Diego," 187.

53. Letter of July 27, 1873 from Father Anthony Dominic Ubach in San Diego to Bishop Thaddeus Amat, from the Archives of the Bureau of Catholic Indian Missions, as cited in Weber, *Documents of California Catholic History*, 143–47.

54. McNeil, "St. Anthony's Indian School," 194–95.

55. McNeil, "Catholic Indian Schools of the Southwest Frontiers," 324.

56. June 30, 1902, letter as cited on p. 325 of McNeil, "Catholic Indian Schools."

57. McNeil, "St. Anthony's Indian School," 195–97.

58. Jacobs, "Maternal Colonialism," 459, 462.

59. Cuero, *Her Autobiography*, 60–61.

60. Massengill and Topkins, "Letters Written from San Diego County," quotes on 152, 167.

61. Cuero, *Her Autobiography*, 9.

62. Mathes, *Helen Hunt Jackson*.

63. The act established by 1895 fifteen separate reservations. Another two were formed in 1931. See "Table 2: San Diego County Native American Population (1860–1880)"; Carrico, *Strangers in a Stolen Land*, 34; and "Table 5: Population of Counties According to the Decennial Censuses," 55–58 and 64 in Cook, *The Population of the California Indians 1769–1970*. On the Mission Indian Relief Act, see Martin, "The First Residents," 57–60.

64. Los Angeles established its health department in 1879, three years after San Diego. Molina, *Fit to Be Citizens?*, 1, fn.1 on p. 190. See Stephens, "The History of Social Welfare Agencies," 4, for the development of San Diego's hospital.

65. Griego, "Rebuilding the California Southern Railroad," 324–37.

66. MacPhail, "San Diego's Chinese Mission," 8–21.

2. Maternal Care

1. These incidents played out from July 1900 to June 1905, and are recorded in SDCC, (specifically SDCCa 266, 271, 344, 437, and 559). SDCC records are divided into four periods: September 1888 to October 1905 (Box 17 and identified by me as SDCCa); 1909–1918 (Box 8, SDCCb); 1919–1921 (Box 9, SDCCc); and 1925–1929 (Box 10, SDCCd). I do not know why the years from 1906 to 1908 are missing from the collection or why the earliest years are in a later box. The numbers for each case

record are my chronological assignments and not official ones assigned by the facility. Matrons recorded information for the first period (September 1888 to October 1905) in a ledger they referred to as the "Register" and listed 591 entries of children. This does not mean that 591 different children entered the CHDN because 85 of these entries represent children returning to the facility for a second, third or even fourth stay. Between 1909 and 1915, records show that 196 households turned to the Home for childcare, and by 1919, the facility annually took in about one hundred children. I first explored some of these cases in "The Power of Maternal Love," 71–79.

2. Scholars have studied day care at the local, state, and national policy level. See Broder, *Tramps, Unfit Mothers, and Neglected Children*; Crocker, *Social Work and Social Order*; Durst, "Day Nurseries and Wage-Earning Mothers in the United States"; Hewitt, *Southern Discomfort*; Lasch-Quinn, *Black Neighbors*; Michel, *Children's Interests/Mothers' Rights*; and Rose, *A Mother's Job*. On San Diego specifically, see Breitenbach, "The Development of the Role of the Community Welfare Council," 28; Sexton, "The San Diego Woman's Home Association," 41–53.

3. Moehring, *Urbanism and Empire in the Far West*, 66–73; and Molina, *Fit to Be Citizens?* for population figures. Molina's table 1 on page 7 notes that in 1880 the Los Angeles population was 11,183 and jumped to 50,395 by 1890.

4. Henry H. Weddle interviews, February 25, August 20, and December 30, 1959, and Earnest Morgan interview, November 13, 1958, interviews by Edgar F. Hastings, Oral History Historical Collection, Documents Archives, San Diego History Center Research Archives (OHHC).

5. Oral History of Gertrude Gildos, 1958, OHHC; and Carlton, "Blacks in San Diego County," 84.

6. The number of people considered Mexican American in this era is difficult to tally because until the 1970s census enumerators for the state and city included Mexican Americans in their counts of "Whites." In 1920 the county's population totaled 112,248, with 4,104 enumerated as Mexican-born immigrants living in the U.S. The city population was 74,683 in 1920, with 2,741 enumerated as Mexican-born immigrants. See Broadbent, pages 27 and 28 of "Table 7: Distribution in the United States of White Persons Born in Mexico by Counties and Cities, 1919–1920," in *The Distribution of Mexican Populations in the United States*; and page 41 of "Table S104: City, Municipality, and County Populations, 10 S, 1900–90," in Lorey, *United States–Mexico Border Statistics since 1900: 1990 Update*.

7. Pryde, "Water Supply for the County," 115; and Hennessey, "The Politics of Water in San Diego 1895–1897," 367–383.

8. McGrew, *City of San Diego and San Diego County*, 129. On the transformations due to increased rail traffic, see Carlton, "Blacks in San Diego County," 86; Lowell, "The California Southern Railroad and the Growth of San Diego," 245–60; Mayo, *Los Angeles*; Newmark and Newmark, *Sixty Years in Southern California*; Woods, *Recollections of Pioneer Work in California*.

9. *First Annual Report of the County Hospital and Poor Farm of San Diego, California, for the Year Ending June 30, 1889* (San Diego, 1889) in Stephens, "The History

of Social Welfare Agencies," 4, 8. The report notes that three hundred families were part of the SDBA assistance.

10. See Stephens, "The History of Social Welfare Agencies," 5, for the quote taken from Benevolent and Protective Order of Elks, *Fourteenth Annual Benefit: San Diego Lodge* (San Diego: Benevolent and Protective Order of Elks, 1904), 26.

11. *Book of By Laws and Record of Minutes of Associated Charities, San Diego CA, 1889*, Box 1, Family Services Association of San Diego Collection (FSASD); and Stephens, "The History of Social Welfare Agencies," 14.

12. Stephens, "The History of Social Welfare Agencies," 16.

13. Helping Hand Home for Children, Ephemera Collection, Documents Archive, SDHCRA; and Stephens, "The History of Social Welfare Agencies," 23.

14. There is conflicting evidence to the opening of the Door of Hope, known as the Girls Home of San Diego. The endorsement "Application—Door of Hope" lists the facility at 729–20th Street and opening in May 1911. However, the 1893 date is used by Stephens, "The History of Social Welfare Agencies," 13, and is verified by evidence from Charlotte Baker. The home's purpose was to provide temporary shelter to girls and women under the age of thirty who were "desirous of reformation and who [were] not otherwise objectionable." It did not admit "negroes" and averaged five admits per month. Their records indicate they averaged sixty girls and babies per year. Endorsement applications are located in the FSASD, Box 1A, Malcolm A. Love Library, Special Collections, San Diego State University (SDSU) [hereafter, Endorsements].

15. Neil Larry Shumsky points to how red-light districts, downtown entertainment zones, and Chinatowns often occupied the same urban space, so that the "thrills of the forbidden and the erotic were frequently combined with those of the distant and the exotic." See his "Tacit Acceptance" quote on page 666; and Keire, *For Business and Pleasure*.

16. Census information shows that some of these single women resided in well-kept houses, but most of the women shared one-room rentals (commonly known as cribs) that could easily be construed as places where prostitution operated. MacPhail, "Shady Ladies in the 'Stingaree District,'" 7; Subject File Collection, Box 21, "Prostitution," Documents Archive, SDHCRA; and Census 1870, 1880, 1890.

17. *Report of the Woman's Home Association & Day Nursery for the Year Ending February 1, 1890* [hereafter, *Report, 1890*], Box 10, folder (Mixed Programs, notes), SDCC.

18. WCTU chapters in San Diego, Denver, Baltimore, and Poughkeepsie, and Hamilton in Ontario, Canada, opened day nurseries or crèches for children who needed full-day care, and for teachers to gain experience with small children. Michel, *Children's Interests/Mothers' Rights*, 34.

19. Butler, *Gendered Justice in the American West* and *Daughters of Joy, Sisters of Misery*; Goldman, *Gold Diggers and Silver Miners*; and Rosen, *The Lost Sisterhood*.

20. County of San Diego, California, "Coroner's Inquest Papers," 1853–1904 [hereafter, Coroner's Inquest], Public Records Collection PR2.69, Documents Archive, SDHCRA.

21. Donovan, *White Slave Crusades*, 38.

22. Sharon E. Wood notes how sexual experience was assumed among working-class girls as young as six years of age. See *The Freedom of the Streets*, 132–57.

23. Donovan, *White Slave Crusades*, 39. On the fears of white slavery, see also Keire, *For Business and Pleasure* and "The Vice Trust," 5–42; Meyerowitz, *Women Adrift*; Mumford, *Interzones*; Strange, *Toronto's "Girl Problem"*; Wood, *The Freedom of the Streets*.

24. Odem, *Delinquent Daughters*, 9–15, quote on page 15.

25. *San Diego Union*, May 3, 1887 and May 6, 1887.

26. Scientific studies emphasized that lesbian interactions were highly unnatural and that women who engaged in such acts did so accidentally or through manipulation by sinister criminals. This contributed to the fears about women's growing sexuality in an urban world and included madams luring young women into prostitution and a supposed lesbian life. See Gilman, "Black Bodies, White Bodies," 204–42.

27. *San Diego Union*, June 29, 1887, p. 5; June 30, 1887, p. 6; July 2, 1887, p. 3; July 3, 1887, p. 1; July 8, 1887, p. 1; and August 9, 1887, p. 5.

28. San Diego City Directories list Kate Clark living at Sixth between J & K (1886–87) and at 355 Sixth (1887–88).

29. *San Diego Union*, August 12, 1887, p. 1; August 24, 1887, p. 1; August 25, 1887, p. 2; August 27, 1887, p. 1; September 2, 1887, p. 4; September 21, 1887, p. 1; April 8, 1888, p. 6; April 9, 1888, p. 4; May 1, 1888, p. 1; and July 7, 1888, p. 5.

30. In 1915 William H. Slingerland recorded three homes in the Los Angeles area and none in San Diego for girls who had "erred," which means he overlooked the Girls Rescue Home, otherwise known as the Door of Hope. The Los Angeles area homes were the Florence Crittenton Home (1894), Truelove Home (1899), and Beulah Home (1890). See Slingerland, *Child Welfare Work in California*, 123–24.

31. *San Diego Union*, April 3, 1887, and February 18, 1888.

32. *San Diego Union*, February 18, 1888, p. 1.

33. Gilman, "Black Bodies, White Bodies," 237.

34. *San Diego Union*, February 17, 1888, p. 3. John Callahan, property owner of the house Kate Clark ran, was arrested, perhaps in a move more political than legal.

35. San Diego Justice Court Case Files, 1889 and 1890, SDHCRA.

36. Coroner's Inquest, "Mary A. Monroe," November 16, 1897, SDHCRA; *San Diego Union*, November 15, 1897, p. 1, and November 16, 1897, p. 1; and Carlton, "Blacks in San Diego County," 134.

37. MacPhail, *The Story of New San Diego*, 101–2, cited in Alma Kathryn Robens, "Charlotte Baker," 38–39.

38. *Report of the Woman's Home Association and Day Nursery, February 1, 1891* [hereafter *Report, 1891*], Box 14, folder 17, SDCC; and Stephens, "History of Social Welfare Agencies," 9.

39. Abrams, "Guardians of Virtue," 436–52.

40. Hennessey, "George White and Anna Gunn Marston," 96–105.

41. Information on Baker derives from Robens's thesis, "Charlotte Baker," unless otherwise noted. For specifics on the Bakers' arrival to San Diego and their connections with other San Diegans from Newburyport, Massachusetts, see pages 34–35 and 41.

42. Jewish women united their relief in 1905 under the umbrella organization Federated Jewish Aid Society. On Catholic and Jewish benevolence, see Stephens, "History of Social Welfare Agencies," 27; Karsh, "San Diego Pioneering Ladies and Their Contributions to the Community," 21–32; Casper, "The Blochman Saga in San Diego," 64–79.

43. Sander, *The Business of Charity*; and Wood, *The Freedom of the Streets*, 73–74.

44. The Dallas Exchange used a similar tactic. See Enstam, *Women and the Creation of Urban Life*, 62–64. On the development of saloons and taverns as spaces that provided domestic services to men, see Chudacoff, *The Age of the Bachelor*, 109–10.

45. Phillips, "Secretary's Report," 7, Ephemera Collection, pamphlet, Documents Archive, SDHCRA.

46. Sexton, "The San Diego Woman's Home Association," 45.

47. To my knowledge, no one has tackled the project of systematically calculating these increases. My assessment is derived from working with the directories to verify data gathered from the CHDN child registration cards and Associated Charities records. These combined sources support the finding that most women seeking aid worked in the service sector. Figures for the year 1920 in "Table 118—Women Employed in Certain Selected Occupations, for Cities Having from 25,000 to 100,000 Inhabitants: 1920," in Hill, *Women in Gainful Occupations*, 216. Businesses in San Diego employed 7,603 women in all occupations in 1920. The three highest occupations were clerks and saleswomen (in stores), 730; servants, 732; and teachers, 634.

48. On January 17, 1889, members of the Woman's Industrial Exchange filed incorporation papers with the State of California. See *Woman's Industrial Exchange* (San Diego: Pacific Printing, October 31, 1888), 1–13, as cited in Stephens, "History of Social Welfare Agencies," 10–11.

49. In the 1930s the San Diego Society for Crippled Children challenged WHA's full ownership rights to the land after WHA refused to share their facility with the society. A series of rulings found the city had deeded the land to Bryant Howard on December 2, 1887, who then deeded five acres to the WHA. The organization's Articles of Agreement, dated July 22, 1890, stipulate WHA "agrees to provide in the building now being erected by the said Woman's Home Association upon the city park within the city of San Diego in said County, suitable accommodation for the care and maintenance of the classes of indigent sick or otherwise dependent poor of the said County of San Diego." However, the 1934 rulings found the city did not have the authority to deed part of the Howard acreage to a separate body. See WHA, "Articles of Agreement, July 22, 1890," Documents File, WHA; "Deed from City of San Diego, California to the Woman's

Home Association," December 30, 1887, WHA; "Rule to Children's Home Site Is Ruled Illegal," 1934 (newspaper unknown), Box 5 Series IV–Scrapbooks, 1923–40, SDCC; and "$1000 Fund Gives Start to San Diego Children's Home," *San Diego Union*, circa 1937, Box 6 Scrapbook 1923–40, SDCC.

50. These figures are derived from my review of all of the CHDN case records.

51. "Indigent Gentlewomen Make Way for Needy Children," undated newspaper article, Box 10, folder (Mixed Programs, notes), SDCC.

52. *Report, 1890.*

53. Quote from January 1, 1898, newspaper article (newspaper unknown), Box 5, Series IV–Scrapbooks, SDCC.

54. Robens, "Charlotte Baker," 71–76.

55. *Report, 1890,* 5.

56. Durst, "Day Nurseries and Wage-Earning Mothers," 143.

57. "Articles of Agreement Organizing Woman's Home Association as a Corporation," July 22, 1890, Box 1, folder 1, SDCC (MS227); and *Report, 1890.*

58. Gullet, *Becoming Citizens*; Simpson, *Selling the City*; and Rafferty, "Los Angeles Clubwomen and Progressive Reform," 144.

59. Rose, "From Sponge Cake to *Hamentashen*," 3–23.

60. *Report, 1890.*

61. SDCCa 167; and *San Diego City Directory,* 1895.

62. From September 1888 to October 1905, sixteen women made this arrangement. Eleven mothers had only one child, which likely made it cost effective for the organization to offer them this aid. Three of these mothers asked CHDN to take in their two children, and two mothers needed help with their three children. Records 70; 104/105; 123/124; 202; 258; 264; 268; 274; 284; 320/321/322; 365/366/367; 377; 385; 390/391; 449; and 560, SDCCa.

63. *Report, 1891,* 5.

64. Aiken, *Harnessing the Power of Motherhood*; Solinger, *Wake Up Little Susie,* 149–52; and Wood, *The Freedom of the Streets,* 186–212.

65. Kunzel, *Fallen Women, Problem Girls,* 26.

66. Perhaps her contact with unmarried mothers at CHDN convinced Charlotte Baker that San Diego needed a separate facility to help these women. Robens, "Charlotte Baker," 76, and quote on p. 128.

67. SDCCa 103, 112, and 116 are examples of single women delivering at CHDN and putting their children up for adoption. After a married woman delivered her son on March 2, 1891, the new mother and her baby stayed free of charge through their time of confinement; see SDCCa, 69.

68. "$1000 Fund," SDCC; and Woman's Home Association, *Review of the Work, 1899* [hereafter *Review, 1899*], p. 7, in Box 5, Series IV–Scrapbooks, SDCC. The CHDN received funds, clothing, food, and volunteer help from women associated with the aid societies of the Presbyterian, Congregational, Lutheran, German Methodist, Baptist, and Episcopal Churches, as well as the Ladies Hebrew Aid and King's Daughters.

69. Minutes of the Advisory Council Committee Meetings for the Associated Charities (1909–1912) in San Diego reflect these practices. Minutes are located in Box IA, FSASD. As with the Children's Home records, I use fictitious names for families discussed by the Associated Charities. In all cases I have adopted a name that fits ethnically with the real name of the family.

70. *Report, 1890*.

71. See Slingerland, *Child Welfare Work in California*, 98–99; Pascoe, *Relations of Rescue*, 13–17.

72. Liu, "Celestials in the Golden Mountain"; and Yung, *Unbound Feet*, 293, 296.

73. This exclusion may extend to 1929. I limited my review of the 1919–29 case records to a 50 percent sample, which did not reveal any Asian children.

74. SDCCa 229.

75. SDCCa 315/316.

76. For example, SDCCa 6, SDCCa 7, SDCCa 9, SDCCa 10.

77. The children entered CHDN on March 27, 1903, and stayed for over a year until their mother remarried and claimed them on September 5, 1904; see SDCCa 396/397/398.

78. Carlton, "Blacks in San Diego County," 83, 87, 91, 140–41.

79. SDCCa 151.

80. SDCCa 380.

81. *San Diego Union*, October 19, 1931, in Box 5 Series IV–Scrapbooks, Scrapbook 1923–1940, SDCC.

82. SDCCa 12, 85, 32, and 54.

83. T. L. to Mr. James Ross, Chief of Police, Santa Barbara, CA, dated February 24, 1906, Box 5, Series IV–Scrapbooks, SDCC.

84. SDCCa 101; SDCCa 102.

85. Historians have not fully assessed how Americans handled fatherly care in this era. See Willrich, "Home Slackers," 460–89.

86. SDCCa 295.

87. SDCCa 10/11.

88. Tentler, *Wage-Earning Women*, 139, 142–43.

89. Tentler, *Wage-Earning Women*, 133.

90. I explored women in Detroit entering the paid workforce as domestic day workers in "Hidden Laborers," 23–51. Book-length studies include Clark-Lewis, *Living In, Living Out*; Cooper, *Once a Cigar Maker*; Deutsch, *Women and the City*; Hunter, *To 'Joy My Freedom*; Katzman, *Seven Days a Week*; Kleinberg, *The Shadow of the Mills*; Pleck, *Black Migration and Poverty*; and Tentler, *Wage-Earning Women*.

91. SDCCa 371.

92. SDCCa 34/35.

93. *Report, 1890*, p. 7; and January 1, 1898, newspaper article (newspaper unknown), Box 5, Series IV–Scrapbooks, SDCC.

94. *Review, 1899*.

95. In 1904 Mr. and Mrs. Ernest White donated funding to furnish an addition that expanded kitchen and dining space; in 1909 a boys dormitory was added, and Mr. and Mrs. J. W. Sefton financed the Holly Sefton Memorial Hospital in honor of their son Holly; in 1912 Mr. and Mrs. F. S. Jennings donated in memory of two little daughters to build the Nellie Inez cottage for infants and children under five; Mrs. Julius Waggenheim initially furnished the cottage and continued to offer funding for renovating and renewing supplies; and in 1914, contributions from Mrs. Oliver H. Hicks of Redlands built an isolation ward. See "$1000 Fund," SDCC.

96. H. P. Wood to San Diego Chamber of Commerce, cited in Shragge, "'I Like the Cut of Your Jib,'" 230–55.

97. Woman's Home Association pamphlet, December 1901, Ephemera Collection, pamphlet, Documents Archives, SDHCRA.

3. Court-Appointed Care

1. County of San Diego, Superior Court, Order of Commitment, no. 9, 1897–1904, Public Records Collection, PR3.91 (OC), Document Archives, SDHCRA.

2. Wrigley, "Children's Caregivers and Ideologies of Parental Inadequacy," 291.

3. Steven Schlossman offers the best overview of how reformers dealt with the problems of juvenile delinquency in *Transforming Juvenile Justice*. See also Clapp, *Mothers of All Children*; Getis, *The Juvenile Court and the Progressives*; Wolcott, *Cops and Kids*.

4. Alexander, *The "Girl Problem,"* 22–28 and 33–66; Foley, *White Scourge*, especially 79, note 44 on page 240; Kevles, *In the Name of Eugenics*; Kline, *Building a Better Race*; Lunbeck, *The Psychiatric Persuasion*; and Stern, *Eugenic Nation*.

5. Peiss, *Cheap Amusements*, 56–76. See also Odem, *Delinquent Daughters*; Strange, *Toronto's "Girl Problem"*; Wood, *The Freedom of the Streets*.

6. Broder, *Tramps, Unfit Mothers, and Neglected Children*, 64–67; Chávez-García, "Youth, Evidence, and Agency," 55–83, "Intelligence Testing at Whittier School," 193–228, and *States of Delinquency*; Gordon, *Heroes of Their Own Lives*, 84; and Wrigley, "Children's Caregivers and Ideologies of Parental Inadequacy."

7. Chávez-García, *States of Delinquency*, 30–31.

8. Chávez-García, *States of Delinquency*, 30, 33–35. While youth from all over the state were sent to these institutions, I have not found evidence in San Diego's records that youngsters from the area were sent north in this era (1860s and 1870s).

9. Parr, "From Crooked to Straight," 29.

10. Slingerland, *Child Welfare Work in California*, 43.

11. Parr, "From Crooked to Straight," 28.

12. Chávez-García, "Youth, Evidence and Agency," 66–67.

13. Parr, "From Crooked to Straight," 28.

14. Superintendent Mrs. C. M. Weyman wrote in October 1915: "It is not likely that we will move before February or March of next year. We consider it inadvisable to take 75 girls up there during the construction of the seven buildings now

being erected ... it is too great a hazard to move in while there are so many work-men on the premises." Quoted in Slingerland, *Child Welfare Work in California*, 44.

15. A.M., *Special Report of the Whittier State School*, 39; "State School Shake-Up to Be Investigated," *Los Angeles Times*, October 16, 1912; and "Tell of Ice to Cure Bad Girls," *Los Angeles Times*, January 16, 1919, as cited in Parr, "From Crooked to Straight," 63, 66.

16. San Diego County (Calif) Board of Supervisors, *Fact-Finding Study of Social and Economic Conditions of Indians of San Diego County and Reports from Special-ists in Allied Fields* (np: publisher unknown, 1932), 11. This collaborative study was published in 1932 and involved San Diego County's Board of Supervisors and Wel-fare Commission, the state Department of Social Welfare, and the Office of Indian Affairs. On the importance of these collaborative studies conducted in this era, see James, "Rhetoric and Resistance." In 1892, Perris Indian School had opened with eight students. Located about twenty miles south of Riverside, over the course of ten years, it expanded to 350 students, but the lack of a clean and adequate water supply prompted its closure. Perris students were transferred to the Sherman Insti-tute and formed its student body core when it opened in 1902. Perris remained open for two more years. See Keller, *Empty Beds*; Gilbert, *Education Beyond the Mesa*.

17. "Fact-Finding Study," 84.

18. Slingerland, *Child Welfare Work in California*, 39–41.

19. Dutschke, "A History of American Indians in California," 44.

20. "Fact-Finding Study," 93.

21. On the 1903 statute (1903 Cal. Stats., ch. 43, § 2), see Sutton, "The Juvenile Court and Social Welfare," 113; *Delinquent Daughters*, 74.

22. Chávez-García, *States of Delinquency*, 53–54, 62–75.

23. Stephens, "History of Social Welfare Agencies," 26.

24. Cahn and Bary, *Welfare Activities of Federal, State and Local Governments in California*, 31.

25. Stephens, "History of Social Welfare Agencies," 27.

26. 12 April 1900, no. 8, OC.

27. Peiss, *Cheap Amusements*, 50–51.

28. Odem, *Delinquent Daughters*, 45.

29. One-fourth of the County Indigents expenditures for 1893 had supported abandoned, orphaned, and half-orphaned children, which highlights the ongo-ing problems of both funding and managing childcare for certain children in San Diego. The County Indigents report for 1893 provided separate line items for abandoned, whole orphans, and half orphans. While the majority of county expenditures went toward "outside hospital" expenses ($3,101.71), children's needs formed the remainder of payouts: abandoned children ($350.00); whole orphans ($112.50); and half orphans ($615.00). See County of San Diego, *Indigents Ledger, 1893*, PRC, PR2,161, Documents Archive, SDHCRA.

30. On education in Mexico, see Vaughan, *State, Education, and Social Class in Mexico*; and "Rural Women's Literacy and Education during the Mexican Revo-

lution," 106–24. On limited educational opportunities for Mexican-heritage children, see Chávez-García, "Intelligence Testing at Whittier School, 1890–1920," 193–228; González, *Chicano Education in the Era of Segregation*; Raftery, *Land of Fair Promise*. On the integration of manual and vocational education into San Diego city schools, see Kantor, *Learning to Earn*.

31. September 8, 1897, no. 1, OC. The chaperone is listed as Mrs. E. C. Chambers (her first name is never referred to in court documents or other records, such as the city directories). *San Diego City Directory for 1897* lists E. C. Chambers as the superintendent of the Diamond Livery Stable at 744 D Street, and his wife, Mrs. E. C. Chambers, as performing "Spanish drawing work." Because of her listed profession and the use by the juvenile court as transport for girls sent to Whittier, she probably spoke both English and Spanish, and may even have been of Mexican ancestry, thus serving as both chaperone and interpreter for girls coming before the court. She probably worked in vocational education (perhaps with the programs implemented by San Diego's public school system in 1891 and the Free Industrial School), but I have found no evidence of these connections.

32. One of San Diego's oldest neighborhoods, Sherman Heights was established in 1867 and located east of downtown, between Fifteenth and Twenty-Fourth Streets and Market and Commercial Streets. Sherman School was one of two schools built in the city in 1870. See Crane, "Matthew Sherman: Pioneer San Diegan," 22–27.

33. Others present at the hearing included T. H. Blackledge, the individual who submitted the case to the court, and Carmichael and Mrs. Rodríguez. The relationship between the Rodríguez couple and Frank Vasqúez is unknown. February 8, 1898, no. 2, OC.

34. Even though persons of Mexican descent constituted only 3 to 5 percent of San Diego's total population (17,700 in 1900), two of the twelve adolescent commitment cases (or nearly 17 percent) involved Mexican immigrants. For rich analysis of prejudice against Mexican people in the Southwest and how whites translated that bias into incarceration or eugenic sterilization (especially for young adults considered "feeble-minded), see Chávez-García, "Intelligence Testing at Whittier School," and *States of Delinquency*; and Foley, *The White Scourge*, especially 40–63.

35. August 11, 1899, no. 5, OC.

36. Scholars have made excellent use of local court records in assessing what contemporaries termed the "girl problem." See Alexander, *The "Girl Problem"*; Odem, *Delinquent Daughters*; Strange, *Toronto's "Girl Problem"*; Wood, *The Freedom of the Streets*.

37. The Mann Act of 1908 restricted the interstate movements of single women accompanied by men as a preventative to the spread of prostitution. It had a racialized directive to it, as the women being monitored tended to be white, and the men stopped for questioning were often African American. See Mumford, *Interzones*.

38. Mary Detrick, August 12, 1898, no. 3, OC; Olive Casna, January 23, 1899, no. 4, OC; Bessie Henry, July 18, 1899, no. 6, OC; and Virginia Ybarra, September 8, 1897, no. 1, OC.

39. Royal Stark told authorities that he "tried to learn shoemakers trade;" Russell Jones, fourteen at the time of his court hearing, had earned wages by gardening; and Frank Vasquéz had worked in a factory. Records are incomplete for two of the youths charged with delinquent behavior, both of whom were seventeen at the time of their convictions and sent to Preston School of Industry: Charles H. Begley was sentenced on February 17, 1900, by Judge J. W. Hughes to one year at Preston for petit larceny (no. 7, OC); and Clarence Eaton, born in Vicksburg, Mississippi, was charged with "embezzlement" on February 24, 1904 (no. 11, OC). Neither record indicated employment history.

40. Nunn and Cleary, "From the Mexican California Frontier to Arnold-Kennick," 3–31.

41. On development of vocational education in the United States, see Kantor and Tyack, *Work, Youth, and Schooling*; Kliebard, *Schooled to Work*.

42. Kantor, *Learning to Earn*, 48–49.

43. Endorsement Forms, Endorsements, FSASD; and Atherton, "Vocational Side Lights," 12.

44. See San Diego State University Oral History (SDSUOH).

45. Endorsements; Atherton, "Vocational Side Lights," 12.

46. Lindenmeyer, *"A Right to Childhood"*; and Sklar, *Florence Kelley and the Nation's Work*.

47. Trattner, *Crusade for Children*, 45–67; and Sarbaugh-Thompson and Zald, "Child Labor Laws," 25–53.

48. Nasaw, *Children of the City*, 62–87; and Trattner, *Crusade for the Children*, 110.

49. Postol, "Hearing the Voices of Working Children," 4, 6.

50. Shatto King and King, *Pathfinder Social Survey*, 31–32.

51. Shatto King and King, *Pathfinder Social Survey*, 21

52. Shatto King and King, *Pathfinder Social Survey*, 32.

53. January 9, 1914, "Minutes of Advisory Meeting, 1911–1916 and January 1914–May 1914," FSASD; Ciani, "The Power of Maternal Love," 71–79.

54. SDCCb 6.

55. Endorsement Application, 12 April 1920, Endorsements. The Children's Home Society of California (CHSC) was established in 1891 by Dr. and Mrs. J. R. Townsend out of concern for homeless and abandoned children in Los Angeles, San Bernardino, and Santa Clara Counties. In 1892 it expanded operations to include California's Bay Area. In 1911 CHSC received the state's first permit as a licensed child placement agency from the newly created BCC.

56. SDCCb 12.

57. Cabeza de Baca and Cabeza de Baca, "The 'Shame Suicides' and Tijuana," 603–35; Curtis and Arreola, "Zonas de Tolerancia on the Northern Mexican Border," 333–46; Guzmán, "El régimen jurídico de la prostitución en México," 85–134;

Sandos, "Prostitution and Drugs," 621–45; Schantz, "All Night at the Owl," 549–602; and Taylor, "The Wild Frontier Moves South," 204–29.

58. FSASD minutes for September 28, 1917; October 5, 1917; October 12, 1917; October 19, 1917; October 26, 1917; November 2, 1917; November 9, 1917; November 16, 1917; November 23, 1917; December 21, 1917; December 28, 1917; January 4, 1918.

59. SDCCb 39.

60. Alexander, The "Girl Problem," 102–22; and Odem, Delinquent Daughters, 182–84.

61. Odem, Delinquent Daughters, 159–61.

62. The first Italians were fishermen who arrived in 1871; a larger migration followed in the 1880s, including Italian families displaced by the San Francisco fire and earthquake of 1906. Most were fishing families and settled in homes in the "vicinity of India, Columbia, and State Streets and Kettner Boulevard." Richardson, "Fishermen of San Diego," 213–26.

63. Prior to 1920 most families using the Children's Home spoke English, worshipped in a Protestant church, and claimed American citizenship. There is no evidence that personnel spoke any language other than English. In a sampling of forty-three households using the CH between 1909 and 1919, staff described 70 percent of the sample (or thirty households) as "American." They registered children from three Mexican households; two Italian families; two German households; and children from one family each of Irish, Serbian, English, Canadian, and Swedish heritage. They listed only one family as Catholic, and one other as Jewish.

64. The most thorough analysis of how expositions in San Diego influenced urban change is Bokovoy, The San Diego World's Fairs and Southwestern Memory.

65. Shumsky, "Tacit Acceptance," 671; Putnam, Class and Gender Politics in Progressive-Era Seattle, 121.

66. For how San Diego officials attempted to clean up their red-light district in the early twentieth century, see McKanna Jr., "San Diego's Stingaree," 56–59, and "Hold Back the Tide," 55–56; and MacPhail, "Shady Ladies," 2–28.

67. Robens, "Charlotte Baker," 24–128.

68. Los Angeles authorities hired Alice Stebbins Wells as the first female permanent, full-time police office in the country, on September 13, 1910. Odem, Delinquent Daughters, 110–11.

69. San Diego Union, October 10, 1912.

70. Robens, "Charlotte Baker," 129.

71. Pourade, Gold in the Sun, 224.

72. Robens, "Charlotte Baker," 132–33. Baker and Allen led the effort and were joined by Dr. Mary A. Ritter and Florence Toll in hosting the luncheon at the U. S. Grant Hotel.

73. Dummer, Why I Think So, 84.

74. Lichtman, Ethel Sturges Dummer, 74.

75. Rosen, Reproductive Health, Reproductive Rights, 40–41; and Stokes, "Ethel Sturges Dummer," 209–10.

76. Lichtman, *Ethel Sturges Dummer*, 31.

77. February 22, 1910, FSASD.

78. For instance, she and her four sisters underwrote the first five years of the Juvenile Psychopathic Institute, established in Chicago in 1908. Advocates appreciated her involvement and respected her requests for anonymity. Juvenile court chief probation officer Joel D. Hunter sent Dummer the Juvenile Court Report for 1916 and thanked her for "her assistance in signing the indemnity bond for the court's operation: "You deserve a great deal more thanks than anyone else." Lichtman, *Ethel Sturges Dummer*, 16; and Getis, *The Juvenile Court and the Progressives*, 1–2.

79. Guy V. Whaley letter, May 15, 1919, Endorsements.

4. Professional Care

1. Payments of $10 per month found in Register 1914, Box 17, SDCC; and information on the man who made those payments found in *San Diego City Directory, 1914*.

2. San Diego History Center staff, "Timeline of San Diego History," July 1, 2018, http://www.sandiegohistory.org/archives/biographysubject/timeline/1900–1929/.

3. Lotchin, *Fortress California 1910–1961*, especially 23–41; Pourade, *Gold in the Sun*, 111; and Shragge, "'I Like the Cut of Your Jib.'"

4. See Bridges, *Morning Glories*, 47–51.

5. Subject File Collection, Box 12, "Associations—YWCA" and "Associations—Women's Clubs and Societies," Documents Archive, SDHCRA; Stephens, "History of Social Welfare," 28 and 35–36. Stephens notes that the TASSD opened in 1900, but it did not become active until 1910, and records for the chapter do not begin until 1915. See TASSD records in SDSU.

6. Box 3, folder 11 (Board Minutes, Circa 1914–45), TASSD. On the international development of the Travelers Aid Society, see Meyerowitz, *Women Adrift*; Strange, *Toronto's Girl Problem*.

7. Worchester, *Grim the Battles*, 151.

8. Worchester, *Grim the Battles*, 9.

9. On the NCLC advocacy, see Trattner, *Crusade for Children*, especially 69–93; Sarbaugh-Thompson and Zald, "Child Labor Laws," 25–53.

10. Worchester, *Grim the Battles*, 9, 149–51; Shelton, "The Neighborhood House of San Diego," 32; and Stephens, "History of Social Welfare Agencies," 44.

11. The first meeting was held on October 8, 1896, when thirteen women and eighteen men met at the Bakers' medical office. Flanigan, "Social and Intellectual Affiliation," 40–43.

12. Edwina B. Sample, a partner in San Diego's first all-woman press relations company, admitted to storming the club during the 1950s as a show of protest against banning women from membership. Miss Sample passed in May 2006, and the anecdotes derive from numerous conversations between Sample and myself over the span of a twenty-year friendship. In her history of the group, Syl-

via Flanigan noted how the University Club remained off-limits to women as late as 1975 and voted to expand membership to include women only for financial stability. Flanigan, "Social Intellectual Affiliation," 48.

13. For an overview of California suffrage, see Gullet, *Becoming Citizens*.

14. Robens, "Charlotte Baker," 88–120.

15. Lowe, *Looking Good*; Palmieri, *In Adamless Eden*; Smith-Rosenberg, *Disorderly Conduct*, 245–96; and Solomon, *In the Company of Educated Women*, 47–61.

16. Jensen, "Helen Marston and the California Peace Movement," 118–31; and Ciani, "Revelations of a Reformer," 102–23.

17. In her study of female college graduates, including those from Wellesley, Joyce Antler found that many of these women remained devoted to their families throughout their lives and often returned to their homes to secure their professions. While referring to an earlier generation than Helen Marston's, Antler's findings are relevant for understanding Helen and her elder sister's return to San Diego. Mary Gilman Marston graduated from Wellesley in 1903, never married, and remained devoted to her parents, the family home, her siblings' families, and Neighborhood House. See Antler, "After College, What?" 409–34; Palmieri, *In Adamless Eden*, 238–44.

18. December 1, 1909, FSASD. In one of her first actions as AC secretary, Mary Anderson Hill asserted this strategy by assigning a friendly visitor to a case where a "missionary nurse" was tending a sick Mexican mother and her baby while the father searched for work. The committee also voted to table the investigations of seven new cases, deciding instead to focus on raising money for their wavering budget.

19. December 31, 1909, FSASD.

20. September 8, 1911, FSASD.

21. Peggy Pascoe's thorough analysis of miscegenation law throughout the United States indicates that prior to the 1920s, no "white person" could secure a marriage license if their partner was a "negro, mulatto, or mongolian." See pages 131–32 for a synopsis of this law, in *What Comes Naturally*.

22. *First Report of the Associated Charities of San Diego County, Inc., February 1, 1910–March 1, 1911*, cited in Breitenbach, "Development of Community Welfare Council," 29; and January 27, 1911, FSASD, where the details of the visiting-nurse hiring process—done by a committee composed of Dr. Charlotte Baker, Mrs. German, and Miss Dietzler, registrar of the Associated Charities—can be reviewed. Five women applied for the position, all with good experience in poverty relief work and carrying the recommendations of respected authorities in San Diego.

23. August 19, 1910, FSASD; the minutes referred to School Law, Section 1618 and Section 1662 subdivision 2, and page 202, section 10.

24. January 27, 1911, and April 21, 1911, FSASD.

25. The group also sought advice from more-experienced societies such as New York's Charity Organization Service. By writing to New York, the San Diego Charities could demonstrate to the eastern body that they were not a

naive backwater agency; rather, their advice gathering signaled a movement toward professional oversight. Minutes from November 18, 1910; April 21, 1911; and December 8, 1911, FSASD.

26. See Endorsement Forms, and Letter from Board of Investigation to Mr. John S. Akerman, January 22, 1919, Endorsements.

27. August 19, 1910, FSASD.

28. For examples of this aid, see SDCCC 17, 56, and 58; SDCCd 54/55/56 and 57.

29. Letter from Leslie S. Everts, Chairman, Sidney J. Wines and (Mrs. L. A.) Haidee G. Blochman to Board of Directors, Community Welfare Council, January 11, 1922, San Diego Community Chest Records 1920–25, Volume I, UWSD.

30. Numbers derived from SDCCb case records, and earlier noted in Ciani, "Power of Maternal Love."

31. "Annual Report of Public Health, 1915," SDPH in SDSU; Stone, Price, and Stone, *City Manager Government in Nine Cities*, 151.

32. Walter Bellon manuscript, 1956, SDHCRA.

33. Shatto King and King, *Pathfinder Social Survey*, 11.

34. October 17, 1913, FSASD.

35. May 12, 1911, and May 19, 1911, FSASD.

36. January 2 and 9, 1914, FSASD.

37. Gardner, *The Qualities of a Citizen*, 50.

38. Hirata, "Free Indentured, Enslaved," 3–29; and Peffer, "Forbidden Families," 28–46.

39. Gardner, *Qualities of a Citizen*, 92–93.

40. Gardner, *Qualities of a Citizen*, 73, 81.

41. Gardner, *Qualities of a Citizen*, 63, 75–79.

42. March 20, 1914, FSASD.

43. June 19, 1914, FSASD.

44. September 28, 1917, FSASD; 12 October 1917, FSASD.

45. Calexico lies on the United States/Mexico border in Imperial County, which is directly east of San Diego County and runs to Arizona's southwestern line. Using the term *border* when describing Calexico is deceptive for this era, since people in Calexico accepted the fluid culture of both U.S. and Mexican nationals moving in and out of the two countries.

46. September 22, 1910, FSASD.

47. Lui, *The Chinatown Trunk Mystery*; and Strange, *Toronto's "Girl Problem."*

48. February 9, 1912, FSASD.

49. Trattner, *Crusade for the Children*, 110.

50. Supervision changed in 1925 to the Department of Public Welfare, and again in 1927 to the Department of Social Welfare. Cahn and Bary, *Welfare Activities of Federal, State and Local Governments in California*, 28.

51. Survey notes, Endorsements.

52. Ladd-Taylor, *Mother-Work*, 43–103; Lindenmeyer, *A Right to Childhood*, especially 9–52; and Schlossman, "End of Innocence," 209.

53. Scholars understand the success of passing mothers' pension agendas to be linked to urbanization and women's changing position and authority in the culture, such as the spread of female literacy. Skocpol, *Protecting Soldiers and Mothers*, 459; Gordon, *Pitied but Not Entitled*; and Goodwin, *Gender and the Politics of Welfare Reform*.

54. Skocpol, *Protecting Soldiers and Mothers*, 465, 467.

55. Mink, *Wages of Motherhood*, 49–51.

56. SDCCb 9. The Oakes moved to California from Chattanooga, Tennessee, in 1911. At the time of his death, her husband was forty-one, and Justine was thirty-two.

57. July 31, 1913, FSASD.

58. Box 17, Register 1914, SDCC. According to the Home Register, staff admitted three children on June 30, 1913, with an agreement that their mother would pay $10 per month.

59. November 21, 1913, FSASD.

60. March 27, 1914; April 3, 1914; and April 17, 1914, FSASD.

61. April 24, 1914; and May 8, 1914, FSASD.

62. November 29, 1912; April 25, 1913; and October 10, 1913, FSASD.

63. Slingerland, *Child Welfare Work in California*, 220–23.

64. July 21, 1916, FSASD.

65. "Orphans Flourish in Atmosphere of Kindness: Motherliness and Sympathy Make Children's Home Beloved by Little Ones," January 1, 1915, *San Diego Union*, Box 14, folder 18, SDCC.

66. Quote from page 6, *Report of the San Diego Children's Home Association, May 1, 1913*, Ephemera Collection, Associations, San Diego Children's Home, Documents Archive, SDHCRA.

67. "Children's Home Association Reviews Year of Achievement," July 9, 1927, Box 5, Series IV–Scrapbooks, SDCC.

68. Durst, "Day Nurseries and Wage-Earning Mothers," 247–49.

69. Stadum, "A Critique of Family Case Workers," 78.

70. "Children's Home Association Reviews Year of Achievement," July 9, 1927, Box 5, SDCC.

71. "Report of Travelers Aid Department of YWCA for July 1922," TASSD.

72. Travelers Aid Society of San Diego, *First Annual Report for the Year Ending December 31, 1915*, in Box 2, TASSD.

73. "Report of Master Forrest Holmes, September 3, 1915," Box 2, folder 3 (Case histories, circa 1915), TASSD; Ciani, "Power of Maternal Love."

74. "Stat Reports, November 1921," Box 2, folder 21 (Statistical Reports, Case histories, Circa 1921), TAASD.

75. Ella Thomas, Anna V. Speer Travelers' Aid Workers, "Travelers Aid Department of the U.W.C.A. Report for June–1921," TASSD.

76. "Report of Travelers Aid Department for July 1926," Box 2, folder (Statistical Reports, Case Histories, circa 1926), TASSD.

77. "Report for June 1921," Box 2, folder 25 (Statistical Reports, Circa 1922), TASSD.

78. "Report of August 1920," Box 2, folder 25 (Statistical Reports, Case Histories, Circa 1922), TASSD.

79. "First Annual Report, San Diego County Welfare Commission, July 1, 1920 to July 1, 1921," Minutes of County Welfare Commission, Box PR2. 167, folder 1, Documents Archives SDHCRA.

80. Shatto King and King, *Pathfinder Social Survey*, 30.

81. SDCCd 5.

82. "Meeting No. 9," San Diego County Welfare Commission Annual Reports, July 1, 1920 to July 1, 1921, SDCWC.

83. "Meeting No. 11," August 3, 1920, and "Meeting No. 13," August 17, 1920, SDCWC.

84. E. B. Gould served as the chair of the organizing committee, and members included Mrs. Homer Oatman and Miss McLeod for the CH; Mr. J. D. Smith and Ed Davidson for the BGAS; George W. Marston for the YMCA; and his youngest child, Helen Marston, for NH. "Minutes of Agency Representatives RE: Community Welfare Council, San Diego Hotel, August 31, 1920," Volume 1, 1920–25, SDCCUW.

85. "Minutes of Meeting of the Board of Directors of the Community Welfare Council, October 23, 1923," SDCCUW.

86. "Meeting of the Community Welfare Council," November 20, 1923, SDCCUW.

87. "1937 Annual Narrative Report," Box 2, folder 30 (Narrative Report, Circa 1926), TASSD.

88. "80 Years of Service," *San Diego Children's Home Newsletter*, May 1968, Ephemera Collection, Associations, San Diego Children's Home, Document Archives, SDHCRA.

89. "Everybody Helps, 1938," Scrapbook 1923–40, Box 6, SDCC.

5. Neighborhood Care

1. Worchester, *Grim the Battles*, 154.

2. Muncy, *Creating a Female Dominion in American Reform*; and Hewitt, *Southern Discomfort*.

3. Shatto King and King, *Pathfinder Social Survey of San Diego*.

4. Shelton, "The Neighborhood House of San Diego," 36. Unfortunately, in 1970 most of the NH archives perished in a fire, making Shelton's oral interviews with Helen D. Marston Beardsley and Laura Rodriguez, who worked at the Chicano Community Clinic in the 1970s, an important resource. Garcia, *La Neighbor*, provides the history of the settlement from the perspective of those people who used its programs. Over a span of several years, Garcia interviewed dozens of people who grew up in Barrio Logan from the 1930s through the 1970s, providing some of the only firsthand accounts of how the primarily Mexican-descent people interacted as neighbors, friends, and family. See also Dittmyer and Grant, "Historical Study of Neighborhood House."

5. Shelton, "The Neighborhood House of San Diego," 55 and 60.

6. A sampling of analysis on settlement house agendas includes Carson, *Settlement Folk*; Hewitt, *Southern Discomfort*; Lasch-Quinn, *Black Neighbors*; and Trolanger, *Settlement Houses and the Great Depression*.

7. Gordon, "Social Insurance and Public Assistance," 19–54, and Hewitt, *Southern Discomfort*, highlight how these practices influenced communities with racially diverse populations.

8. Page 3 of Youth Services Division, Community Welfare Council, "A Study of Casa de Salud," June 9, 1949, in Box 26, folder (California, San Diego, Neighborhood House, 1926–49), NFSDNC, Social Welfare History Archives (SWHA), University of Minnesota Libraries.

9. Shatto King and King, *Pathfinder Social Survey*, 3–4.

10. Literature on the Mexican Revolution is extensive, and its historiography is complex, as noted in Alan Knight's two-volume chronological analysis, *The Mexican Revolution*.

11. Dittmyer and Grant, "Historical Study of Neighborhood House," 32.

12. Shatto King and King, *Pathfinder Social Survey*, 11–12.

13. Mead's report did not include other minority groups, such as the Chinese and African American populations. See "Minutes of the Advisory Council, November 18, 1910," Box 1A, folder (Minutes of Advisory Council Meetings, 1909–1912), FSASD.

14. Page 6 of "Annual Report of the Department of Public Health for the Year 1916," SDPH; and Shatto King and King, *Pathfinder Social Survey*, 9 and 18.

15. Koslow, "Putting It to a Vote," 111–44, and *Cultivating Health*; and Rafferty, "Los Angeles Clubwomen and Progressive Reform," 144–74.

16. See, for example, *The California Club Woman*, ed. Mrs. M. D. Hamilton vol. 1, no. 5 (September and October 1900), Box Serials C, folder California Club Woman, Document Archives, SDHCRA.

17. Shatto King and King, *Pathfinder Social Survey*, 4.

18. From that point, NH staff took on the work originally provided solely by FIS volunteers, and gradually FIS conceded its standing in the community. See Neighborhood House pamphlet, 1916, California Collection, in San Diego Central Library (SDCL); Arline Fay, "History of the College Woman's Club 1911–1932," unpublished paper, 1936, in Dittmyer and Grant, "Historical Study," 33.

19. NH 1916.

20. NH 1916. Helen Marston probably recruited Andrews, since she and her siblings had all attended the Bishop's School, but I found no evidence of that connection.

21. NH 1916.

22. "Annual Report of the Departments of Public Health for the year 1916," p. 7, Box 40, SDPH.

23. Worchester, *Grim the Battles*, 155–56.

24. Worchester, *Grim the Battles*, 156–57.

25. Even when Worchester penned her memoir in the early 1950s, the distribution of birth control remained a taboo subject to discuss with acquaintances. Linda Gordon, *The Moral Property of Women*; Reagan, *When Abortion was a Crime*; and Schoen, *Choice and Coercion*.

26. Hajo, *Birth Control on Main Street*, 28–29.

27. Marston, "Mexican Traits," 562.

28. Marston, "Mexican Traits," 562.

29. Figures for 1900 through 1970 calculated by Harris, "The Other Side of the Freeway," Table A and Table 1, pages 7 and 8.

30. The investigators discovered a home at 3035 Greeley Street where apparently people lived in back. Reverend Williams lived opposite the home, which seemed to give the residence and its residents some credibility, but white officials continued to be skeptical about the Greeley Street neighbors. A cryptic telegram sent at 11:30 a.m. on August 9, 1919, sent by W. F. Harper, authorizes William R. Carter, Superintendent of Negroe [*sic*] Work for the Southern Baptist Convention to raise money for local churches. See the correspondence in Endorsements.

31. Clare Crane, *The San Diego YWCA*, 15.

32. Madyun, "In the Midst of Things," 30.

33. Hewes, *Intergroup Relations in San Diego*, 21.

34. Ladd-Taylor, "'My Work Came out of Agony and Grief,'" 324. For a rich analysis of the bureau, see Lindenmeyer, *"A Right to Childhood."*

35. Ladd-Taylor, *Raising a Baby*, 44.

36. Ladd-Taylor, "'My Work Came out of Agony and Grief,'" 322.

37. Michel, *Children's Interests/Mothers' Rights*; and Sealander, *Private Wealth and Public Life*.

38. Smith-Hughes represented the second of two federal acts designed to assist rural communities. The first, the Smith-Lever Act, passed into law in May 1914 and expanded farm demonstration work initiated by the General Education Board eight years earlier. The Smith-Lever Act committed the federal government to supplying $4 million a year to extension work and mandated that state governments match the figure each received from the federal source. Sealander notes the growing savvy of state officials to take advantage of federal resources, especially in funding parent education classes in California public schools. See Sealander, *Private Wealth and Public Life*, 35–36, 52, 94–98 for debates.

39. Shelton, "Neighborhood House of San Diego," 41.

40. "Annual Report of the Department of Public Health for the Year 1921," SDPH; and Dittmyer and Grant, "Historical Study of Neighborhood House," 34.

41. Dittmeyer and Grant, "Historical Study of Neighborhood House," 39.

42. Shelton, "Neighborhood House of San Diego," 45.

43. Garcia, *La Neighbor*.

44. Amanda Mathews Chase, *Second Annual Report of the CIHC*, 139–46, cited in Gullet, "Women Progressives and the Politics of Americanization in California," 83.

45. Shelton, "The Neighborhood House of San Diego," 55.

46. Rose, "From Sponge Cake to *Hamentashen*," 4–5.

47. Chambers, *Paul U. Kellogg and the Survey*.

48. An index search of volumes 30 (1911) through 47 (1922) of the *Survey* indicates only a handful of articles devoted to topics in San Diego, including the presence of Japanese in the city and the importance of building the structures in Balboa Park for the 1915 exposition. Thanks to Jason Kaplan for his research assistance in validating this point.

49. Ciani, "Revelations of a Reformer," 102–23.

50. Shatto King, "My Mexican Neighbors," 624.

51. Marston, "Mexican Traits," 562.

52. Shatto King, "My Mexican Neighbors," 624.

53. Shatto King, "My Mexican Neighbors," 624.

54. Bokovoy, *The San Diego World's Fairs and Southwestern Memory*. For the area north of San Diego, see Haas, *Conquests and Historical Identities in California*; Engstrand, "In Search of the Sun," 53–59; Starr, *Inventing the Dream*.

55. Marston, "Mexican Traits," 563.

56. Hennessey, "Creating a Monument, Re-creating History," 139.

57. "Minutes of Meeting of the Board of Directors Community Welfare Council," July 28, 1925, San Diego Community Chest Records, 1920–25, Volume I, UWSD.

58. For example, Carson, *Settlement Folk*; and Crocker, *Social Work and Social Order*.

59. Marston, "Mexican Traits," 564.

60. Ciani, "Revelations of a Reformer," 116.

61. "Minutes of the Advisory Council, March 24, 1916," Box IA, folder (Minutes of the Advisory Council Meetings, November 1911–April 1916), FSASD.

62. Dittmyer and Grant, "Historical Study of Neighborhood House," 39–40; and Shelton, "The Neighborhood House of San Diego," 39, 44.

63. Richard H. Peterson, "The Spanish Influenza Epidemic in San Diego," 89–105. On October 13, ten cases of influenza were treated at the county hospital and seven at the county jail. Those cases caused the city board of health to initiate the quarantine. By October 24, reports counted 488 cases of the flu with eighteen deaths. Seven percent translates to 4,392 cases and 324 deaths in 1918, and 648 cases and 44 deaths in 1919.

64. After King's resignation, it became difficult to secure a head resident. From 1916 to 1918, Florence Shields, Mrs. D. G. Barnett, Daisy Worchester, and Grace Bissell all served in the position. See Dittmeyer and Grant, "Historical Study," 37; Alice Pratt, "Neighborhood House: Its History and Its Activities, 1927," delivered before the AAUW, San Diego, 1927, page 1 as cited in Shelton, "Neighborhood House of San Diego," 39.

65. Worchester, *Grim the Battles*, 150, 154.

66. In 1920 the Labor Council "sought and received the support of San Diego's Mexican community in its fight against drugs, liquor, and prostitution," and helped stage the celebrations of Mexico's Independence Day in Balboa Park

rather than in Tijuana. Miller, "Attitudes of the San Diego Labor Movement toward Mexicans, 1917–1936," 18.

67. Shelton, "Neighborhood House of San Diego," 52–53.

68. Shelton, "Neighborhood House of San Diego," 40.

69. Neighborhood House pamphlet, 1921, in San Diego Heritage Collection, SDCL.

70. NH 1921.

71. Crane, *The San Diego YWCA*, 15–16.

72. "1937 Annual Narrative Report," Box 2, folder 30 (Narrative Report, Circa 1926), TASSD.

73. Madyun, "'In the Midst of Things,'" 32; and Madyun and Malone, "Black Pioneers in San Diego," 109.

74. Shelton, "Neighborhood House in San Diego," 50.

75. "Annual Report of the Department of Health to the Mayor of the City of San Diego for the Year 1921," page 7 in SDPH.

76. Francis Parker School, *Gold & Brown* (school yearbook), 1922, page 30, and 1923, page 36, in Francis Parker School Archives, San Diego.

77. Letter from Mary Hart Taylor, RN, to Dr. Alex M. Lesem, Health Officer and Superintendent, January 31, 1922, Department of Health Report, 1921, SDPH.

78. In *Social Housekeepers*, pages 47–56, Schackel explains how Spanish-speaking women in New Mexico preferred using *curanderas* and *parteras*, and the San Diego evidence shows a similar culture.

79. "Annual Report of the Department of Health to the Mayor of the City of San Diego for the Year 1924," SDPH.

80. Shelton, "Neighborhood House of San Diego," 71.

81. Shelton, "Neighborhood House in San Diego," 42.

82. "Field notes for Mexican Labor in the United States," as cited in Guerin-Gonzales, *Mexican Workers and American Dreams*, 69–70.

83. "Annual Report of the Neighborhood House," September 1, 1929, to August 31, 1930, page 2; and *The Neighborhood House*, Bulletin 1, May 1929, both in Vertical File: Neighborhood House, SDCL. Lenore Panunzio would continue with the San Diego Public Schools through World War II and chair San Diego's Defense Council's Child Care Committee to solve problems during the war era. See California Citizens Committee of the White House Conference on Children in a Democracy, *Day Shift Orphans* (Los Angeles, 1942), 18.

84. As outlined on page 5 of the report, "the families visited were either personally known to the investigator or were neighbors or relatives of families already included." Heller Committee, *How Mexicans Earn and Live*, 4–5. At the time of the report, Mexican-heritage families were counted at 9,266 people, or 6.3 percent of San Diego's total population.

85. "Standard of Living of Employees of the Ford Motor Company in Detroit," *Monthly Labor Review*, 1209–52.

86. Heller Committee, *How Mexicans Earn and Live*, 5.

87. Heller Committee, *How Mexicans Earn and Live*, 11.

88. García, *Mexicans in the Midwest*, 228–35; and Guerin-Gonzales, *Mexican Workers and American Dreams*.

89. Guerin-Gonzales, *Mexican Workers and American Dreams*, 84, 143 (Appendix, Table 4).

90. Dittmyer and Grant, "Historical Study of Neighborhood House," 48; and *San Diego Union*, September 30, 1930.

91. After visiting NH, Robbins contributed the funds to allow for membership in the National Federation of Settlements. See correspondence between Miss Lillie M. Peck, National Federation of Settlements, and Anita Jones, Neighborhood House, April 25, 1934 and May 12, 1934, Box 26, folder 244 (California, San Diego, Neighborhood House 1926–1949), (NFSNC), SWHA.

92. Shelton, "Neighborhood House of San Diego," 101. Data on the clinic do not indicate whether staff distributed contraceptive devices, but even if the counseling entailed only education, the program was controversial, considering the stance of the Catholic Church.

93. Letter from Anita Jones to Lillie M. Peck, April 25, 1934, Box 26, folder 244: California, San Diego, Neighborhood House, 1926–49, NFSNC; and Dittmeyer and Grant, "Historical Study of Neighborhood House," 45–46.

94. Michel, *Children's Interest/Mothers' Rights*, 119.

95. Metropolitan Life Insurance Company, *A Review of Health Conditions and Needs in San Diego County*.

96. National office field notes documented that average attendance was sixteen children. "Field Notes, Children's Field/Day Nursery," 1, Box 68, folder 688, Associated Junior League of America (AJLA), SWHA; and "Minutes of June 10, 1931," Volume 3, San Diego Community Chest Records, 1929–31, UWSD.

97. Metropolitan Life Insurance Company, *A Review of Health Conditions and Needs in San Diego County*, 11.

98. Metropolitan Life Insurance Company, *A Review of Health Conditions and Needs in San Diego County*, 24.

99. Minutes of VNB, April 7, 1932, FSASD.

100. Hajo, *Birth Control on Main Street*, 24; and Hajo, "Appendix," http://www.press.ullinois.edu/books/hajo/appendix.php (site discontinued). Hajo found four clinics: Hoffman Memorial Hospital, 1932–1937; San Diego Marital Relations Clinic, 1936–1938; San Diego Mothers Clinic, 1937–1940; and San Diego Clinic, 1938.

101. Metropolitan Life Insurance Company, *A Review of Health Conditions and Needs in San Diego County*, 24–25.

102. Dittmeyer and Grant, "Historical Study of Neighborhood House," 41.

103. Alvarez, "The Lemon Grove Incident," 116–35.

104. Guerin-Gonzales, *Mexican Workers and American Dreams*; and Daniel, *Bitter Harvest*, especially Chapter 7 (pages 222–57), which explains efforts to unionize the Imperial Valley in 1934.

105. Weber, *Dark Sweat, White Gold*, 148–49.

106. Larralde, "*El Congreso* in San Diego," 17–29; and Larralde and Griswold del Castillo, "San Diego's Ku Klux Klan," 68–88.

107. Larralde, "*El Congreso* in San Diego," 19–23.

108. Larralde and Griswold del Castillo, "San Diego's Ku Klux Klan," 72.

109. Larralde, "*El Congreso* in San Diego," 17–29; and Alvarez, "The Lemon Grove Incident," 116–35.

110. San Diego County Department of Public Welfare and Emergency Relief Association, "Report of the Work Relief Program of the San Diego County Department of Public Welfare, January 1, 1930–December 1, 1933," San Diego, California, 17, MS 53, Folder 8 (County Emergency Relief Administration, 1930–1935), San Diego County Public Welfare and Emergency Relief Association (PWERA), in SDHCRA.

111. Alice Byrd Hoskins interview by Linda Barron, February 17, 1980, page 2, OHHC. Hoskins (b. 1885) moved to San Diego from Mississippi with her husband in 1913. A graduate of Meridian Women's College, Hoskins had organized a Travelers Aid office in that community and then immersed herself in the TASSD. She had three children, and in her interview she made a point of noting that she continued to work for TASSD throughout her pregnancies and returned to her position when her babies were still infants.

6. Emergency Care

1. Case 22, SDCCD.

2. "Report of the Work Relief Program of the San Diego County Department of Public Welfare," January 1, 1930, to December 1, 1933, Box 1, Folder 8, San Diego County Department of Public Welfare and Emergency Relief, PR2, 170, Documents Archives, SDHCRA.

3. Lotchin, *Fortress California*; Shragge, "'I Like the Cut of Your Jib,'" 230–55.

4. Lotchin, *Fortress California*, 3.

5. County-managed work relief programs alleviated some unemployment in the early 1930s. Men were assigned to the County Planning Commission and completed "several pieces of valuable work" that included "listing all streets within the various subdivisions in unincorporated parts of San Diego County" and conducting an analysis of the highway system. See "Report of the Work Relief Program," 19.

6. Shelton, "The Neighborhood House of San Diego," 93; Dittmyer and Grant, "Historical Study of Neighborhood House Association," 86; and correspondence between Miss Anita Jones and Miss Lillie Peck, National Federation of Settlements in Box 26, Folder 244: California, San Diego, Neighborhood House, 1926–1949, NFSNC.

7. "Minutes of Visiting Nurses Bureau for April 1930," Box 10, folder-Visiting Nurse Committee Minutes/Reports 1931–34, FSASD.

8. Dr. Rieta Campbell Hough interview by Billie Jean Meade, February 19, 1977, SDSUOH.

9. Visiting Nurses Bureaus date to 1893, when Lillian Wald established Henry Street Settlement in New York City with the express goal to provide medical care to immigrants living in Lower East Side tenement housing. Bureaus expanded throughout the Progressive Era to cities and in rural communities, and were often connected to an area's settlement house programs. See Keeling, "Carrying Ointments and Even Pills!" 7–30.

10. Visiting Nurses Bureau Monthly Reports, 1930–1934, Box 10, folder Visiting Nurse Committee minutes/Reports 1931–34, FSASD.

11. Upon accepting the position, Seeger had asked for a second visiting nurse and within two months reported the vital need for a third nurse. Hiring decisions and patient care data found in "Minutes of Visiting Nurses Bureau," for April 1930; May 7, 1930; and June 30, 1930, in Box 10, folder Visiting Nurse Committee Minutes/Reports 1931–34, FSASD.

12. Visiting Nurses Bureau Monthly Reports, 1930–1934, Box 10, folder Visiting Nurse Committee minutes/Reports 1931–34, FSASD.

13. Ann Seeger, R.N., "Memorandum to Members of the Board of Supervisors and the Members of the City Council," June 19, 1931, pages 1–2, Box 10, folder Visiting Nurse Committee Minutes/Reports 1931–34, FSASD.

14. Katherine Tuttle, RN, "VNB Report for January 1933," Box 10, FSASD.

15. "Report of Emergency Relief Office Activities, Week Ending September 20, 1934," Box 1, Folder 8, PWERA.

16. Howard G. Eddy, "Report of Assistant Director, San Diego County S.E.R.A., May 14 to November 1, 1934," Box 1, Folder 8, PWERA.

17. See Starr, *Endangered Dreams*; and *The Dream Endures* for an overview of this era.

18. "Travelers Aid Report, February 1932," Box 2, folder (Statistical Reports, circa 1932), TASSD.

19. Clyde Parker, "Depression Days (A Narrative of One Man's Experience on WPA)," typed script, no date, page 3, Document Archives, SDHCRA; and Branton, "The Works Progress Administration in San Diego County, 1935–1943," 16–17.

20. Eddy, "Report of Assistant Director," 1–4.

21. San Diego County, *Fact-Finding Study*, 24.

22. The family's tribal affiliation is not noted in the report. *Fact-Finding Study*, 45–47.

23. San Diego County, *Fact-Finding Study*, 29.

24. San Diego County, *Fact-Finding Study*, 24.

25. Elizabeth V. Duggan, Assistant Supervisor of Nurses, *Fact-Finding Study*, 14, 123.

26. "To Replace April 1, 1934 Budget Memo at S.E.R.A.," June 15, 1934, Box 1, Folder 9, PWERA.

27. "Report on the Nutritional and Housing Conditions of One Hundred Families Receiving Relief from San Diego County from the Department of Public Welfare," Box 1, Folder 8, PWERA.

28. Day and Zimmerman, book 2, vol. 3, page 18.

29. William G. Bray, "A Doomed Local Industry," *San Diego Sun*, December 6, 1933.

30. Caterina (Katie) Asaro interview by Robert G. Wright, March 24, 1990, Oral History Program, SDHCRA.

31. Ruiz, *Cannery Women, Cannery Lives*, 33.

32. Caterine Bregante Ghio (Mrs. Michael Cotardo Ghio) interview by Robert G. Wright, April 27, 1980, OHHC.

33. Ghio interview.

34. Asaro interview.

35. Ruiz, *Cannery Women, Cannery Lives*, 35.

36. Richard Griswold del Castillo, ed., *Chicano San Diego: Cultural Space and the Struggle for Justice* (Tucson: University of Arizona Press, 2007), 93.

37. Ethel D. Mintzer, typescript, "The Emergency Nursery School," 1–5, for October issue of *PTA Council*. Shared with author by Ethel M. Lichtman.

38. Massachusetts had the most at 167, and Washington and Ohio had each established 72. Pennsylvania also had 71 schools; however, its enrollment of 1,935 students was significantly lower than California's. See Appendix B in Michel, *Children's Interests/Mother's Rights*, 302–3.

39. Mintzer, "Nursery Schools Have Many Objectives," 4. Mintzer cites bulletin NS-0 of California State Department of Education, Division of Adult and Continuation Education.

40. For analysis of the early childhood movement, see Beatty, *Preschool Education in America*; Julia Grant, *Raising Baby by the Book*.

41. Michel, *Children's Interests/Mothers' Rights*, 121–22.

42. Ethel Dummer Mintzer was born in Chicago, Illinois, in 1895. She entered the University of Wisconsin in 1914 and graduated four years later. Lichtman, *Ethel Sturgis Dummer*, 64–65.

43. Lichtman, *Ethel Sturgis Dummer*, 135.

44. Beatty, *Preschool Education in America*, 132–68; and Ciani, "Training Young Women in the 'Service' of Motherhood," 103–32.

45. Mintzer, "Nursery Schools Have Many Objectives," 13.

46. Dummer, *Why I Think So*, 2.

47. Mintzer, "The Emergency Nursery School," 1–5; and Mintzer, "Nursery Schools Have Many Objectives," 4 and 13.

48. Mintzer, "The Emergency Nursery School," 4.

49. Mintzer, "The Emergency Nursery School," 5.

50. For example, in Philadelphia, women applying for free day care did not see it as relief, since they did not receive cash in return, yet social workers understood it as in-kind relief. Rose, "Maternal Work," 250–56.

51. "Field Notes, Children's Field/Day Nursery," and "Field Notes, Project/Day Nursery," Box 68, folder 688, AJLA.

52. Mangold, *Community Welfare in San Diego*, 130.

53. "Field Notes, Project/Day Nursery," 1–2, Box 68, folder 688, AJLA.

54. Michel, *Children's Interests/Mothers' Rights*, 118–19.

55. "Field Notes, Project/Day Nursery," 4, Box 68, folder 688, AJLA.

56. "Field Notes, Project/Day Nursery," 2, Box 68, folder 688, AJLA.

57. Mrs. Bradner W. Lee Jr. (Region IX), "Regional Director's Report on Junior League of San Diego, January 3–4, 1938," Box 68, folder (San Diego, Cal. 1934–1944), AJLA.

58. Lee, "Regional Director's Report."

59. Jones to Peck, October 16, 1935, NFSDN.

60. Quote in Lotchin, *Fortress California*, 8–9. See also Amero, "San Diego Invites the World to Balboa Park a Second Time," 261–79; Bokovoy, *San Diego World's Fairs and Southwestern Memory*, 165–221.

61. Hough interview, 12, SDSUOH.

62. Bokovoy, *San Diego World's Fairs and Southwestern Memory*, 195–221.

63. *San Diego Union*, March 29, 1936. I thank Balboa Park historian Richard W. Amero for sharing this citation with me.

64. Hammack retired from State College in 1957 as associate professor of education. See Heather Kufchak interview of Isabella Hammack and Beryl Campbell, November 5, 1985 in SDSUOH. For information on the California Children's Centers, see Grub and Lazerson, "Child Care, Government Financing, and the Public Schools," 5–37.

65. Florence, "Palomar, after 50 Years," 212–43.

66. Ethel D. Mintzer, typescript, "2nd Installment of San Diego Teacher's Association Bulletin," March 1936, shared with author by Ethel M. Lichtman.

67. WPA funds helped build most of the exposition buildings that remain permanent structures in Balboa Park; however, the nursery school and its equipment were housed only temporarily in the park. See Michael Milligan interview of Aileen Birch and Beryl Campbell, July 22, 1994, page 7; and Heather Kufchak interview of Isabella Hammack and Beryl Campbell, November 5, 1985, pages 117–19, SDSUOH.

68. Born Blanca Rosa Rodríguez López on August 30, 1907, in Guatemala City, the labor activist changed her name to protect her family's upper-class reputation. Moreno became awakened to union benefits in 1928 when she took a job at a garment factory near Spanish Harlem in New York City. By 1935 the American Delegation of Labor (ADL) had hired her as an organizer, a position that involved her in some of the most provocative labor strikes in the twentieth century as she tried to organize workers with the United Cannery, Agricultural, Packing, and Allied Workers of America. College-educated and bilingual, Moreno provided ADL with a smart and savvy voice that could communicate with Anglo and Latino employers. Cannery operatives, many of whom were Latinas, related to Moreno because of her gender, ethnicity, and status as a working mother. Her position brought her to cities and towns throughout the Southwest, including a stop in San Diego to help organize cannery operatives in 1937. See Ruiz, "Una mujer sin fronteras"; Larralde and Griswold del Castillo, "Luisa Moreno," 284–311.

69. "Annual Narrative Report for 1939," Box 2, Folder (Narrative Report, circa 1926), TASSD.

70. Pages 3–4, "Study of Women and Children Known to San Diego Travelers Aid Society in 1945," Box 2, folder 34, TASSD.

71. Eleanor Mead to Linton B. Swift (General Director), December 25, 1940, Box 41, folder (San Diego CA 1940–41), Family Welfare Services Association of America records (FWSAA), SWHA.

72. Eddy, "War Comes to San Diego," 50–120.

73. Killory, "Temporary Suburbs," 35, 47.

7. Wartime Care

1. Nakamura, "San Diego and the Pacific Theater," 221–46; and Lotchin, *Fortress California*, 120–24.

2. Taschner, "Boomerang Boom, 3.

3. The county population increased as dramatically, posting a 44 percent change, from 289,348 in 1940 to 415,875 in 1944. The metropolitan population nearly doubled, growing by 46 percent, from 256,368 in 1940 to 374,940 in 1944. Statistics from Day and Zimmerman report "Population and Labor Force," Book 1, Vol. 1, *Summary of Industrial and Commercial Survey*, 87; and Abraham J. Shragge, "Boosters and Bluejackets: The Civic Culture of Militarism in San Diego, California, 1900–1945" (dissertation, University of California, San Diego, 1998), 532.

4. Killory, "Temporary Suburbs," 34.

5. Lotchin, *Fortress California*; Killory, "Temporary Suburbs"; Shragge, "'A New Federal City'"; and Taschner, "Boomerang Boom."

6. U.S. Department of Labor, Bureau of Labor Statistics, "Changes in Cost of Living in San Diego, Cal. to October 1941," in "Union Matters (AFL)," Box 85, American Tuna Association Archives (ATA) in Scripps Institute of Oceanography Archives.

7. Clark, "Women Aircraft Workers in San Diego during the Second World War," 30, 73.

8. Female laborers in San Diego County increased from 24,448 in April 1940 to 69,795 workers by March 1944. Figures found in Lotchin, *Fortress California*, 120–24.

9. The shift in workforce demographics occurred among married women with no children under the age of ten (61 percent in 1940 to 66 percent in 1944) and with single women workers (29 percent in 1940 to 24 percent in 1944). Clark, "Women Aircraft Workers," 45–48.

10. Clark, "Women Aircraft Workers," 45–48.

11. Louise Johnston interview, SDSUOH. Johnston graduated from the University of Oklahoma in 1937, married in 1940, and joined her husband in San Diego seven months later when he had secured a job that her parents considered a living wage.

12. Oakland and Los Angeles attracted nonwhite residents from the Midwest through employment opportunities and because train routes ran directly from

Chicago, St. Louis, and Kansas City to those California cities. See Johnson, *The Second Gold Rush*; Lemke-Santangelo, *Abiding Courage*; and Ruiz, *Cannery Women, Cannery Lives*. On census findings, see Day and Zimmerman, "Population and Labor Force," Book 2, Vol. 3, *Summary of Industrial and Commercial Survey*, 4, 16–17.

13. For her master's thesis, "Women during War," Kimberly A. Hall interviewed a number of women who experienced San Diego during the war years. Those interviews may be found in the oral history collection, "Women during World War II," SDSUOH.

14. Ethelwyne S. Harrinton, Social Worker for Children's Homes, "Notes on Intake, May 26, 1942," Box 10, Folder (1940–43), FSASD. On women war workers, see Anderson, *Wartime Women*; Gluck, *Rosie the Riveter Revisited*.

15. Peck, "San Diego's Parachute Manufacturers," 134–37.

16. Day and Zimmerman, "Population and Labor Force," Book 2, Vol. 3, 18.

17. García, *La Neighbor*, 188–89, 204.

18. Weiss, *To Have and to Hold*.

19. Letter from Ruth Martin to Kimberly A. Hall, February 1993, SDSUOH. Ruth and Frank had grown up in Lowell, Massachusetts, and knew each other from childhood. They married in 1939 at the age of nineteen. Five years later, Ruth found herself and their three children moving to San Diego via a five-night, four-day train ride.

20. Taschner, "Boomerang Boom," 3.

21. Lotchin, *Fortress California*, 120–24.

22. "Plans for Small Parts Plant Told," *Consolidated News*, November 26, 1942, page 1 in Clark, "Women Aircraft Workers," 31, 34.

23. Gouveia, "'We Also Serve,'" 153–82.

24. Day and Zimmerman, "Population and Labor Force," Book 2, Vol. 3, *Summary of Industrial and Commercial Survey*, 4, 16–17.

25. Estes and Estes, "Further and Further Away," 1–31.

26. Day and Zimmerman, "Population and Labor Force," Book 2, Vol. 3, 17.

27. Eddy, "War Comes to San Diego," 50–51.

28. Photographer Russell Lee documented many of these problems for the Office of War Information, including in-migrant families living in tents and converted streetcars. His photos are part of the Farm Security Administration/Office of War Information Collection at the Library of Congress Prints & Photographs Division. See also Eddy, "War Comes to San Diego"; Killory, "Temporary Suburbs," 31–49; Taschner, "Boomerang Boom."

29. Taschner, "Boomerang Boom."

30. Carey McWilliams, "The Boom Nobody Wanted," *New Republic* 104, no. 26 (June 30, 1941), 882, as cited in Mary Taschner, "Boomerang Boom."

31. Rental problems were common among the interviewees in the SDSUOH collection.

32. "List of Eligible Companies for PFHA War Housing," Box 10, Folder 1940–43, FSASD.

33. Killory, "Temporary Suburbs," 36.

34. Lotchin, *Fortress California*, 132.

35. Weiss, *To Have and to Hold*.

36. Kimberly A. Hall cites Mary Jane Babcock's experience in her article "Women in Wartime," 261–79. I first encountered Babcock as an anonymous woman interviewed by Hall for her master's thesis, "Women during War." Those interviews may be found in the oral history collection, "Women during World War II," SDSUOH. Since Hall used Babcock's name, I adopted it as well, rather than referring to her as "anonymous" as in the full oral history transcript.

37. Hough interview, 14–15.

38. Gubar, "'This Is My Rifle, This Is My Gun,'" 227–60.

39. Hough interview, 10.

40. Harrinton, "Notes on Intake, May 26, 1942."

41. Eleanor Mead, "Report of Executive Secretary," January 19, 1944, Box 2: Board of Directors Minutes, January 1939–1945, FSASD.

42. California Citizens Committee of the White House Conference on Children in a Democracy, *Day Shift Orphans*, 11.

43. Eleanor Mead, "Report of Executive Secretary," January 19, 1944, Box 2: Board of Directors Minutes, January 1939–1945, FSASD.

44. Page 2 of "Memo to FWSAA Staff from MBB regarding War Effects on San Diego CA," October 29, 1942," Box 41, folder (Assoc. Charities San Diego CA), FWSAA.

45. "FSASD roster, March 1, 1943," Box 10, Folder (1940–43), FSASD.

46. "FSASD roster, May 1, 1943," Box 10, Folder (1940–43), FSASD.

47. Clark, "Women Aircraft Workers," 76–77.

48. Clark, "Women Aircraft Workers," 76–77

49. Mrs. Belloff notes, "Requirements for Home Entry—Parent–Child Homes," 1943, Box 10, FSASD.

50. Clark, "Women Aircraft Workers," 79.

51. Garcia, *La Neighbor*, 223; and José Rodolfo Jacobs and Richard Griswold del Castillo, "World War II and the Emerging Civil Rights Struggle," *Chicano San Diego*, 98–103.

52. "Memo to FWSAA Staff from MBB regarding War Effects on San Diego CA," FWSAA.

53. Natalie Fousekis, *Demanding Child Care*, 30.

54. California State Department of Education (CSDE), Bulletin of the California State Department of Education, *California Program for the Care of Children of Working Parents* 12, no. 6 (August 1943), 2–3, 10–11.

55. CSDE, "Child Care by California School Districts," ii, as cited in CSDE, *Report on Child Care Centers Administered and Operated by California School Districts* (1949), 1.

56. Fousekis, *Demanding Child Care*, 34.

57. Sonya Michel explains that while the Lanham Act was passed in 1941 to fund "community facilities in 'war-impacted areas' . . . it was not until early 1943

that these provisions were interpreted as being applicable to child care centers," Michel, *Children's Interests/Mothers' Rights*, 132.

58. Grubb and Lazerson, "Child Care, Government Financing, and the Public Schools," 12.

59. Table 6 notes the other districts in San Diego County that received Lanham Act funding over the course of the war to develop its CCCS.

60. Clark, "Women Aircraft Workers," 75–76.

61. CSDE Child Care Centers Office, "Child Care by California School Districts" (Sacramento, December 1945), 4, 10, 33–36.

62. Karen Anderson, *Wartime Women*, 122–23.

63. Stoltzfus, *Citizen, Mother, Worker*, 138, 141.

64. Mrs. R. H. Sundberg, "President's Annual Report," January 21, 1943, Box 2: Board of Directors Minutes, January 1939–January 1945, FSASD.

65. Employers like Ryan Aeronautics helped advertise the centers and emphasized health and safety features as well as the happy disposition of the children in these centers. See "Child Care Centers Opened in San Diego," *Ryan Flying Report*, July 9, 1943, 6.

66. CSDE, "Child Care by California School Districts," 10.

67. CWLA, "General Report Survey of Child Welfare Resources of San Diego" (September 1944), 4–5, in Box 33-Surveys, folder 9 (California 1943–44, 52), CWLA.

68. CWLA, "General Report Survey of Child Welfare Resources of San Diego," 27.

69. At a time when the Child Welfare League of America (CWLA) assumed control of the National Association of Day Nurseries, and the Children's Bureau wrangled with the Federal Security Agency for jurisdiction of childcare programs, parents were the ones forced to make uncomfortable decisions about day care. Box 37, FWSAA, holds numerous reports, memoranda, and correspondence among national childcare leaders regarding who should assume responsibility for wartime childcare. See also Michel, *Children's Interests/Mothers' Rights*'; and Lindenmeyer, *A Right to Childhood*.

70. CWLA, "General Report Survey of Child Welfare Resources of San Diego," 31.

71. CWLA, "A Ten Year Experiment in Foster Day Care," Bulletin No. 15 (February 1939), 47, CWLA.

72. CWLA, "General Report Survey of Child Welfare Resources of San Diego," 5–10.

73. CWLA, "Day Care of Children in Post-War United States," May 16, 1945, pages 1–5, Box 37, folder (Wartime Problems-Industrial Expansion Day Care for Children), FWSAA.

74. FWSAA notes.

75. Day and Zimmerman, "Population and Labor Force," 89; CSDE, *Child Care by California School Districts*, 23.

76. Mrs. Barbara E. Shenko, Intake Worker, "Discussion of Community Relief Problems," August 31, 1945, Box 10, Folder (Unsorted), FSASD. Agencies represented at the meetings included the Department of Public Welfare, Travelers Aid Soci-

ety of San Diego, American Red Cross, Catholic Welfare Bureau, Community Welfare Council, and the Family Service Association.

77. "Study of Women and Children Known to San Diego Travelers Aid Society in 1945," TASSD.

78. Community Welfare Council of San Diego, "Day Care," in *The Job at Hand* (June 18, 1956), 28–29, in Box 33 (Surveys), folder 9, CWLA.

79. Fousekis, *Demanding Child Care*, 39–66.

Conclusion

1. Child Welfare League of America, Inc., "General Report Survey of Child Welfare Resources in San Diego," (September 1944), 32–33, in Folder 9, Box 33, CWLA.

2. Department of Research and Publicity of the Community Welfare Council, "Family Services Association Chart," in Box 10: Unsorted Materials, FWSAA.

3. Mrs. M. M. Clancy, "Day Care," *The Job at Hand* (San Diego: Community Welfare Council of San Diego, June 18, 1956), 28–29, in Folder 9, Box 33, CWLA.

4. Mohanty, Russo, and Torres, "Cartographies of Struggle," 1–47, and Anderson, *Changing Woman*, 3–16, emphasize how racial ethnic identities define labor issues, especially for mothers.

5. Kids Count Data Center, "Selected KIDS COUNT Indicators for Cities in California," August 7, 2018, https://datacenter.kidscount.org/data/customreports /90/43,6795.

6. Levy and Michel, "More Can Be Less," 239–63.

7. Human Rights Watch, *Failing Its Families*, 32.

8. Institute for Women's Policy Research, "Maternity, Paternity, and Adoption," 3.

9. State of California, Employment Development Department, "About Paid Family Leave," https://www.edd.ca.gov/Disability/About_PFL.htm; and O'Leary, Firestein, and Savitsky, *A Guide to Implementing Paid Family Leave*, 6.

10. Bodenhorn and Reidy, "Implementation of California's Children and Families First Act of 1998," 151–57; and First 5 San Diego, "First 5 San Diego Strategic Plan, 2015–2020," http://first5sandiego.org/wp-content/uploads/2013/11/F5SD _Final-SP_06–19–14.pdf.

Abrams, Laura S. "Guardians of Virtue: The Social Reformers and the 'Girl Problem,' 1890–1920." *Social Service Review* 74, no. 3 (September 2000): 436–52.

Adams, David Wallace. *Education for Extinction: American Indians and the Boarding School Experience, 1875–1928*. Lawrence: University of Kansas Press, 1995.

Alexander, Ruth M. *The "Girl Problem": Female Sexual Delinquency in New York, 1900–1930*. Ithaca: Cornell University Press, 1995.

Almaguer, Tomás. *Racial Fault Lines: The Historical Origins of White Supremacy in California*. Berkeley: University of California Press, 1995.

Alvarez, Robert R. "The Lemon Grove Incident: The Nation's First Successful Desegregation Court Case." *Journal of San Diego History* 32, no. 2 (Spring 1986): 116–35.

A. M., *Special Report of the Whittier State School*. November 18, 1896.

Amero, Richard W. "San Diego Invites the World to Balboa Park a Second Time." *Journal of San Diego History* 31, no. 4 (Fall 1985): 261–79.

Anderson, Karen. *Changing Woman: A History of Racial Ethnic Women in Modern America*. Oxford: Oxford University Press, 1996.

———. "Changing Woman: Maternalist Politics and 'Racial Rehabilitation' in the U.S. West." In *Over the Edge: Remapping the American West*, edited by Valerie J. Matsumoto and Blake Allmendinger, 148–59. Berkeley: University of California Press, 1999.

———. *Wartime Women: Sex Roles, Family Relations, and the Status of Women during World War II*. Westport CT: Greenwood Press, 1981.

Antler, Joyce. "'After College, What?' New Graduates and the Family Claim." *American Quarterly* 30, no. 4 (Autumn 1980): 409–34.

Atherton, Lucien C. "Vocational Side Lights," *Parent-Teacher Courier* (February 1943): 12.

Bahr, Diana. "Cupeño Trail of Tears: Relocation and Urbanization." *American Indian Culture and Research Journal* 21, no. 3 (1997): 75–82.

Barr, Juliana. *Peace Came in the Form of a Woman: Indians and Spaniards in the Texas Borderlands*. Chapel Hill: University of North Carolina Press, 2007.

Beatty, Barbara. *Preschool Education in America: The Culture of Young Children from the Colonial Era to the Present.* New Haven: Yale University Press, 1995.

Blair, Karen. *The Clubwoman as Feminist: True Womanhood Redefined, 1868–1914.* New York: Holmes and Meir, 1980.

Block, Sharon. *Rape and Sexual Power in Early America.* Chapel Hill: University of North Carolina Press, 2006.

Bodenhorn, Karen A., and Deborah Reidy. "Implementation of California's Children and Families First Act of 1998." *Future of Children* 11, no. 1 (Spring–Summer 2001): 151–57.

Bokovoy, Matthew F. "Humanist Sentiment, Modern Spanish Heritage, and California Mission Commemoration, 1769–1915." *Journal of San Diego History* 48, no. 2 (Summer 2002): 177–203.

———. *The San Diego World's Fairs and Southwestern Memory, 1880–1940.* Albuquerque: University of New Mexico Press, 2005.

Bonifaz de Novelo, Maria Eugenia. "Ensenada: Its Background, Founding and Early Development." *Journal of San Diego History* 30, no. 1 (Winter 1984): 14–28.

Boris, Eileen. *Home to Work: Motherhood and the Politics of Industrial Homework in the United States.* New York: Cambridge University Press, 1994.

Bouvier, Virginia M. *Women and the Conquest of California, 1542–1840: Codes of Silence.* Tucson: University of Arizona Press, 2001.

Boydston, Jeanne. *Home and Work: Housework, Wages, and the Ideology of Labor in the Early Republic.* Oxford: Oxford University Press, 1990.

Breitenbach, Marjorie N. "The Development of the Role of the Community Welfare Council of San Diego County, 1914–1963: An Exploratory Study." Master's thesis, San Diego State College, 1964.

Bridges, Amy. *Morning Glories: Municipal Reform in the Southwest.* Princeton: Princeton University Press, 1997.

Broadbent, Elizabeth. *The Distribution of Mexican Populations in the United States.* Dissertation, University of Chicago, 1941.

Broder, Sherri. *Tramps, Unfit Mothers, and Neglected Children: Negotiating the Family in Late Nineteenth-Century Philadelphia.* Philadelphia: University of Pennsylvania Press, 2002.

Brooks, James. *Captives and Cousins: Slavery, Kinship, and Community in the Southwest Borderlands.* Chapel Hill: University of North Carolina Press, 2002.

Butler, Anne M. *Daughters of Joy, Sisters of Misery: Prostitutes in the American West, 1865–90.* Urbana: University of Illinois Press, 1985.

———. *Gendered Justice in the American West: Women Prisoners in Men's Penitentiaries.* Urbana: University of Illinois Press, 1997.

Cabeza de Baca, Vincent, and Juan Cabeza de Baca. "The 'Shame Suicides' and Tijuana." *Journal of the Southwest* 43, no. 4 (Winter 2001): 603–35.

Cahn, Frances, and Valeska Bary. *Welfare Activities of Federal, State and Local Governments in California, 1850–1934.* Berkeley: University of California Press, 1936.

California Citizens Committee of the White House Conference on Children in a Democracy. *Day Shift Orphans*. Los Angeles: August 1, 1942.

California State Department of Education (CSDE), Bulletin of the California State Department of Education, *California Program for the Care of Children of Working Parents* 12, no. 6, August 1943.

Cameron, Ardis. *Radicals of the Worst Sort: Laboring Women in Lawrence, Massachusetts, 1860–1912*. Urbana: University of Illinois Press, 1995.

Carlton, Robert Lloyd. "Blacks in San Diego County, 1850–1900." Master's thesis, San Diego State University, 1977.

Carrico, Richard L. "A Brief Glimpse of the Kumeyaay Past: An Interview with Tom Lucas, Kwaaymii, of Laguna Ranch." *Journal of San Diego History* 29, no. 2 (Spring 1983): 115–39.

———. *Strangers in a Stolen Land: American Indians in San Diego, 1850–1880*. Sacramento: Sierra Oaks, 1987.

Carrico, Richard L., and Florence C. Shipek. "Indian Labor in San Diego County, California, 1850–1900." In *Native Americans and Wage Labor: Ethnohistorical Perspectives*, edited by Alice Littlefield and Martha C. Knack, 198–217. Norman: University of Oklahoma Press, 1996.

Carson, Mina. *Settlement Folk: Social Thought and the American Settlement Movement, 1885–1930*. Chicago: University of Chicago Press, 1990.

Casper, Trudie. "The Blochman Saga in San Diego." *Journal of San Diego History* 23, no. 1 (Winter 1977): 64–79.

Castañeda, Antonia I. "Engendering the History of Alta California, 1769–1848: Gender, Sexuality, and the Family." *California History* 77, nos. 2–3 (1997): 230–59.

Chambers, Clarke A. *Paul U. Kellogg and the Survey: Voice for Social Welfare and Social Justice*. Minneapolis: University of Minnesota Press, 1971.

Chan, Sucheng. "A People of Exceptional Character: Ethnic Diversity, Nativism, and Racism in the California Gold Rush." In *Rooted in Barbarous Soil: People, Culture and Community in Gold Rush California*, edited by Kevin Starr and Richard J. Orsi, 44-85. Berkeley: University of California Press, 2000.

Chandler, Robert J., and Ronald J. Quinn. "Emma Is a Good Girl." *Californians* 8, no. 5 (January/February 1991): 34–37.

Chávez-García, Miroslava. "Intelligence Testing at Whittier School, 1890–1920." *Pacific Historical Review* 76, no. 2 (2007): 193–228.

———. *Negotiating Conquest: Gender and Power in California, 1770s to 1880s*. Tucson: University of Arizona Press, 2004.

———. *States of Delinquency: Race and Science in the Making of California's Juvenile Justice System*. Berkeley: University of California Press, 2012.

———. "Youth, Evidence, and Agency: Mexican and Mexican American Youth at the Whittier State School, 1890–1920." *Aztlán: A Journal of Chicano Studies* 31, no. 2 (Fall 2006): 55–83.

Child, Brenda J. *Boarding School Seasons: American Indian Families, 1900–1940*. Lincoln: University of Nebraska Press, 1998.

Chudacoff, Howard P. *The Age of the Bachelor: Creating an American Subculture.* Princeton: Princeton University Press, 1999.

Ciani, Kyle E. "A 'Growing Evil' or 'Inventive Genius': Anglo Perceptions of Indian Life in San Diego, 1850 to 1900." *Southern California Quarterly* 89, no. 3 (Fall 2007): 249–84.

———. "The Power of Maternal Love: Negotiating a Child's Care in Progressive-Era San Diego." *Journal of the West* 41, no. 4 (Fall 2002): 71–79.

———. "Revelations of a Reformer: Helen D. Marston Beardsley and Progressive Social Activism." *Journal of San Diego History* 50, no. 3–4 (Summer/Fall 2004): 102–23.

———. "Training Young Women in the 'Service' of Motherhood: Early Childhood Education at Detroit's Merrill-Palmer School, 1920–1940." *Michigan Historical Review* 24 (Spring 1998): 103–32.

Cicero, Dawn Marie. "Passing the Talking Stick: American Indian Women's Voices Heard." Master's thesis, San Diego State University, 1999.

Clapp, Elizabeth J. *Mothers of All Children: Women Reformers and the Rise of Juvenile Courts in Progressive Era America.* University Park: Pennsylvania State University Press, 1998.

Clark, Marilyn N. "Women Aircraft Workers in San Diego during the Second World War." Master's thesis, San Diego State University, 1977.

Clark-Lewis, Elizabeth. *Living In, Living Out: African American Domestics in Washington, D.C., 1910–1940.* Washington: Smithsonian Institution Press, 1994.

Cook, Sherburne F. *The Conflict between the California Indian and White Civilization: The American Invasion, 1848–1870.* Berkeley: University of California Press, 1943.

———. *The Population of the California Indians 1769–1970.* Berkeley: University of California Press, 1976.

Cooper, Patricia A. *Once a Cigar Maker: Men, Women, and Work Culture in American Cigar Factories, 1900–1919.* Urbana: University of Illinois Press, 1987.

Crane, Clare B. "Matthew Sherman: Pioneer San Diegan." *Journal of San Diego History* 18, no. 4 (Fall 1972): 22–27.

———. "The Pueblo Lands: San Diego's Hispanic Heritage." *Journal of San Diego History* 37, no. 3 (Spring 1991): 104–27.

———. *The San Diego YWCA: A Short History, 1907–1982.* YWCA of San Diego County, 1982.

Crocker, Ruth Hutchinson. *Social Work and Social Order: The Settlement Movement in Two Industrial Cities, 1889–1930.* Urbana: University of Illinois Press, 1992.

CSDE Child Care Centers Office. "Child Care by California School Districts." Sacramento, December, 1945.

Cuero, Delfina. *Her Autobiography: An Account of Her Last Years and Her Ethnobotanic Contributions.* Edited by Florence Connolly Shipek. Menlo Park CA: Ballena Press, 1991.

Curtis, James R., and Daniel D. Arreola. "Zonas de Tolerancia on the Northern Mexican Border." *Geographical Review* 81, no. 3 (July 1991): 333–46.

Daniel, Cletus. *Bitter Harvest: A History of California Farmworkers, 1870–194.* Ithaca: Cornell University Press, 1981.

Darnall, Thomas Ryan. "Letters of Thomas Ryan Darnall." *Southern California Quarterly* 16 (1934): 58–66.

Davis, Mike, Kelly Mayhew, and Jim Miller. *Under the Perfect Sun: The San Diego Tourists Never See.* New York: New Press, via W.W. Norton, 2003.

Day and Zimmerman, "Population and Labor Force," Book 1, Volume 1, *Summary of Industrial and Commercial Survey, City of San Diego and San Diego County,* March 31, 1945.

———. "Population and Labor Force," Book 2, Volume 3 *Summary of Industrial and Commercial Survey, City of San Diego and San Diego County.* February 21, 1945.

Delgado, Grace Peña. "Border Control and Sexual Policing: White Slavery and Prostitution along the U.S.–Mexico Borderlands, 1903–1910." *Western Historical Quarterly* 43 (Summer 2012): 157–78.

Deutsch, Sarah. *No Separate Refuge: Culture, Class, and Gender on an Anglo-Hispanic Frontier in the American Southwest, 1880–1940.* Oxford: Oxford University Press, 1987.

———. *Women and the City: Gender, Space and Power in Boston, 1870–1940.* New York: Oxford University Press, 2000.

Deverell, William, and Tom Sitton, eds. *California Progressivism Revisited.* Berkeley: University of California Press, 1994.

Dittmyer, Scott, and Kathryn Grant. "Historical Study of Neighborhood House." Master's thesis, San Diego State University, 1978.

Donovan, Brian. *White Slave Crusades: Race, Gender, and Anti-Vice Activism, 1887–1917.* Urbana: University of Illinois Press, 2006.

Dummer, Ethel Sturgis. *Why I Think So: The Autobiography of a Hypothesis.* Chicago: Clarke McElray, 1935.

Durst, Ann. "Day Nurseries and Wage-Earning Mothers in the United States, 1890–1930." Dissertation, University of Wisconsin-Madison, 1989.

Dutschke, Dwight. "A History of American Indians in California." In *Five Views: An Ethnic Sites Survey for California.* Department of Parks and Recreation, Office of Historic Preservation. Sacramento: State of California, December 1988.

Eddy, Lucinda. "War Comes to San Diego." *Journal of San Diego History* 39, nos. 1–2 (1993): 51–119.

Engstrand, Iris H. W. "In Search of the Sun." In *California Light, 1900–1930,* edited by Patricia Trenton and William H. Gerdts, 53-60. Laguna CA: Laguna Art Museum, 1990.

Enstam, Elizabeth York. *Women and the Creation of Urban Life: Dallas, Texas, 1843–1920.* College Station: Texas A&M University Press, 1988.

Estes, Donald H., and Matthew T. "Further and Further Away: The Relocation of San Diego's Nikkei Community, 1942." *Journal of San Diego History* 39, nos. 1 & 2 (Winter/Spring 1993): 1–31.

Fernandez, Ferdinand F. "Except a California Indian: A Study in Legal Discrimination." *Southern California Quarterly* 50, no. 4 (Fall 1968): 161–75.

First 5 San Diego. "First 5 San Diego Strategic Plan, 2015–2020." http://first5sandiego .org/wp-content/uploads/2013/11/F5SD_Final-SP_06-19-14.pdf.

Fischer, Kirsten. *Suspect Relations: Sex, Race, and Resistance in Colonial North Carolina*. Ithaca: Cornell University Press, 2002.

Flanigan, Sylvia K. "The Baja California Gold Rush of 1889." *Journal of San Diego History*, 26, no. 1 (Winter 1980): 11–20.

———. "Social and Intellectual Affiliation: Formation and Growth of San Diego's University Club." *Journal of San Diego History* 31, no. 1 (Winter 1985): 40–50.

Flannigan, Kathleen. "The Ranch House at Warner's." *Journal of San Diego History* 42, no. 4 (Fall 1996): 208–39.

Flannigan, Maureen A. *Seeing with Their Hearts: Chicago Women and the Vision of the Good City, 1871–1933*. Princeton: Princeton University Press, 2002.

Florence, Ronald. "Palomar, after 50 Years." *Journal of San Diego History* 44, no. 4 (Fall 1998): 212–43.

Foley, Neil. *The White Scourge: Mexicans, Blacks, and Poor Whites in Texas Cotton Culture*. Berkeley: University of California Press, 1997.

Fousekis, Natalie. *Demanding Child Care: Women's Activism and the Politics of Welfare, 1940–1971*. Urbana: University of Illinois Press, 2011.

Fraser, Nancy, and Linda Gordon. "A Genealogy of *Dependency*: Tracing a Keyword of the U.S. Welfare State." *Signs* 19, no. 2 (1994): 309–36.

García, Juan R. *Mexicans in the Midwest, 1900–1932*. Tucson: University of Arizona Press, 1996.

García, Maria E. *La Neighbor: A Settlement House in Logan Heights*. np: by the Author, 2016.

Garcia, Mario T. "Merchants and Dons: San Diego's Attempt at Modernization, 1850–1860." *Journal of San Diego History* 21, no. 1 (Winter 1975): 52–80.

Gardner, Martha. *The Qualities of a Citizen: Women, Immigration, and Citizenship, 1870–1965*. Princeton: Princeton University Press, 2005.

Getis, Victoria. *The Juvenile Court and the Progressives*. Urbana: University of Illinois Press, 2000.

Gilbert, Matthew Sakiestewa. *Education beyond the Mesa: Hopi Students at Sherman Institute, 1902–1929*. Lincoln: University of Nebraska Press, 2010.

Gilman, Sander L. "Black Bodies, White Bodies: Toward an Iconography of Female Sexuality in Late Nineteenth-Century Art, Medicine, and Literature." *Critical Inquiry* 12, no. 1 (1985): 204–42.

Gluck, Sherna Berger. *Rosie the Riveter Revisited: Women, the War, and Social Change*. Boston: Twayne, 1987.

Gochenaur, D. M D, *Health Department First Annual Report of the Board of Health of the City of San Diego for the Year Ending December 31, 1888*. San Diego: C. J. Hildreth, 1889.

Goldman, Marion S. *Gold Diggers and Silver Miners: Prostitution and Social Life on the Comstock Lode*. Ann Arbor: University of Michigan Press, 1981.

González, Deena J. *Refusing the Favor: The Spanish-Mexican Women of Santa Fe, 1820–1880*. Oxford: Oxford University Press, 1999.

González, Gilbert G. *Chicano Education in the Era of Segregation*. Philadelphia: Balch Institute Press, 1990.

González, Michael J. *This Small City Will Be a Mexican Paradise: Exploring the Origins of Mexican Culture in Los Angeles, 1821–1846*. Albuquerque: University of New Mexico Press, 2005.

Goodwin, Joanne L. *Gender and the Politics of Welfare Reform: Mothers' Pensions in Chicago, 1911–1929*. Chicago: University of Chicago Press, 1997.

Gordon, Linda. *The Great Arizona Orphan Abduction*. Cambridge: Harvard University Press, 1999.

———. *Heroes of Their Own Lives: The Politics and History of Family Violence*. New York: Penguin Books, 1988.

———. *The Moral Property of Women: A History of Birth Control Politics in America*. 1st ed. Urbana: University of Illinois Press, 1974.

———. *Pitied but Not Entitled: Single Mothers and the History of Welfare*. New York: Free Press, 1994.

———. "Social Insurance and Public Assistance: The Influence of Gender in Welfare Thought in the United States, 1890–1935." *American Historical Review* 97, no. 1 (February 1992): 19–54.

Gouveia, Grace Mary. "'We Also Serve': American Indian Women's Role in World War II." *Michigan Historical Review* 20, no. 2 (Fall 1994): 153–82.

Grant, Julia. *Raising Baby by the Book: The Education of American Mothers*. New Haven: Yale University Press, 1998.

Griego, Andrew, ed. "Rebuilding the California Southern Railroad: The Personal Account of a Chinese Labor Contractor, 1884." *Journal of San Diego History* 25, no. 4 (Fall 1979): 324–37.

Griswold Del Castillo, Richard, ed. *Chicano San Diego: Cultural Space and the Struggle for Justice*. Tucson: University of Arizona Press, 2007.

Grub, W. Norton, and Marvin Lazerson. "Child Care, Government Financing, and the Public Schools: Lessons from the California Children's Centers." *School Review* 86 (November 1977): 5–37.

Gubar, Susan. "'This Is My Rifle, This Is My Gun': World War II and the Blitz on Women." In *Behind the Lines: Gender and the Two World Wars*, ed. Margaret Randolph Higonnet, Jane Jenson, Sonya Michel, and Margaret Collins Weitz, 227–59. New Haven: Yale University Press, 1987.

Guerin-Gonzales, Camille. *Mexican Workers and American Dreams: Immigration, Repatriation, and California Farm Labor, 1900–1939*. New Brunswick: Rutgers University Press, 1994.

Gullet, Gayle Ann. *Becoming Citizens: The Emergence and Development of the California Women's Movement, 1880–1911*. Urbana: University of Illinois Press, 2000.

———. "Women Progressives and the Politics of Americanization in California, 1915–1920." *Pacific Historical Review* 64, no. 1 (1995): 71–94.

Gutierrez, Ramón A. *When Jesus Came, the Corn Mothers Went Away: Marriage, Sexuality, and Power in New Mexico, 1500–1846*. Stanford: Stanford University Press, 1991.

Guzmán, Ricardo Franco. "El régimen jurídico de la prostitución en México." *Revista de la Facultad de Derecho de Mexico* 22, no. 85–86 (1972): 85–134.

Haas, Lisbeth. *Conquests and Historical Identities in California, 1769–1936*. Berkeley: University of California Press, 1995.

Hackel, Steven W. *Children of Coyote, Missionaries of Saint Francis: Indian-Spanish Relations in Colonial California, 1769–1850*. Chapel Hill: University of North Carolina Press, 2005.

Hajo, Cathy Moran. "Appendix," http://www.press.illinois.edu/books/hajo/appendix.php.

———. *Birth Control on Main Street: Organizing Clinics in the United States, 1916–1939*. Urbana: University of Illinois Press, 2010.

Hall, Kimberly A. "Women during War: Responses to Situations in San Diego, 1941–45." Master's thesis, San Diego State University, 1993.

———. "Women in Wartime: The San Diego Experience, 1941–1945." *Journal of San Diego History* 39, no. 4 (Fall 1993): 261–79.

Harris, LeRoy E. "The Other Side of the Freeway: A Study of Settlement Patterns of Negroes and Mexican Americans in San Diego, California." Dissertation, Carnegie Mellon University, 1974.

Heizer, Robert F. *The Destruction of California Indians: A Collection of Documents … of the Things That Happened to Some of the Indians of California*. Santa Barbara CA: Peregrine Smith, 1974.

Heller Committee for Research in Social Economics of the University of California and Constantine Panunzio. *How Mexicans Earn and Live: A Study of the Incomes and Expenditures of One Hundred Mexican Families in San Diego, California*. Publications in Economics 13, Cost of Living Studies 5. Berkeley: University of California, 1933.

Hennessey, Gregg R. "Creating a Monument, Re-creating History: Junipero Serra Museum and Presidio Park." *Journal of San Diego History* 43, no. 3 (Summer 1999): 136–63.

———. "George White and Anna Gunn Marston: A Sketch." *Journal of San Diego History*, 36, nos. 2–3 (Spring/Summer 1990): 96–105.

———. "George White Marston and Conservative Reform in San Diego." *Journal of San Diego History* 32, no. 4 (Fall 1986): 230–53.

———. "The Politics of Water in San Diego 1895–1897." *Journal of San Diego History* 24, no. 3 (Summer 1978): 367–83.

Hewes, Laurence I. Jr. *Intergroup Relations in San Diego: Some Aspects of Community Life in San Diego Which Particularly Affect Minority Groups.* San Francisco: American Council on Race Relations, 1946.

Hewitt, Nancy. *Southern Discomfort: Women's Activism in Tampa, Florida, 1880s–1920s.* Urbana: University of Illinois Press, 2001.

Hickey, Georgina. *Hope and Danger in the New South City: Working-Class Women and Urban Development in Atlanta, 1890–1940.* Athens: University of Georgia Press, 2003.

Hill, Joseph A. *Women in Gainful Occupations 1870 to 1920. U.S. Bureau of Census Monographs* IX. U.S. Bureau of the Census: Washington DC, 1929.

Hirata, Lucie Cheng. "Free, Indentured, Enslaved: Chinese Prostitutes in Nineteenth-Century America." *Signs* 5, no. 1 (1979): 3–29.

Hughes, Charles. "The Decline of the *Californios*: The Case of San Diego, 1846–1856." *Journal of San Diego History* 21 (Summer 1975): 1–31.

Human Rights Watch, *Failing Its Families: Lack of Paid Leave and Work–Family Supports in the US.* New York: Human Rights Watch, 2011.

Hunter, Tera W. *To 'Joy My Freedom: Southern Black Women's Lives and Labors after the Civil War.* Cambridge: Cambridge University Press, 1997.

Hurtado, Albert L. *Indian Survival on the California Frontier.* New Haven: Yale University Press, 1988.

———. *Intimate Frontiers: Sex, Gender, and Culture in Old California.* Albuquerque: University of New Mexico Press, 1999.

Institute for Women's Policy Research, "Maternity, Paternity, and Adoption Leave in the United States Summary," IWPR # A142, May 2013.

Jacobs, Margaret D. "Maternal Colonialism: White Women and Indigenous Child Removal in the American West and Australia, 1880–1940." *Western Historical Quarterly* 36 (Winter 2005): 453–76.

———. *White Mother to a Dark Race: Settler Colonialism, Maternalism, and the Removal of Indigenous Children in the American West and Australia, 1880–1940.* Lincoln: University of Nebraska Press, 2009.

James, Thomas. "Rhetoric and Resistance: Social Science and Community Schools for Navajos in the 1930s." *History of Education Quarterly* 28, no. 4 (Winter 1988): 599–626.

Jameson, Elizabeth. "Dancing on the Rim, Tiptoeing through Minefields: Challenges and Promises of Borderlands." *Pacific Historical Review* 75, no. 1 (2006): 1–24.

———. "Women as Workers, Women as Civilizers: True Womanhood in the American West." In *The Woman's West*, edited by Susan Armitage and Elizabeth Jameson, 145–64. Norman: University of Oklahoma Press, 1987.

Jeffredo-Warden, Louise. "Expressing the Sacred: An Indigenous Southern Californian View." In *Over the Edge: Remapping the American West*, edited by Valerie J. Matsumoto and Blake Allmendinger, 329–38. Berkeley: University of California Press, 1999.

Jensen, Joan M. "Helen Marston and the California Peace Movement, 1915–1945." *California History* 67 (1988): 118–31.

Johnson, Marilynn S. *The Second Gold Rush: Oakland and the East Bay in World War II*. Berkeley: University of California Press, 1993.

Kantor, Harvey A. *Learning to Earn: School, Work, and Vocational Reform in California, 1880–1930*. Madison: University of Wisconsin Press, 1988.

Kantor, Harvey A., and David B. Tyack, eds. *Work, Youth, and Schooling: Historical Perspective on Vocationalism in American Education*. Stanford: Stanford University Press, 1982.

Karsh, Audrey R. "San Diego Pioneering Ladies and Their Contributions to the Community, 1881–1905." *Western States Jewish History* 31, no. 1 (Fall 1998): 21–32.

Katzman, David. *Seven Days a Week: Women and Domestic Service in Industrializing America*. Urbana: University of Illinois Press, 1981.

Keeling, Arlene W. "'Carrying Ointments and Even Pills!' Medicines in the Work of Henry Street Settlement Visiting Nurses, 1893–1944." *Nursing History Review* 14 (2006): 7–30.

Keire, Mara L. *For Business and Pleasure: Red-Light Districts and the Regulation of Vice in the United States, 1890–1933*. Baltimore: Johns Hopkins University Press, 2010.

———. "The Vice Trust: A Reinterpretation of the White Slavery Scare in the United States, 1907–1917." *Journal of Social History* 35, no. 1 (Fall 2001): 5–42.

Keller, Jean A. *Empty Beds: Indian Student Health at Sherman Institute, 1902–1922*. East Lansing: Michigan State University Press, 2002.

Kelly, Michael, ed. "First Annual Report of the Board of Health of the City of San Diego for the Year Ending December 31, 1888." *Journal of San Diego History* 48, no. 4 (Winter 2002): 282–348.

———. "First Annual Report of the San Diego County Hospital and Poor Farm to the Board of Supervisors, for the Year Ending June 30, 1889." *Journal of San Diego History* 48, no. 4 (Winter 2002): 362–89.

Kevles, Daniel J. *In the Name of Eugenics: Genetics and the Uses of Human Heredity*. Cambridge: Harvard University Press, 1995.

Kids Count Data Center. "Selected KIDS COUNT Indicators for Cities in California." https://datacenter.kidscount.org/data/customreports/90/43.6795.

KidsData.Org: A Program of Lucile Packard Foundation for Children's Health. http://www.kidsdata.org/search?#q/san+diego+county.

Killory, Christine. "Temporary Suburbs: The Lost Opportunity of San Diego's National Defense Housing Projects." *Journal of San Diego History* 39 (Winter/Spring 1993): 31–49.

King, Edith Shatto. "My Mexican Neighbors." *Survey* 37 (March 3, 1917): 624–26.

King, Edith Shatto, and Frederick King. *Pathfinder Social Survey of San Diego: Report of Limited Investigations of Social Conditions in San Diego, California*. San Diego: Labor Temple Press, 1914.

Kleinberg, S. J. *The Shadow of the Mills: Working-Class Families in Pittsburgh, 1870–1907*. Pittsburgh: University of Pittsburgh Press, 1989.

Kliebard, Herbert M. *Schooled to Work: Vocationalism and the American Curriculum, 1876–1946*. New York: Teachers College Press, 1999.

Kline, Wendy. *Building a Better Race: Gender, Sexuality, and Eugenics from the Turn of the Century to the Baby Boom*. Berkeley: University of California Press, 2001.

Knight, Alan. *The Mexican Revolution*. New York: Cambridge University Press, 1986.

Knott, Beatrice. "Reading between the Lines (of a Business Ledger)." *Journal of San Diego History* 35, no. 3 (Summer 1989): 206–20.

Koslow, Jennifer Lisa. *Cultivating Health: Los Angeles Women and Public Health Reform*. New Brunswick: Rutgers University Press, 2009.

———. "Putting It to a Vote: The Provision of Pure Milk in Progressive Era Los Angeles." *Journal of the Gilded Age and Progressive Era* 3, no. 2 (April 2004): 111–44.

Koven, Seth, and Sonya Michel, eds. *Mothers of a New World: Maternalist Politics and the Origins of Welfare States*. New York: Routledge, 1993.

Kropp, Phoebe S. *California Vieja: Culture and Memory in a Modern American Place*. Berkeley: University of California Press, 2006.

Kunzel, Regina G. *Fallen Women, Problem Girls: Unmarried Mothers and the Professionalization of Social Work, 1890–1945*. New Haven: Yale University Press, 1993.

Ladd-Taylor, Molly. *Mother-Work: Women, Child Welfare, and the State, 1890–1930*. Urbana: University of Illinois Press, 1994.

———. "'My Work Came out of Agony and Grief': Mothers and the Making of the Sheppard-Towner Act." In *Mothers of a New World: Maternalist Politics and the Origins of Welfare States*, edited by Seth Koven and Sonya Michel, 321–42. New York: Routledge, 1993.

———. *Raising a Baby the Government Way: Mothers' Letters to the Children's Bureau, 1915–1932*. New Brunswick: Rutgers University Press, 1986.

Larralde, Carlos M. "*El Congreso* in San Diego: An Endeavor for Civil Rights." *Journal of San Diego History* 50, no. 1 (March 2004): 17–29.

Larralde, Carlos M., and Richard Griswold del Castillo. "Luisa Moreno and the Beginnings of the Mexican American Civil Rights Movement in San Diego." *Journal of San Diego History* 43, no. 3 (Summer 1997): 158–75.

———. "San Diego's Ku Klux Klan." *Journal of San Diego History* 46, no. 2–3 (2000): 68–88.

Lasch-Quinn, Elizabeth. *Black Neighbors: Race and the Limits of Reform in the American Settlement House Movement, 1890–1945*. Chapel Hill: University of North Carolina Press, 1993.

Lemke-Santangelo, Gretchen. *Abiding Courage: African American Migrant Women and the East Bay Community*. Chapel Hill: University of North Carolina Press, 1996.

Levy, Denise Urias, and Sonya Michel. "More Can Be Less: Child Care and Welfare Reform in the United States." In *Child Care Policy at the Crossroads:*

Gender and Welfare State Restructuring, edited by Sonya Michel and Rianne Mahon, 239–66. New York: Routledge, 2002.

Lichtman, Ethel M. *Ethel Sturges Dummer: A Pioneer of American Social Activism*. Bloomington IN: iUniverse, 2009.

Lim, Julian. *Porous Borders: Multiracial Migrations and the Law in the U.S.–Mexico Borderlands*. Chapel Hill: University of North Carolina Press, 2017.

Limerick, Patricia Nelson. *Legacy of Conquest: The Unbroken Past of the American West*. New York: Norton, 1987.

Limerick, Patricia Nelson, and Clyde A. Milner II, and Charles E. Rankin. *Trails: Toward a New Western History*. Lawrence: University of Kansas Press, 1991.

Lindenmeyer, Kriste. *"A Right to Childhood": The U.S. Children's Bureau and Child Welfare, 1912–46*. Urbana: University of Illinois Press, 1997.

Liu, Judith. "Celestials in the Golden Mountain: The Chinese in One California City, San Diego, 1870–1900." Master's thesis, Sociology, San Diego State University, 1977.

Loewen, James W. *Sundown Towns: A Hidden Dimension of American Racism*. New York: New Press, 2005.

Lomawaima, K. Tisianina. *They Called It Prairie Light: The Story of Chilocco Indian School*. Lincoln: University of Nebraska Press, 1994.

Lorey, David E., ed. *United States–Mexico Border Statistics since 1900: 1990 Update*. Los Angeles: UCLA Latin American Center Publications, 1993.

Lotchin, Roger W. *Fortress California 1910–1961: From Warfare to Welfare*. New York: Oxford University Press, 1992.

Lowell, Douglas L. "The California Southern Railroad and the Growth of San Diego." *Journal of San Diego History* 31, no. 4 (Fall 1985): 245–60.

Lugones, María. *Pilgrimages/Peregrinajes: Theorizing Coalition against Multiple Oppressions*. Lanham MD: Rowman and Littlefield, 2003.

Lui, Mary Ting Yi. *The Chinatown Trunk Mystery: Murder, Miscegenation, and Other Dangerous Encounters in Turn-of-the-Century New York City*. Princeton: Princeton University Press, 2005.

Lunbeck, Elizabeth. *The Psychiatric Persuasion: Knowledge, Gender and Power in Modern America*. Princeton: Princeton University Press, 1994.

MacPhail, Elizabeth C. "San Diego's Chinese Mission." *Journal of San Diego History* 23, no. 2 (Spring 1977): 8–21.

———. "Shady Ladies in the 'Stingaree District': When the Red Lights Went Out in San Diego." *Journal of San Diego History* 20, no. 2 (Spring 1974): 2–28.

———. *The Story of New San Diego and of Its Founder, Alonzo E. Horton*. San Diego: San Diego Historical Society, 1979.

Madyun, Gail. "'In the Midst of Things': Rebecca Craft and the Women's Civic League." *Journal of San Diego History* 34 (Winter 1988): 29–37.

Madyun, Gail, and Larry Malone. "Black Pioneers in San Diego, 1880–1920." *Journal of San Diego History* 27, no. 2 (Spring 1981): 91–114.

Magliari, Michael. "Free Soil, Unfree Labor: Cave Johnson Couts and the Binding of Indian Workers in California, 1850–1867." *Pacific Historical Review* 73, no. 3 (August 2004): 349–89.

Mangold, George B. *Community Welfare in San Diego*. San Diego: Dove and Robinson, 1929.

Marston, Helen D. "Mexican Traits." *Survey* 44 (August 2, 1920): 562–63.

Marston, Mary Gilman. *George White Marston: A Family Chronicle, Volume I*. San Diego: Ward Ritchie Press, 1956.

Martin, Kenneth R. "The First Residents." In *San Diego: An Introduction to the Region*, 2nd ed., edited by Philip R. Pryde, 47–60. Dubuque: Kendall/Hunt, 1984.

Massengill, Stephen E., and Robert M. Topkins, eds. "Letters Written from San Diego County, 1879–1880, by Rufus Morgan, North Carolina Apiarist and Photographer." *Journal of San Diego History* 40, no. 4 (Fall 1994): 143–77.

Mathes, Valerie Sherer. *Helen Hunt Jackson and Her Indian Reform Legacy*. Norman: University of Oklahoma Press, 1997.

May, Ronald V. "Dog-Holes, Bomb Lances and Devil Fish: Boom Times for the San Diego Whaling Industry." *Journal of San Diego History* 32, no. 2 (Spring 1986): 73–91.

Mayo, Morrow. *Los Angeles*. New York: Knopf, 1932.

McGrew, Clarence A. *City of San Diego and San Diego County: The Birthplace of California*, Vol. 1. Chicago: American History Association, 1922.

McKanna, Clare V. Jr. "Hold Back the Tide: Vice Control in San Diego, 1870–1930." *Pacific Historian* 28, no. 3 (1984): 55–56.

———. "San Diego's Stingaree." *True West* (July 1985): 56–59.

McNeil, Teresa. "Catholic Indian Schools of the Southwest Frontiers: Curriculum and Management." *Southern California Quarterly* 72, no. 4 (Winter 1990): 321–38.

———. "St. Anthony's Indian School in San Diego, 1886–1907." *Journal of San Diego History* 34, no. 3 (Summer 1988): 194–95.

Metropolitan Life Insurance Company. *A Review of Health Conditions and Needs in San Diego County, California (Including San Diego City)*. New York: Printed for the General Federation of Women's Clubs, Department of Public Welfare, 1932.

Meyerowitz, Joanne J. *Women Adrift: Independent Wage Earners in Chicago, 1880–1930*. Chicago: University of Chicago Press, 1988.

Michel, Sonya. *Children's Interests/Mothers' Rights: The Shaping of America's Child Care Policy*. New Haven: Yale University Press, 1999.

Michel, Sonya, and Rianne Mahon, eds. *Child Care Policy at the Crossroads: Gender and Welfare State Restructuring*. New York: Routledge, 2002.

Miller, Mary Catherine. "Attitudes of the San Diego Labor Movement toward Mexicans, 1917–1936." Master's thesis, San Diego State University, 1974.

Mink, Gwendolyn. *Wages of Motherhood: Inequality in the Welfare State, 1917–1942*. Ithaca: Cornell University Press, 1995.

Mintzer, Ethel D. "The Emergency Nursery School." Typescript, 1–5, for October issue of *PTA Council*.

———. "Nursery Schools Have Many Objectives." *San Diego Teachers' Association Bulletin* 2, no. 5 (February 1936): 13.

Moehring, Eugene P. *Urbanism and Empire in the Far West, 1840–1890*. Reno: University of Nevada Press, 2004.

Mohanty, Chandra Talpade, Ann Russo, and Lourdes Torres, eds. *Third World Women and the Politics of Feminism*. Bloomington: Indiana University Press, 1991.

Molina, Natalia. *Fit to Be Citizens? Public Health and Race in Los Angeles, 1879–1939*. Berkeley: University of California Press, 2006.

Monroy, Douglas. *Thrown among Strangers: The Making of Mexican Culture in Frontier California*. Berkeley: University of California Press, 1990.

Moore, Shirley Ann Wilson. "'We Feel the Want of Protection': The Politics of Law and Race in California, 1848–1878." In *Taming the Elephant: Politics, Government, and Law in Pioneer California*, edited by John F. Burns and Richard J. Orsi, 96–125. Berkeley: University of California Press, 2003.

Mumford, Kevin J. *Interzones: Black/White Sex Districts in Chicago and New York in the Early Twentieth Century*. New York: Columbia University Press, 1997.

Muncy, Robyn. *Creating a Female Dominion in American Reform, 1890–1935*. New York: Oxford University Press, 1991.

Nakamura, Natalie. "San Diego and the Pacific Theater: Consolidated Aircraft Corporation Holds the Home Front." *Journal of San Diego History* 58, no. 4 (Winter 2012): 221–46.

Nasaw, David. *Children of the City: At Work and at Play*. New York: Oxford University Press, 1985.

Newmark, Maurice H., and Marco R. Newmark, eds. *Sixty Years in Southern California, 1853–1913, Containing the Reminiscences of Harris Newmark*. Boston: Houghton Mifflin, 1930.

Nunn, Diane, and Christine Cleary. "From the Mexican California Frontier to Arnold-Kennick: Highlights in the Evolution of the California Juvenile Court, 1850–1961." *Journal of the Center for Families, Children and the Courts* 5 (2004): 3–31.

Odem, Mary. *Delinquent Daughters: Protecting and Policing Adolescent Female Sexuality in the United States, 1885–1920*. Chapel Hill: University of North Carolina Press, 1995.

O'Leary, Ann, Netsy Firestein, and Zoe Savitsky. *A Guide to Implementing Paid Family Leave—Lessons from California*. Berkeley: Labor Project for Working Families Berkeley Center for Health, Economic and Family Security, 2011. https://www.issuelab.org/resource/a-guide-to-implementing-paid-family-leave -lessons-from-california.html.

Palmieri, Patricia Ann. *In Adamless Eden: The Community of Women Faculty at Wellesley*. New Haven: Yale University Press, 1995.

Parr, Deborah Jean. "From Crooked to Straight: The Girls' Department at Whittier State Reformatory, 1891–1913." Master's thesis, University of California, Riverside, June 2005.

Pascoe, Peggy. *Relations of Rescue: The Search for Female Moral Authority in the American West, 1874–1939*. New York: Oxford University Press, 1990.

———. *What Comes Naturally: Miscegenation Law and the Making of Race in America*. New York: Oxford University Press, 2009.

Peck, Wallace R., "San Diego's Parachute Manufacturers: Visionaries and Entrepreneurs." *Journal of San Diego History* 60, no. 3 (Summer 2014): 121–44.

Peffer, George Anthony. "Forbidden Families: Emigration Experiences of Chinese Women under the Page Law, 1875–1882." *Journal of American Ethnic History* 6 (Fall 1986): 28–46.

Peiss, Kathy. *Cheap Amusements: Working Women and Leisure in Turn-of-the Century New York*. Philadelphia: Temple University Press, 1986.

Peterson, Richard H. "The Spanish Influenza Epidemic in San Diego, 1918–1919." *Southern California Quarterly* 71, no. 1 (Spring 1989): 89–105.

Phelps, Robert. "'All Hands Have Gone Downtown': Urban Places in Gold Rush California." In *Rooted in Barbarous Soil: People, Culture and Community in Gold Rush California*, edited by Kevin Starr and Richard J. Orsi, 113–40. Berkeley: University of California Press, 2000.

Pleck, Elizabeth Hafkin. *Black Migration and Poverty, Boston 1865–1900*. New York: Academic Press, 1979.

Ports, Uldis. "Geraniums and Smokestacks: San Diego's Mayoralty Campaign of 1917." *Journal of San Diego History* 21, no. 3 (Summer 1975): 50–56.

Postol, Todd Alexander. "Hearing the Voices of Working Children: The NRA Newspaperboy Letters." *Labor's Heritage* 1, no. 3 (July 1989): 4–19.

Pourade, Richard F. *Gold in the Sun, The History of San Diego*. Vol. 5. San Diego: Union-Tribune, 1965.

———. *The Glory Years, The History of San Diego*. Vol. 4. San Diego: Union-Tribune, 1964.

———. *The Silver Dons, The History of San Diego*. Vol. 3. San Diego: Union-Tribune, 1963.

Pryde, Philip R. "Water Supply for the County." In *San Diego: An Introduction to the Region*. 2nd ed. Edited by Philip R. Pryde, 103-127. Dubuque: Kendall/Hunt, 1984.

Putnam, John C. *Class and Gender Politics in Progressive-Era Seattle*. Reno: University of Nevada Press, 2008.

Raftery, Judith. "Los Angeles Clubwomen and Progressive Reform." In *California Progressives Revisited*, edited by William Deverell and Tom Sitton, 144–74. Berkeley: University of California Press, 1994.

Raftery, Judith Rosenberg. *Land of Fair Promise: Politics and Reform in Los Angeles Schools, 1885–1941*. Stanford: Stanford University Press, 1992.

Ramey, Jessie B. *Child Care in Black and White: Working Parents and the History of Orphanages.* Urbana: University of Illinois Press, 2012.

Rawls, James J. *Indians of California: The Changing Image.* Norman: University of Oklahoma Press, 1984.

Reagan, Leslie J. *When Abortion Was a Crime: Women, Medicine, and Law in the United States, 1867–1973.* Berkeley: University of California Press, 1997.

Richardson, William C. "Fishermen of San Diego: The Italians." *Journal of San Diego History* 27, no. 4 (Fall 1981): 213–26.

Robens, Alma Kathryn. "Charlotte Baker: First Woman Physician and Community Leader in Turn of Nineteenth Century San Diego." Master's thesis, San Diego State University, 1992.

Roediger, David. *The Wages of Whiteness: Race and the Making of the American Working Class.* New York: Verso, 1991.

Rose, Elizabeth R. "From Sponge Cake to *Hamentashen:* Jewish Identity in a Jewish Settlement House, 1885–1952." *Journal of American Ethnic History* 12, no. 2 (Spring 1994): 3–23.

———. *A Mother's Job: The History of Day Care, 1890–1960.* New York: Oxford University Press, 1999.

Rosen, Robyn L. *Reproductive Health, Reproductive Rights: Reformers and the Politics of Maternal Welfare, 1917–1940.* Columbus: Ohio State University Press, 2003.

Rosen, Ruth. *The Lost Sisterhood: Prostitution in America, 1900–1918.* Baltimore: Johns Hopkins University Press, 1982.

Rubin-Kurtzman, Jane R., Roberto Ham-Chabde, and Maurice D. Van Arsdol Jr. "Population in Trans-Border Regions: The Southern California-Baja California Urban System." *International Migration Review* 30, no. 4 (1996): 1020–45.

Ruíz, Vicki L. *Cannery Women, Cannery Lives: Mexican Women, Unionization, and the California Food Processing Industry, 1930–1950.* Albuquerque: University of New Mexico Press, 1987.

———. "Una mujer sin fronteras: Luisa Moreno and Latina Labor Activism." *Pacific Historical Review* 73, no. 1 (2004): 1–20.

Sander, Kathleen Waters. *The Business of Charity: The Woman's Exchange Movement, 1832–1900.* Urbana: University of Illinois Press, 1998.

San Diego City Directories, 1886–1920.

San Diego County and First Annual Report 1888, City of San Diego. San Diego: C. J. Hildreth, 1889.

San Diego County (Calif) Board of Supervisors. *Fact-Finding Study of Social and Economic Conditions of Indians of San Diego County and Reports from Specialists in Allied Fields.* Np: publisher unknown, 1932.

San Diego History Center Staff. "Timeline of San Diego History." http://www.sandiegohistory.org/archives/biographysubject/timeline/1900-1929/.

Sandos, James A. "'Because He Is a Liar and a Thief': Conquering the Residents of 'Old' California, 1850–1880." In *Rooted in Barbarous Soil: People, Culture*

and Community in Gold Rush California, edited by Kevin Starr and Richard
J. Orsi, 86–112. Berkeley: University of California Press, 2000.

———. "Prostitution and Drugs: The United States Army on the Mexican-
American Border, 1916–1917." *Pacific Historical Review* 49, no. 4 (November
1980): 621–45.

Sarbaugh-Thompson, Marjorie, and Mayer N. Zald. "Child Labor Laws: A Historical Case of Public Policy Implementation." *Administration and Society*
27, no. 1 (May 1995): 25–53.

Schackel, Sandra. *Social Housekeepers: Women Shaping Public Policy in New Mexico,
1920–1940.* Albuquerque: University of New Mexico Press, 1992.

Schantz, Eric Michael. "All Night at the Owl: The Social and Political Relations
of Mexicali's Red-Light District, 1913–1925." *Journal of the Southwest* 43, no.
4 (Winter 2001): 549–602.

Schlossman, Steven. "End of Innocence: Science and the Transformation of Progressive Juvenile Justice, 1899–1917." *History of Education Quarterly* 7, no. 3
(1978): 207–18.

———. *Transforming Juvenile Justice: Reform Ideals and Institutional Realities, 1825–
1920.* DeKalb: Northern Illinois University Press, 1977; 2005.

Schoen, Joanna. *Choice and Coercion: Birth Control, Sterilization, and Abortion in Public Health and Welfare.* Chapel Hill: University of North Carolina Press, 2005.

Schwartz, Henry. "The Uneasy Alliance: Jewish-Anglo Relations in San Diego,
1850–1860." *Journal of San Diego History* 20, no. 3 (Summer 1974): 53–60.

Sealander, Judith. *Private Wealth and Public Life: Foundation Philanthropy and the
Reshaping of American Social Policy from the Progressive Era to the New Deal.*
Baltimore: Johns Hopkins University Press, 1997.

Sexton, Richard D. "The San Diego Woman's Home Association: A Volunteer Charity Organization." *Journal of San Diego History* 24, no. 1 (Winter 1983): 41–53.

Shelton, Cynthia Jane. "The Neighborhood House of San Diego: Settlement
Work in the Mexican Community, 1914–1940." Master's thesis, San Diego
State University, 1975.

Sherer Mathes, Valerie. *Helen Hunt Jackson and Her Indian Reform Legacy.* Norman: University of Oklahoma Press, 1990; 1997.

Shipek, Florence C. *Pushed into the Rocks: Southern California Indian Land Tenure, 1769–1986.* Lincoln: University of Nebraska Press, 1988.

———, ed. *Lower California Frontier, Articles from the San Diego Union, 1870.* Los
Angeles: Dawson's Book Shop, 1965.

Shragge, Abraham J. "Boosters and Bluejackets: The Civic Culture of Militarism in San Diego, California, 1900–1945." Dissertation, University of California, San Diego, 1998.

———. "'I Like the Cut of Your Jib': Cultures of Accommodation between the
U.S. Navy and Citizens of San Diego, California, 1900–1951." *Journal of San
Diego History* 48, no. 3 (Summer 2002): 230–55.

———. "'A New Federal City'": San Diego during World War II." *Pacific Historical Review* 63, no. 3 (August 1994): 333–61.

Shumsky, Neil Larry. "Tacit Acceptance: Respectable Americans and Segregated Prostitution, 1870–1910." *Journal of Social History* 19, no. 4 (1986): 665–79.

Simpson, Lee M. A. *Selling the City: Gender, Class, and the California Growth Machine, 1880–1940*. Stanford: Stanford University Press, 2004.

Sklar, Kathryn Kish. *Florence Kelley and the Nation's Work: The Rise of Women's Political Culture, 1830–1900*. New Haven: Yale University Press, 1995.

Skocpol, Theda. *Protecting Soldiers and Mothers: The Political Origins of Social Policy in the United States*. Cambridge: Cambridge University Press, 1992.

Slingerland, William H. *Child Welfare Work in California: A Study of Agencies and Institutions*. New York: Russell Sage Foundation, 1916.

Smith-Rosenberg, Carroll. *Disorderly Conduct: Visions of Gender in Victorian America*. New York: Oxford University Press, 1985.

Smythe, William E. *History of San Diego 1542–1907*. San Diego: History Company, 1907.

Solinger, Ricki. *Wake Up Little Susie: Single Pregnancy and Race before Roe v. Wade*. New York: Routledge, 1992.

Solomon, Barbara Miller. *In the Company of Educated Women: A History of Women and Higher Education in America*. New Haven: Yale University Press, 1985.

Spain, Daphne. *How Women Saved the City*. Minneapolis: University of Minnesota Press, 2001.

Stadum, Beverly A. "A Critique of Family Case Workers 1900–1930: Women Working with Women." *Journal of Sociology and Social Welfare* 17, no. 3 (September 1990): 73–100.

"Standard of Living of Employees of the Ford Motor Company in Detroit." *Monthly Labor Review* 30 (1930): 1209–52.

Starr, Kevin. *Americans and the California Dream, 1850–1915*. New York: Oxford University Press, 1973.

———. *The Dream Endures: California Enters the 1940s*. New York: Oxford University Press, 1997.

———. *Embattled Dreams: California in War and Peace*. New York: Oxford University Press, 2002.

———. *Endangered Dreams: The Great Depression in California*. New York: Oxford University Press, 1996.

———. *Golden Dreams: California in an Age of Abundance, 1950–1963*. New York: Oxford University Press, 2009.

———. *Inventing the Dream: California through the Progressive Era*. New York: Oxford University Press, 1985.

———. *Material Dreams: Southern California through the 1920s*. New York: Oxford University Press, 1990.

Starr, Raymond. "Philanthropy in San Diego, 1900–1929." *Southern California Quarterly* 71, no. 2–3 (1989): 227–73.

State of California. Employment Development Department. "About Paid Family Leave." https://www.edd.ca.gov/Disability/About_PFL.htm.

Stephens, Cyrus Wayne. "The History of Social Welfare Agencies in San Diego County, 1872–1914." Master's thesis, Social Work, San Diego State College, 1966.

Stern, Alexandra Minna. *Eugenic Nation: Faults and Frontiers of Better Breeding in Modern America*. Berkeley: University of California Press, 2005.

Stokes, G. Allison. "Ethel Sturges Dummer." *Notable American Women: The Modern Period, A Biographical Dictionary*. Cambridge: The Belknap Press of Harvard University, 1980.

Stoler, Ann Laura. "Tense and Tender Ties: The Politics of Comparison in North American History and (Post) Colonial Studies." *Journal of American History* 88, no. 3 (December 2001): 829–65.

Stoltzfus, Emilie. *Citizen, Mother, Worker: Debating Public Responsibility for Child Care after the Second World War*. Chapel Hill: University of North Carolina Press, 2003.

Stone, Harold A., Don K. Price, and Kathryn H. Stone. *City Manager Government in Nine Cities*. Chicago: Committee on Public Administration of the Social Science Research Council, 1940.

Strange, Carolyn. *Toronto's "Girl Problem": The Perils and Pleasures of the City, 1880–1930*. Toronto: University of Toronto Press, 1995.

Sundue, Sharon Braslaw. *Industrious in Their Stations: Young People at Work in Urban America, 1720–1810*. Charlottesville: University of Virginia Press, 2009.

Sutton, John R. "The Juvenile Court and Social Welfare: Dynamics of Progressive Reform." *Law & Society Review* 19, no. 1 (1985): 107–45.

Taschner, Mary. "Boomerang Boom: San Diego 1941–1942." *Journal of San Diego History* 28, no. 1 (Winter 1982): 1–10.

Taylor, Lawrence D. "The Wild Frontier Moves South: U.S. Entrepreneurs and the Growth of Tijuana's Vice Industry, 1908–1935." *Journal of San Diego History* 48, no. 3 (Summer 2002): 204–29.

Tentler, Leslie Woodcock. *Wage-Earning Women: Industrial Work and Family Life in the United States, 1900–1930*. Oxford: Oxford University Press, 1979.

Tomlins, Christopher. "Indentured Servitude in Perspective: European Migration into North America and the Composition of the Early American Labor Force, 1600–1775." In *The Economy of Early America: Historical Perspectives and New Directions*, edited by Cathy D. Matson, 146–82. University Park: Pennsylvania State University Press, 2006.

Trattner, Walter. *Crusade for Children: A History of the National Child Labor Committee*. Chicago: University of Chicago Press, 1970.

Trennart, Robert A. *The Phoenix Indian School: Forced Assimilation in Arizona, 1891–1935*. Norman: University of Oklahoma Press, 1988.

Trolanger, Judith Ann. *Settlement Houses and the Great Depression*. Detroit: Wayne State University Press, 1975.

Turner, Elizabeth Hayes. *Women, Culture, and Community: Religion and Reform in Galveston, 1880–1920*. New York: Oxford University Press, 1997.

Van Kirk, Sylvia. *Many Tender Ties: Women in Fur-Trade Society 1670–1870*. Norman: University of Oklahoma Press, 1980.

Varzally, Allison. *Making a Non-white America: Californians Coloring outside Ethnic Lines, 1925–1955*. Berkeley: University of California Press, 2008.

Vaughan, Mary Kay. "Rural Women's Literacy and Education during the Mexican Revolution: Subverting a Patriarchal Event?" In *Women of the Mexican Countryside, 1850–1990*, edited by Heather Fowler-Salamini and Mary Kay Vaughan, 106–24. Tucson: University of Arizona Press, 1994.

———. *State, Education, and Social Class in Mexico, 1880–1928*. DeKalb: Northern Illinois University Press, 1982.

Wachi, Yasuko Amemiya. "What Comes Next? Native Americans of San Diego County: A Study of Uncertainty for an Ethnic Minority Group of Southern California." Dissertation, University of California, San Diego, 1994.

Weber, David J. *The Spanish Frontier in North America*. New Haven: Yale University Press, 1992.

Weber, Devra. *Dark Sweat, White Gold: California Farm Workers, Cotton, and the New Deal*. Berkeley: University of California Press, 1994.

Weber, Francis J. *Documents of California Catholic History*. Los Angeles: Dawson's Book Shop, 1965.

Weiss, Jessica. *To Have and to Hold: Marriage, the Baby Boom, and Social Change*. Chicago: University of Chicago Press, 2000.

Welter, Barbara. "The Cult of True Womanhood: 1820–1860." *American Quarterly* 18 (Summer 1966): 151–74.

West, Eliot. "Reconstructing Race." *Western Historical Quarterly* 34, no. 2 (Spring 2003): 7–28.

White, Richard. *"It's Your Misfortune and None of My Own": A History of the American West*. Norman: University of Oklahoma Press, 1991.

Willrich, Michael. "Home Slackers: Men, the State, and Welfare in Modern America." *Journal of American History* 87, no. 2 (September 2000): 460–89.

Wolcott, David B. *Cops and Kids: Policing Juvenile Delinquency in Urban America, 1890–1940*. Columbus: Ohio State University Press, 2005.

Wood, Sharon E. *The Freedom of the Streets: Work, Citizenship, and Sexuality in a Gilded Age City*. Chapel Hill: University of North Carolina Press, 2005.

Woods, Reverend James. *Recollections of Pioneer Work in California*. San Francisco: Joseph Winterburn, 1878.

Worchester, Daisy Lee Worthington. *Grim the Battles: A Semi-Autobiographical Account of the War against Want in the United States during the First Half of the Twentieth Century*. New York: Exposition Press, 1954.

Wrigley, Julia. "Children's Caregivers and Ideologies of Parental Inadequacy." In *Circles of Care: Work and Identity in Women's Lives*, edited by Emily K. Abel and Margaret K. Nelson, 290–312. Albany: State University of New York, 1990.

Yung, Judy. *Unbound Feet: A Social History of Chinese Women in San Francisco*. Berkeley: University of California Press, 1995.

INDEX

Page numbers in italic indicate illustrations.

abuse, 3–4, 6, 16, 32, 59, 79, 171; sexual, 14, 32, 226
AC. *See* Associated Charities
Acasan Garcia, Mercedes, 160
Act for the Government and Protection of Indians (1850), 2
activism, xxii; antislavery, 35; civic, 215; legal, 160; social, 147
Addams, Jane, 34, 94, 138, 157
adoption, 46, 47–48, 50
Advisory Council, 95, 247n69
African American children, 46, 118; jobs for, 62; mortality rate for, 231
African Americans, xxvii, 16, 23, 24, 27, 39, 45, 70, 139–40, 152, 165, 168, 250n37; population of, 4, 197; social services for, 151; survival of, 212
African American women, 151, 197, 198; pension reformers and, 109
age-of-consent laws, 31, 56, 226
Allen, Ellen B., 83, 84, 93–94
Almaguer, Tomás, 235n12
Alvarez, Luis, 177, 178
Amador, José María, 239n27
Amat, Bishop, 13
American Child Hygiene Association, 152
American Civil Liberties Union (ACLU), 148–49
American Delegation of Labor (ADL), 266n68
American Indian children, 39, 44, 60, 118;

caring for, 20; conversion tactics for, 240n44; custody of, 3; indenturing, 2; racism/prejudice/segregation and, 20
American Indians, 2, *17*, 27, 29, 173, 201, 226, 238n15; controlling, 3; imprisonment of, 58; isolation of, xxvi
Americanization, 19, 57, 65, 143, 150, 226; Christianization and, 122; cultural agendas of, 129
Amero, Richard M., 266n63
Anderson, Amelia (pseud.), 50
Anderson, Joseph (pseud.), 50
Andrews, Alice, 134, 258n20
Anglos, 4, 239n22, 240n44; population of, 4; term, 238n17
Anthony's Fish Grotto, 177
Antler, Joyce, 254n17
apprenticeships, 3, 4, 12, 70, 201, 224
Asaro, Andrew, 176, 177
Asaro, Caterina (Katie), 176, 177
Asian Americans, 27, 165
Asian children, 39, 44, 118, 247n73
Asian immigrants, 45, 160
Associated Charities (AC), xxii, 76, 78, 79, 85, 95–96, 97, 100–101, 103, 110, 112, 118, 127, 130, 133, 139, 149, 152, 166, 167, 185, 191, 208, 228, 245n47, 254n22; Cantero and, 105–6; CH and, 111, 113; committee meetings for, 247n69; funding and, 99; monitoring by, 104; oversight by, 90, 105; resource distribution and, 95; return of, 91; running, 92; VNB and, 169

Associated Junior League of America, 185

Babcock, Mary Jane, 205, 206, 208, 217, 218, 269n36
Bade, Elizabeth Marston, 234n4
Bahr, Diana, 238n18
Baker, Charlotte, 34, 35, 36, 43, 84, 92, 166, 243n14, 253n11, 254n22; CHDN and, 41, 246n66; CWC and, 93–94; Purity League and, 83; Robens and, 245n41; work of, 40, 46
Baker, Fred, 36, 92, 93, 253n11
Balboa Park, 150, 176, 187, 188, 260n48, 260n66, 266n63, 266n67
Balch, Emily Greene, 94
Barnett, Mrs. D. G., 260n64
Barrio Logan, 24, 45, 100, 119, 128, 129, 130, 133, 138, 139, 145, 149, 177, 199
BCC. See Board of Charities and Corrections
Beardsley, Helen D. Marston. See Marston, Helen
Begley, Charles H., 251n39
behavior: anti-social, 182; bad, 29, 53, 64, 65, 66, 67, 76, 220, 225; gender-specific, 56–57; immoral, 50, 102, 103; parental, 76–77; problems with, 70
Bellon, Walter, 100
Benevolent and Protective Order of Elks, 26
Beulah Home, 244n30
BGAS. See Boys and Girls Aid Society
"Big Girl Revue," 192
birth control, 138, 159, 259n25
Bishop's School, 94, 258n20
Bissell, Grace, 260n64
Black Infant Health program, 231
Blackledge, T. H., 250n33
Blair (probation officer), 134
Blochman, Haidee Goldtree, 34, 36
Blochman, Lucien, 36
boarding, 155; long-term, 47–48
boarding homes, 44, 208, 225; foster, 210, 218; licensing for, 106; organizing, 22; parent-child, 195, 212; socialization at, 115
boarding schools, xxvi, 18, 201
Board of Charities and Corrections (BCC), 106, 107, 108, 122
Board of Directors (Children's Home), 47

Board of Education Department, 213
Board of Health, 136
Board of Prison Directors, 58
Boys and Girls Aid Society (BGAS), 62–63, 97, 124, 257n84
Boy's Dormitory, 24
Brackett, Mrs. Charles, 152
Brooklyn Street ENS, 181, 188, 189
brothels, 28, 31, 84
Bureau of Catholic Indian Missions (BCIM), 14
Burr, Lizzie (pseud.), 42

CAC. See Consolidated Aircraft Corporation
Cahuilla, 4, 9
Calexico, 104, 255n45
California Child Care Centers (CCCC), 195, 213, 214, 216, 217, 218, 219, 221, 229, 270n59
California Children's Centers, 266n64
California Club Woman, 132
California Immigration and Housing Commission (CIHC), 143
California Institute of Technology, 188, 189
California-Pacific International Exposition (1935–1936), xxvii, 165, 186, 187
California School for Girls (Ventura), 59, 62, 123
California Southern Railroad, 19
California State Bureau of Labor, 73
Californios, 4, 5, 6, 9, 58, 239n23, 239n24
Callahan, Darlene (pseud.), 163
Callahan, John, 244n34
Campbell Machine Company, 204
Camp Kearney, 149, 150
Camp Pendleton, 164
canneries, 156, 160, 175, 176, 177, 178, 186; workers at, 189–90, 189, 198–99
Cantero, Maddie (pseud.), 105–6
Carey, J. F., 71
Carter, Bobby Joe (pseud.), 123
Carter, William R., 259n30
Casa de Salud (CS), 130, 159–60, 160, 164, 228
Case Work Department, 171
caseworkers, 114, 122, 170, 183
Catholic Charities, 26, 118, 119, 124, 125, 214
Catholic Church, 46, 95, 262n92
Catholic League, 44

CCCC. See California Child Care Centers

CH. See Children's Home

Chambers, Mrs. E. C., 250n31

chambers of commerce, 51, 90, 158

charities, 29, 96, 120, 139, 186

Charities Endorsement Board, 124

Charity Organization Service, 254–55n25

Chase, Amanda Mathews, 143, 144

Chase, Andrew Jackson, 1, 9

Chase, Mrs., 10, 11

Chavez children (pseud.), CHDN and, 45

CHDN. See Children's Home and Day Nursery

cherry packing, 75

Chicano Community Clinic, 257n4

Child Care Center Act (1943), 214

Child Care Center program, xxvii, 213

Child Care Committee (Defense Council), 261n83

child labor, 20, 55, 74, 106, 107; eliminating, 56, 73; laws, 128; parental consent for, 3

Child Welfare League of America (CWLA), 193, 217, 218, 219, 223, 229, 270n69

childcare, xviii, xxvi, xxvii, 64, 86, 87, 102, 108, 182–83, 186, 188, 190, 192, 200, 221, 226, 270n69; accommodating, xxviii; advocates, 126, 215, 216, 229; benevolent, 46–47; choices about, 99; concerns about, 27, 161, 195, 224; daily operation of, 230; development of, xxii–xxiii, 22, 42, 225; employer-sponsored, 224; finding, xxi, 49, 63, 79, 90, 91, 194, 205, 208, 210, 214, 217, 221, 223; help with, xxii, 25–26, 57, 199, 208, 212, 231; licensed, 210; long-term, 115; need for, 178, 196, 200, 208–9, 214; options for, 210, 232; paying for, 40; problems with, xxiii, 47, 197, 205, 218, 219, 220–21; professional standards for, xxi, 228–29; providing, xxviii, 220, 223, 228; public, 212, 215; resources for, xx, xxii, 208, 209, 226; shared, 177, 206; social welfare and, xx, xxi–xxii; societal expectations of, 227; solutions to, 231–32; state-sanctioned, 2; types of, xxviii, 224; working class and, xix, 225

childcare centers, xxvii, 211, 213, 218, 270n57

childcare workers, xxvii, 47, 113–14, 227

Children and Families First Act, 231

Children's Bureau, 140, 270n69

Children's Home (CH), 48–49, 68, 86, 91, 109, 112, 114, 115, 118, 124, 126, 130, 163, 164, 168, 228, 232, 247n69, 252n63, 257n84; AC and, 111, 113; admission to, 89, 104; Board of Directors of, 47; boy from, 114; Boy's Dormitory at, 24; children at, 76, 77–78, 80–81; cleanup campaign and, 100; economic necessity of, 98–99; housing at, 98, 100, 110, 111; mission of, 63; problems at, 123; staff at, 39, 82; using, 81, 82

Children's Home and Day Nursery (CHDN), xvii, xviii, xxiii, xxvi, 23, 36, 37, 54, 113, 224, 226, 234n1, 242n1, 245n47, 245n66, 246n50, 246n67, 246n68; baby care by, 21–22; boarding at, 39, 40, 41–42, 46–47, 47–48; daycare at, 47–48; establishment of, xxiv, 26; inspections of, 51–52; motivation of, 40–41; payment schedules at, 41–42; success for, 43–44; using, 38, 44–45, 48, 49–50, 51

Children's Home Society of California (CHSC), 27, 77, 251n55

Chinatowns, 105, 243n15

Chinese, 19, 24, 32, 44, 105, 167, 168; population of, 197

Chinese Exclusion Act (1882), 102

Chinese Home for Girls, 46

Christianization, 19, 122

CHSC. See Children's Home Society of California

citizenship, xxiii, 3, 11, 100–101, 120, 136, 252n63

City Heights, 71

Civic Association, 90

civic leaders, xx, xxiv, 19, 22, 27, 28, 55, 83, 87, 146, 228

Civil Code of California, 140

Civilian Defense Council, 213, 261

Clancy, Mrs. M. M., 223

Clark, Kate, 31, 244n34

Clinton, Bill, 231

Clubs for Boys and Girls, 151

collaboration, xxvi, xxvii, 142, 218, 232; encouraging, 90–91

College Graduate Club (CGC), 93
College Woman's Club (CWC), xxvii, 36,
85, 86, 128–29, 130, 131, 132, 133, 138, 139,
152, 156, 178; launching of, 93–94; study
by, 73–74
Columbian Exposition, 188
Committee on Children in Wartime, 213, 214
Community Chest, 124, 125, 159, 178, 184
Community Music Association, 125
Community Welfare Council, 99, 124, 125,
221, 223, 224
Comstock Act (1873), 159
Congregational Church, 35, 246n68
Conrad, James "Bull," 29
Consolidated Aircraft Corporation (CAC),
193, 194, 196, 197, 201
Cook, Sherbourne, 4
Cooley, George H., 64
Coronado, 165, 179, 185
County Parent Teacher Federation, 125
County Planning Commission, 263n5
County Welfare Department, 210
Couts, Cave Johnson, 7, 8, 16, 236n1
Couts, Ysidora Bandini de, 7
Craft, Rebecca, 151
crimes, 29, 57, 68; sexualized, 67; violent, 28
CS. See Casa de Salud
Cuero, Delfina, 15, 16, 17, 18
Culfa, Ramón, 12, 13, 16, 18
cultural boundaries, xix, 16, 143
culture, 9, 15, 144, 202, 237n4; American, 57,
143; American Indian, xxiii; Asian, xxiii;
family, 64; immigrant, 65; maternalism
and, xxiii; Mexican, xxiii, 128, 143; work-
ing class and, 64
Cupeño, 4, 17, 238n18
curanderas (community healer), 153,
261n78
custody, xix, 1, 3, 22, 41, 48, 67, 76, 77, 79,
82, 97, 99, 106, 110, 111, 112, 121, 126, 158, 158,
214, 227
Cuyamaca Dam, 25
CWC. See College Woman's Club
CWLA. See Child Welfare League of
America

Daily Bee, 234n1
Darnall, Thomas Rylan, 7

Daughters of the American Revolution, 143
Davidson, Ed, 257n84
Davis, Mike, 235n9
day care, xxvi, xxvii, 47–48, 128, 130, 182, 219,
224; adequate, 223; expansion of, 126;
foster, 209–10; free, 265n50; full, 243n18;
licensed, 195, 210; operating, 211; problems with, 220–21; quality, 191; responsibilities for, 208; space for, 221
day care centers, xxii, xxvii, 214, 216
day laborers, 8, 11, 170, 247n90
day nurseries, xx, 44, 108, 113, 178, 181, 182,
183, 224, 228; licensing, 51; organizing,
22; voluntary, 183
Decker, Claire (pseud.), 113
defense industry, employment in, 198,
214, 221
Del Monte cannery, 177
demographics, 65, 98, 99, 230, 267n9
Denison House, 128
Department of Commerce and Labor, 140
Department of Public Health, 131
Department of Social Welfare, 216, 224,
249n16
deportation, 102, 103
Detention Home (DH), 63, 64, 65, 78, 81,
82, 97, 118, 122, 164, 218; admission to, 104;
children at, 76; cleanup campaign and,
100; conditions at, 106; environment at,
96; housing at, 98, 100; problems at, 123
Dietzler, Mary, 96, 254n22
Dillingham Commission, 103
discrimination, xxii, 125, 130, 137, 140, 213,
226; educational, 128; housing, 193, 204;
job, 161, 200; racial, 212; sexual, 94
diseases, xxv, 1, 11, 26, 84, 85, 127, 141, 149, 150,
167, 158, 169, 224, 235n9, 237n1, 260n63;
childhood, 163, 181–82; communicable,
153; preventing, 98; spread of, 4
divorce, 47, 50, 77, 100, 115, 120, 121, 123, 163,
179, 206
Dixon, Jessie, 33
domestic service, 4, 38, 48, 49–50, 102, 165,
212, 245n44
domestic troubles, 4, 117
Donovan, Brian, 30
Door of Hope, 122, 232, 243n14, 244n30

Douglas, Mrs., 211
D Street, 38
Dummer, Frank, 85, 86

Eaton, Clarence, 70, 251n39
economic growth, 18, 90
economic issues, xxv, 3–4, 25, 66, 98, 164, 184, 203, 224, 235n7, 235n9; childcare payments and, 41–42; working class and, 227–28
education, 60, 71, 85, 90, 141, 143, 158, 169, 187, 189, 191, 208, 216, 219; bilingual, 130; early childhood, xxvi, xxvii, 214, 225, 265n40; evaluating, 106; health, 140, 151; law, 70; maternal, 153; nursery school, xxii, 180, 186, 188; quality, 134; sex, 211; university, 86; vocational, xxvi, 52, 54, 58, 62, 70, 71, 72–73, 75, 128, 134, 145, 151, 201, 250n30, 251n41
Eisel, Gretchen, 31, 32, 33
El Congreso del Pueblo de Habla Española (Congress of Spanish-Speaking Peoples), 160, 190
Electric Laundry Company, 39
Electrical Equipment Co., 109
Eleventh Naval District Headquarters, 165
emergency nursery schools (ENS), xxvii, 157, 158, 178, 180–83, 185, 188, 189, 208, 227
Emergency Relief Association, 164
employment, xxii, 22, 54, 91, 128, 160, 161, 190, 202, 217; access to, 197; child, 62, 69; defense industry, 198, 221; military service and, 196; secure, 151; service, 166; social welfare and, 221; stable, 90; unskilled, 9; urban, 65; women and, xxi, 4, 37, 40, 113–14, 135, 136, 196, 200, 201, 213, 223, 224, 229
employment agency, establishment of, 42
ENS. See emergency nursery schools
Ensenada, xvii, 103, 167, 234n1, 235n7
ethnicity, 68, 105, 109, 120, 136, 145, 151, 153, 155, 176, 197, 204, 237n14; impact of, 47; individual, 238n17
Exalted Cyclops, No.64, 160
Executive Order 9066 (1942), 199, 202

familial care, xx, xxii, 53, 199, 208
Family and Medical Leave Act, 231

Family Services Association of San Diego (FSASD), 208, 209, 210, 211, 216, 217, 219
Family Welfare Services Association of America (FWSAA), 210, 213, 220, 229
Farm Security Administration, 268n28
Federal Emergency Relief Act (FERA), 229
Federal Security Agency, 270n69
Federal Works Agency, 214
Federated Jewish Aid Society, 245n42
Fiedler, Mrs. (pseud.), 112
Filipinos, 155, 168, 197, 199
Fine, C. F., 171
First 5 San Diego, 231
First Annual Report of the Board of Health, xvii
First Methodist Church, 39
FIS. See Free Industrial School
fishing industry, 175, 202
Forsythe, Charles E., 33
Fort Rosecrans, 150
foster care, xxvi, 208, 209–10, 219, 224; homes, 76, 195
Fousekis, Natalie, 213
Fox Theater, 192, 213
Fran Ross and her All Girl Band, 192
Francis W. Parker School, 152, 179, 180, 188
Franciscans, 2, 6
Fraser, Nancy, 237n14
Frederico, 9, 11, 12, 16
Free Industrial School (FIS), 71, 72, 131, 133, 134
Frémont, Jessie Benton, 5
Frontier Homes Housing Project, 204
FSASD. See Family Services Association of San Diego
FWSAA. See Family Welfare Services Association of America

Gale, Anita, 5
Galindo, Frank, 212
gambling, 19, 28, 29, 102, 239n25
Garcia, Mrs., 137, 257n4
Gardner, Martha, 102
General Education Board, 259n38
General Federation of Women's Clubs (GFWC), 56, 158, 159
German, Mrs., 254n22
Ghio, Caterine (Caty) Brigante, 176, 177

Gildos, Gertrude, 24

girl problem, 69, 250n36

Girls Home of San Diego, 243n14

Girls Rescue Home, xxvi, 27, 43, 67, 83, 84, 244n30

Gochenaur, David, xvii, xxv

González, Jorge, 104

González, Michael, 2

Gordon, Charley, 28

Gordon, Linda, 237n14

Gould, E. B., 257n84

Grand Army of the Republic, 26

Great Depression, 160, 164, 165, 166, 167, 179, 185, 186, 229; federal programs of, xxvii; San Diego and, 158, 170, 171, 172, 187; surviving, 176

Gunn, Douglas, 34

Guy, Judge, 96

Hackel, Stephen, 2

Hall, G. Stanley, 56

Hammack, Isabella, 188, 266n64

Harper, Howard, 64

Harper, J. H., 64

Harper, W. F., 259n30

Hart Taylor, Mary, 142, 152, 153, 181–82

Hawley, Edna, 184, 185

Headley, Harriet Marston, 234n4

health care, xxv, xxvii, 26, 36, 50, 90, 98, 125, 136, 140, 143, 144, 167, 173, 208; access to, 128; growth of, 207; lectures on, 153; preventive, 141; public, xxii, 95, 226

health issues, 140, 141, 151, 158–59, 160

Heinig, Christine, 178

Heller Committee for Research in Social Economics, 154, 155, 156, 172

Helping Hand Home (HHH), xxvi, 26–27, 106, 107, 118, 119, 120; scrutiny for, 107, 108

Hedrick, Mrs. (pseud.), 110, 111, 112

Henry, Bessie, 69–70

Henry Street Settlement, 264n9

HHH. See Helping Hand Home

Hicks, Mrs. Oliver H., 248n95

Hill, Archibald, 92

Hill, Kay, 193, 194

Hill, Mary Anderson, 92, 93–94, 254n18

Hoffman Memorial Hospital Mother's Clinic, 159

Holly Sefton Memorial Hospital, 248n95

Holmes, Forrest, 116–17

Holmes, Versa, 118, 120

homelessness, xxvii, 226

homeworkers, 49, 74

Hoskins, Alice Byrd, 161, 263n111

Hough, Rieta Campbell, 166, 167, 187, 207, 229

housing, 90, 98, 128, 190, 191, 192, 202, 207, 208, 232; access to, 197; affordable, 170, 193–94, 203, 205; discrimination in, 193, 204; lack of, 66, 183, 200; long-term, 63; military service and, 205; private places for, 151; problems with, 153, 203–4, 205, 220; tenement, 264n9

Howard, Bryant, 37, 245n49

How Mexicans Earn and Live: A Study of the Incomes and Expenditures of One Hundred Mexican Families in San Diego, California, 154

Hughes, J. W., 68, 251n39

Hull House, 85, 128, 138, 147, 157

Human Rights Watch, 230

Hunt, Ethel M., 33

Hunter, Joel D., 253n78

hygiene, xxvii, 85, 139, 141, 142, 143, 153, 160, 200

identity, 198; class, xix; ethnic, xix, 145, 271n4; gender, xix; legal, xxi; national, 238n17; public, 237n14; racial, xix, 145, 197, 238n17, 271n4

illegitimate children, 43, 50

immigrants, 72, 212, 226; anxieties about, 69; medical care for, 264n9

immigration, 170; controlling, 102–3; federal, 101; laws, 104; policies, 69, 230

Immigration Act (1875), 102

Immigration Act (1882), 102

immoral practices, 13, 69

Imperial Valley, 149, 262n104

incarceration, 79, 99; juvenile, 58, 59, 62

indentured service, xxv, xxvi, 1, 3, 6, 224

Indian Health Bureau, 173

Indian problem, 13, 15

Indian removal, 6, 8

Indian Service, 201

Inez, Nellie, 248n95

infant care, xxvii, 141, 211, 216, 224

influenza, xxv, II, 127, 141, 149, 150, 167, 169, 260n63
in-migrants, 194, 195, 197, 200, 201, 209, 212, 220; housing problems for, 205
Italians, 39, 156, 199, 252n62

Jackson, Helen Hunt, 17–18
Jacobs, Margaret D., 15, 239n21
Jameson, Elizabeth, 235n9
Japanese, 156; internment of, 202; population of, 197; work for, 198–99
Jennings, Mr. and Mrs. F. S., 248n95
Jewish Hebrew Society, 99
Jews, 144, 155, 241n47, 245n42
JLSD. See Junior League of San Diego
Johnson, Carrie, 33
Johnson, Clara Sturgis, 179
Johnson, Hiram, 143
Johnson, William Templeton, 179
Johnston, Luise, 196, 197, 267n11
Jones, Anita, 157–58, 166, 186
Jones, Ellen, 53, 54
Jones, Russell, 53, 54, 251n39
Junior League of San Diego (JLSD), 158, 164, 165, 166, 178, 183, 184, 185, 186; day nursery by, 182, 183, 228; thrift shop, 185
justices of the peace, 2
Juvenile Court Laws (1909), 63, 106, 112
Juvenile Court Laws (1913), 112
Juvenile Court of San Diego, 218
Juvenile Court Report (1916), 253n78
juvenile courts, 55, 57, 61, 81, 85, 96, 118, 123, 130, 218; establishment of, 64
juvenile delinquency, xxvi, 52, 54, 59, 60, 70, 85–86, 228
juvenile justice, xxvi, 52, 54–58, 61, 72–73, 86, 112–13, 212–13, 228; reform of, 62–63, 85, 98
juvenile law, changes in, 98
Juvenile Protective League, 85
Juvenile Psychopathic Institute, 253n78

Kallenberg, Frederic (pseud.), 77, 80
Keeley, Mary, 223
Kettenburg Boat Works, 201
kids.data.org, 230
Killory, Christine, 194
King, Fred, 93, 96, 131, 132, 133, 134

King's Daughters of Home, 91, 246n68
kinship networks, xxviii, 16, 190
Knight, Alan, 258n10
Knights of Pythias, 26
Kropp, Phoebe, 238n17
Ku Klux Klan, 160
Kumeyaay, 4, 10, 11, 12, 17, 238n18
Kunzel, Regina G., 43
Kuupangaxwichem, 4, 5, 6, 9

La Jolla Elementary School, 181
La Jolla Episcopalian private school, 134
La Mesa Women's Club, 158
La Neighbor (Garcia), 257n4
labor, 83, 119, 190, 224; advocates, 232; female, 195–96, 197; indentured, 4, 8; issues, xx, 221, 266n68, 271n4; laws, 128; semicaptive, 2; skilled/unskilled, 165, 201; volunteer, 225; women and, 196
Lack, Levi, 240n41
Ladies Hebrew Aid Society, 44
Lanham Act (1941), 203, 214, 215, 216, 269n57, 270n59
laundries, 38, 105–6
Lawson, Evelyn N., 89, 113
Lee, Jim, 105
Lee, Mrs. Bradner W., Jr., 185
Lesem, Theresa Greenbaum, 34, 36, 47
Letters from California, 6
licensing requirements, 51, 106, 107, 195, 210, 211
Lichtman, Ethel M., 265n37, 266n66
Lincoln Elementary, 39
Linda Vista Housing Project, 203, 204
Lindsey, Ben, 55, 56
literacy, 66, 145, 226, 236n21
Little Italy, 81–82
Little Mothers Club, 142
Logan Heights, 24, 45, 128, 139, 140, 151, 226
Logan Heights School, 79
Los Angeles, 13, 139, 188, 198; budgetary concerns for, 170; health department for, 241n64; hearings in, 213; in-migration and, 197; nonwhite residents in, 267–68n12; population of, 242n3
Los Angeles County, 251n55
Los Angeles School District, 215
Los Angeles Times, 59

Lower California Fisheries Company, 117
Lugones, Maria, 240n40
Luiseño, 7, 238n18
Luzo, Angelina, *18*
Lying-In Hospital, 207

Magdalene Asylum, 58
Magliari, Michael, 8, 240n34
"The Maiden Tribute of Modern Babylon"
    (Stead), 29
Mangold, George, 183
Mann Act (1908), 69, 250n37
Manufacturers' and Employers' Associa-
    tion, 124
Marino, Anthony (pseud.), 81, 82
Marino, Helena (pseud.), 81
Marino, Josie (pseud.), 81
Marino family (pseud.), 80, 81–82
Marital Relations Clinic, 157
Marshall, Lucille, 184, 185
Marston, Anna Lee Gunn, xviii, 36, 94;
    activism of, 147–48; birth of, 35; social
    problems and, 34
Marston, Arthur, 234n4
Marston, George White, xviii, 26, 35, 94,
    257n84; activism of, 147–48
Marston, Helen, 128, 129, 139, 147, 166, 234n4,
    254n17, 257n4, 257n84, 258n20; activism of,
    149; advocacy by, 138; discrimination and,
    138; essay by, 144, 145; humanness of, 148;
    NH and, 94, 143, 148; social justice and,
    145; Worchester and, 150
Marston, Mary Gilman, 94, 148, 234n4,
    254n17
Marston Department Store, 35, 149
Martin, Frank, 200, 268n19
Martin, Leonard (pseud.), 78–79, 79–80
Martin, Luther, 268n19
Martin, Mrs. (pseud.), 79
Martin, Ruth, 200, 204, 206
Marysville Industrial School, 58
Masons, 26
maternalism, xxvi, 140, 141, 210; culture
    and, xxiii
maternity homes, 43, 224
matrons, 21, 22, 40, 50, 97, 98, 100, 111, 113,
    114, 234n13, 242n1

Mayhew, Kelly, 235n9
McClun, Marah, 234n3
McCutcheon, Maggie (Maggie Bangs), 28
McLeod, Miss, 257n84
McNellis, Father, 95
Mead, Eleanor, 191, 209, 219, 220, 229,
    258n13
Mead, Francis, 131, 132
Mead, W. D. B., 139
Memorial Junior High School, 185, 212
Mesa Grande government school, chil-
    dren at, *174*
Metropolitan Life Insurance Company,
    109, 152, 158
Mexicali, 102, 235n7
Mexican American children, 101, 105
Mexican Americans, 39, 70, 119, 129, 130,
    156, 157, 212; dependency of, 109; jobs for,
    161; population of, 242n6; surveillance
    of, 103
Mexican children, 118, 146, 250n30; educat-
    ing, 105; jobs for, 62; mortality rate for,
    152; poverty for, 159
Mexican immigrants, xxvii, 25, *101*, 104,
    143, 144–45, 148, 242n6, 250n34, 261n84;
    arrival of, 45; funds for, 101; work for, 160
Mexican Immigrants Protection League, 157
Mexican Revolution, xx, xxvii, 78, 103, 126,
    130, 142, 148, 160–61; impact of, 101–2; lit-
    erature on, 258n10; refugees from, 91
Mexicans, 70, 119, 130, 132, 156, 157, 158, 168,
    174, 176, 260n66; County Hospital and,
    153; imprisonment of, 58; population of,
    153; stereotypes about, 138, 145
*Mexicans in California: Report of Governor
    C. C. Young's Mexican Fact-Finding Com-
    mittee*, 154, 157
"Mexican Traits" (Marston), 144
Mexican women, 67, *174*, *175*, 197; deporta-
    tion of, 103; marriage of, 96; struggles of,
    123; work for, 199
Michel, Sonya, 183, 269n57
middle class, childcare and, xix, 60
Miles, Mrs., 98, 100, 113
military installations, xxii, 90, 202, 230
military service, 190, 199, 200, 201, 207, 217;

employment and, 196; housing and, 205; population growth and, 194
Millar, Stanley, 151
Miller, George, 34
Miller, Jim, 235n9
Mink, Gwendolyn, 109
Minority Report, 8, 240n36
Mintzer, Ethel Sturgis "Happy" Dummer, 85, 86, 180, 182, 189, 265n42; canneries and, 178; leadership from, 179
Mintzer, L. Murney, 179
miscegenation, 96, 254n21
Mission Indians, 4, 6, 13, 172–73, 201, 238n18, 240n36, 240n37; government aid and, 172; poverty of, 5; reservations for, 18, 19
Mission Relief Act (1891), 18
Mission San Diego de Alcalá, 14
Mission Valley Hospital, 84, 85, 86
Mitchell, Adina, 59
Monroe, Mary W., 34
Monroy, Douglas, 239n23
Monthly Labor Review (MLR), 155, 156
moral reform, xxii, 29, 71, 82
Morena, Luisa, 190
Morgan, Catherine Fauntroy, 23
Morgan, Noah, 23
Morgan, Rufus, 16, 17
Morse, Ephraim Weed, 1, 9–10, 16, 240n41
mortality rate, 131–32, 133, 152, 153
Mosher, Eliza, 35
motherhood, xxiii, 66; paid, 108; single, 43, 77, 109, 121
mothers' pension, 108–9, 109–10, 112, 256n53
Mrs. Watson's Home for Stray Girls, 31, 32
"My Mexican Neighbors" (Shatto King), 127, 144

National Association of Colored Women, 56
National Association of Day Nurseries, 270n69
National Child Labor Committee (NCLC), 73, 92, 106, 107
National City, 47, 68, 130, 159, 160, 215
National Compensation Survey, 230
National Council of Jewish Women, 56

National Federation of Day Nurseries, 186
National Federation of Settlements, 166, 262n92
National Geographic, 202–3
National Housing Authority, 204
National Negro Business League, 198
National Recovery Administration, 175
nativists, 102, 142
Naval Hospital, 207
Navy Relief, 99
NCLC. *See* National Child Labor Committee
Neighborhood House (NH), xxiii, xxvii, 36, 94, 119, 124, 126, 127, 128, 129, 130, 133, 134, 135, 136, 138, 139, 140, 141, 143, 148, 152, 154–55, 160, 161, 164, 166, 168, 178, 181, 186, 199, 213, 229, 232; activities at, 212; day nursery by, 228; health/education and, 153, 158; leadership of, 150, 156–57; living at, 145, 146, 147; Mexicans and, 155; opening of, 27, 72; as parent substitute, 212; service by, 142
Nelles, Fred, 62
Neptune cannery, 177
New Deal, 166, 174, 183, 187
newsboys, 74, 74–75
"New Town" venture, 239n29
New Woman, 147
New York School of Philanthropy, 92
NH. *See* Neighborhood House
Normandy Company, *15*
North Island, 150, 205
nurseries, 2, 184, 215. *See also* day nurseries
nursery schools, 179, 181, 182, 186, 188, 211; government, 215. *See also* emergency nursery schools
nurses, xx, 207; public health, 166; school, 152; visiting, *169*, 225, 228

Oake, Justine, (pseud.): mothers' pension and, 109–10
Oake, Theodore (pseud.), 110, 256n56
Oakland: budgetary concerns for, 170; hearings in, 213; in-migration and, 197; nonwhite residents in, 267–68n12
Oatman, Mrs. Homer, 257n84
Odem, Mary, 81

Office of Indian Affairs, 249n16
Office of War Information, 268n28
Old Mission Olive Factory, *136*
Old Town, 14, 17, 159, 240n41
O'Malley, Marie (pseud.), xvii, xviii, 234n1
O'Neall, Charles, 83
Orange County, 202
Order of Commitment, 53, 54, 64–70
Oregon Boot, 59
orphans, xxii, xxv, 3, 8, 11, 23, 25, 27, 37, 47, 60, 100, 124, 164, 249n29; caring for, 41, 42
Ortega, Elizabeth, 137–38, 201

Pacific Beach, 118, 119, 196, 216
Pacific Parachute Company, 197; workers and, *198*
Paid Family Leave Insurance Program (PFL), 231
Paiute villages, raids on, 2
Palace of Education, 188
Palmer, Mrs., 124
Palomar Observatory, 189
Panama-California Exposition (1915), 81, 116, 128, 146
Panama-Pacific Exposition, 82, 100
Panunzio, Constantine, 154–55, 156, 157
Panunzio, Lenore, 154, 156, 157, 261n83
parent-child homes, 211, 218
Parent Teacher Association, 152, 159, 214, 215
Parent Teacher Association Council, 180
parental rights, 3, 12, 111, 224, 226
parenting, 5, 105, 115, 227
Parents' Association, 216
Parker, Clyde, 171
parteras, 153, 261n78
Pascoe, Peggy, 254n21
Pathfinder Social Survey of San Diego: Report of Limited Investigations of Social Conditions in San Diego, California (CWC), 73–74, 75, 128, 129, 130, 131, 132, 133, 142
Payómkawichum, 7
Pearce, Josephine (pseud.), 76
Peery, Bessie, 40
peonage, 8, 237n9
Pest Hospital, 237n1
Phillips, D. L., 6
Pico family, 5

Piña sisters, 199
Pinkerton, Merlin, 212, 213
Point Loma, 150, 185, 198, 204
Police Gazette, 32
Polinsky Children's Center, 232
politics, xxii, 3, 204; gendered, xxiii; property ownership and, 5
population growth, xxv, 4, 23, 25, 89–90, 229; Mexican, 153; military service and, 194
Porter, Otis, 193, 194
Portuguese, 156, 199
Poston Internment Camp, 202
Pourade, Richard F., 235n9
poverty, xix, xxii, 5, 15, 33, 66, 68, 69, 76, 118, 121, 129, 145, 147, 149, 159, 171, 199; alleviating, 165; children in, 230; homelessness and, xxvii; stereotypes and, 57
Poyomkawish, 9, 238n18
prejudices, 19, 119, 130, 132, 137, 197, 226; Anglo, 13; ethnic, xxv, 141, 145, 153
Preston School of Industry (Preston), 58, 59, 60, 64, 70, 123, 251n39
private organizations, 25, 91, 161, 210
professionalism, 86, 93, 122
Progress Club, 158
Progressive Era, 29, 54, 65, 94, 136, 157, 232; activists of, 92–93
Progressive reform, xxvi, 91, 92, 179–80, 186
Prohibition, xx, 78
promiscuity, 56–57, 67
Proposition 10 (California) (1998), 231
prostitution, xxvi, 6, 7, 14, 19, 28–29, 33, 68–69, 83–84, 102, 226, 239n25, 243n16, 244n26, 260n66; life of, 31; shelter from, 32; spread of, 30, 250n37; suspicion of, 112
public agencies, 89–90, 161; private organizations and, 91
Public Buildings Administration, 203
Public Health Department, xxiii, 135–36
Public Health Report for the City, 152
public officials, 171, 172
public schools, 60, 66, 70, 75, 86, 89, 133, 145, 180, 181, 214, 215, 216, 250n31
Public Welfare Department, 170, 213
Purity League, 83

race, 68, 109, 151, 152, 153, 204, 237n14; impact of, 47; politics of, xxiii

racial boundaries, 3, 139, 140, 197
racism, 19, 24, 141, 161, 197, 200, 212, 213; experiencing, 45–46; violence and, 160
Rae, Rebecca (pseud.), 46
railroads, 13, 23, 116, 242n8
Rancho Cereza Loma, 75
Rawls, James, 3, 237n9, 238n15
Red Cross, 101, 180, 191
red-light district, 18, 27, 28, 33, 82, 83, 243n15, 252n66
reformatories, 55, 57, 62, 65, 224; at-risk youth, 68; rehabilitation at, 58
reformers, xx, xxii–xxiii, 52, 55, 71, 80, 127–28, 143, 226; benevolent/professional, xxi; female, xxvi, 91, 108, 140, 229–30; flexibility and, 229–30; middle-class, 64; pension, 109; problems for, 75
rehabilitation, 51, 52, 58, 59, 64
repatriation, 156, 157, 160, 161
reservations, 18, 19, 241n63
Riley, Mirabel, 116
Ritter, Mary A., 252n68
Riverside. See Sherman Institute
Riverside County, 173
Robbins, Jane, 157, 262n91
Robertson, Alice Adams, 92
Rockwood Home, 118, 119
Rodríguez, Laura, 129, 257n4
Rodríguez López, Blanca Rosa, 266n68
Roosevelt, Franklin D., 202
Roosevelt, Theodore, 94
Rosario, Dolores, 11, 16
Rosario, José, 11
Rose, Elizabeth, 144
Ross, Fran, 192
Ross, James, 47
Ruiz, Leticia (pseud.), 45
Ruiz, Vicki, 176, 177
Russell, Edna, 31, 268n28
Ruth, Hattie, 29
Ryan Aeronautics, 216, 270n65

safety issues, 106, 121, 227, 270n65
Salvation Army, 27, 43, 124, 190, 232
Sample, Edwina B., 253–54n12
San Diego: birthrate in, 208; budgetary concerns for, 170; cost of living in, 194; militarization of, 203; population of, xxv,

4, 23, 25, 54, 89–90, 115, 153, 192, 194, 197; social conditions of, 52
San Diego Benevolent Association (SDBA), 25, 243n9
San Diego Board of Education, 96
San Diego-California Club, 90
San Diego Center for Children, 232
San Diego Chamber of Commerce, 158
San Diego Charities, 254–55n25
San Diego City Council, 36
San Diego City Directory, 253n1
San Diego City Schools, 86, 154, 155, 224, 261n83
San Diego County, 8, 9, 10, 11, 16, 54, 157, 175, 188, 231, 245n49, 255n45, 263n5, 270n59; African American families in, 24; city directories for, 37; federal aid in, 174; female labor in, 221, 267n8; growth of, 195; Japanese in, 202; Mexican immigrants in, 24; reservations in, 18
San Diego County Board of Supervisors, 12, 25, 26, 122, 150, 168, 173, 249n16
San Diego County Department of Public Welfare, 164
San Diego County Federation of Women's Clubs, 158
San Diego County Grand Jury, 8
San Diego County Health Department, 158, 159
San Diego County Hospital, 26, 47, 98, 122, 137, 152, 153, 158–59, 166, 167, 169
San Diego County Medical Society, 84
San Diego County Welfare Commission (SDCWC), 91, 122, 149, 249n16; meeting of, 121
San Diego Electric Railway Company, 217
San Diego Flume Company, 25
San Diego History Center, 234n1
San Diego Labor Council, 150
San Diego Mission, 6
San Diego Police, 103
San Diego Public Schools. See San Diego City Schools
San Diego School District, funding for, 214–15
San Diego Society for Crippled Children, 245n49
San Diego State College, 154

San Diego State Normal College, 184, 188, 189

San Diego Sun, 175; newsboys for, 74

San Diego Teacher's Association Bulletin, 180

San Diego Tent and Awning Company, 25

San Diego Union, 13, 30, 34, 113, 165, 234n1

San Diego Union-Tribune Publishing Company, 235n79

San Francisco, 188, 239n31; budgetary concerns for, 170; fire/earthquake, 252n62

San Francisco Exposition (1915), 188

San Francisco Industrial School (SFIS), 58

San Gabriel mission, 239n27

San José mission, 239n27

San Juan Capistrano, 236n1

San Luis Rey, 14, 238n15

San Quentin, 58

Sanger, Margaret, 159

Santa Anita Assembly Center, 202

Santa Fe Depot, 104, 116, 151, 202

Santa Ysabel, 171, 172

Saturday Evening Post, 202

Schiller, Hannah, 11

Schiller, Rebecca, 240n37

Schlossman, Steven, 248n3

school districts, 161, 201, 214–15, 226

Scott, Andres, 11–12

Scott, Charles (pseud.), 77–78, 80

Scott, Henry (pseud.), 77–78

SDBA. *See* San Diego Benevolent Association

SDCWC. *See* San Diego County Welfare Commission

Section 316 policy, 33

Seeger, Ann, 166, 167, 168–69, 264n11

Sefton, Holly, 248n95

Sefton, Mr. and Mrs. J. W., 248n95

segregation, xxvi, 4, 13, 19, 27, 54, 82, 146, 151, 152, 160, 226; housing, 202; job, 202; occupational, 94; racial, xxv, 161

Seiler, Julia, 31, 32, 33

Senate Bill 1661 (2002), 231

separation, 16, 54, 56, 76, 100, 117, 120, 121, 219, 232

SERA. *See* State Emergency Relief Administration

Serra, Father Junípero, 239n27

settlement houses, xx, xxvii, 27, 72, 91, 94–95, 128, 129, 130, 138, 141, 143, 144, 151, 160, 224, 228, 258n6, 264n9

sexual relations, 15, 30, 33, 56–57, 62, 65, 67, 69, 103, 212, 244n22

Shatto King, Edith, 92, 93, 128, 131, 132, 133, 134, 145, 146; essay by, 127, 144; NH and, 147; prejudices and, 145; resignation of, 260n64

Sheppard-Towner Maternity and Infancy Act (STMIA) (1921), 140, 141

Sherman Heights Elementary, 67–68, 154, 250n32

Sherman Institute (Riverside), 15, 59–60, 61, 123, 201, 249n16

Shields, Florence, 260n64

Shipek, Florence, 240n36

Shong, Esther, 168, 169

Shumsky, Neil Larry, 82, 243n15

Silver Gate Lodge, 99

Sisters of Mercy Hospital, 26, 159, 207, 209

Sisters of the St. Joseph of Carondelet, 13

Sisters School, 14

slavery, 3, 5, 7, 226

Sleepy Lagoon murder trial, 212

Slingerland, William H., 244n30

Smith, Howard "Skippy," 197, 198

Smith, J. D., 257n84

Smith, Jedediah, 5

Smith, Joseph, 1, 11

Smith-Hughes Act (1917), 140, 141, 142, 259n38

Smith-Lever Act (1914), 140, 259n38

Smithson, Lydia (pseud.), 50

Smithson, Mabel (pseud.), 50

Snyder, Mary, 150–51, 154

social agencies, 122, 165, 223

social conditions, 52, 172, 237n4

Social Gospel, 147

social issues, xxiii, 34, 35, 159, 203

social networks, 120, 183, 211, 212

social programs, xxiii–xxiv, 134, 143, 230

social reform, xix, xxviii, 55–56, 144, 225, 226

social services, xix, 54, 131, 151, 183, 192, 206, 224; unemployment and, 51

social welfare, xxv, 22, 36, 52, 55, 90, 91, 94, 122, 126, 128, 129, 147, 166, 170, 179, 210,

216, 228; advocates, 232; childcare and, xx, xxi–xxii, 224; employment and, 221; influencing, 124

social workers, xix, xx, xxiii, 56, 77, 95, 114, 118, 125, 166, 182, 183, 184, 212, 217, 225, 227, 228, 229; volunteers and, 115–16

Social Workers Association, 85

Solar Aircraft, 201

Solinger, Ricki, 43

Southern California–Baja California, 234–35n7

Speer, Anna, 118–19, 120, 122

Sr. Octavia, 15

Stadum, Beverly, 114

St. Anthony's Industrial School, 13, 14, 15, 44

Stark, Royal, 68, 251n39

Starr, Kevin, 235n10

State Agricultural Extension Service, 172

State Disability Insurance Fund, 231

State Emergency Relief Administration (SERA), 174, 182

State Reform School for Juvenile Offenders (Whittier), 36, 53, 58, 59, 60, 62, 64, 67, 68, 123

State War Council, 214

Stead, William T., 29

Stearns, Abel, 236n1

Steel cannery, 177

Stephens, Cyrus Wayne, 253n5

stereotypes, 10, 19, 138, 146, 148, 171; cultural, 57, 109; ethnic, 143; learning, 146; Mexican, 138, 145; of nonwhite women, 67; pension reformers and, 109; poverty and, 57; racial, 143; strength of, 147

Stingaree, 28, 30, 31, 32, 33, 34, 82, 83, 84, 100, 105, 220

St. Joseph's Sanitarium, 26

STMIA. See Sheppard-Towner Maternity and Infancy Act

Stoltzfus, Emilie, 216

St. Paul's Episcopal Church, 36

Sturgis family, 85

Sullivan, Michael, 125

Survey, 138, 144, 147, 260n48

Sweeney, Ellen, 214

Swift, Linton B., 191

Takhtam, 4

Taschner, Mary, 203

TASSD. See Travelers Aid Society of San Diego

Tavares Construction Company, 204

Taylor, Mrs., 48

Taylor, Paul S., 154

Temple Beth Israel, 36

Thomas, Ella, 116, 120

Thuli, Irene F., 179

Tijuana, 78, 101, 102, 103, 150, 167, 195, 235n7

Tilton, Edwin B., 154

Toll, Florence, 252n72

Torrance, E. S., 67

tourism, xxiv, 83, 97, 187, 190, 221, 225

Townsend, Dr. and Mrs. J. R., 251n55

Travelers Aid Society, xxiii, 84, 87, 116, 117, 118, 125, 151, 161, 168, 171, 190, 191, 228

Travelers Aid Society of San Diego (TASSD), 91, 119–20, 120–21, 122, 139, 163, 170–71, 190, 191, 220, 253n5, 263n111; help from, 116, 118; Los Angeles Society, 120

Trejos, Armida, 199

Trejos, Obdulia "Tulie," 199

truancy, 55, 57, 212

Truelove Home, 244n30

tuberculosis, xxv, 26, 92, 123, 124, 127, 141, 167

Tuttle, Katherine, 168, 169

Ubach, Father Anthony Dominic, 13, 14, 44

Underhill, Lizzie, 68

unemployment, 51, 71, 95, 101, 172, 181, 190, 227, 263n5

United Cannery, Agricultural, Packing, and Allied Workers of America (UCAP-AWA), 190, 266n68

United States Employment Service, 211

United States v. Bitty (1908), 103

United Way, 125

University Club, 93, 94, 254n12

U.S. Department of Labor, survey by, 230

U.S. Grant Hotel, 252n72

U.S. Marine Corps, 90

U.S. Navy, 90, 163

U.S. Supreme Court, 2, 103

vagrancy, 2, 6, 7, 29, 53, 57, 67

Vásquez, Frank, 53, 67, 68, 251n39

Ventura. *See* California School for Girls
Vice-Suppression League, 83, 84
Visiting Nurses Association, xxiii, 87
Visiting Nurses Bureau (vnb), 159, 166, 167, 168–69, *169*, 170, 264n9

Waggenheim, Mrs. Julius, 248n95
Wald, Lillian, 264n9
Walker's Department Store, 217
Walling, Mrs. (pseud.), 111, 112
War Manpower Committee, 213
Warner, J. T. (Jonathan Trumball Warner; Don Juan José Warner), 5–6, 8
Washington Elementary School, 181
wcc. *See* Women's Civic Center
wctu. *See* Women's Christian Temperance Union
welfare, 104, 116, 125, 157, 164, 219, 221, 231; abuses of, 171; child, 41, 76, 223
Wells, Alice Stebbins, 252n68
Welpton, Martha, 167
West, Eliot, 237n10
Weyman, Mrs. C. M., 248n14
wha. *See* Woman's Home Association
Whaley, Guy V., 86
What Comes Naturally, 254n21
White, Mr. and Mrs. Ernest, 248n95
white slavery, 29–30, 69, 244n23
whites, population of, 197, 242n6
Whittier. *See* State Reform School for Juvenile Offenders
wie. *See* Woman's Industrial Exchange
Willard, Frances, 28, 29
Williams, Reverend, 259n30
Wilson, Keno, 83
Wissner, Francine (pseud.), 48
Wissner, Peter (pseud.), 48
Wissner (pseud.), Sara, 48
Woman's Home Association (wha), xviii, 21, 26, 27, 28, 34, 35, 36, 37, 51, 71, 103–4, 245n49, fund-raising by, 42; legacy of, 84; ownership rights for, 245n49; religious foundations of, 36; work of, 44
Woman's Industrial Exchange (wie), 36, 37, 41, 245n48

women adrift, 29, 33–34, 69
Women's Bureau, 195
Women's Christian Temperance Union (wctu), 26, 27, 28, 29, 30, 33, 34, 37, 124, 243n18; child labor and, 56; consent campaign of, 32
Women's Civic Center (wcc), 84, 152
Women's Civic League, 151
women's clubs, 84–85, 132, 159
Women's Federated Clubs, 152
Women's International League for Peace and Freedom, 148
Women's Missionary Society of Southern California, 35
Women's Welfare Commission, 84
Wood, Sharon E., 93, 127, 244n22
Worchester, Daisy Lee Worthington, 91, 92, 93, 128, 136, 137, 138, 159, 259n25, 260n64; Marston and, 150
Worchester, Wood F., 92
Worchester vs. State of Georgia (1832), 2
working class, 56, 69, 230; childcare and, xix, 225; economic issues and, 227–28; family culture and, 64; sexual experience and, 244n22
Work Relief Program, 161
Works Progress Administration (wpa), 161, 176, 178, 179, 180, 190, 266n67; Emergency Nursery Schools, xxvii
World's Fair, 187
World War I, 127, 139, 142
World War II, xxii, xxv, 43, 151, 192, 216, 220, 229, 261n83
Wright, Senator: visit by, 96–97

Ybarra, Charlotte, 66
Ybarra, Virginia, 66, 67, 68, 69, 70
Young, Governor, 172
Young Men's Christian Association (ymca), 26, 139, 257n84
Young Women's Christian Association (ywca), 91, 116, 124, 151, 166

Zolezzi, Rose, 72
zoot suit riots, 212

CPSIA information can be obtained
at www.ICGtesting.com
Printed in the USA
LVHW111113160819
627783LV00005BA/35/P